W9-BCJ-030

The Berlin Blockade

A STUDY IN COLD WAR POLITICS

BY W. PHILLIPS DAVISON
THE *RAND* CORPORATION

PRINCETON, NEW JERSEY
PRINCETON UNIVERSITY PRESS
1958

L.C. CARD: 58-6103

PRINTED IN THE UNITED STATES OF AMERICA
BY PRINCETON UNIVERSITY PRESS, PRINCETON, N.J.

ACKNOWLEDGMENTS

So MANY persons and organizations have assisted the writer in preparing this study over the course of the past seven years that it is almost impossible to acknowledge fully all the advice and information so generously given. A particular debt is owed to Dr. Hans Speier, Chief of the Social Science Division of The RAND Corporation, who contributed invaluable encouragement and advice during all phases of the research, and whose writings in political sociology have provided many of the concepts used in the analysis.* Thanks are also due to Dr. Herbert Goldhamer, whose penetrating criticisms have been most helpful, and to Joseph Goldsen, Alexander George, Leon Gouré, Anne Jonas, Paul Kecskemeti, Herbert Dinerstein, Frederick Sallagar, Bernard Brodie, and Victor Hunt of The RAND Corporation, all of whom read and commented on sections of the manuscript. The Chronology at Appendix B was prepared by Evelyn Moore. Emmanuel Mesthene and Sibylle Crane have edited the manuscript with both firmness and diplomacy.

Great assistance on many portions of the study was received from Dr. Paul F. Lazarsfeld of Columbia University, whose interest in social-scientific approaches to historical problems has been particularly stimulating to the author.† Valuable criticisms and suggestions on several sections of the manuscript were made by Professors Shepard Clough, Herbert Hyman, Philip C. Jessup, and Robert Merton, also of the Columbia faculty.

Former officials of the United States and British military governments and the Department of State have been generous with both critical comments and information but do not, of course, bear any responsibility for errors in fact or interpretation which may be contained in this study. Among the many who have been of assistance to the author are General Lucius D. Clay, General Frank L. Howley, Jack Bennett, Ulrich Biel, Alfred V. Boerner, Leo Crespi, Alexander Forest, Max Kimental, J. Burke Knapp, Melvin Lasky, Charles Lewis, J. A. N. McEwan, Richard Scammon, Boris Shub, John E. Sommers, and Adolphe Warner. The writer is also indebted to Mrs. Eleanor Dulles, David Linebaugh, Karl Mautner, and Deputy Under Secretary Robert Murphy of the Department of State.

* E.g., Hans Speier, *Social Order and the Risks of War*, Stewart, New York, 1952.

† See especially his "Public Opinion and the Classical Tradition," *Public Opinion Quarterly*, Spring, 1957.

Numerous Air Force officers, both active and retired, have contributed a great deal to various aspects of the study. Generals Samuel E. Anderson, Robert W. Harper, August W. Kissner, Oliver S. Picher, and Joseph Smith; Colonels Joseph Dasher, Raymond Sleeper, and Russell W. Tarvin; Lt. Colonels William F. Sprague, Raymond L. Towne, and Robert Hogg; and Major Alexander Bebenin have been helpful in answering questions. A number of airlift pilots and crew members have also contributed valuable advice and information.

Thanks are due to officials and former officials of the Berlin city government, political parties, and trade unions, as well as to numerous private citizens, whose co-operation proved invaluable. The late Mayor Otto Suhr, Dr. Ferdinand Friedensburg, Mayor Willy Brandt, Dr. Rolf May, Ernst Scharnowski, Karl Hubert Schwennicke, Theodor Thiele, Ernst Tillich, and many others have been of assistance in gathering information. A number of West German officials, newspapermen, and other private citizens have also been generous with their time.

The writer owes a particular debt to Publisher Hans Sonnenfeld of *Der Abend*, and to the editors of *Der Abend*, for their assistance in making important source materials available. *Abend* staff member Jürgen Reiss read and commented on portions of the manuscript. Dr. Eberlein of the *Tagesspiegel*, Mr. Fodor of *Die Neue Zeitung*, and staff members of RIAS also contributed valuable information to the study. Heinz König, formerly of the HICOG Reactions Analysis Staff, and interviewers working with him, gave expert assistance in the interpretation of public opinion during the blockade. A number of stimulating observations on public opinion were also provided by Günter Neumann. Large quantities of extremely valuable material and numerous penetrating observations were contributed by Harold Hurwitz; these have been acknowledged more explicitly in the text.

Finally, the contribution of a great many Berliners, whose assistance it has not been possible to acknowledge individually, should be mentioned. Former airlift workers and professional men, civil servants and housewives, businessmen and employees, have all been willing to recall the days of the blockade and to give the author the benefit of their experiences. Their generosity, expressiveness, and humor have helped to make the author's task a pleasant one.

This study was prepared as part of the research program undertaken for the U.S. Air Force by The RAND Corporation.

Washington, D.C. W. Phillips Davison

CONTENTS

MAPS

MAPS

INTRODUCTION

In June 1948, the Soviet Union cut overland communications between Berlin and West Germany. By this action Moscow created one of the most interesting crises of the cold war. The Berlin blockade brought the Western Powers into direct conflict with the Soviet Union, it placed Berlin's population in a position of having to choose between East and West, and it involved the use of a massive airlift to fly food to the beleaguered Berliners. The blockade thus provides an excellent opportunity to observe in some detail and in convenient compass the operation of Soviet and Western diplomacy, the behavior of a population under physical and psychological stress, and, in general, the part played by public opinion in a cold war crisis.

Soviet actions before and during the blockade are consistent with the often stated thesis that Moscow regards Germany as the key to the balance of power in Europe. According to this view, a strong, pro-Western Germany would force the Soviet Union on the defensive, while a communist Germany would place Europe at Russia's mercy. Following World War II, the Soviets appear to have decided that, if all Germany could not be united under communism, it should be kept in a divided state, with East Germany as strong as possible and West Germany as weak as possible. The objective of the Berlin blockade was to prevent West German economic recovery and formation of a West German government or, failing this, to incorporate the population and resources of West Berlin into East Germany, thus depriving the democracies of a valuable outpost behind the iron curtain and invaluable prestige throughout the world.

The Soviets lifted the blockade when they found that its net effect was to reduce rather than increase their power relative to that of the West. Moscow suffered a particularly serious defeat in West Germany, where the net effect of the assault on Berlin was to promote the formation of a stable government rather than to impede it.

During the blockade, even minor moves by Soviet and German Communists appear to have been governed by similar power calculations. In the borough administrations of Berlin, in the various departments of Berlin's government, and in the *Länder* of West Germany, the Communists conducted a drive to capture positions from which authority could be exercised. Once having gained any such position, they ordinarily refused to give it up unless compelled to do so by military or police power.

Soviet actions indicated thoroughness in planning and preparation. All available instruments were pressed into service to achieve chosen objectives. Diplomatic moves on the international scene were coordinated with mob action in the streets, with massive propaganda campaigns, and with the tactics of communist deputies in representative bodies. Efforts were even made to wear down the physical and mental ability of German office holders to resist communist demands by subjecting them to marathon conferences, veiled threats and irritating surveillance.

While tireless in the pursuit of power, the Soviets also showed that there were well-defined limits beyond which they would not take risks. Having apparently determined in advance not to allow the Berlin crisis to flare up into war, Moscow accepted numerous affronts to its prestige, and made several withdrawals when determined resistance was encountered.

The variety of gains which the Soviets achieved through the use of international negotiations was particularly striking. By maintaining almost continuous conversations with the Western powers, they were able to cause delays when this suited their purposes, to take precautions against the possibility that war might break out, to secure political intelligence, to conduct propaganda, and to state demands and receive concessions. There were no indications that the Soviets looked at international negotiations primarily as a means of solving differences through bargaining.

The Soviets used propaganda for a similarly wide range of purposes. In addition to trying to create attitudes favorable to their current policies, and attempting to clothe their actions with the appearance of legality, they employed mass media to convey diplomatic communications, to launch trial balloons in advance of official negotiations, and to inform communist leaders throughout the world of the Kremlin's current line. They also used propaganda to balance their policy of caution. While their overt actions were cautious, propaganda in the media they controlled was blatantly aggressive. In this way, Moscow was able to play on the fear of war while at the same time refraining from moves which would increase the risk of war.

Western policy in the Berlin crisis, as contrasted with that of the Soviets, was characterized by vagueness, indecisiveness, and lack of planning. There were few among the Allied leaders who gave evidence of appreciating the magnitude of the threat posed by the Soviet blockade until several weeks or even months after the crisis had been in existence. The Western powers appeared to be unable to turn international negotiations to their own advantage; indeed, they allowed themselves repeatedly to be outmaneuvered by the Soviets. This was partially because of domestic pressures on Allied negotiators for a quick settlement, and partially because of prevailing Western attitudes toward international conferences; namely, that it was necessary to show good faith by suspending other types of action while negotiations were in progress, and that the sole purpose of negotiations was to arrive at an agreement.

But the Western powers also showed a number of positive characteristics. Prominent among these was the ability to improvise, as exemplified by the airlift. Another was the ability of key Western leaders to make rapid and firm decisions, even if at the last possible minute. Probably most important, however, was the reputation for fundamental decency enjoyed by the Allies, particularly when contrasted with the Soviets. This assured the Western powers of the almost unanimous support of the Berliners and the co-operation of German leaders in Berlin and West Germany. Without this German support the West could not have emerged victorious from the crisis.

The airlift itself did a great deal more than transport supplies. Above all, it emphasized to both Russians and Germans that the democracries were determined to defend their position in Berlin. In addition, airlift planes served to reassure Berliners; without the sight and sound of aircraft to remind them that they had powerful friends, many of them would have despaired during the long winter. Similarly, Germans felt more secure and hence were better able to resist communist pressure as a result of the movement of U.S. B-29 bombers to Britain, and the strengthening of the Allied air forces in Germany.

Western ground forces in Berlin also proved to have a substantial political value, even though they were in a militarily hopeless position. As long as these forces were there the Soviets could not resort to armed intervention without invoking greater risks of war than they were willing to assume.

The behavior of West Berlin's civilian population during the blockade is one of the most striking aspects of the crisis. In this century, peoples threatened by totalitarianism have not always been eager to fight for their own freedom, but Berlin is an example of a community that was willing to defend itself vigorously. In spite of the fact that they knew their city could be overrun by Russian troops in a mater of hours, Berliners remained firm in the face of Soviet threats and promises. They learned to live with danger, and even to live fairly comfortably.

Berlin's ability to hold out during the blockade seems to have been based on a combination of four major factors. First, the will to resist was widely shared throughout the population, and exemplary behavior was enforced by social pressure. (Before most people were willing openly to identify themselves with the cause of the democracies, however, it was necessary for them to be convinced that there was some hope of successful resistance.) Second, Berlin had a corps of able political leaders who were willing to run personal risks and refused to be intimidated by Soviet threats. Third, these leaders controlled efficient political institutions, including most of the civil administration, police, political parties, trade unions, and some media of communication. Finally, a material basis for resistance was provided by airlifted supplies. These four factors were closely interrelated, and the absence or insufficiency of any one of them could easily have made the other three ineffective, thus precipitating the fall of Berlin.

It was possible to improvise the airlift and to whip up resistance spirit among the public at large at the last minute, but it had taken several years to develop leadership, the machinery of administration, and a hard core of those who were willing to defend themselves at all costs. Berlin's political and trade union leaders had been toughened by almost continuous struggles with the Communists since 1945, and those who lacked the necessary personal courage had been winnowed out. Between 1946 and 1948, these leaders had with infinite labor captured control of the democratic political parties, the vital institutions of government, and some of the trade unions. Then they had set out to convince the previously apathetic populace that freedom was worth a fight. Berlin's continued existence as an oasis of freedom behind the iron curtain is in large part a monument to their vision and hard work.

THE BERLIN BLOCKADE

ILLUSTRATIONS

1. U.S. Military Governor, General Lucius D. Clay, and British Military Governor, General Sir Brian Robertson. (U.S. Army Photo)

2. Commandants of the Four Sectors of Berlin meet in the Kommandatura building before the blockade. Left to right, left side of table: Colonel Frank Howley, U.S. Sector Commandant, and members of the American Staff. Right side of table, front to rear: General Jean Ganeval, French Sector Commandant; General Alexander Kotikov, Soviet Sector Commandant. General E. O. Herbert, British Sector Commandant, is on the left side of the table just outside the camera's field of vision. (U.S. Army Photo)

3. Berlin's Mayor, Ernst Reuter, standing before the ruins of the old Reichstag building, addresses a mass meeting during the blockade. (U.S. Army Photo)

4. Thousands of Berliners jam the square before the burned-out Reichstag building to protest Soviet actions in disrupting the City Assembly. (U.S. Army Photo)

5. A four-engine Skymaster passes over the junction of the British, American, and Soviet sectors as it approaches Tempelhof Air Base. (ACME Photo)

6. The first U.S. C-74 Globemaster to be used in the Berlin airlift landed at Gatow Air Base on August 20, 1948, carrying 20 tons of flour. (ACME Photo)

7. The airlift is the center of "their conversations, their games, and perhaps their dreams." (U.S. Air Force Photo)

8. Exultant over the news that agreement to end the blockade has been reached, German loaders welcome the crew of an airlift plane arriving at Tempelhof, May 5, 1949. (ACME Photo)

9. Top U.S. Air Force officials at the start of the Berlin airlift leave the operations building at Rhein/Main Air Base. Left to right: Secretary of the Air Force W. Stuart Symington; Air Force Chief of Staff General Hoyt S. Vandenberg; and Lt. General Curtis E. LeMay, Commander of the U.S. Air Forces in Europe. (U.S. Air Force Photo)

1

2

3

4

5

6

7

8

9

CHAPTER I

SETTING THE STAGE: GERMANY FROM 1945 TO 1948

THE end of World War II found the continent of Europe divided as it had not been since Turkish armies beat against the gates of of Vienna in 1683. A line running through the center of Germany and Austria separated Western Europe from the vast hinterland controlled by the forces of the Soviet Union and its satellites.

In 1945 there were many in the West, and perhaps also in the East, who attached only limited significance to this tortuous demarcation line. The Soviet Union and the Western powers were allies who had learned to work together under the pressure of war. With good will they could certainly find harmonious solutions to the problems of peace. Instrumentalities such as the United Nations and the Council of Foreign Ministers would be able to resolve differences and to frame common policies when necessary.

These hopes were speedily dashed. From the cessation of hostilities in 1945 to the time of the Berlin blockade in 1948, the gulf between East and West became increasingly difficult to bridge. And it was especially in Germany, which the Soviets and the Western democracies had planned to govern jointly, that signs of growing tension between the erstwhile allies could be observed most clearly.

Early Agreements Regarding Germany

A succession of agreements on Germany had been reached by the Big Three at Teheran and Yalta, and at other conferences during the war, although there were still areas of vagueness and disagreement. Germany was to be denazified, demilitarized, and democratized. Reparations were to be exacted from her, but the extent and manner of reparation payments had not been defined. Poland was to receive territorial compensation from the eastern areas of Germany to make up for land she was to relinquish to the Soviet Union, but precise boundary lines had not been established. Zones of occupation had been drawn up, and the city of Berlin was to be divided into pie-shaped sectors, each of which was to be garrisoned by one of the occupying powers. During the immediate postwar period, supreme authority was to be exercised in Germany by an Allied Control Council, sitting in Berlin and operating under the principle of unanimity.

Although Berlin was an enclave in the zone of Germany allotted to the Soviet Union, the Western powers did not secure any formal agreement that they could have free access to the city. Indeed, during wartime negotiations the question was never raised with Soviet representatives, because it was felt in Washington that the question of access could be settled later on a military level. But the Soviet representative on the European Advisory Commission (the top level inter-allied planning staff) repeatedly insisted that "the presence of American and British forces in Berlin 'of course' carried with it all necessary facilities of access. . . ."[1]

Throughout the wartime discussions on Germany, Soviet representatives had behaved in a manner which encouraged the Western powers to believe in their good faith. Stalin and Molotov frequently made blunt statements in favor of their own position, and sometimes resorted to temporization and vagueness, but at no point were the Soviets regarded as the *enfants terribles* that they came to be in postwar negotiations.

Almost as soon as Russian forces entered the territory of the defeated German Reich, however, the Western powers found themselves faced with a series of unilateral actions. First, the Soviets detached the entire area of Germany east of the Oder-Neisse line and handed it over to Polish administration. Stalin had asked at Yalta that this territory be given to Poland, but the Western powers had not agreed.[2] Other unilateral Soviet moves affected the political and economic structure of Germany. On June 10, 1945, Soviet Marshal Zhukov authorized the establishment in East Germany of "anti-fascist, democratic parties," "free" trade unions, and other workers' organizations. A German Communist Party, led by former German Communists who had returned from Moscow on the heels of the Red Army, was formed in Berlin almost immediately. Organization of the Social Democratic Party, the Christian Democratic Union, the Liberal Democratic Party, and a centralized trade union under communist control followed in quick succession.[3] Meanwhile, Soviet troops and industrial specialists descended on the territories of Germany under Soviet control, and even on the sectors of Berlin earmarked for occupation by the West, and appropriated almost everything of value that could be transported.

These unilateral Soviet moves cast a shadow on the third meeting of the Big Three, which took place in Potsdam during July 1945.

Potsdam

Nevertheless, the conference proceeded relatively smoothly, and Stalin showed himself accommodating in a number of respects. To Western protests about the transfer of such large territories to Poland, he replied that the question of Germany's eastern border was still open, and that the Soviet Union did not feel itself bound to support the Oder-Neisse line in a final settlement. It was decided to defer further consideration of this question to a later peace conference, and that in the meantime the territory should remain under Polish administration.

A compromise was reached on the subject of reparations. Since the Soviets had already extracted large quantities of goods from the region under their control, it was agreed that each occupying power would satisfy its reparations requirements primarily from its own zone, provided enough resources were left to enable the Germans to subsist without external assistance. The Soviets assented to this after being promised 25 per cent of the industrial plants to be dismantled in West Germany; in return, they agreed to make certain deliveries to the West of raw materials and manufactured goods from East Germany. They also agreed to satisfy Poland's reparations requirements from the Soviet share. When Bevin objected to a Soviet proposal for international control of the Ruhr, Stalin personally withdrew the proposal. General principles governing the occupation of Germany were agreed upon at Potsdam—largely in accord with previous conversations at Teheran and Yalta—and a permanent Council of Foreign Ministers was formed to consider questions arising from the war, including the preparation of a peace treaty for Germany.[4]

In addition to the negative provisions for demilitarization, denazification, and reparations, the general principles laid down at Potsdam included certain positive ones:

> Supreme authority in matters affecting Germany as a whole was to be exercised jointly by the commanders-in-chief of the occupying powers in their capacity as members of the Control Council.
>
> So far as practicable, there was to be uniformity of treatment of the German population throughout Germany.
>
> Subject to the necessity of maintaining military security, freedom of speech, press, and religion were to be permitted, as well as the freedom to form free trade unions.

During the period of occupation, Germany was to be treated as a single economic unit. To this end, common policies were to be established in regard to:

a. Mining and industrial production
b. Agriculture, forestry, and fishing
c. Wages, prices, and rationing
d. Import and export programs
e. Currency and banking, taxation, and customs
f. Reparation and removal of industrial war potential
g. Transportation and communications

All democratic political parties, with rights of assembly and of public discussion, were to be allowed and encouraged throughout Germany.[5]

Thus, the Big Three seemed to have reached a *modus vivendi* with regard to Germany, although decisions were reached only in principle on some questions, and were deferred on many others.

Failure to Achieve Common Occupation Policies

Even before the conclusion of the Potsdam conference, Western elements had moved into Berlin, and the machinery of four-power government had been set up for the capital and for the country as a whole. General Clay, at that time Deputy U.S. Military Governor, and his British opposite number, General Weeks, had agreed verbally with Marshall Zhukov that a main highway, a rail line, and two air corridors would be used for the entry of Allied personnel into Berlin. They did not wish to accept a permanent allocation of specific routes, since this might later be interpreted as limiting the right of access over any and all routes.[6] When the first contingent of American occupation personnel under Colonel Howley moved up the road to Berlin, however, they found the Soviets extremely jealous of their right to supervise traffic entering the capital.[7] Soviet officers also showed themselves reluctant to turn over control of the U.S. sector of Berlin to American personnel.[8]

There soon were further indications that all would not be smooth sailing for the Allied Control Council. Part of the difficulty stemmed from the fact that France, though invited to take part in the occupation as a result of the Yalta conference, had not been represented at Potsdam. Consequently, her officials did not regard themselves bound by the Potsdam Agreement, and the French Military Governor felt free to veto the establishment of central German administrative agencies.[9]

More disturbing was the attitude of Soviet officials. While agreeing in principle to the establishment of central German agencies and on the need for measures to promote German economic reconstruction, the Soviets waged a campaign of delay and obfuscation. When in December 1945, General Clay and British Military Governor General Robertson advanced a proposal to open all zonal boundaries to the passage of Germans, Soviet General Sokolovsky said that he agreed in principle but that practical application at the present moment was impossible. His colleagues were unable to determine his reasons.[10] Earlier, General Clay had proposed the establishment of certain German administrative agencies; General Zhukov's response had been that he was satisfied with the proposal but would have to withhold his concurrence until it had been referred to his government.[11] Only after they had been assured that France would oppose central German agencies did the Soviet representatives vote in favor of them.

Again, when the Western powers asked that the Soviets place the manufactures from East Germany in a common pool to meet the cost of essential imports, as provided by the Potsdam Agreement, the Soviets did not deny the agreement but put up a successful delaying action.[12] General Clay concluded that while Soviet representatives supported the establishment of central administrative agencies in principle, they did not intend to remove the zonal barriers or even to place the resources of East Germany in a common pool except on terms highly unfavorable to the West.[13]

Under these conditions the work of the Control Council was severely limited in scope. During the initial months of its existence, the Council concluded numerous agreements, concerned for the most part with undoing the work of the Nazis. In addition, it issued some directives of an administrative nature (e.g., concerning the rationing of electricity and gas) and a smaller number of more positive laws (such as a law establishing German labor courts).[14] As the months went on, fewer and fewer agreements were reached. The last issue of the Control Council *Gazette* covers seven months but shows only one piece of legislation: "Repealing Certain Laws, Ordinances, and Decrees Promulgated by the Nazi Government Concerning Churches."[15] With one exception, the four powers were never able to agree on any measures which would have resulted in curtailing the absolute power of the Soviets in East Germany or in promoting to a significant degree unification of the country as a whole.

The exception, however, was an important one. At the end of 1945 the U.S.S.R. agreed to the establishment of three flight corridors leading from West Germany into Berlin, and shortly afterwards to certain flight rules governing operations in these corridors. This agreement will be discussed in Chapter II.

Soviet Policies in East Germany

While the Control Council was stalled, the Soviets retained an almost completely free hand in the administration of East Germany. After a brief period during which emphasis was placed on dismantling industrial equipment and shipping it east, Moscow began to build its zone of occupation into something resembling an East European satellite state. This involved consolidating the hold of local Communists on East Germany's political life and coordinating the economy with that of the Soviet bloc.

The first step taken to build up the strength of communism in East Germany was to install German Communists, some of pre-1933 vintage and some trained during the war in Moscow, in key positions in Berlin and throughout the zone.[16] Schools for training new communist leaders were established,[17] and a series of communist-controlled "mass organizations" and blocs was built up to permit complete and centralized control of all political activities.[18]

Early in 1946 a merger of the Communist Party and the Social Democratic Party was forced by the Soviet military authorities, apparently in an effort to assure communist control of a large bloc of votes. The resulting combination was christened the Socialist Unity Party (SED).[19] In spite of the fact that the SED enjoyed strenuous Soviet backing, it received, together with several tiny, communist-dominated farmers' groups, only slightly more than half of the votes cast in zonal elections held in the fall of 1946. Nevertheless, this election permitted the SED, with a semblance of legality, to assume effective control of all the state governments in the Soviet zone.

During 1947 the Soviets placed still more emphasis on political organization. The establishment of paramilitary "people's police" units was announced in December of that year, although actual formation of these units may have started some months earlier.[20] The last elements of real opposition to communist policy in the two "bourgeois" parties were stamped out, at about the same time, and from then on the East German branches of the Christian

Democratic Union and the Liberal Democratic Party functioned principally as democratic window dressing.

Meanwhile Soviet economic officials had been working toward the reconstruction of a part of East German industry. A large proportion of the major industrial enterprises in East Germany were converted into Soviet-owned corporations, which, together with many smaller, privately-owned firms, now devoted their production efforts to the delivery of reparations to the Soviet Union. Some of the enterprises that the Soviets had seized were later transferred to the German communist authorities, possibly as a move to strengthen the hand of the SED, but reparations continued to be extracted from their current production.[21] In the summer of 1947 a German Economic Commission (DWK) was established in East Germany with the task of mobilizing the resources and reestablishing the economic potential of the Soviet zone.[22] Other German administrative agencies, working on a zonal level under the watchful eye of Soviet Military Government, gave central direction to the communist-controlled *Land* (state) administrations.

In pursuing their goals of economic reconstruction and political consolidation, the Soviets enjoyed certain advantages that were denied the Western powers in their respective zones. The Soviet zone ordinarily produced a surplus of agricultural products, so that the occupation forces were able to live off the land and still avoid the necessity of importing food supplies for the civilian population. Furthermore, decisions affecting East Germany could be made by the Soviets alone, without the concurrence of Western authorities. The Western powers, on the other hand, occupied zones that ordinarily required more food than they produced, and the major steps toward economic recovery in West Germany presupposed the cooperation of two or more of the occupying powers and thus became matters for international negotiation. The Soviets could argue that for a zonal commander to take a decision in his own zone was one thing, but that discussions among two or more zonal commanders infringed upon agreements providing for four-power government. Finally, most moves by the Western powers were subject to criticism from groups within Germany as well as to the influence of public opinion in Great Britain, France, and the United States. The Soviet Union, with its tight system of political control both in East Germany and at home, was able to move more freely.

Efforts to Reconstruct the West German Economy

At first, postwar economic reconstruction in West Germany proceeded at a snail's pace. Western authorities, striving to preserve the wartime alliance and to reach four-power agreement on common policies to be followed in Germany, were reluctant to take unilateral action in their own zones, although reports of Soviet unilateral action in East Germany became increasingly frequent. West Germany's communications system was repaired, and a start was made on rehabilitating industrial facilities. But with the difficulty of interzonal trade and the hopelessly inflated currency, the economic situation remained one of apathy and stagnation. Only a succession of relief measures by the Western powers, largely the United States, prevented it from becoming catastrophic.*

Those who studied the economic situation in West Germany during 1945 and 1946 were often at a loss for words in which to describe its bleakness. At the end of 1946 a Conservative member of the British House of Commons reported that it was almost impossible to exaggerate how utterly shattered was the German economy and how completely collapsed was the morale of the German people.[23] A comprehensive survey of conditions in the U.S. and British zones undertaken at the request of President Truman by Herbert Hoover in 1946 painted an even darker picture:

> The housing situation in the two zones is the worst that modern civilization has ever seen. . . . The coal famine all over Western Europe and the unprecedented severity of the winter have produced everywhere the most acute suffering. As an example in Germany, no household coal has been issued in Hamburg since October. . . .
>
> Over half of the 6,595,000 children and adolescents, especially in the lower-income groups, are in a deplorable condition. . . . In some areas famine edema . . . is appearing in the children. . . . The increasing death toll among the aged is appalling.[24]

* As of July 1946 the "out-of-pocket" expenses of the United States for emergency economic support in Germany were estimated by Assistant Secretary of State Hilldring at 200 million dollars per year. (*The New York Times*, July 30, 1946.) If indirect supports had been included, the total would have been considerably larger. At the end of 1947, Secretary of State Marshall estimated that Great Britain and the United States were spending approximately 700 million dollars a year to provide food for West Germany. (Boris Meissner, *Russland die Westmächte und Deutschland*, H. H. Nölke Verlag, Hamburg, 1953, p. 149.)

This situation concerned the Western powers both for humanitarian reasons and because they realized that only an economically healthy Germany would permit the recovery of Western Europe as a whole. As long as economic stagnation continued in Germany, it would be necessary to pump dollar assistance not only into the west zones but into most of Western Europe.

Particularly irritating to American officials was the fact that, while the United States was spending substantial amounts to prevent starvation in West Germany, the Soviets, in violation of the Potsdam Agreement, were taking reparations from the current production of East German factories without even consulting the Western powers.*

The first countermove by the West came almost a year after the end of the war, on May 3, 1946, when General Clay halted delivery to the Soviet Union of dismantled plants from West Germany.[25] Under the Potsdam Agreement the Soviets were to have received 25 per cent of all dismantled plants in West Germany as reparations; but since they had refused to agree on the common utilization of German resources in the four zones, General Clay wished to avoid a situation in which, as he put it, the West would be "without plants and without an agreement."

A more positive move toward the economic reconstruction of West Germany was taken two months later. Despairing of achieving four-power implementation of German economic unity, Secretary of State Byrnes invited each of the other three occupying powers to join the economic administration of its zone with that of the U.S. zone. This invitation was accepted by the British, denounced by the Soviets, and not acted upon by the French.[26] Thereafter measures to merge the economies of the U.S. and British zones moved steadily ahead. During the next two years the French also allowed the economy of their zone to be integrated more and more closely with that of the "bizone."

A still more positive policy was outlined by Secretary Byrnes in a major address delivered in Stuttgart on September 6, 1946. Byrnes

* Paragraph 19, Section III, of the Potsdam Agreement reads as follows: "Payment of reparations should leave enough resources to enable the German people to subsist without external assistance. In working out the economic balance of Germany the necessary means must be provided to pay for imports approved by the Control Council in Germany. The proceeds of exports from current production and stocks shall be available in the first place for payment of such imports." (Reprinted in *Occupation of Germany—Policy and Progress, 1945-1946,* Department of State Publication 2783, Government Printing Office, Washington, 1947, p. 160.)

emphasized that the solution of economic problems in Germany was necessary for the future well-being not only of Germany but of Europe. He recalled that the Potsdam Agreement had provided for the treatment of Germany as an economic unit, but pointed out that, as a result of the inability of the Allied Control Council to carry out this agreement, industrial production in Germany had not reached even those levels which the occupying powers had agreed were essential for a minimum German peacetime economy. "So far as many vital questions are concerned," he said, "the Control Council is neither governing Germany nor allowing Germany to govern herself." Byrnes therefore advocated the economic unification of as large a portion of Germany as possible, the establishment of central German economic agencies, and the early formation of a provisional German government.[27]

In line with the new British-American policy of treating their two zones as an economic unit, bizonal German administrative agencies for economics, food, transport, communications, finance, and certain other functions were established in a number of cities of West Germany during the fall of 1946.[28] The agencies purposely were not concentrated in one place in order that they might not be construed as a German government. This arrangement proved weak, however, and the two military governors authorized an improved and strengthened German administration for the bizonal area on May 29, 1947. The new organization provided for an Economic Council in Frankfurt composed of delegates elected by the various state parliaments. This body convened for the first time on June 25, 1947. Decisions of the Economic Council were to be carried out by an Executive Committee. Administrative machinery was strengthened still more early in 1948 with the establishment of a central banking system for the two zones.[29]

While the bizonal economic administration was being formed, the European Recovery Program was also taking shape. Secretary of State Marshall, in an address delivered at Harvard on June 5, 1947, called for a combined economic effort on the part of all European states and promised U.S. assistance. Somewhat over a month later, Washington sent General Clay a new policy directive which envisaged the integration of West Germany into the European Recovery Program. When delegates of the sixteen participating powers met in April 1948, to conclude administrative arrangements for the program, they were joined by experts from West Germany.[30]

All these measures did not immediately provide food for the

hungry population. Indeed, the situation seemed to become worse rather than better. A major drought in the summer of 1947 caused a serious water shortage, and the harvest was 20 per cent less than that of the previous year. "It seemed as if the fates had conspired against the defeated Germany," wrote a German historian.[31] In January 1948, food stocks were down to a dangerously low level. Hamburg had supplies of grain and flour for only seventeen days.[32] One strike wave after another broke out, and the authorities seemed powerless to improve the situation.[33] Anti-Allied sentiment was reported to be on the increase in West Germany. Konrad Adenauer, later to become the first postwar chancellor of Germany, bitterly criticized military government, saying that it knew how to give orders but not how to govern.[34] Other German leaders made even stronger attacks on the occupying authorities.

Soviet Obstruction of West German Recovery

Under pressure of the serious situation in West Germany, the Western military governors made repeated and vigorous attempts to achieve a major economic measure—currency reform. Until the runaway inflation could be checked, there was little hope for German economic recovery.

The prospects for an agreement on currency reform for all four zones at first appeared relatively favorable, and in the fall of 1946 some Allied officials were hopeful that anti-inflation measures could be carried out. But then the Soviets started to introduce complications by making the reform conditional on the solution of other questions, such as reparations, and the negotiations dragged on for many months.[35] In August 1947 General Clay was reported to have made his "one last effort" to come to an agreement with the Soviets on the sorely-needed reform.[36] However, in February of 1948 he was still trying, although the Soviet-controlled German press had begun to allege that the Americans were only talking about a general monetary reform in order to cloak their real intentions of establishing a separate reform in the Western zones.[37] The London *Times* commented that, on the face of it, this charge foreshadowed the end of Russian participation in four-power discussions of the matter, but that both British and American circles were reluctant to adopt this unfavorable view with its implication of still further difficulties in the Control Council.[38]

According to General Clay, the Soviets did not directly refuse the final Western proposals, but by delaying tactics prevented agreement and drew the discussions out for almost a year. One of their principal demands was that they be allowed to print some of the currency themselves from a duplicate set of the plates, instead of having all the money printed at a central point under four-power control. American representatives rejected this demand, since it would have permitted the Soviets to re-create inflation simply by running their printing presses. They remembered all too well how, in 1945, the Soviets had used a duplicate set of plates for occupation currency to flood Germany with paper money, much of which later had to be redeemed in dollars by the U.S. Treasury.[39] In the end, four-power agreement on currency reform proved impossible, and inflation in West Germany was not checked until after the Control Council had broken up in the spring of 1948. Similarly, the Soviets opposed almost every other measure designed to promote political integration or economic recovery in West Germany.

The principal weapons that the Soviets used in opposing the policies of the Western powers in Germany were obstruction, delay, and vituperation in the Allied Control Council and the Council of Foreign Ministers; but they also made use of propaganda attacks in the press, appeals to German nationalism, protests from the satellite states of Eastern Europe, and finally, pressure on West Berlin. Each of these modes of opposition will be discussed below.

By the end of 1946, it was obvious that the Control Council would not agree on any major constructive measures, and during 1947 the atmosphere at Council meetings became more and more stormy. General Clay notes that Soviet representatives used meetings of the Control Council with increasing frequency to launch vicious and unfounded propaganda attacks on the Western powers.[40] The Soviet Military Governor alleged that the British and American zones were being militarized, that the Allies had sabotaged the reparations program, that West Germany was being exploited by the capitalist powers, that Nazi and criminal elements were being rehabilitated in the west zones, that the SED and other "democratic" elements were being persecuted, and that the bizonal fusion was deliberately designed to break up quadripartite government and split Germany. The British representative on the Allied Control Council finally was driven to remark that he had been trying to find a reason why he had listened to so much invective, and that the only reason he could find was courtesy, and even that was severely taxed.[41]

Soviet obstruction in the Council of Foreign Ministers was

marked primarily by delay. In 1945, the problem of making peace with Germany was bypassed by mutual consent, and four-power efforts were concentrated on questions concerning the Far East and Germany's former satellites. Early in 1946, French Foreign Minister Bidault proposed a discussion of the German question at a meeting of the Council of Foreign Ministers in Paris, but this was refused by the Soviets.[42] Molotov also opposed the appointment of deputies to study German problems in detail and to prepare recommendations for action by the Council of Foreign Ministers. Instead, he proposed that the Council assemble again later in the year to consider those problems. At this, U.S. Secretary of State Byrnes forecast, correctly, that at such a meeting the Soviets would then suggest referring German questions to a committee of deputies.[43] He had concluded, after successive rebuffs by the Soviets, that they were not eager to obtain an early peace settlement: "Particularly in the case of Germany, the Soviet Union was content with any policy that contributed to delay."[44] Byrnes quotes from one of Molotov's speeches at the Paris conference:

> Before talking about a peace treaty with Germany it is necessary to solve the question of setting up an all-German government. . . . But even when a German government has been set up it will take a number of years to check up on what this new German government represents and whether it is trustworthy. . . . A future German government must be such a democratic government as will be able to extirpate the remnants of Fascism in Germany and which will at the same time be able to fulfill Germany's obligations toward the Allies. Amongst other things and above all it will be bound to carry out reparations deliveries to the Allies.[45]

As Byrnes had prophesied, the conference of foreign ministers in New York at the end of 1946 made little progress toward a four-power agreement on Germany. Instead, deputies were appointed to study the German question, which was referred to another meeting to be held in Moscow in the spring of 1947.

The Moscow conference at first showed promise of reaching agreement on the formation of central German agencies, but even this was prevented by Molotov's insistence on reparations in the amount of ten billion dollars to be taken from current German production, was well as by his demand that each zonal commander should have the right to overrule decisions of central German agencies which affected his zone.[46] Meanwhile, economic conditions in West Germany were becoming catastrophic and the consolidation of Soviet power in East Germany and Eastern Europe continued. The Moscow conference thus served to delay still more the reconstruction of Germany and Western Europe.

The four foreign ministers met again in London at the end of 1947. It was to be the last meeting of the Council until after the blockade. Molotov pressed his previous demands for reparations, and Secretary of State Marshall countered by pointing out that the United States could not pump economic support into one side of Germany for an indefinite period while the Soviets extracted reparations from the other side. Molotov also, while ostensibly supporting creation of a central German government, continued jealously to guard the independence of the Soviet command in East Germany. When Marshall pressed him for an accounting of goods removed from East Germany, Molotov replied that the Allies had no right to demand information about the economic policies in any individual zone.[47] In addition, he reiterated the Soviet demand that a zonal commander be given the right to overrule the decisions of central German agencies affecting his zone.[48] The London conference broke up at the motion of Secretary Marshall, after Molotov had leveled "almost every conceivable charge" against the policies of the Western powers in Germany,[49] and the Allies had become convinced that the Soviet Union simply did not want an agreement.

A third method by which the Soviets sought to obstruct Allied policies in West Germany was by agitating vigorously for German unity—but under conditions that the Western powers could not possibly accept. Moscow thus attempted to turn German nationalism against schemes for improving conditions in West Germany, while at the same time blocking any quadripartite unification plan that did not assure substantial communist control of the whole country. In a speech at the Allied Control Council on February 26, 1947, for instance, Marshal Sokolovsky charged the United States and Great Britain with trying to split their zones from the rest of Germany, and then called for immediate unification of the country and a plebiscite to consult Germans on their desires. His proposal was echoed by the Soviet-controlled German press and became the basis for a campaign by German authorities in the Soviet zone.

One of the principal elements in this campaign was the "People's Congress" movement. The first "German People's Congress," which was completely communist-controlled although it purported to represent all democratic elements in the east zone, met in Berlin on December 6 and 7, 1947. On December 15, Soviet Foreign Minister Molotov showed an official Soviet interest in this activity by attempting to have a delegation from the Congress appear before the Council of Foreign Ministers then meeting in London. But the Western powers refused to receive the delegates.[50]

On January 15, 1948, the Standing Committee of the People's Congress adopted a resolution condemning the establishment of a bizonal economic executive at Frankfurt and advocating a plebiscite on the question of German unity. It also announced that a draft German constitution would be prepared, and called for the election of a new People's Congress to represent all Germany.[51]

Political parties and other organizations in the east zone immediately went through the motions of electing delegates to the Congress. In the west zones, the appeal was studiously ignored by nearly all German organizations except those controlled by the Communists.[52] Nevertheless, the second People's Congress, claiming to speak for all Germans, met in Berlin as scheduled on March 18, 1948. It took two principal measures. First, it elected a People's Council, which was to carry on the activities of the Congress between meetings, and was to have committees to deal with questions of a peace treaty, a constitution, economics, justice, culture, and welfare.[53] The Council looked very much like a shadow government.

The second action of the Congress was to launch a campaign to collect signatures to a petition advocating the immediate unification of Germany. Allied military authorities forbade the circulation of this petition in West Germany and West Berlin. A British official statement characterized it as "unnecessary and undesirable," and concluded that it "is not a genuine attempt to ascertain the wishes of the German people, but aims at hiding the responsibility of its promoters for the present division of Germany."[54] Nevertheless, by the end of the campaign, the Communists claimed to have collected over thirteen million signatures, hundreds of thousands of them from West Germany.[55]

A fourth method used by the Soviets to oppose Allied plans for reconstruction in West Germany was to organize pressure from the East European satellites. One important exemplification of this tactic was a three-power conference on Germany which met in Prague on February 17, 1948—a week before the coup which was to snuff out democratic liberties in that city. Communist Deputy Foreign Minister Clementis of Czechoslovakia told the delegates of the three powers (Czechoslovakia, Yugoslavia, and Poland) that it was high time to call such a conference in view of violations of the principles of the Potsdam Agreement, the disruption of the London conference of foreign ministers, and the preference accorded to Germany under the Marshall Plan. He added that many "doubtful occurrences" in West Germany directly affected the states that had been the first victims of German imperialism.[56] The conference issued a declaration attacking the policies of the Western powers in Germany, which Marshal Sokolovsky introduced at the last meeting of the Allied Control Council on March 20, 1948.[57]

London Agreements and Breakup of the Allied Control Council

Soviet intransigence in the Control Council and the Council of Foreign Ministers, as well as communist policies in East Germany, convinced the Western powers that the Soviet Union had no intention of coming to an agreement on the administration of Germany, except on terms that would give her substantial control of the whole country. Indeed, Molotov's behavior at the London conference late in 1947 was one of the final considerations which precipitated the French decision to merge her zone with that of Great Britain and the United States. As a result, the three Western powers were able to agree to discuss the establishment of a West German Government.[58]

Accordingly, representatives of the United States, Great Britain, and France convened again in London in February 1948. Holland, Belgium, and Luxembourg, as interested parties, were also invited. The talks lasted until early June, although the conference recessed during much of March and April. The Western powers arrived at several agreements which were announced on June 2 in a series of documents known as the London Recommendations. Economic policies in the three west zones were to be coordinated, West Germany was to be enabled to play a full part in the European Recovery Program, and German state authorities were to be authorized to take steps to draft a constitution for a German Federal Republic. Another major decision provided for control of the Ruhr by an international authority, which was to include the six powers assembled in London and also the Germans.[59]

The initial communiqué of the London six-power conference, issued on March 8 at the end of the first session, indicated a continued desire to achieve agreement with the Soviet Union on the

German question, but made it clear that the Western powers would move ahead even in the absence of such agreement:

> The continuous failure of the Council of Foreign Ministers to reach quadripartite agreement has created a situation in Germany which, if permitted to continue, would have increasingly unfortunate consequences for western Europe. It was therefore necessary that urgent political and economic problems arising out of this situation in Germany should be solved. The participating powers had in view the necessity of ensuring the economic reconstruction of western Europe including Germany, and of establishing a basis for the participation of a democratic Germany in the community of free peoples. While delay in reaching these objectives can no longer be accepted, ultimate Four Power agreement is in no way precluded.[60]

In spite of this expression of hope that four-power agreement might yet be attained, the Soviets reacted to the first session of the London conference by walking out of the Allied Control Council in Berlin. Toward the end of the Council meeting of March 20, 1948, Marshal Sokolovsky suddenly demanded to be advised of all agreements on West Germany reached by the London conference in February and March. Representatives of the Western powers replied that this conference had been held among governments and that the Western military governors had not yet been officially informed of its results. Sokolovsky then read a long statement, repeating his former charges against the Western powers in even stronger language. As the British representative started to reply, the Soviet commander, who was in the chair, interrupted him and declared the meeting adjourned. General Clay notes that the Soviet delegation rose as one and walked out, following what must have been a prearranged plan.[61] Two days later, the Soviets announced that their representatives would not be able to attend meetings of seven subsidiary groups of the Control Council because of illness.[62] Marshal Sokolovsky retained the Council chairmanship through the end of March, but did not call a meeting.

Although one or another of the Western military governors who served as chairman of the Control Council in April, May, and June could have tried to call another meeting, none did so, on the grounds that no items had been submitted for the agenda.[63] By this time, Allied authorities were convinced that the Soviets would only engage in further wrangling in an effort to perpetuate economic chaos in the western zones. The Control Council was dead.

The end of the Control Council made it possible to proceed with currency reform in the western zones. The British and Americans were quick to reach agreement, and, after a few weeks' hesitation, were joined by the French. The first law governing currency reform was announced on June 18, 1948, and others followed in quick succession. By and large, the effect of this legislation was to substitute one new *Deutsche Mark* (DM) for every ten of the old *Reichsmark* (RM).[64] Currency reform touched off an almost magical process of recovery in West Germany. It also was part of a chain of events which led directly to the Berlin blockade.

An Interpretation of Soviet German Policy, 1945-1948

Ever since Prussia rose to the status of a great power, Russian rulers have been deeply concerned about their policy toward this vigorous neighbor. With the triumph of communism in Russia, this concern about relations with Germany became even more intense than it had been under the Czars. Germany was the birthplace of Marx and the hope of Lenin. She was the most highly industrialized state on the continent of Europe. As a friend of the Soviet Union she could help to balance the power of the Western capitalist nations; as an unfriendly power she could provide a bridgehead leading to the heart of Russia.

After World War I, Karl Radek, one of the Soviet leaders most concerned with the formulation of policy toward Germany, summarized his attitude at the fourth congress of the Comintern in November 1922, as follows:

> A Russia weakened to the utmost by the war could neither have remained a great Power nor acquired the economic and technical means for her industrial reconstruction, unless she had in the existence of Germany a counter-weight to the preponderance of the Allies.[65]

A year later Radek wrote in *Izvestiia*:

> If Entente capital, having torn Germany to pieces, were to establish its hegemony over her, on the backs of the conquered German workers, this would signify the greatest danger for Soviet Russia.[66]

At the end of World War II, although Russia was then in a relatively more favorable power position than she had been after the war of 1914-1918, her concern with German affairs was in no wise diminished. At first Stalin apparently felt that the best solution would be to destroy Germany as a great power once and for all. This view may have been based in part on the Russians' hate and fear of the Germans after the latter's brutal and successful operations in the Soviet Union from 1941 to 1943. In addition, Stalin had a profound contempt for the German working class, which he regarded as too submissive to authority to constitute a suitable revolutionary instrument.* He was without question profoundly disturbed by the thought that, after the war, the Western capitalist nations (whom he never ceased to regard as enemies) might incorporate Germany's military and economic strength into their total potential.

Accordingly, Soviet policy toward post-war Germany appears to have been initially directed toward weakening and pauperizing the whole country. During 1945 and early 1946, however, the Soviets modified their policies toward East Germany and their tactics toward West Germany. Instead of continuing to dismantle East German industry, thereby arousing the antagonism of even pro-communist East Germans, they started to strengthen the economic and political structure of this area. As for West Germany, the Soviets still tried to ensure that the Western powers would obtain as little value as possible from their zones of occupation, but they used new means to achieve this objective. Instead of demanding openly that West Germany be kept weak, they now presented themselves as champions of a reunited Germany with a substantial industrial capacity, while at the same time insisting on the imposition of political and economic controls that would enable them to profit relatively more from the reconstituted Reich than would the Western powers.†

* At the Teheran conference Stalin cited an instance in 1907 when two hundred German workers failed to appear at an important mass meeting because there was no railroad employee at a station platform to punch their tickets. (Robert E. Sherwood, *Roosevelt and Hopkins*, Harper and Brothers, New York 1948, p. 782).

† Since most of Germany's steel capacity is located in the western part of the country, the postwar change in the Soviet attitude toward the level of German steel production may have reflected this change in tactics toward West Germany. At discussions in the Allied Control Council in 1945 the Soviets proposed 4,900,000 tons a year as the maximum steel production that should be allowed. This was more than two million tons lower than the next lowest proposal, that of the French. Yet only a few months later Molotov proposed that German steel capacity be raised to 10,000,000 tons a year, or a million tons higher than the next highest figure, which had been advanced by the British. (Lucius D. Clay, *Decision in Germany*, Doubleday & Company, New York, 1950, pp. 108 and 130.)

If the United States, Britain, and France refused to accede to the controls which the Soviets desired, Moscow was prepared to use every available instrument to perpetuate the economic chaos in the three west zones.

The Warsaw Declaration

This new approach to Germany was revealed piecemeal by Soviet spokesmen at international conferences, from the Paris meeting of the Council of Foreign Ministers in the summer of 1946 to the London conferences of the Council at the end of 1947. Its most succinct statement was contained in the Warsaw Declaration, issued in June 1948 by a conference of Soviet and satellite foreign ministers meeting in the Polish capital.

The Warsaw Declaration, which may have been intended as a counterblast to the London Recommendations released by the six-power conference in London some three weeks earlier, was published the day after the blockade was imposed. Since this Declaration represents the most complete official statement of the Soviet position on the German question at the time of the Berlin blockade, it is perhaps worth considering in more detail. Most of the text is devoted to attacks on the London Recommendations and the policies of the Western powers. The Declaration concludes, however, with the following demands:

> 1. The implementation of the measures insuring the final demilitarization of Germany, by agreement among Great Britain, the USSR, France and the United States.
> 2. The institution for a definite time of control by the Four Powers—Great Britain, USSR, France and the United States—over the Ruhr heavy industry, with a view to developing the peace branches of the Ruhr industry and preventing the re-establishment of Germany's war potential.
> 3. The establishment, by agreement among the Governments of Great Britain, the USSR, France and the United States, of a provisional, democratic peace-loving government for the whole of Germany, composed of representatives of democratic parties and organizations of Germany, for the purpose of creating a guarantee against the repetition of German aggression.
> 4. The conclusion of a peace treaty with Germany, in accordance with the Potsdam decisions, so that the occupation troops of all the Powers should be withdrawn from Germany within one year after the conclusion of the peace treaty.

5. The elaboration of measures for the fulfillment by Germany of her reparations obligations toward the states which suffered from German aggression.[67]

This statement embodies a policy which, if accepted, could have given the Soviet Union a continued veto over the economic reconstruction of West Germany, and might have resulted in the creation of a communist government for all Germany. In analyzing the statement, one should remember that it is based on the "principle of unanimity" by which any one power could stop action by the other three.* Also implicit in the statement is the concept of control and enforcement by all four powers. The implementation of any program based on the Warsaw Declaration, would, therefore, have been supervised by Soviet personnel as well as by the Western Allies. Whether this would have permitted Allied inspectors to penetrate East Germany is uncertain. It is clear, however, that Soviet inspectors would have been strategically located in the Ruhr.

With the principle of unanimity and the principle of supervision in mind, one can see that the program embodied in the Warsaw Declaration would have enabled the Soviets to exercise a powerful voice in West German affairs, and to prevent the Western powers from harnessing West German economic and military potential in the service of their own policies. Demilitarization (Point 1) would presumably have enabled Soviet inspectors to enter industrial plants throughout West Germany and to interfere with the manufacture of any articles which they might interpret as military supplies. Four-power control of the Ruhr (Point 2) would have given the Soviets an opportunity to place inspectors in the industrial plants of the Ruhr and to make more difficult the participation of this area in the economic recovery of Europe as a whole. The elaboration of measures for Germany's fulfillment of her reparations obligations (Point 5) would have given the Soviets a voice in all West Germany's economic policies. Since the Soviet Union claimed ten billion dollars in reparations from current production, she could, in effect, have ensured that a major part of West Germany's industry worked to fill reparations orders rather than take part in the European Recovery Program.

Point Three, concerning the establishment of a German government, deserves special mention. The Declaration specified that this

* Soviet representatives stubbornly defended the "principle of unanimity" at all international discussions affecting Germany. (Cf. Meissner, *op. cit.*, pp. 101, 125, 193-196.)

government was to be composed of "representatives of democratic parties and organizations of Germany." In other words, the many communist front organizations, which had been systematically organized in East Germany, were to be given representation, thus ensuring the Communists a much larger share in the government than that to which their proportion in the total population would have entitled them. Inclusion of these communist-dominated "mass organizations" in any central German authority was a demand emphasized by Molotov at the London meeting of the Council of Foreign Ministers in December 1947.[68] When the first "German People's Congress" met in Berlin earlier that month, the SED—actually a minority group—had been able to dominate the Congress in part through the use of such mass organizations.* The phrase "democratic parties and organizations" not only permitted the Soviets to give representation to communist-dominated groups in the east zone; it also afforded them an opportunity to veto any parties or groups from West Germany which they chose to define as "undemocratic." Furthermore, since the Soviets would have been in a position to maintain a state of chaos in West Germany's economy, they could easily have given the Germans to understand that election of a communist-dominated government was a prerequisite for an improvement in their economic condition. In other words, the Soviet program, as elaborated in successive four-power meetings and summarized in the Warsaw Declaration, might well have led to a pro-communist government for all Germany.†

With regard to Point Four, which demanded conclusion of a peace treaty and withdrawal of all occupation troops within a year, one need only recognize that this provision did not apply to civilian or military control personnel, who presumably would stay at their posts. Furthermore, withdrawal of Soviet troops meant withdrawal only to the Oder River line, forty miles from Berlin. Withdrawal of American troops probably meant withdrawal across the Atlantic.

A final word should be said about Point Five, which dealt with

* Meissner observes that the SED never would have achieved a majority in anything approaching a free election, but with the help of the "mass organizations," which were dependent on the SED and Communists from the west zones, an SED majority in the People's Congress was easily achieved. (*Op. cit.*, p. 157.)

† Secretary Marshall recognized this at the London conference, when he observed that the power to exact continuing reparations would mean in fact a power of life and death over every German government. He had noted earlier that payment of reparations out of current production for an indefinite period would prevent the economic reconstruction of Germany and delay European recovery for many years. (Meissner, *op. cit.*, pp. 149 and 151.)

reparations. From the time of the Yalta conference right up to the blockade of Berlin, the Soviets continued to demand ten billion dollars in reparations from Germany. Some Allied observers have seen this particular Soviet demand as the principal stumbling block on which the four-power conferences broke down. It is possible to maintain, however, that Soviet demands for reparations represented less a desire for goods with which to reconstruct the war-shattered economy of Russia than a screen behind which political control of Germany was to be exercised.

One strange aspect of the Soviet reparations demands is that, no matter how much Moscow had already extracted from East Germany or had received from West Germany, the figure of ten billion dollars remained the same. At the Paris meeting of the Council of Foreign Ministers, Secretary Byrnes pointed out that the East German territories under Polish administration had formerly contained properties with a tax valuation of more than eleven billion dollars, and that properties in the East German territory annexed by the Soviets had been valued at two-and-one-half billion.[69] Seen from this point of view, the Soviet and Polish reparations demands had been met even before the fighting had stopped. Estimates as to the exact value of reparations received by the Soviets from the remaining area of Germany differ widely, but they agree that it was very high. One specialist estimates that by the end of 1948 the Soviets had received about eight billion dollars' worth of reparations from the four zones, about one-half in removals and the other half in current production.[70] Another expert computes the approximate value of Soviet reparations taken from the German economy by July 1948, as over eleven billion marks.*

Whatever their arithmetical peculiarities, the reparations demands must have had great political merit from the Soviet point of view. First, they provided an excellent stumbling block to four-power agreement, and thus contributed to their policy of delay. Second, if the Allies had assented to ten billion dollars in reparations, this would have provided an excuse to impose controls which would have given the Soviets a major voice in the West German economy.†

* Nettl, *op. cit.*, p. 237. These were "1937 marks," and hence more valuable than postwar German currency. To convert this value into dollars is a difficult task. One may hazard a guess that this figure represented a value on the order of three billion dollars.

† General Clay reports an American offer at the Moscow conference which would have gone a considerable way toward meeting the Russian reparations

The Warsaw Declaration came at a time when Moscow was facing a basic decision. The sovietization of East Germany had progressed to a point at which German communist authorities were in charge of the administration of the whole zone, although under close Soviet supervision. As for West Germany, it was now clear that the policy of delay would serve no longer. With or without Soviet agreement, the Allies intended to proceed with political consolidation and economic reconstruction. The basic decision for the Soviets, therefore, was whether to complete the bolshevization of East Germany and eliminate the Western enclave in Berlin, or whether to try to force upon the Allies a four-power agreement on Germany along the lines of the Warsaw program.

There were, however, two unusual features about the alternative courses of action which faced the Soviets. One was that either course could presumably be pursued by blockading the west sectors of Berlin. The second was that the decision on which course to follow would depend in large measure on the reaction of the Western powers to such a blockade. It would be up to the Allies to decide whether to stay in Berlin and accept the Soviet program for Germany, or to withdraw from Berlin and leave Germany east of the Elbe an exclusive Soviet preserve. The immediate Soviet purpose in imposing the blockade on the west sectors of Berlin was thus to force a difficult decision on the Western powers, with the prospect that their prestige would be severely shaken whichever course they chose.

---

demands. This offer was "either overlooked by the Soviet delegation or else, more probably, the Soviet delegation did not desire that any real agreements be reached in this conference." (Clay, *op. cit.*, p. 150.)

CHAPTER II

BERLIN FROM 1945 TO 1948

THE main themes of German history from 1945 to 1948 were reflected in the Berlin microcosm. When personnel of the Western powers entered the city at the end of World War II, some two months after it had been taken by Soviet forces, they were concerned chiefly with preventing a resurgence of Nazism and militarism. They were also determined to cooperate peacefully with the Soviet Union, and to make four-power government of Berlin a successful venture. The Soviets accepted the concessions tendered by the West, but made few in return, all the while attempting to maintain their political grip on the city. Faced with Soviet intransigence and provocation, the Western powers reluctantly defended their own political position with increasing stubbornness. By the time the complete blockade was imposed in June 1948, a vest-pocket cold war within the former German capital was in full swing.

Initial Soviet Policy in Berlin

Berlin fell to the Soviets in April 1945. Flushed with victory, and remembering the atrocities of which the Nazis had been guilty in Russia, the men of the Red Army gave vent to their emotions at the expense of the hapless Berliners. The precise extent of the raping, looting, and violence which took place during April and May will never be known, but it was very great.

While the soldiery of the Red Army terrorized Berlin, technicians from Moscow systematically stripped the area of industrial equipment and other articles of value, especially the western sectors of the city, which were earmarked for occupation by the Allies. When American and British elements arrived, they found that machinery had been removed from mills and factories, stoves and pipes had been torn from restaurant kitchens, and all available livestock had been driven away, including 7,000 cows.[1] To paraphrase General Sherman's words, a crow flying over West Berlin would have had to carry its own provisions.

Even more important, in the long run, were the measures taken by the Soviet occupation forces to secure control of the political life of Berlin. On May 17 the executive branch of the city government (known as the Magistrat) was reconstituted by Soviet order. The new mayor was a non-Communist, and many of the technical functions of the city were placed in the hands of competent technicians of varying political persuasions. Close control over the city government was maintained, however, through the deputy mayor, a pre-1933 Communist who had returned to Berlin with the Red Army, and through other seasoned Communists who were placed in strategic posts. The director of personnel for the city government was a Communist, and the personnel directors in eighteen out of Berlin's twenty borough administrations were Communists or communist sympathizers.[2]

The banking system established by the Soviets is worthy of special note. When the Red Army entered Berlin, all banks were closed by Soviet order. In their place the Soviet commandant decreed the establishment of a commercial bank and a savings bank, which were to serve all banking requirements in the city, and were completely owned by the municipality. When the Western powers arrived, they were thus confronted with a centralized banking system under communist control.[3]

The Soviets also had established a police force, headed by Colonel Paul Markgraf, a former German army officer who had been captured and indoctrinated in the Soviet Union. As everywhere in the city government, key police posts were occupied by Communists or those who sympathized with them.[4]

In addition, the Soviets created a trade union structure and authorized four political parties in Berlin. The trade union, known as the Free German Trade Union Association (*Freier deutscher Gewerkschaftsbund*), was organized from the top down on a strongly centralized basis. It soon had 1,240 functionaries, of whom over 1,000 were Communists. The union executive committee was composed of 45 members, of whom 34 later proved to be Communists or communist sympathizers.[5] This committee controlled the financial transactions of all individual unions and received the dues of their members.[6]

The Soviet order authorizing the formation of German political parties was dated June 10, 1945. Two days later, a Communist Party was established for Berlin and the east zone, and the organization of three other parties—the Social Democratic Party (SPD), the Christian Democratic Union (CDU), and the Liberal Democratic Party (LDP)—followed in quick succession.[7] These three parties, as it later proved, were well suited to represent the principal political aspirations of non-Nazi Germans, and the action of the Soviet command in permitting their formation seemed both wise and equitable. It soon became clear, however, that the Soviets had no intention of treating all parties impartially. They showed marked favoritism toward the Communist Party, but hampered the free development of the other parties in an increasingly stringent fashion.

A number of newspapers were established in Berlin before Western military government teams entered the city. The largest of these was the *Tägliche Rundschau*, a German-language daily published by the Red Army. Another, the *Berliner Zeitung*, served as an organ of the city government. Each of the four political parties was authorized to publish a paper, but the journalistic efforts of the three noncommunist political parties were strictly circumscribed by two limitations. First, they received a very limited allocation of newsprint, and their circulation was therefore small. Second, Soviet officers exercised strict prepublication censorship, with the result that in news treatment and political coloration the noncommunist papers differed only slightly from the communist press.[8]

The Berlin radio, which had started functioning again shortly after the Red Army arrived, was operated by a German staff under close Soviet supervision. It reinforced the themes of the communist press.

Finally, the Soviets instituted a rationing system which enabled them to use the allocation of food as an instrument for controlling Berlin's political and cultural life. The German population was divided into five categories. Civilians in the highest category were allowed 2,485 calories a day, while those in the lowest category received only 1,248 calories. (The average American consumes approximately 3,000 calories each day.) Unemployed old people and those who had incurred Soviet displeasure received the lowest rations. Those with the most generous ration card included many politicians, officials, intellectuals, and teachers, as well as persons doing heavy physical labor. A German official or intellectual who displeased the Soviets and consequently lost his job was faced with the loss not only of his income but also of his preferential ration card. The lowest two categories were insufficient to sustain a normal existence, and one million people, or approximately one-third of the population, lived on the borderline of starvation.[9]

When the Western powers assumed responsibility for their sectors of Berlin in July 1945, they thus found a communist-dominated city administration, and a political life in which Soviet influence was very strong. Western entry into Berlin was synchronized with the withdrawal of British and American forces from parts of central

Germany which had been designated as part of the Soviet zone of occupation. Many in the West felt later that to give up this fertile area in exchange for a precarious position in the former capital had been a bad bargain.

Early Policies of the Western Powers in Berlin

It had been agreed that the area of Greater Berlin would be divided into four sectors, each to be occupied by one of the victorious powers. A governing authority, consisting of four city commandants appointed by their respective commanders-in-chief, would be established to direct its administration on a joint basis,[10] and would be known by its Russian designation as the "Kommandatura." Nothing more specific had been decided in advance about the way the city was to be run.

Details about the functions of the Kommandatura were discussed by the British, American, and Soviet commanders on July 7 and 11.* At the first meeting, the U.S. and British authorities accepted a Soviet draft outlining operating procedures for the Kommandatura, and providing that all resolutions be passed unanimously. They also agreed, at Soviet insistence, that America and Britain would provide food and coal for the west sectors of the city. The second meeting resulted in an announcement that orders already issued by the Soviet authorities or by the German city government would remain in force until further notice.[11] Since, under these agreements, all orders issued prior to the arrival of Western personnel remained in effect until otherwise ordered by the Kommandatura, and since Kommandatura decisions had to be unanimous, it later proved difficult for the Western powers to achieve basic changes in the pattern of political life which the Soviets had already imposed on Berlin.

At the time, however, the Western powers were not greatly concerned about their own political position in Berlin vis-à-vis the Soviets. Official American opinion was that the chief problem in Berlin was to get along smoothly with the Russians. Colonel (later

* French officials, although present in Berlin, were not invited to the first meeting because it was feared that this might offend the Soviets. At the meeting on July 7, however, General Zhukov recognized the right of the French to participate, and they attended meetings of the Kommandatura after the latter had been established. A French sector was carved out of the British sector, which, in turn, received compensations from the American sector.

General) Howley,* chief of Military Government in the U.S. sector, wrote about the meeting of July 7:

> I think it was a good indication of the policy which we were to follow in Berlin for many months, doing almost anything to win over the Russians, allay their suspicions, and convince them we were their friends.[12]

From all indications, the French and British initially followed a similar policy.

The possible military implications of their position in Berlin appear to have entered very little into the calculations of the Western powers in their early dealings with the Soviets. Neither the Western representatives on the European Advisory Commission nor the Western military commanders attempted to obtain a written agreement assuring Allied personnel access to Berlin by land or air.[13] Indeed, a former American diplomat recalled that, in the course of discussions on the delimitation of a French sector of occupation, one proposal, which was almost accepted by the Western powers, would have surrendered to the Soviets territory adjoining Tempelhof airfield in exchange for certain territory in the northern part of Berlin. If the proposal had been adopted, it would have made the airlift next to impossible, since the Soviets could have obstructed landing at Tempelhof by the simple device of constructing a number of tall buildings on the eastern border of the airfield.

Allied efforts to promote good relations with the Soviets included measures which effectively prevented Germans in West Berlin as well as in the East from criticizing Soviet policy or the conduct of Russian personnel. Military Government Ordinance No. 1, promulgated by the Supreme Commander of the Allied Expeditionary Forces, listed as a punishable offense "conduct hostile or disrespectful to the Allied Forces or to any of the United Nations."[14] U.S. Military Government Regulations specified as of 1945 that

> Any hostile discussion of announced Military Government policies or of Military Government personnel, or any attempt to create division among or to foster disrespect for the Allied Occupying Powers or for the United Nations, will be considered as a danger to military security.[15]

* Colonel Howley was promoted to Brigadier General in March 1949. Since documents from the time of the blockade usually refer to him as "Colonel Howley," his earlier rank will be used in the historical discussion.

German applicants for positions in the civil administration or in any of the information services were usually rejected out of hand by U.S. Military Government if they showed hostility toward any of the four occupying powers.

In spite of the efforts of the Western powers to show good will toward the Soviets, points of friction soon became evident. The borough administrations in the west sectors, which had been established under communist auspices with communist personnel in strategic positions, were reluctant to follow the orders of Western military authorities, and in some cases openly defied them. In each of the Western sectors it became necessary to remove one or several of the Soviet-appointed borough mayors. In one borough of the American sector it was discovered that the local Communist Party was issuing orders directly to members of the borough administration, and two members of the Party were subsequently convicted of violating military government ordinances.[16]

The issue of public safety produced even greater friction between East and West. For several months after British, French, and American troops had entered the city, Red Army personnel continued their depredations in West Berlin; they were finally halted only after Allied military police began to use force to restrain the marauders. Furthermore, agents from East Berlin kidnaped a number of Germans from the west sectors, some of them important city officials.[17] The Western powers found it very difficult to get the facts about such cases because the German police force, under the direction of the Soviet-appointed Colonel Markgraf, refused to give information and the Soviet authorities remained silent.

A third area of friction was in the field of press and radio. According to former U.S. and British Military Government officials, the Western powers believed that four-power rule entitled them to share in the control of Radio Berlin, as well as of the national German transmitter (*Deutschlandsender*), which was located in the Soviet zone. The Soviets maintained that these stations were needed to provide service for the east zone and therefore should be under exclusive Soviet control. Similarly, the Western powers suggested that four-power control be established over the *Berliner Zeitung*, the organ of the German city government, and possibly over the Soviet-published *Tägliche Rundschau*. The Soviets refused both requests, denying that the *Berliner Zeitung* was an official organ of the Magistrat, and arguing that the *Tägliche Rundschau* was published primarily for readers in the Soviet zone. On the other hand, when

British Military Government wanted to publish a German-language newspaper in Berlin, the Soviets countered with the suggestion that a single paper sponsored jointly by all the occupying powers would be preferable.[18] As it developed, there were no jointly-sponsored information media. Each power controlled the media located in its own sector, with the important exception of Radio Berlin, which had its studios in the British sector and its transmitter in the French sector, but continued to broadcast under exclusive Soviet control. The U.S. Military Government started its own radio station (known as "RIAS"*) in the American sector during 1946.

In spite of such disagreements, the four-power administration of Berlin proceeded with relative smoothness for approximately a year. Though this was due in large part to the accommodating attitude of the Western powers, the Soviets were not always intransigent. Russian authorities cooperated, after a fashion, in curbing the misbehavior of Red Army troops in the West sectors.[19] They also agreed to a procedure whereby each power could remove borough officials in its own sector,[20] and they cooperated reluctantly in the establishment of three air corridors between Berlin and points in West Germany. Although agreement on reorganization of the police department could not be reached, a compromise measure approved by the Control Council in October 1946 gave the Western powers authority over the police in their individual sectors through the establishment of sector assistants to the police president.[21] Social relations among Western and Soviet personnel remained fairly cordial, and formal and informal working arrangements between them enabled the city to function and to start the long and painful process of repairing war damage.

The Air Corridor Agreement†

On November 30, 1945, the Allied Control Council in Berlin approved a paper which provided that three corridors were to be set up for communication between Berlin and West Germany, and that flights through these corridors could proceed without advance

* The initials stood for "Rundfunk im amerikanischen Sektor."

† Published material on this agreement is confined to a few paragraphs from a magazine article by General Robert W. Harper (Chief of the U.S. Element of the Four Power Air Directorate prior to the blockade), "Let's Not Waste Our Fighting Man Power," *Saturday Evening Post*, December 11, 1954, and occasional references in other sources. Most of the information used here was obtained in interviews with U.S. military and civilian specialists who were concerned with air policy in Germany during 1945 and 1946.

notice. It provided further that responsibility for drawing up safety measures and flight rules in the corridors would rest with the Air Directorate of the Control Council. The paper was thus in the nature of a preparatory agreement, and the air corridors were not actually established until several months later when the four-power Air Directorate issued a set of specifications and rules for flights in and out of Berlin. This later document described the location of the three corridors and provided that they were to be twenty miles wide. It also established a "Berlin control zone," extending twenty miles in every direction from the Allied Control Authority building in Berlin and including all air space up to 10,000 feet. Aircraft entering this zone were to give certain identifying information to a four-power Berlin Air Safety Center, also provided for in the agreement. Finally, the document laid down a number of safety rules for flights in and out of Berlin.

The impetus behind this agreement seems to have come largely from the U.S. element of the Air Directorate. Shortly after Western forces entered Berlin, the Allies had begun to receive Soviet protests charging violations of air-safety regulations and digressions from the air corridor to Berlin.[22] At that time there existed no formal agreement concerning access to Berlin by air or any other avenue, but British and American officers had a verbal agreement with the Soviets, by which Western pilots en route to Berlin were to follow the line of the railroad or the highway across the Soviet zone from Helmstedt in the British zone. This meant that American planes coming from South Germany had to fly north to Helmstedt and then make a right-angle turn. It also required visual navigation. Since there were no navigational aids in the Soviet zone to facilitate bad-weather entries into Berlin, all pilots—including Soviet pilots—had occasional difficulties.

When Soviet protests reached General Robert W. Harper, chief of the U.S. element of the four-power Air Directorate, he first ascertained that no regulations governing flights in and out of Berlin were in existence. He then suggested to the representatives of the other powers on the Air Directorate that a uniform flying code be established for all Germany.

The U.S. proposal was based on the assumption that Berlin would again become the German capital and would resume its position as national air center. Six airways, or corridors, were to radiate out from Berlin in every direction—to Hamburg, Braunschweig, Frankfurt, Copenhagen, Prague, and Warsaw. Navigational aids were to be constructed on the Berlin approaches, and uniform rules for greater flying safety were to be adopted by all four powers and administered by a quadripartite Berlin Air Safety Center.

The Soviet representatives on the Air Directorate seemed sympathetic to this proposal, but made it clear that it would have to be reviewed in Moscow. There, the Copenhagen, Warsaw and Prague corridors were immediately declared unacceptable. But even after the Western representatives had agreed to the elimination of these corridors, at least for the time being, the Soviets put off signing the agreement.

American negotiators could never be sure which of the remaining Soviet objections were genuine and which were primarily devices for postponing final agreement. One problem related to the use of the air corridors by commercial aircraft. The Soviets at first demanded that flights be limited specifically to aircraft serving the needs of the military forces of occupation, but American representatives insisted that the corridors should be open to all air traffic, subject only to agreed safety regulations.[23] The Soviets finally dropped their objections to unrestricted use of the air corridors, only to revive them at the time of the blockade.

Another reason for the delay in concluding the negotiations may have been the Russians' fear that some of the proposed navigational aid stations would impair the secrecy surrounding militarily sensitive areas in East Germany. Though they never mentioned this point specifically, they certainly expressed less opposition to the corridor agreement after U.S. representatives suggested rearranging the proposed navigational aid stations in such a way as to avoid those areas presumed to have major Soviet military installations in them.

The agreement was finally concluded early in 1946, and the four-power Berlin Air Safety Center was established in February of that year. Working on a twenty-four-hour basis, it continued to function with remarkably little friction even after relations among the occupying powers had deteriorated.[24]

It is of course impossible to determine why the Soviets eventually signed, but several reasons may be suggested. First, the agreement gave Moscow very appreciable benefits. The new safety measures promised to assist Soviet aviation even more than Allied aviation, since at that time the Soviets engaged in more flying in the Berlin area. Furthermore, the United States was to build the navigational aid stations on the approaches to Berlin and offered to train Soviet personnel to man them. Finally, the terms of the agreement facilitated Russian flights to the west as well as Allied flights to Berlin. The Soviets may have felt that it was a good bargain to allow Western aircraft to approach Berlin freely in exchange for their own unrestricted access to Hamburg, Braunschweig, and Frankfurt.

Also, the Soviet air representatives apparently set considerable store on maintaining the existing cordial relationship with their British and American opposite numbers, which General Harper and other Western personnel had worked hard to foster. American officials took advantage of this mutual good feeling when it came to explaining to the Soviets the safety features of the proposed corridor agreement. A number of U.S. training films on air safety and navigation were obtained, and Soviet air officers were invited to see them. They seemed much impressed by the system of airways and beacons which was explained in the training films, and asked to have the showings repeated. Soviet officers were also invited to visit the U.S. control tower at Tempelhof Air Base and study its operation.

At that time, the Soviets' own training in navigation and air safety lagged considerably behind that of the Western powers, and they may have been anxious to maintain good relations in order to benefit from training information which U.S. officers could supply. Even after the corridor agreement was signed, the Soviets showed an interest in learning how these matters were handled in other countries, frequently surprising American officers by their ignorance of some of the most elementary safety procedures and devices used in the United States. For instance, the four-quadrant range had to be explained to them, and they had no clear idea of what went on in a control tower. Shortly after the agreement was concluded, a Russian-speaking officer from the U.S. element of the Air Directorate was invited to fly to Moscow and give lectures on air safety and related subjects to Soviet officers. For three weeks, the American officer lectured in Moscow, where he was royally entertained.

A third factor that may have been instrumental in obtaining Soviet consent was General Harper's determination to push the corridor agreement through. According to several accounts, he was always polite but extremely persistent, and his determination was clear to all. At the time, Soviet policy was apparently opposed to any action that would give serious offense to the United States, and it must have been evident that American representatives would take a grave view of continued obstruction of the air-corridor agreement.

Finally, circumstances surrounding air activity in the Berlin area during 1945 and 1946 were such that the Soviets did not actually appear to be making any far-reaching concessions when they signed the corridor agreement. Although the informal Anglo-U.S.-Soviet understanding required pilots to follow the road or rail line into Berlin, in practice Soviet authorities ordinarily authorized other flights over East Germany without extensive red tape. American Air Force officers who were stationed in Berlin during this period have reported that they had no particular difficulty in arranging "flying time," although there were certain areas over which the Soviets did not authorize flights.

Whatever may have been the reasons for Soviet concurrence, the fact that the corridor agreement was concluded makes it appear unlikely that early in 1946 Moscow was planning a blockade of Berlin. It also shows that the Soviets were willing, at that time, to participate in four-power arrangements with at least a degree of cooperativeness.

*Formation of the SED and the 1946 Elections**

The first major conflict between East and West in Berlin came when the Communists and a number of Social Democrats attempted to merge the Social Democratic Party with the Communist Party. To understand the issues at stake in this conflict one must examine the reconstitution of political life in the city during the months immediately following the war.

Allied personnel who moved into the western sectors of Berlin in July 1945 had been more than mildly surprised at the warm welcome given them by the Germans. In the heavily-bombed capital of the defeated Reich they had expected to encounter the greatest bitterness; instead, they were greeted almost as liberators, come to free as least a portion of the population from the Soviet yoke. The measures of Western military governments were stern; their efforts to remove all Nazis from positions of influence and to prevent a resurgence of militarism can scarcely have aroused enthusiasm. Nevertheless, these measures were at least comprehensible to the Germans,

* The following summary is based primarily on two categories of source material: (1) conversations with former U.S. military government personnel and with German residents of Berlin, and (2) material made available in memorandum form by Mr. Harold Hurwitz, an American scholar working in Berlin. Mr. Hurwitz' material was based on interviews and observations which he made personally in Berlin from 1946 to 1948, and also on documents dating from that period.

and they contrasted sharply with the seemingly random violence and destruction meted out by the Red Army. Furthermore, such instances of misbehavior on the part of Allied troops as occurred were viewed less seriously when compared to the excesses of the Soviets. American, British, and French military police soon found that they were expected to protect Germans from Soviet personnel. The offices of Western military governments were flooded by people who claimed that they had been injured or robbed by the Russians.

It was a severe shock to many Berliners to find that the Western powers did not share their attitude toward the Soviets. When told coldly that they were the victims of Nazi propaganda, or that they could scarcely expect better treatment in view of the behavior of the Nazis in countries they had occupied, Berliners turned away with a mixture of disillusionment and indignation. In vain did they protest (quite correctly) that the city of Berlin had been less pro-Nazi than almost any other area in Germany. And when they saw that Western military government authorities were not only co-operating with Soviet officials but were making special efforts to accommodate them, most Berliners sank back into hopelessness and apathy. It was generally agreed that the Americans, British, and French were preferable as occupying powers—if one had to be occupied—but that they certainly were sadly misinformed about the Soviets.

Political apathy, then, was one of the dominant characteristics of Berliners during 1945 and early 1946. Most people held strong opinions about the occupying powers, but the physical problems of daily existence were in the forefront of their attention. Approximately 40 per cent of the city's dwellings had been made uninhabitable by bomb damage during the war.[25] To procure materials with which to patch a roof or repair a wall was a major undertaking. To find a new dwelling either through the housing authorities or through private channels required days of negotiation, and even if a roof and four walls were available, there was still the problem of obtaining furniture and bedding. Food and fuel were also in short supply. A bare minimum of rationed goods was available to those with time and energy to stand in line. Those who had salvaged possessions which they could barter were able to supplement their rations by transactions on the black market, others made foraging trips to the countryside around Berlin. Fighting off hunger and cold was a full-time job for many people, and the inflated German currency robbed most Berliners of the incentive to earn money.

But the communist activists in Berlin were neither apathetic nor destitute. From the beginning party workers and propagandists received the best housing available and generous supplementary food rations. Their energy, and the preferential treatment given them by the Soviet authorities, enabled this small group to exercise an influence far out of proportion to their numbers.

In contrast, the three noncommunist political parties received little encouragement and few favors from Western authorities, who attempted to treat all non-Nazi Germans equally. But in spite of this disadvantage, the noncommunist parties managed to build a nucleus of leaders and a political framework, and within a few months became vigorous contenders in the political arena.

By far the most important of the three noncommunist groups was the Social Democratic Party (SPD), the only one of the democratic parties which had been in existence in pre-Nazi days. In spite of Nazi persecution and concentration camps, there remained a core of old Social Democrats who knew one another, were politically experienced, and could go about the business of reorganizing the party immediately after the occupation of Berlin in 1945. (The other two democratic parties were new combinations without the benefit of a vestigial organization.) Furthermore, Berlin was traditionally a Social Democratic stronghold, and many workers rallied to their old party. By March 1946 the Berlin SPD could count over 50,000 members.

When it was first reestablished after the war, the SPD was interested in cooperating with the Communist Party. Members of the two groups had struggled together against the Nazis, they had been thrown together in concentration camps, and the idea was widespread that the Nazis could never have come to power if the working-class parties had been united. Also, Berlin's postwar problems were so immediate and overwhelming that cooperation among political parties seemed a more sensible course than competition. Indeed, some Social Democratic leaders approached the Communists with suggestions for a merger to form a single workers' party.[26]

The Communists rejected these overtures as "premature." They may have feared that a merger, at a time when they had not yet perfected their own organization, would have meant their being swallowed up by the more numerous Social Democrats. The Communist Party, with the support of the Soviet Military Administration, preferred to follow an "anti-fascist bloc" policy, arguing that all four political parties should work together, and pressing for the formation of supra-party coordinating groups in which all non-Nazi points of view would be represented.[27]

This approach had a strong attraction for many of the noncommunist political leaders. Most of them were older men of wide experience who, while far from enamored of the Soviets, did not share the strong anti-Russian sentiments of the masses. They were inclined to excuse the violence of the Red Army as a reaction to Nazi atrocities, and as excesses typical of troops at the end of any long war. It was also clear to them that, like it or not, Germany's future would depend to a large degree on the Soviet Union. This was particularly true of Berlin, not only because it was an island in the Soviet zone, but also because Berlin could once again become the German capital only if the four zones were united; and such a union would depend on cooperation among all the occupying powers. Consequently, in the beginning, most of these democratic leaders believed that the only intelligent course open to German politicians was to attempt to get along with *all* the occupying powers, including the Soviets. And since the Communist Party clearly was the favorite of the Soviets, cooperation with the Communists and support of their "anti-fascist bloc" policy seemed necessary. As time went on, however, more and more of the noncommunist politicians became disillusioned with the "bloc" policy. They found that four-party bodies somehow had a way of becoming communist instruments.

A few of the Social Democrats had been doubtful about the possibility of cooperating with the Communists from the first. A senior member of the SPD has related that, shortly after the Soviet army occupied Berlin, he and a few friends went to Military Government headquarters to ask permission to reorganize the Social Democratic Party. They were eventually given the necessary permission. But first they received a stiff lecture from a young Soviet officer, who said to the amazed SPD men: "We finished off the Trotskyites and we'll finish you off too," and then went on to use the same arguments against the Social Democrats that had been used by the German Communist Party in the 1920's. When Moscow-trained German Communists began to arrive in Berlin, the old Social Democrats heard the same lecture again. The SPD member who told this story was forced to conclude that his party had the choice only of resisting the Communists or being totally absorbed by them.

The struggle over the location of SPD headquarters in Berlin, while in itself a relatively minor matter, was another indication of the way the wind was blowing. During the first few weeks after the Soviet entry into Berlin, the SPD set up its headquarters in a building, somewhat away from the center of town, which it had used in pre-Nazi times. It then developed that this building was in the sector which was to be occupied by the British. The day before British forces arrived, Soviet Military Government loaded all the furniture and supplies from the building into trucks, drove them to the Soviet sector, and ordered the SPD to set up its headquarters there. Apparently Soviet Military Government wished to have all party headquarters in a position where they could be carefully supervised. This move, however, increased the suspicions among the Social Democratic leaders, who therefore arranged to maintain a duplicate headquarters in the old building in the British sector, where they gradually accumulated furniture and built up new files, and where they could make decisions with relative freedom from Soviet pressure.

In the course of 1945, the SPD leaders were able to observe the policies of Soviet Military Government and the Communists in both Berlin and the east zone, and what they saw dashed their earlier hopes that Germans might be allowed to work out democratic solutions to their own problems. Soviet personnel intervened in German political life at all levels. When, late in 1945, communist policy shifted in favor of a merger with the Social Democrats, the merger was pushed directly by Soviet military authorities. It soon became clear both that Moscow intended to force through the merger, and that the resulting party would be completely communist-dominated.

At first there was every indication that the merger plan would be successful. Not only the Soviet Military Administration, but also the chairman of the Social Democratic Party for Berlin and the east zone, Otto Grotewohl, actively promoted amalgamation of the two groups. It is not clear whether Grotewohl really favored the merger or had capitulated to Soviet pressure. In any case, the higher echelons of the SPD were in the hands of pro-merger forces.

This was the situation on February 14, 1946, when a number of anti-merger officials from the SPD borough organizations in Berlin met informally in the living room behind a textile shop owned by one of their number. They conceded that merger in the Soviet zone could not be stopped, but went on to discuss whether anything could be done to save at least the Berlin SPD. A majority of the functionaries believed that there was little they could do themselves, and that action was up to the Western powers. But would the Western powers acually intervene? Some of those present thought they would not; others argued that the Americans and British were democrats and would never permit a democratic German party to be liquidated in this way, at least not in the west sectors. A determined minority finally convinced the group that the only hope of preventing their absorption by the Communists lay in taking a firm stand. Unless the German Social Democrats strongly opposed the merger and spoke out clearly against it, they argued, the Allies would not raise a finger. It was thereupon decided to oppose the merger at a formal gathering of borough and section leaders in the party headquarters three days later.

Accordingly, at this gathering, the opposition attempted to pass a resolution of no confidence in the pro-merger leadership. The resolution was barely defeated, after Chairman Grotewohl had made an impassioned two-hour appeal against it, and a vaguely-worded compromise resolution was adopted instead.

The two meetings, while not decisive, at least allowed the principal points of view to be stated. In addition, they called the attention of West German Social Democratic leaders and Western occupation officials to the situation. Kurt Schumacher, the sour and forceful leader of the West German SPD, immediately traveled to Berlin and threw his support to the anti-merger forces, which were greatly encouraged by it. American and British Military Government officials backed the opposition group to the extent of attempting to ensure their physical safety, at least in the west sectors. One anti-merger SPD official, who was believed to be in danger, was flown to West Germany. Reprisals against the anti-merger group, which up to this time had been carried out by the communist-controlled police in all four sectors of the city, were halted by military authorities in West Berlin. Indeed, eleven Communists who had been accused of intimidation methods in one borough were arrested. According to a correspondent of the *Manchester Guardian,* this was the first visible sign that the Western powers were determined to see that democracy in Berlin was not swept away by threats of force.[28]

On March 1 the anti-merger forces won their first solid victory. A meeting of Berlin's Social Democratic functionaries voted, over the strenuous opposition of Otto Grotewohl and his supporters, that no merger could take place without approval from the individual members. A five-man committee was set up to organize a referendum, Kommandatura permission was secured, and voting was set for March 31.

The conference of March 1 had been a stormy one, and had been attended by some two thousand Germans as well as by representatives from the occupation forces. It aroused the interest of a large part of the city's population, and also brought about a sympathetic adjustment in the attitude of the Western powers. The anti-merger Social Democrats had no publicity media of their own, but the editors of the U.S.-licensed *Tagesspiegel* agreed to present the views of the SPD opposition. In addition, British authorities procured several tons of newsprint for the opposition, and granted a license for publication of an independent Social Democratic paper, *Der Sozialdemokrat,* which began to appear shoftly thereafter. The opposition received further encouragement from a visiting deputy of the British Labour Party and from German emigre groups abroad. The Committee for a Democratic Germany in New York provided important information about the Soviet Union, including a chapter from Koestler's *The Yogi and the Kommissar.* Individual members of the British and American military governments, working largely in an unofficial capacity, did what they could to lend private and informal assistance to the independent SPD leaders, mostly in the form of moral support.

The importance of this moral support should not be underestimated. Then as later, one of the key questions facing Berlin democrats was: To what extent will the United States back us up? The fact that a number of junior American personnel encouraged anti-merger forces, albeit in a private capacity, gave hope that official support and recognition would be forthcoming later. Informal gatherings of Germans, Americans and British, usually in cold, badly-lighted, plaster-cracked parlors (since military government regulations made unofficial conferences in military quarters difficult) seemed at the time a pitifully inadequate answer to the threat to which democracy in Berlin was exposed. Yet in the long run they probably exerted a significant influence.

The first official American position, though apparently not a very emphatic one, was taken the day before the referendum when a United States spokesman announced that no merger would be recognized that had not been agreed to by a majority of both parties. However, Colonel Howley reports that, at the time, Americans "even at the top level" were divided on whether the merger was a good or a bad thing, and that U.S. Military Government policy was that "politics was a German question and our interest was confined to safeguarding democratic processes."[29] Colonel Howley's own view was that it was a healthy sign for a group of individuals who disagreed with their leaders to insist on arguing the issue on an open and democratic basis.[30]

The anti-merger Social Democrats thus had two West Berlin newspapers through which to present their views, and could count on moral support from the West German SPD and certain Western officials. They enjoyed at least the benevolent neutrality of U.S. Military Government and received somewhat more tangible backing from the British. Against them, however, were arrayed a formidable combination of determined foes. Pro-merger forces still controlled the east zone SPD organization, which included Berlin. The Soviets threw their weight firmly behind the merger, with the result that at least five newspapers and the Berlin radio strongly supported it. Pro-merger forces could also use the extensive propaganda capabilities of the Communist Party and could brandish the ever-present threat of the Soviet and East German police.

Nevertheless, the anti-merger forces won a smashing victory on March 31. Balloting took place only in West Berlin. In the Soviet sector the polls were closed by order of the Soviet commandant shortly after they had opened, on the grounds that certain undefined regulations had not been complied with. In the west sectors, some 75 per cent of the registered SPD members voted approximately 19 to 2 against the merger. An alternative proposal, calling for close cooperation with the Communist Party, was also opposed by a large majority. Grotewohl and the Communists had suffered a severe defeat.[31]

On April 7, at the SPD regional party convention, anti-merger Social Democrats followed up their victory by electing three chairmen who were in favor of maintaining the SPD's independence: Franz Neumann, Klaus Peter Schulz, and Kurt Swolinsky. Thus, a large group of middle and lower functionaries, with the aid of the rank and file, was able to wrest control of the Berlin SPD from the pro-merger leadership.

Despite their resounding defeat in West Berlin, the pro-merger minority of the Social Democrats and the leaders of the Communist Party proceeded formally to combine the two groups to form the Socialist Unity Party (SED). This new party, which was completely under communist control, was immediately recognized by

Soviet Military Government in the east zone, and the SPD was thereupon prohibited from functioning in that area.

In Berlin itself, the situation was not so simple. Both the new SED and the independent SPD applied to the Kommandatura for permission to operate in the city. The Soviet Commandant, General Kotikov, advocated recognizing the SED at once and deferring discussion about whether to recognize the reorganized SPD. The other sector commanders, headed by French General Lançon, insisted that the SED be recognized merely as the old Communist Party under a new name, and argued that there was thus no objection to recognizing the Berlin SPD as well. Since the Kommandatura was unable to come to any agreement, the issue was referred to the higher authority of the Control Council, which in turn tossed it back to the Kommandatura. After additional wrangling the Kommandatura decided to recognize both the SED and the reorganized SPD in the city of Berlin.[32]

This looked like a compromise, by which the Western powers agreed to let the newly-formed SED operate in West Berlin, while the Soviets allowed the SPD to be active in East Berlin. Actually, however, it was a Soviet defeat, because it meant that the strategy of eliminating Social Democratic opposition to the Communist Party had failed, at least in Berlin. Indeed, the fact that pro-merger Social Democrats had been absorbed by the SED actually left the SPD leadership more united, and the publicity which the anti-merger forces had enjoyed gained them thousands of votes in the municipal elections that followed several months later.

Furthermore, the struggle had forced many SPD leaders to take a stronger and more independent stand than they might otherwise have taken. At first, only a relatively small minority had favored an active fight against merger; a larger number, including some who later were to play an outstanding role in defeating the blockade, remained passive or neutral. Gradually, more and more of the functionaries showed active opposition to the merger plan. After the referendum of party members on March 31, the middle ground, on which so many had sought to stand, no longer existed. Forced to make a choice, most functionaries chose the SPD rather than the SED.

The next major political issue to plague the four-power Kommandatura concerned the municipal elections. At first the Soviets appeared to be opposed to them, and General Kotikov, commandant of the Soviet sector, would not agree to even a tentative election date. After a three-month delay, the matter was referred to the Allied Control Council. There General Clay threw his full weight on the side of early elections, and four-power agreement on this subject was obtained in June 1946.[33] The date set for Berlin's first postwar elections was October 20, 1946.

While the debate about elections was going on, representatives of the four powers were drafting a temporary constitution for the city. It was finished in July, and Colonel Howley characterized it as "a brief but good document, entirely democratic, and from the legal point of view full of flaws." He believed, however, that it would be adequate as a basis for the forthcoming elections and until Berlin's elected representatives could write their own constitution. General Kotikov, without opposing it outright, refused to give the document his formal approval, and the issue once again was referred to the Allied Control Council, where General Sokolovsky approved it for the Soviets,* and the three Western powers also gave their assent.[34] The provisional constitution went into effect in the fall of 1946.

In the election campaign that followed, the SED engaged in more propaganda than the other three parties combined. Its election posters were everywhere; food was provided and drinks were served at parties in SED offices; notebooks were distributed to school children with the compliments of the SED; coal briquettes with "SED" stamped on them were given away; the Soviet-controlled press and radio inundated the city; and communist speakers harangued Berliners wherever they could find an audience.

The scales were further weighted in favor of the SED by the fact that Soviet occupation authorities took an active part in the campaign. They hampered the democratic political parties, and especially the SPD, in their efforts to conduct election propaganda in East Berlin. SPD speakers were banned on security grounds, and halls in which SPD meetings were to be held suddenly became "unavailable." Some SPD meetings were cancelled on Soviet orders only

* Thus Sokolovsky had "overruled" Kotikov twice in a row. Colonel Howley suggests that Kotikov suspected that the Communists would not do well in Berlin elections and wanted to protect himself. (Frank Howley, *Berlin Command,* Putnam, New York, 1950, p. 121.) Another possible interpretation is that this maneuver was simply a Soviet device to gain time in which to build up the SED organization and make elaborate preparations for the election campaign without appearing to be unduly stubborn and thereby provoking the Allies to countermeasures. In a third case—the SED-SPD recognition dispute—Sokolovsky did not overrule Kotikov but voted to send the issue back to the Kommandatura, where Kotikov reversed himself.

a few minutes before they were scheduled to begin. Conversely, the SED received powerful direct and indirect assistance, designed to help it win over the voters not only in East Berlin, but in the west sectors as well. The Soviet Military Administration announced that, at the request of the SED, fruit and vegetables were to be supplied the whole city. The SED received plentiful allotments of paper and other supplies for propaganda purposes, while, even in West Berlin, the resources of the democratic parties were strictly limited.

In addition, the Soviets made it clear to Berliners that their future lay with the East. The amount of electric power allowed to flow into West Berlin from Soviet-controlled areas was sharply restricted, and a highly-placed Soviet official started the rumor that the Western powers would leave Berlin two months after the elections.[35]

Nevertheless, the results of the election were another serious blow to the Communists. The SED received only 19.8 per cent of the vote in the entire city, and 21 per cent in the Soviet sector. By far the strongest party was the SPD, with 48.7 per cent of the vote. The other two noncommunist parties divided the remainder, the CDU receiving 22.2 per cent, and the LDP 9.3 per cent. The election was carried out under the supervision of four-power election teams, and all the occupying powers accepted the results of the election, although the Soviets claimed that there were abuses.[36] The SPD emerged from the elections as a dominating force in Berlin politics.

During the struggle that accompanied the formation of the SED and the reorganization of the SPD, as well as during the election campaign itself, more and more Berliners became concerned with political affairs. When SPD members went to the polls to vote on the merger question at the end of March, thousands of their fellow citizens watched attentively from the sidelines. And nearly every Berliner became deeply involved in the municipal election campaign: of the some 2,300,000 persons who were entitled to vote, more than 92 per cent cast their ballots.[37] Though many of those who voted for one of the democratic parties were probably doing little more than registering their dislike and fear of the Soviets, it can be said that, by the end of 1946, political interest was no longer confined to a few thousand party leaders and members.

Soviet Efforts To Retain Power in Berlin: The "Burgomaster Crisis"

Having cooperated with the Western powers to the extent of

agreeing to the elections and providing joint supervision over their conduct, the Soviets now turned their efforts to maintaining the preeminent position in Berlin's political life which they had acquired by being first on the scene. In general, they followed three lines of action: they attempted to keep in office as many communist and procommunist German officials as possible; they tried to keep out of office those German leaders whom they believed to be particularly unpliable; and, with the help of German Communists, they moved toward the creation of a majority bloc in the City Assembly which would be friendly to Russia and in which the SED would play a dominant role.

They began by trying to limit the authority of the newly-elected city government, basing themselves on the provisional constitution, which stated that "resignation of the Magistrat or one of its members, as well as appointment and discharge of leading persons in the city government, may take place only with the permission of the Allied Kommandatura of Berlin."[38] The Soviets interpreted the "leading persons in the city government" as including the mayor and the councilmen. The Western powers took the view that this provision applied only to appointed and not to elected officials. When the newly-elected City Assembly chose a Magistrat—an executive body consisting of a mayor and department heads—from among its members, the Soviets would neither accept the resignation of the old Magistrat nor agree to seat the new one. After about six weeks, a compromise was worked out by which the new Magistrat was allowed to take office, but the Western powers agreed to support Soviet objections to three of its members. One of these was Professor Ernst Reuter, later to become mayor of Berlin.[39]

The new government was a coalition of all four parties. A Social Democrat, Dr. Otto Ostrowski, was installed as mayor, and members of the three noncommunist parties occupied a majority of the other seventeen top positions. The SED was given three positions.

Having finally agreed to seat the new Magistrat, the Soviets sought to use their power and that of the SED to build a majority coalition in the City Assembly in which the Communists would have a dominant influence. This tactic precipitated what has been called the "burgomaster crisis" of 1947.*

This crisis started to develop early in 1947 shortly after Dr.

* This account of the "burgomaster crisis" is based on Howley, *op. cit.*, pp. 143-149, personal interviews with American and German officials, and background information provided by Mr. Hurwitz, except as otherwise noted.

Ostrowski took office. The new mayor's announced policy was to follow a middle course between East and West and to devote his primary efforts to reconstructing the badly-damaged city. One of his first moves was to approach the Soviets in an effort to find a way to replace some of the leading communist-appointed administrative officials by men of the new Magistrat's choosing. The Soviets told him that he would have to cooperate with the SED on this as indeed on any other issue. Concluding that he would be unable to administer the city efficiently without at least a minimum of co-operation from the Soviets and the German Communists, Ostrowski accordingly worked out with the SED an arrangement whereby the latter consented to the removal of five leading communist officials from the city administration on condition that the SPD and the SED pursue a common program during the following three months. Both parties were to cease all polemical attacks on each other.[40]

Soviet pressure on the mayor personally may have played a substantial role in his decision to work with the SED. According to Colonel Howley, it was the practice of the Soviets to summon Ostrowski to their headquarters two or three nights a week. There they would alternately ply him with liquor and goodfellowship and subject him to endless interrogations and veiled threats. They also investigated his private life and threatened to expose family skeletons unless he gave in to their demands.

Having agreed to cooperate with the Communists, the unfortunate mayor found himself exposed to vigorous attacks from the other side. The SPD, and the other democratic parties as well, immediately raised a storm of protest. SPD leaders pointed out that Dr. Ostrowski had acted without consulting his own party. CDU spokesmen added that a majority of the Magistrat no longer had confidence in him. In the City Assembly, the chairman of the Berlin SPD, Franz Neumann, submitted a motion of no confidence in the mayor, which was passed by a vote of 85 to 20.[41] Dr. Ostrowski argued that the only way to get any legislation approved by the Soviets was to cooperate with the Communists. The Social Democratic leaders replied that their continued existence as a separate party depended on their ability to maintain a line independent of Moscow.[42]

Ostrowski finally submitted his resignation to the Kommandatura, where Kotikov was willing to accept it on condition that any new mayor be approved in advance by the four powers. Kotikov's proposal was apparently designed to forestall the nomination of Ernst

Reuter, who was at that time city councilman in charge of transportation and public services. It was generally known that the SPD would favor Reuter as successor to Ostrowski, and to this the Soviets were strongly opposed. The Soviet bargain was rejected by the Western powers at the Kommandatura level, and the matter was referred to the Allied Control Council. There the Western powers agreed that Ostrowski's successor would have to be approved in advance.[43] General Clay emphasized, however, that this concession to Soviet demands did not constitute a precedent, but applied to the individual case only.[44]

While the principle of prior approval was still being debated, the Soviets made strenuous efforts to prevent Reuter's nomination. Through the SED, and also directly, they brought pressure on the Social Democrats to select a candidate more acceptable to the Communists, but the SPD refused to do so. In a meeting of the City Assembly on June 24, 1947, SED Deputy Maron complained:

> We have again made the proposal to cooperate and to make use of the socialist majority of this chamber. . . . Unfortunately, we again have met with a refusal. . . . The leaders of the SPD insist on the election of a candidate who is known to us as one of the strongest opponents of unity and even of cooperation between the parties representing the workers.[45]

Pressure was also brought to bear on the smaller democratic parties in Berlin. A Soviet liaison officer told LDP officials that Reuter was known for his anti-Soviet attitude, and that the LDP deputies in the City Assembly could not vote for him without thereby showing anti-Soviet tendencies. Karl Hubert Schwennicke, chairman of the Berlin LDP, replied that no question of an anti-Soviet attitude was involved, but that his party would vote for the man whom they believed to be best qualified for the job. The acting chairman of the LDP organization in the Soviet zone, however, opposed Schwennicke's stand on the grounds that their party could not afford to pursue a policy in opposition to the Soviets.[46] This issue prepared the ground for the later split between the LDP organization in the Soviet zone and the Berlin LDP. Soviet emissaries also approached the Berlin CDU with similar arguments, but met with refusal there as well.

Soviet opposition to Reuter was probably based on two grounds. He was known as a strong personality, a man very unlikely to succumb to Soviet pressure, who would lead his party on an independent course. Also, he had once been a high-ranking Communist, but had broken with the party and become a Social Democrat in the early 1920's, and the Soviets may have felt that he knew too much about them.[47]

In spite of the knowledge that the Soviets were opposed to Reuter, and the suspicion that the Western powers might not back them up, the Social Democrats in the City Assembly—supported by the other two democratic parties—put Reuter forward as their candidate for the mayor's office. He was elected by an overwhelming majority of the Assembly, but, as expected, the Soviets vetoed his confirmation. Berlin was thus without a mayor during much of 1947 and all of 1948; the functions of the office were carried on by First Deputy Mayor Louise Schroeder, also a Social Democrat.

Soviet efforts to retain their power in the Berlin city administration were thus only partially successful. They were able to prevent Reuter from becoming mayor, but they did not succeed in bending the democratic parties or the new city government to their will. Nevertheless, the grip of the Communists on a large number of city departments was still strong, and their position in the central police organization and in the trade unions was unshaken. In the Soviet sector, the new borough mayors were told, shortly after they had taken up their duties, that each change in personnel would require approval by the competent Soviet borough commander.[48] In the borough administrations of the west sectors, the new Magistrat had less difficulty in enforcing its authority, since it could usually count on the support of the Western military governments, but even in West Berlin prior agreements hampered the freedom of both the military and the civilian authorities. When American public-safety officials sought to remove three police officials who were judged to be incompetent, they found that an agreement between the communist-controlled trade union and the former city government prohibited such dismissals.[49] A high U.S. official was quoted as saying early in 1947 that the Communists were still running Berlin, in spite of their defeat at the polls.[50] However, this became less true as the months went on.

By June 1948, despite the regulation that appointment and discharge of principal executive officials required the approval of the Kommandatura, some important changes in key personnel had been made. The communist deputy chiefs of the Labor and Welfare offices had been replaced by Social Democrats, though SED deputy chiefs still remained in the offices of Education, Housing, and

Personnel. In the borough administrations the process was similar. When the blockade came, numerous key posts in the city administration were still held by Communists, but it was often possible to circumvent these officials. Also, some communist officials were imbued with the spirit of German bureaucracy even more deeply than with their sense of political allegiance, and performed their work in a manner satisfactory to their noncommunist superiors.

Democratic control of the police proved more difficult to obtain, and was not achieved until a new police headquarters was set up in West Berlin after the blockade had started. The police had been established by Soviet order in 1945, and Police President Markgraf believed himself responsible to the Kommandatura alone. The city government, on the other hand, maintained that the Magistrat had supervisory authority over the police; for if it did not, this "would mean in practice that two independent German administrations were existing side by side in Berlin."[51]

The Magistrat regarded control of the police as urgently necessary, because it was known that German policemen had been involved in the abduction of a number of anti-Communists from West Berlin.[52] After the particularly notorious kidnaping of journalist Dieter Friede of *Der Abend,* a majority in the City Assembly expressed the view that in this and similar cases the police had not performed their duties properly, and in November 1947 a resolution voicing lack of confidence in the police president was passed.[53] Nothing came of this protest. Police headquarters were in the Soviet sector, and there was no way that the Magistrat and the Assembly could enforce their desires.

Nevertheless, the Magistrat continued to press for control. At the end of January 1948, the city government urged Police President Markgraf to report to the mayor's office all cases of citizens who had been arrested by agencies of the occupying powers.[54] When Markgraf failed to provide this information, the Magistrat summoned him to answer publicly at a press conference. The conference was never held. On the first two dates scheduled, Markgraf reported that he was sick. On the third date, his time was reportedly taken up by one of the occupying powers (presumably the Soviet Union). On March 3 Markgraf told the Magistrat that he did not consider himself obligated to accept any orders from the city government. This led to a series of protests from the Magistrat to the Kommandatura, which were of no avail since the Soviets could prevent any four-power action. Markgraf continued to operate independently of the city government until shortly after the beginning of the blockade.[55]

Nevertheless, the Western powers were able to exercise effective authority over most police activities in their sectors through liaison between military public-safety officers and the German police. This led to strenuous protests from Soviet spokesmen. At the Kommandatura meeting of April 23, 1948, General Kotikov charged that the American sector commander, by unilateral order, had withdrawn the German police in the U.S. sector from control of the central police headquarters, that he was recruiting fascist and other criminal elements for the police service, and that he was using this police force to suppress democratic organizations.[56]

At the same time that it assailed police practices in the west sectors, Soviet Military Government jealously protected the activities of Police President Markgraf from scrutiny by the Western powers. When British officials demanded, at a meeting of the four-power Public Safety Committee, that the police president appear before the committee to answer questions about his personnel policy, the Soviet representatives refused agreement and, after a brief argument, walked out of the meeting.[57]

The Struggle for Nongovernmental Institutions

In order to exercise effective power, Berlin's democratic leaders needed control not only of the formal apparatus of government, but of numerous nongovernmental institutions. Their first problem was to ensure that their own political parties were reliable anti-communist instruments. In some respects, the Social Democrats had the easiest task. The merger struggle of 1946, which had preceded the formation of the SED, had automatically syphoned off those party members who were susceptible to pressure, or who leaned toward the Communists, and had strengthened the rest. The "burgomaster crisis" of 1947 had a similar effect, and the violent attacks by the SED hardened the SPD leaders still more.

The CDU and the LDP, which had not undergone so dramatic a purge, nevertheless became hardened democratic instruments in the course of time, partly as a result of the treatment they suffered from the Soviets in the east zone. At the end of 1945, the co-chairmen of the Soviet zone CDU, Dr. Hermes and Dr. Schreiber, had been removed by Soviet order. Both men subsequently played leading roles in the party organization in Berlin.[58] Their successors—Jacob Kaiser and Ernst Lemmer—were removed by Soviet order at the end of

1947, when they opposed Soviet plans for the "People's Congress," and they also became active in the Berlin CDU. Early in 1948 a Soviet liaison officer forced representatives of the Berlin CDU to leave a meeting of the east zone CDU. Shortly thereafter, the Berlin unit of the party declared that cooperation with the zonal organization was becoming impossible and severed formal ties with it. In April 1948 a Soviet-sponsored "CDU Working Group" was set up in Berlin to compete with the city organization.[59] Most of the procommunist members of the Berlin CDU joined this new group, leaving the Berlin CDU organization in a better position to take a strong stand.

Developments in the LDP were similar, but even more rapid. Differences between the Berlin branch of the party and the zonal organization had existed almost from the beginning, and on February 10, 1948 the Berlin unit was formally expelled by party headquarters in the Soviet zone. The expulsion had been preceded on January 19 by efforts of procommunist elements in Berlin to form an "LDP Working Group" with a view to taking over the city organization.[60] The attempt failed, and the procommunist group was forced out of the Berlin unit, leaving the noncommunist party leaders in a strengthened position.[61]

By the time the blockade came all three of Berlin's democratic parties were thus in the hands of men who were committed to preserving Berlin's freedom. They differed on methods, but were agreed on basic aims.

Another political grouping in Berlin, possibly even more powerful than the political parties, was the Free German Trade Union Association (FDGB). Established under communist auspices on a highly centralized basis, the FDGB remained under full communist control long after the democratic parties had assumed the reins of the city government. A senior union official in Berlin later said that, in his opinion, the Soviets would not have found it necessary to impose a blockade on Berlin if they had retained control of the unions. Had they been able to dominate labor, the Communists could have manipulated the economic life of the city and eventually could have regained political control as well.

The idea of a single union of all labor groups was popular with Berlin's labor leaders of all political colorations in the period immediately following World War II. They attributed the rise of Nazism in Germany in part to the fact that the workers had been split into various competing unions, and they were determined to see that a similar disunity would not arise again. Consequently, when the FDGB was set up under Soviet auspices in the summer of 1945, former leaders from the pre-1933 Social Democratic unions, the Christian Trade Union Movement, and the Hirsch-Duncker unions all cooperated with the Communists.* In spite of the fact that a vast majority of its officials were Communists, and especially those in key positions, the new organization functioned to the relative satisfaction of all major labor groups for approximately a year.

During 1946, however, rumblings of dissatisfaction could be heard. Noncommunist labor leaders were particularly displeased by the 1946 May Day celebration, which, instead of being a demonstration of united labor, had been given a specifically communist flavor by FDGB officials and Soviet representatives. Democratic leaders also looked askance at the manner in which communist union functionaries systematically reviewed union measures to make sure that they were in accord with the communist line. Furthermore, union leaders in Berlin saw the non-Communists in the Soviet zone being systematically removed from all key positions in labor organizations, particularly after the forced merger of the Communist Party and the Social Democratic Party in 1946.

The merger, resulting in the formation of the SED, strengthened the Communists' grip on the unions. Prior to the election of the Berlin Executive Committee of the Trade Union Association in 1946, it had been agreed that of the 30 committee seats, the Communists were to receive 13, the Social Democrats 13, and the Christian Democrats 4. After the merger, however, the SED took over the seats of both the Communists and the Social Democrats.[62]

Noncommunist activists in the unions found it difficult to combat the firm control of the Communists, since they were only a tiny minority among the leaders and functionaries. Their situation is illustrated by a report of the Union of Employees of Public Enterprises and Administrations:

> It may only be mentioned that during the years 1946 and 1947 a tiny minority, consisting of four colleagues, conducted what often seemed like an almost hopeless fight in the Executive Committee . . . against the other 31 members, all of whom were members of the SED and for the most part fanatical communists.[63]

* Much of the material on labor activities in Berlin was made available by Mr. Klaus Kundt of the Free University of Berlin, who at the time of this study was preparing a dissertation on the subject and very kindly provided this writer with an extensive memorandum based on his research.

Another reason for their lack of success during 1946 and 1947 was that most unionized workers, although noncommunist, were politically apathetic.[64] Membership meetings were badly attended, and in Berlin almost one-quarter of the members were delinquent in the payment of their dues. In this situation the highly-organized and politically-conscious SED minority had little difficulty in controlling the amorphous mass.[65] Furthermore, the non-Communists knew that the Soviets would give vigorous support to the SED in its effort to retain control, but they did not know whether, in the event of an open conflict, they could count on the support of the Western powers, without which a fight would be hopeless. Finally, and most important, the Communists used the "unity" slogan with great effectiveness. Any effort to disturb the existing arrangements brought the charge from SED members that their opponents were seeking once more to split the labor movement, and the non-Communists were very sensitive to this charge.

All these restraints did not, however, prevent the non-Communists from gradually mobilizing their forces. Part of their lethargy and hopelessness was lifted by the successful struggle of the Berlin SPD against the forced merger with the Communist Party in 1946, which encouraged them to think that it might be possible to wage an equally successful campaign against the Communists in the unions. The noncommunist opposition waged a vigorous campaign in 1947, and succeeded in electing approximately 1,500 shop stewards identified with the democratic parties, as compared to 1,252 affiliated with the SED, and 842 who had no party connection. When it came to the Berlin Union Congress, however, the non-Communists were able to elect at the borough level only about 30 per cent of the delegates, as against some 45 per cent identified with the SED, and another 25 per cent who were without party affiliation. At the city level 361 of the 436 delegates turned out to be members of the SED. And since it was the city-wide trade union conference that elected the 45-man Central Executive Committee, the latter remained firmly in communist hands, although the Social Democrats were allowed six places on it and the Christian Democrats two.[66]

One reason that the opposition found it impossible to gain control of the central organization at that time was that the communist-dominated executive committee made the rules for an extremely complicated election procedure. Unions in each borough of the city elected delegates to a borough trade union conference, which in turn elected delegates to the city-wide conference that elected the

Executive Committee. Election rules forbade the use of party labels, and the elections proceeded so rapidly that the political affiliation of each candidate could not become known to union members at large. As a result, the mass of non-party union members split their votes, while the well-disciplined SED minority always voted as a unit.[67]

The Western powers made several attempts to secure a more equitable election system for the FDGB, but these efforts were blocked by the Soviets. In a seven-and-one-half-hour session on January 31 the Kommandatura failed to agree on rules for the 1947 union elections. On the following day General Kotikov published a sharp attack on American Military Government in the *Tägliche Rundschau*, calling its attitude "a serious threat to the reconstruction of the political life of Germany on a democratic foundation." This was the first time that a high-ranking Soviet officer had criticized his Allied colleagues in a German-language newspaper, and it created a considerable stir. Colonel Howley, the peppery chief of military government in the U.S. sector, thereupon called in reporters from the German press to give them the other side of the story. Meanwhile, the communist-dominated Executive Committee of the FDGB voted to continue in office "as if nothing had happened."[68]

The formula for the elections that was finally agreed upon by the four powers amounted to a surrender on the part of the Allies, for it preserved the indirect procedures, and enabled the SED to retain control of the unions for another year.[69] According to Colonel Howley, the Soviet commander, in discussing union matters with the Western powers, took the point of view that "the FDGB isn't your business."[70]

The SED was able to manipulate the complicated election system efficiently because it had active groups in nearly all shops and factories. The Social Democratic newspaper in Berlin quoted the following speech made by a communist union leader before the 1947 elections:

> The elections will be held in any case according to the election rules, with or without the permission of the Allied Kommandatura. The elections will be a test of strength, and no tolerance can be shown the reactionary Social Democratic Party. The election committees must therefore be composed so as to have a majority of SED union members. Active SED election leadership groups must be formed in all boroughs, and the party

> secretaries and instructors will be at the disposal of these leadership groups. SED fraction meetings should be held in every union in each district and concrete election tasks should be assigned. . . . An adequate supply of paper for handbills and leaflets will be supplied in each borough. Certain printshops can print the necessary materials overnight. The Social Democrats must be unmasked as a divisive force in the unions.[71]

At first the opposition had no comparable machinery with which to fight this massive SED organization. The SPD, which next to the SED had enrolled the most union members, provided moral support for the insurgents, but as yet no systematic leadership. After the elections of 1947, however, the SPD realized that it would have to take a more active role in providing city-wide leadership, if the grip of the Communists was to be broken. The Berlin SPD Executive Committee concerned itself with this question at two meetings, in August and September of 1947, and decided to conduct its fight *within* the unions. Resignation of unionists opposed to the policies of the communist leadership was to be avoided. Instead, the SPD would organize factory groups to rival those of the SED.[72] At the party convention of the Berlin SPD on October 26, 1947, Ernst Reuter advocated stronger organization of party units in the factories as an essential condition for the survival of the SPD in Berlin.

As the time for the 1948 elections to the city-wide union conference approached, activity on both sides rose to fever pitch. Worried by the increasing activity of the opposition, the communist leadership attempted to throw the insurgents out of the FDGB. The independents counterattacked in February 1948 by forming a working group of representatives from the principal noncommunist pre-Nazi unions. Under the dynamic leadership of Ernst Scharnowski and Georg Müller, this working group sent speakers into factories and offices in all parts of the city to appeal directly to the workers. As one of the independent organizers said later, "We met the Communists on their own ground and we beat them." The greater part of the speaking and organizing was carried on by Ernst Scharnowski and half a dozen of his colleagues. Coordination and staff work was provided by the SPD.

The occupying powers behaved according to a now-familiar pattern. The Soviets actively supported the candidates they favored. The Western powers officially kept their hands off, maintaining that this was purely an affair of the Germans, but a number of British and American officials privately gave opposition leaders what help and encouragement they could. These Allied officers assured independent German unionists that Western opinion would support them in their defiance of the communist-controlled FDGB leadership, but they were unable to make any official promises of assistance. The Soviets attempted simultaneously to bribe the workers of several industries with generous offers of food, and to browbeat the opposition leaders with endless interrogations. But when a number of German leaders pleaded with high Allied officials to offer at least a few material inducements to the workers in order to offset the Soviet largesse, they were told coldly that the Western powers did not propose to engage in competition with the Soviets for German favor.

When the time came for elections of union delegates to the 1948 borough and city-wide conferences, the Soviets and German Communists employed a series of almost fantastic devices in an effort to retain control.[73] For example, independent delegates in at least four boroughs of the Soviet sector were ordered to appear at military government headquarters at the very hour when elections were to be held. In another borough the local mayor, who was also an independent delegate from his area, was ordered by the Russian commander to go out and cut wood at the time the elections were to be held. In five west sector boroughs, the communist-controlled central election committees simply refused to recognize the election of sixty-nine delegates to the borough conferences. When it became apparent that independent delegates were about to be elected by the railway workers union, the SED minority first delayed the election by a series of parliamentary devices and then left the meeting, taking with them the election lists, without which the election could not be conducted. In another case an election was prevented by the disappearance of the ballot box.

The communist union leaders also manipulated the electoral system in such a way that shops and areas likely to return communist delegates were given more representation than those in which the independents were strong. In one borough, for instance, several small businesses were formed into an election unit with only 600 members, most of whom were highly apathetic. When an election meeting was called for this unit, only 80 persons appeared, the majority of them Communists. These 80 then proceeded to elect 30 delegates to the borough conference, while other election meetings, representing thousands of workers, were allowed to elect only a handful of delegates.

In spite of the direct intervention of Soviet Military Government, and the skillful manipulation of the indirect electoral system by the communist Executive Committee, the independents achieved a clear popular majority in the 1948 union elections. They claimed from 60 to 75 per cent of the vote in many areas of the west sectors and an average of 40 per cent in the Soviet sector.* When the city conference met on May 21–23, however, the communist leaders proceeded to turn this popular majority into a minority by simply refusing to seat several dozen independent delegates because of alleged irregularities in their election. They also refused to authorize supplementary elections to clear up the supposedly doubtful cases. Instead, a communist-dominated Executive Committee was elected, and the opposition received only minority representation on this all-powerful body.

Seeing that the Communists refused to surrender control of the central FDGB organization regardless of the wishes of the union members, on May 26 the independent leaders called a meeting of representatives of those industrial and geographical union subdivisions which had given a majority to the independent candidates. This meeting resolved that a temporary executive committee would be set up to handle all union business until new elections could be held. In this way, a rival union organization was finally established. As in the case of the SPD, a group of middle-level functionaries had been able to remove the bulk of the membership from the control of the procommunist central apparatus. One union leader later remarked: "We had been talking about labor unity for years, and then with bleeding hearts we had to set out and split the unions."

The new organization was recognized by American Military Government as bargaining agent for labor in the U.S. sector on June 18, 1948 (just prior to the full blockade) and by the British and French during July. But the independent leaders had a long, hard row to hoe before the new union could become a fully-developed, functioning organization. The power of the Communists over labor in the west sectors had been successfully challenged, but it had not been broken completely. A new central union headquarters was established in West Berlin, but it was up to each individual union

* The exact size of this popular majority cannot be determined, in view of the numerous irregularities in the elections. (Cf. *Wir Klagen an!*, a pamphlet published by the Unabhängige Gewerkschaftsorganisation Gross-Berlin, 1948, pp. 19-24, and *passim.*)

to decide whether to give it allegiance. Furthermore, each union member had to decide whether to pay his dues to a union affiliated with the independents or to the communist-controlled FDGB. The break, however, was a decisive one, and the fact that it occurred just before the blockade was of the greatest significance.

The democratic ferment was not limited to the city government, the parties, and the trade unions. Though it affected only a minority of the population, it penetrated into nearly all of Berlin's institutions where the Communists were entrenched.

An important example is provided by events at the University of Berlin, in the Russian sector. The Soviets had initially allowed the university to function in considerable freedom, and the common feeling that all antifascist groups should cooperate to overcome Berlin's postwar misery had caused democratic academicians to lean over backwards in their efforts to get along with the Communists. In 1947, however, the Soviets began to take steps to bring the university completely under their control. Six students, most of whom were affiliated with the CDU, were arrested in March 1947. The chairman of the student council resigned in October 1947 in protest against interference in the affairs of the university by the Soviet Zone Central Agency for Popular Education. But in spite of increased coercion, the student council elections of December 11, for which the SED had nominated its own candidates, turned out well for the anti-Communists.

In April 1948 the two editors of the student magazine, which had served as spokesman for the democratic opposition, were expelled from the university, along with the most outspoken contributor to the magazine, who was an active functionary of the SPD.

The answer was a mass protest meeting in West Berlin, just outside the Soviet sector. Despite a communist threat that students who attended would be expelled, the meeting was well attended. It was the occasion for the first public appeal for the establishment of a Free University in West Berlin. On May 10, 1948 the City Assembly voted 83 to 17 that the Berlin University be removed from the Soviet zone administration and placed under the Magistrat. Since the institution was in the east sector, however, there was no way to enforce this decision.

But the agitation for a Free University in West Berlin increased. A clandestine group of students was formed to distribute information throughout the university and Western authorities were approached with requests for support. The noncommunist students received encouragement from middle-level American and British officials. And shortly before the blockade American Military Government finally acceded to the demands of university professors for assurances that material support would be forthcoming if they followed the lead of the anticommunist student group and severed their ties with the university in the east sector. Thereafter, plans for a Free University in West Berlin moved ahead rapidly.

Prior to the blockade only a minority of the students or professors actively supported the Free University idea. Of the reluctant majority, some believed that conditions in the old university might be improved, others pointed out that it would be a long time before a new university could create the necessary research and laboratory facilities, and still others were politically indifferent. It was the determination of a relatively small number of student leaders, and the promise of Western assistance, that decided the outcome.

The struggle for control of Berlin's political institutions was by no means over at the time the blockade was imposed. But communist power had been curtailed, and democratic institutions had been developed to a point where, in West Berlin at least, the population could no longer be manipulated for Soviet purposes. The three democratic political parties had successfully asserted their right to follow their own programs, an independent trade union federation had been established, and a Free University was in the offing.

Soviet Preparation for the Blockade

Soviet efforts to retain a position of preeminence in Berlin's political life were accompanied to an increasing degree by measures apparently designed to pave the way for the full blockade. They included predictions in the Soviet-controlled press that the Western powers would leave, assertions that Berlin was a part of the Soviet zone, measures which gradually strangled the movement of persons and goods between Berlin and West Germany, and actions intended to discredit the democratic Magistrat and to consolidate Soviet control over Berlin's east sector.

Characteristically, one of the first intimations that the Soviets might be trying to force the Western powers out of the former Reich capital came in the form of protests against alleged Western actions. At a Kommandatura meeting in August 1947 the Soviets charged that the United States and Britain were trying to merge their sectors of the city with their already combined zones. Despite denials, in which the French joined, the Soviet representative persisted in his charge and pointed out that the city government had sent representatives to the bizonal agencies. The Western representatives replied that this was necessitated by the fact that most of the food for the U.S. and British sectors came from West Germany.[74]

In February 1948 the Soviets prevented invited British representatives from attending a German political meeting in the Soviet sector. When the Western powers protested about this at the Allied Control Council, Marshal Sokolovsky replied that Berlin was a part of the Soviet zone, and accused the Allies of using "their position to prejudice their right to remain in Berlin."[75] Several months later at a meeting of the Kommandatura, General Kotikov twice spoke of Berlin as part of the Soviet zone.[76]

During the spring and summer of 1947 the Soviet-controlled press intimated more and more often that the Western powers were about to leave Berlin. A number of rumors—some of them clearly Soviet-inspired—pointed in the same direction.[77]

In October 1947 a report in the Western press that most United States forces would be withdrawn from Berlin after the London conference of foreign ministers in November caused a sensation throughout Germany. According to this report only General Clay and a handful of liaison officers would remain in the city to deal with the Russians. Acting U.S. Military Governor General Huebner quickly denied that there was any plan to withdraw military government forces from Berlin "now or in the foreseeable future." But his denial apparently was not completely convincing. For the same newspaper story which reported the denial added:

> The denial by General Huebner, however, does not fit in with the general sentiment among many Military Government employees, quite aside from the Germans who have long held similar fears. It is a matter of common knowledge that many Military Government officials openly discuss the probability of a three-power withdrawal from this city.
>
> While there is undoubtedly no official plan for the withdrawal of the western allies, there is room for speculation. It is understood that a large number of branch and division personnel, especially in the field of economics, but including others, will be transferred to Frankfurt.[78]

By the beginning of 1948 Soviet hints of Western withdrawal had become more urgent. In the Soviet newspaper *Tägliche Rundschau* a Russian officer editorialized: "There is no room in Berlin for adherents of the partition of Germany."[79] The official SED organ *Neues Deutschland,* under the headline "U.S. Office of Military Government in Berlin Is Dissolving," reported that American and French officials were preparing to leave Berlin.[80] Another headline in *Neues Deutschland,* on June 3, proclaimed that the Western powers were giving up Berlin as a result of the London six-power conference.

These rumors and news stories threatened to do serious damage to the Western position in Berlin because they made many citizens hesitate to identify themselves with democratic institutions. Berliners knew that, if the Western powers actually left, people who had given offense to the Soviets would be subject to reprisals. In addition, the more timid among Western military government personnel were worried by the continued Soviet suggestions that they leave Berlin, and began to think it might be advisable to depart gracefully before being ejected in an undignified manner. As part of the war of nerves, Soviet automobiles carrying high Red Army officers cruised slowly around Allied billeting areas in the spring of 1948, giving some people the idea that the Soviet officers were choosing billets for themselves.

Even more disturbing to the Western powers and the Berliners was the "creeping blockade." Instances of Soviet interference with traffic between Berlin and West Germany became ever more frequent during early 1948. In January the regulations governing German passengers on interzonal trains were tightened.[81] In March a Soviet General affirmed that traffic between Berlin and West Germany had to be more closely regulated in order to protect the Soviet zone against "subversive and terrorist elements."[82] This announcement was followed by a series of restrictions which had the effect of halting all military trains between Berlin and the west zones and of greatly reducing highway traffic into the city.[83] Under these new regulations the Soviets claimed the right to check the baggage and passengers on military trains running through the east zone, ostensibly in order to thwart black market activity.[84] The United States and Great Britain refused to allow Soviet personnel to board their trains for such purposes, however, and canceled military train service altogether.[85] They then instituted a small airlift, capable of carrying from 60 to 100 tons of supplies per day, to provision Allied personnel in West Berlin.[86] After approximately ten days the Soviets relaxed their position sufficiently for Allied rail service to Berlin to be resumed.

From then on new restrictions came thick and fast. Both the United States and Great Britain were asked to withdraw their communications and service personnel located along the highway from West Germany to Berlin.[87] New border searches were imposed on German travelers and freight between Berlin and West Germany on the grounds that these were necessary to prevent looting. In the City Assembly, City Councilman Klingelhöfer denounced the "anti-looting" campaign of the SED and the Soviet-licensed press as propaganda intended to conceal an attempt to choke Berlin's trade.[88] During May and June the Berlin press reported new restrictions on the movement of goods and persons almost every day. Many of these restrictions were relaxed shortly after being imposed, but the total effect was progressively to sever Berlin's ties with the West. Interference with freight was usually justified by "technical reasons" or on the grounds that shipments were improperly labeled; individual Germans were prevented from traveling through the Soviet zone because allegedly their interzonal passes were not in order or they were engaging in "speculation."[89]

At the same time the Soviets also attempted to restrict air traffic between Berlin and West Germany. Ever since the end of 1946 there had been instances of "buzzing" of Allied transport aircraft by Soviet fighters in the air corridors, but these had not been sufficiently frequent to cause serious tension. Early in 1948, however, the Soviets began to advance official proposals designed to restrict air travel in the corridors. According to a *New York Times* report, two of the proposals advanced by the Soviets called for eliminating instrument flights and advocated the banning of night-flying in the corridors. The *Times* added that the Soviets wished to institute a requirement for prior clearance of all flights into Berlin, and to restrict clearance to those planes directly serving the needs of the occupying forces.[90] The Western powers showed no signs of willingness to alter the existing agreement.

On April 5, 1948 there occurred an incident which may have had a significant influence on the policies of both East and West regarding air travel in and out of Berlin. A Soviet fighter plane, which apparently had been stunting over Berlin, suddenly dove into a scheduled British transport aircraft, as the latter was preparing to land at the Gatow airport in the British sector. Both planes crashed.

The Soviet pilot and the fourteen persons in the British plane were killed.[91]

The British Military Governor, General Robertson, immediately ordered fighter escorts for all British passenger planes. General Clay promptly followed suit. Robertson also delivered a vigorous protest personally to Marshal Sokolovsky, who expressed deep regret and assured Robertson that no interference with the passage of British planes through the agreed corridor was "or is" intended. Upon receiving the Soviet commander's apology and reassurance, General Robertson canceled his order for fighter escorts and General Clay did likewise. A news story from London on the same day noted that the decision to provide fighter escorts, even though it had been canceled in view of Sokolovsky's conciliatory tone, showed that Britain and the United States were willing to risk hostilities unless the Soviets ceased their provocation.[92]

Within a day, however, Sokolovsky reversed his position. In a note to General Robertson (also published in the official Soviet *Tägliche Rundschau*) he placed all the blame for the accident on the British plane. The note contained this implicit threat:

> I hope you will issue the necessary orders to British planes for the strict following of air safety directives outlined by the Allied Control Council. This will forestall me from the necessity of taking measures for the protection and security of traffic over the Soviet occupation zone of Germany. . . .[93]

General Robertson thereupon changed his position also, dropping his demand for written guarantees of the safety of Western planes, and assuring the Soviet commander that British planes had been instructed to observe the quadripartite safety rules strictly. A possible reason for this British retreat is suggested by press stories that the British may have committed a technical violation by not transmitting to Soviet officials at the Berlin Air Safety Center a specific report of the departure and arrival times of the transport plane.[94]

The subsequent British investigation showed that the stunting Soviet flier had been responsible for the crash, but found no evidence to show that the collision was anything but an accident. The Soviets' official report on the Gatow incident accused the British of falsifying the facts and of tampering with the aircraft wreckage in an effort to foist blame onto the Soviet flier.[95]

In addition, the Soviets pressed their earlier proposals to curb air travel between Berlin and the west and suggested such new restrictions as stoppage of all flights by commercial aircraft through the corridors, prohibition of night-flying, curbs on instrument-flying, and Soviet approval of all flights through the corridor twenty-four hours in advance.[96] The official Soviet report on the Gatow crash even suggested that there never had been agreement on flying regulations:

> The Commission likewise calls attention to the absence to this day of precise rules approved by the Control Council for air traffic along routes over the Soviet zone.[97]

Implicitly, the report also questioned the existence of four-power agreements defining the air corridors themselves, since it spoke of the corridors as having been "designated by the Soviet authorities."

Meanwhile, the Soviet-sponsored press continued its campaign against Allied fliers. The *Tägliche Rundschau* and other Soviet-controlled media charged that U.S. and British planes constantly violated air regulations and asserted that "British and American pilots are highly inexperienced and badly need stricter control."[98] One story spoke of "disrespect of elementary flying rules" and concluded: "Law and order must be restored in air traffic above the Soviet occupation zone."[99] These allegations were all the more astonishing since, only a year or so earlier, the Soviets had sought and received the assistance of American officers in the air-safety training of Russian air force personnel.

In the face of Soviet proposals and accusations, British and American authorities stood firm on the previous agreement. General Clay stated crisply that U.S. planes would continue to fly into Berlin under the old four-power agreement, regardless of any new, unilateral regulations the Soviet authorities might devise. He also hinted that fighter escorts would be used if necessary.[100] When the Soviets again complained of violations of flight regulations by British aircraft and invited British Military Government to enter into bilateral air-security discussions, the British denied the Soviet allegations and pointed out that any talks on air security would have to be on a four-power basis.[101] This pattern of Soviet pressure and Allied intransigence continued right up to the time of the airlift.

Soviet efforts to restrict air travel appeared to be coordinated with other measures to choke off Berlin's surface communications, but both the British and the Americans seemed more sensitive to the air restrictions than to interference with rail and road traffic. The

Western powers' readiness to assign fighter escorts, if necessary, may have been one reason why the Soviets made no serious attempt to interfere with the air corridors during the blockade. They apparently wished to avoid any incident that would lead to war, and realized that hostile action against Allied aircraft might well be a *casus belli.*

A pre-blockade measure of a somewhat different nature was taken by the Soviets on June 12 when a Russian borough commander assumed direct control of the Klingenberg power plant, one of Berlin's most important sources of electricity, located in the Soviet sector. Social Democratic members of the factory council and the directors of the Berlin Electric Company (Bewag) were ordered to stay off the premises.

In June 1948 the Communists began issuing statements to the effect that food stocks in Berlin's west sectors were alarmingly low. *Neues Deutschland* reported that the city government was seriously concerned about Berlin's food supply and had pressed the Western powers for a larger credit. This report was vehemently denied by City Councilman Füllsack, director of the city Food Office, and the *Tagesspiegel* observed: "The communist central organ, which wants to make Berliners worry about their food supply by citing statements which never have been made, thereby distinguishes itself by the fact that its lack of love for the truth is exceeded by its lack of conscience."[102] A few days later, *Neues Deutschland* published the headline: "GENERAL CLAY SAYS BERLIN CANNOT BE SUPPLIED BY AIR." The story which followed claimed that food stocks in the U.S. sector would last only a few days.[103] The Communists apparently were aware of the possibility of an airlift to supply the city, and wished to discount this measure in advance.

Another series of Soviet maneuvers during the latter part of 1947 and early 1948 appeared to be designed to weaken the authority of the Western powers, the central city government, and the Kommandatura. In October 1947 the Soviets introduced in the Kommandatura a fourteen-point proposal ostensibly designed to improve working and living conditions in Berlin. In commenting on this proposal, the deputy director of Military Government in the British sector noted that it could not be a coincidence that the Soviet industrial plan for the east zone had been published at the same time and that it also consisted of fourteen points. He surmised that the Soviets were trying to create the impression that they alone were concerned with the well-being of the Berliners, that quadripartite rule was a failure, and that the city was really part of the east zone.[104]

The Western powers, while not averse to most of the points in the Soviet paper, nevertheless wanted to consider each one on its merits. General Kotikov, on the other hand, insisted that the whole package be accepted or rejected as a unit. Discussion of this package proposal continued in the Kommandatura up to the time that the Soviets withdrew from that body. In the course of these often acrimonious arguments, General Kotikov accused the Western powers of trying to plunder and starve the Germans and of sundry other misdeeds.[105] His charges were given full coverage by the Soviet-controlled press and radio and were supplemented by even more blatant accusations from German communist spokesmen.[106]

In their efforts to undermine the authority of the Kommandatura and the city government, the Soviets issued a long chain of unilateral orders to municipal agencies. For instance, in May 1947 General Sokolovsky ordered that East Berlin be included in the Soviet zone drive to collect scrap metals. Quick protests from the Magistrat, aided by a press campaign, prevented implementation of the order and saved the city from being drained of scrap. City Councilman Füllsack received a series of similar orders at the Food Office, usually for preferential treatment of the east sector in the distribution of supplies, but most of these orders were successfully nullified by intervention of the Western powers. It was, however, possible for the Soviets to give preferential treatment to many groups of workers in East Berlin. Thus, employees of the Berlin transit system in East Berlin received a warm noon meal, while those in West Berlin did not.

Another tactic used by the Soviets to embarrass the Magistrat was to offer certain benefits to the city and then to hamper city officials in their efforts to take advantage of these offers. For instance, a considerable amount of East German firewood in the Soviet zone was earmarked for Berlin. But when the city government tried to send trucks to pick up this wood it had the greatest difficulty in obtaining authorization for them to drive into the Soviet zone.[107]

In March of 1948 a Soviet liaison officer informed the speaker of the City Assembly, Dr. Suhr, that he would be held responsible for seeing that no anti-Soviet propaganda was tolerated in the Assembly. Dr. Suhr reported this order to the Assembly and announced that he could not obey it, first because he could not accept unilateral orders for the conduct of the Assembly from any of the occupation powers, and secondly because no one had defined for him what constituted "anti-Soviet propaganda." He then offered to resign. The Assembly, however, gave him a vote of confidence, representatives of the Western powers also expressed their confidence in him, and Dr. Suhr continued as speaker.[108] As a matter of record, nearly all speeches in the Assembly during this pre-blockade period, except those of the Communists, were moderate in tone.

An even more blatant case of attempted intimidation occurred in May when a Soviet officer issued orders on a personnel matter to the city councilman in charge of postal services and threatened him with arrest if he did not comply.[109] Only after protests from the mayor's office did the Russian finally back down. Other Soviet moves succeeded in their purpose. For example, new Soviet zone post office regulations governing the forwarding of parcel post to West Germany were applied to all Berlin, despite protests from the Western powers.[110] On June 3, 1948 the Soviet command unilaterally issued an order governing wages and hours in the Soviet sector, although on matters of this type the Kommandatura was supposed to provide uniform laws for the whole city. City Councilman Klingelhöfer called the order "the first unequivocal act to give the Soviet sector a special system of laws."[111] Through these and other measures, the Soviets tried more and more to limit the area of effective authority of the Magistrat and the Kommandatura. But at the same time that the Soviets were taking these measures, Kotikov was interpreting any Western opposition to Soviet policy as an attempt to obstruct the functioning of the Kommandatura and to end quadripartite government.[112]

On June 16 the Soviets walked out of the Berlin Kommandatura. This was scarcely a surprise to political observers. For the walk-out was a logical continuation of previous Soviet policies. Two days before the last meeting of the four-power body, the London *Times* expressed the opinion that the meeting would probably be "another stage in the Kommandatura's dissolution."[113] It was. After thirteen hours of wrangling, Colonel Howley asked the chairman, General Ganeval, for permission to be excused, leaving his deputy to take his place. As soon as he had left the Soviet representative rose and said that he considered it impossible to continue the meeting in view of Colonel Howley's "hooligan action." He then walked out with the whole Soviet delegation, ignoring the remonstrances of the chairman that Colonel Howley had been properly excused.[114]

Yet withal, the Soviets were rarely intransigent; when faced with counterpressure from the Western powers, or even from the German government, they often backed down. Furthermore, they provided a conciliatory justification for almost every aggressive action. Measures interfering with Berlin's traffic to the west were justified as being necessary to prevent looting or black-market activity, or as being merely enforcements of existing regulations. When Soviet representatives left the Kommandatura, they did so allegedly because Colonel Howley had departed first. These justifications were often trivial or even ridiculous, but they left the way open for retreat without sacrifice of principle, if retreat should be desirable. Indeed, many Soviet actions during the pre-blockade period in Berlin appeared to be of a probing nature, as though Moscow were trying to ascertain what kind of response could be expected.* Since Western reactions to interference with ground communications were relatively weak, one may speculate that the Soviets felt safe in imposing a land blockade. On the other hand, the fact that the Western powers seemed to take a strong view of interference with air traffic may have been the reason why the Soviets never seriously attempted to block the air corridors.

The circumspection with which the Soviets advanced is reflected in a *New York Times* dispatch from Berlin dated June 16, little more than a week before the full blockade was imposed. In spite of the economic and political pressure they had been exerting on the west sectors of Berlin, the Russians were reported to have gone out of their way to emphasize the absence of any political significance in these measures, and to placate irate officials of the Western powers. The dispatch cited, as one evidence of the Soviets' conciliatory attitude, a friendly visit from the chief of the Red Army railroad service in Germany to the chief of British rail transport, ostensibly for the purpose of explaining that Soviet restrictions on rail traffic were not intended to harass the Western powers.[115] Yet two days after this visit, the Soviets walked out of the Kommandatura.

Western Reactions to Soviet Behavior in Berlin

Faced with Soviet attempts to maintain their authority over Berlin and to hamstring communications with the west, the Allies

* An observation along these lines was also made in Washington shortly before the blockade. Under Secretary of State Lovett reported in April 1948 that the Soviet Ambassador and members of his staff, in conversation with State Department officials, seemed to have been probing to determine American intentions. The Soviet representative asked, for instance, whether America really intended to stay in Europe. Cf. Walter Millis (ed.), *The Forrestal Diaries*, Viking Press, New York, 1951, p. 424.

reacted spasmodically—sometimes with brave words and military gestures, sometimes with indecision and compromise.

In the early months of 1947 the Soviet-controlled press began to emphasize Russian military strength in Germany, and Soviet fighter planes appeared over Berlin. To counter this demonstration, General Clay ordered a U.S. fighter group to fly over Berlin on May 30, forming the letters "U.S." And on July 2 the American commander ordered several large B-29 bombers over Berlin. To a protest from the Soviet Military Governor, Clay replied that he was merely making sure that the United States could participate in the security arrangements for Berlin.[116] A U.S. liaison officer, who was in Soviet Military Government headquarters when the big bombers came over, reported that several Soviet officers rushed to the window shaking their fists at the planes.

Also during 1947, Colonel Howley came to realize that the Soviets would use food as a political weapon in their efforts to gain control of Berlin. When they refused to deliver fresh milk to Berlin's west sectors as previously agreed, Howley took measures to stock 200 tons of condensed milk and 150 tons of powdered milk, and to ensure that at least a thirty-day supply of food for the German population in the U.S. sector would be available at all times.[117]

Beginning in 1948, stories in the American and British press reported that General Clay and General Robertson were aware of the possibility that the Soviets might attempt to force them out of Berlin. The reports added that it would be most difficult for the Western powers to remain in Berlin if the Soviets moved to incorporate the city into the east zone, because most of Berlin's public utilities were in the Soviet sector.[118] Nevertheless, some officials tended to discount threatening expressions in the Soviet-controlled press. Thus a ranking officer in U.S. Military Government, commenting on one truculent editorial in the *Tägliche Rundschau,* expressed the belief that the article was designed merely to get on the nerves of the Americans and British. As to the possibility of a blockade, he said that he could not "see the Russians being so foolish as to deliberately and publicly starve the people of Berlin and sabotage the lone symbol of unity just to spite us. This is not the way to win friends and influence people. . . ."[119] On the other hand, a source "extremely close to the Russian political directorate," was reported as saying that the editorial in the *Tägliche Rundschau* was written in dead earnest, and not as a means of "needling" the Americans.[120] In Washington, Acting Secretary of

State Lovett told a press conference that the United States would maintain its military representation in Berlin. He noted that there had been a series of incidents, including the delay of trains between Berlin and Frankfurt and the detention of U.S. personnel by Soviet authorities, but saw no indication that such incidents were increasing.[121]

This tendency of American officials to deprecate Soviet threats was abruptly checked when General Clay dispatched the following warning message to the U.S. Army Director of Intelligence on March 5, 1948:

> FOR MANY MONTHS, BASED ON LOGICAL ANALYSIS, I HAVE FELT AND HELD THAT WAR WAS UNLIKELY FOR AT LEAST TEN YEARS. WITHIN THE LAST FEW WEEKS, I HAVE FELT A SUBTLE CHANGE IN SOVIET ATTITUDE WHICH I CANNOT DEFINE BUT WHICH NOW GIVES ME A FEELING THAT IT MAY COME WITH DRAMATIC SUDDENNESS. I CANNOT SUPPORT THIS CHANGE IN MY OWN THINKING WITH ANY DATA OR OUTWARD EVIDENCE IN RELATIONSHIPS OTHER THAN TO DESCRIBE IT AS A FEELING OF A NEW TENSENESS IN EVERY SOVIET INDIVIDUAL WITH WHOM WE HAVE OFFICIAL RELATIONS. I AM UNABLE TO SUBMIT ANY OFFICIAL REPORT IN THE ABSENCE OF SUPPORTING DATA BUT MY FEELING IS REAL. YOU MAY ADVISE THE CHIEF OF STAFF OF THIS FOR WHATEVER IT MAY BE WORTH IF YOU FEEL IT ADVISABLE.[122]

General Clay's telegram came shortly after the communist coup in Czechoslovakia. Tension in the world was rising, and U.S. intelligence services started working at top speed. On March 16 the Central Intelligence Agency could predict only that war was not probable within 60 days, an estimate that was later extended to cover another 60 days.[123] On March 31 General Clay reported having received word from the Soviets that they were going to institute control checks on military personnel and baggage passing through the Soviet zone. Clay advised Washington that he proposed to issue orders to American military personnel on U.S. trains to prevent the Soviets from entering these trains for inspection purposes, and to shoot if necessary, and asked for instructions. The top U.S. military leaders decided to indorse Clay's plan, with the qualifications that the train guards use their weapons only in self-defense, and that the British be contacted to see if they would issue similar instructions. The last point proved superfluous when news was received that the British had already adopted similar measures.[124]

The discussions in Washington took place against a background of marked military weakness. The United States was unable to send more than a division (about 15,000 men) anywhere without partial mobilization.[125] In London, the Foreign Office was prepared to be firm, but did not know precisely what action to take. The British had no desire to see their forces shoot their way in and out of Berlin, but at the same time they were determined to maintain their position in the city.[126] French policy was less firm. One highly-placed French official in Berlin reported a growing feeling in Paris that Berlin was a political liability, from which France would be glad to extricate herself if she could do it gracefully.

While Washington was prepared to support General Clay in his effort to protect the American position in Berlin, there were apparently some doubts that this could be done, and some fears that it might lead to war. On March 30 the Department of the Army requested General Clay to give his views on a proposal to stop the movement of dependents of military government personnel to Germany, and gradually to withdraw those dependents who were already in Berlin and the U.S. zone. Clay opposed this move, observing that it would create hysteria and cause Germans to rush to communism as a form of insurance. He also noted that it would add to communist strength everywhere, particularly in Italy, where elections were only a few days off.[127] Several days later, the Department of the Army reported to General Clay that pressure at home for the return of American families from Berlin was rising. A number of military government personnel had indeed requested that their families be sent home, but when General Clay ruled that staff members who wanted their dependents evacuated would have to accompany them, nearly all these applications were withdrawn. General Clay replied to the Department that Americans in Berlin could be supported indefinitely with a very small airlift, and that dependents should not be sent home. Part of his message read:

> Evacuation in face of the Italian elections and European situation is to me almost unthinkable.[128]

Nevertheless, on April 10, in view of increased traffic restrictions, the Secretary of the Army teletyped the Military Governor once more that, while there was no change in the Department's position that U.S. forces should remain in Berlin, the question was under constant discussion in Washington. General Clay's answer was that the U.S. should not abandon Berlin unless driven out by force. He thought that extension of the blockade to cut off the food supply of the Berliners might succeed in forcing the Western powers out, but he doubted that the Russians would be so foolish as to make a move that would alienate the German population completely.* He continued:

> We have lost Czechoslovakia. Norway is threatened.† We retreat from Berlin. When Berlin falls, Western Germany will be next. If we mean to hold Europe against Communism, we must not budge. . . . I believe the future of democracy requires us to stay. . . .[129]

Although the U.S. Military Governor insisted that the Allied position in Berlin be defended, and although the British Foreign Office, publicly at least, shared this view, there was a lack of consensus among Western officials in Berlin on whether the Soviets would, in fact, attempt to impose a full blockade on the city, and whether in such an event it would be within the limits of possibility for the Allies to remain. Colonel Howley, for example, came to the conclusion that the Soviets would attempt to drive the Western powers out of the city, possibly by a blockade, and he prepared a plan to meet this eventuality. His conclusions, however, were not fully shared by General Clay's political advisory staff or in other quarters. The French sector commandant, General Ganeval, with whom Howley discussed his plan, did not believe the Russians would do such a cruel thing as to blockade the city, but thought of it as a possibility for which it would be well to be prepared. General Herbert, the British sector commandant, took a more pessimistic view. He, too, did not think it likely that the Soviets would blockade the city; but he believed that, if they did, the Western powers would have no choice but to leave.[130] Right up to the time the blockade was imposed, and indeed afterward as well, Allied officials continued to debate whether they *should* try and remain in Berlin and, if so, whether there was any hope that they *could.* As far as can be determined, no top-level decisions about what to do in the event of a Soviet blackade had been made in Washington, London, or Paris.[131]

* A high U.S. official who was in Germany in 1948 sent an even gloomier report to Washington in June. He forecast that a total blockade of Berlin would so affect West Berlin's food supply that the population would turn against the Western powers and make their position in the city untenable.

† The reference to Norway may have been an error. Finland was threatened at that time.

In the United States, a number of factors tended to inhibit careful consideration of the Berlin problem at the highest level. Secretary of Defense Forrestal noted in his diary that during April there was a slackening in Washington's awareness of the Soviet danger, and also that the start of the 1948 presidential campaign rendered basic political decisions more difficult. In addition, certain politically explosive problems such as the recognition of Israel and the level of the military budget were in the forefront of attention.[132]

Yet, in spite of this lack of clarity in Western policy, certain steps were taken during the spring of 1948 to make West Berlin more self-sufficient. On the basis of Colonel Howley's plan, U.S. authorities attempted to build up food stocks. Their efforts were only moderately successful in the face of Soviet transport restrictions. Indeed, stocks of flour in Berlin were very much lower on June 30 than they had been on January 31, 1948.* But stocks of most other staples were increased. Another pre-blockade measure was to start the reconstruction of an electric power plant in the British sector. German authorities had been pressing for this step for some time, and in April 1948 the British gave the order to go ahead.

Measures which, in fact, amounted to preparations for the full blockade, although they were not specifically designed for this purpose, included arrangements for supplying Allied personnel by air. They were begun in April when the Soviets interfered with military rail traffic. Although the tonnage figures in this "baby airlift" were insignificant in comparison with later performance, the experience gained by the Air Force proved valuable. The big Rhein/Main air base outside Frankfurt was equipped as a traffic control point, and arrangements were made for procuring and shipping certain types of rations. Apparently, however, no efforts were made to determine the maximum tonnage which could be transported into Berlin by air if the need were to arise.

Plans to meet contingencies that might result from the impending currency reform in West Germany were somewhat more extensive. Realizing that currency reform was bound to come in East Germany also, and suspecting that the Soviets might try to include Berlin, the Western powers made arrangements to provide Berlin with Western currency if necessary. A sufficient quantity of the new currency was stamped with a "B" and held in readiness for shipment to Berlin.[133]

* According to officials of the Berlin Food Office, the U.S. sector had flour for 64 days on January 31 and for only 22 days on June 30. In the British sector the figures were 64 and 20, and in the French sector 26 and 37.

Nevertheless, numerous problems were not anticipated, such as the inevitable difficulties of the German city government in the face of two competing currencies in Berlin.

Furthermore, Western officials did not agree on a course of action to take account of the fundamental changes which West German currency reform was bound to cause in the political status of Berlin. The Western powers had decided not to include the city in the West German currency reform, but were prepared to introduce Western-sponsored currency as a stop-gap measure if the Soviets tried to include Berlin in a Soviet zone reform. They did not want to see Berlin become a part of the Soviet zone economy, but they did not believe that it could be integrated successfully into the West German economy. The prevailing view seems to have been that after West German, and possibly also East German, currency reform, one would have to work out with the Russians an arrangement that would allow Berlin's economy to function efficiently under four-power control. But nobody could envisage what the details of such an arrangement might be. In the opinion of a senior American financial expert, no practicable solution based on four-power control of Berlin's economy was possible once different currencies had been adopted in East and West Germany. "We could have worked it out with the British," he said, "but even so there would have been friction. With the Russians it was impossible."

During the last weeks before the blockade, top Western officials in Berlin were faced with conflicting estimates of Soviet intentions. On the one hand, there were reports of the possibility of further interference with communications to the west. On the other hand, restrictions did not seem to be increasing, and some of the existing ones appeared to be justified. On June 19 the Soviets turned back a number of freight cars with supplies for the Berlin civilian population on the grounds that the cars were so old as to be unsafe.[134] The following day, since the Soviets reasserted their right to inspect military freight, U.S. authorities again stopped military rail shipments, and once more began to rely on a small airlift to supply the requirements of Allied personnel.[135] Still, when the complete blockade began on June 24, it came as a surprise to most officials.

To summarize, the West did not really believe that the Soviets would attempt to blockade the civilian population in West Berlin. But if there were to be a blockade, the Allies were not certain that they could maintain their position in the city, and, with certain exceptions, they had made no preparations to meet the contingency.

They had somewhat more extensive plans for meeting the eventuality of a Soviet effort to gain control of Berlin's currency, but they had not faced up to its long-term implications for the city. When the blockade came, a great many vital decisions remained to be made.

Changing Political Viewpoint of Berlin's Democratic Leaders

In 1946 and early 1947 it was generally accepted by Berlin's leaders that a formula would have to be found which would enable the city government to cooperate with all four powers. Rejecting as unrealistic the idea that they could identify themselves exclusively with the West, they fought instead to preserve their city's unique status as a ward of all four powers, and to encourage the reunification of Germany.

There were, of course, different shades of opinion among the various political groups. The CDU tended to believe that Berlin might serve as a bridge, or mediator, between East and West; that four-power cooperation, if achieved in Berlin, might gradually be extended to all Germany. Some of the CDU leaders also believed that they could "handle" the Soviets by a policy of firm politeness. The SPD, on the other hand, tended to see the issue as a struggle for power: Only if the Berliners and the Western Allies strenuously resisted all Soviet and German communist efforts to dominate the city's political life could there be a dynamic balance in which Berlin and all Germany could achieve a degree of freedom.

These differences were accentuated by CDU efforts to arrange "bridge-building" talks among German leaders of all shades of opinion, and SPD skepticism about these efforts. In 1946 CDU leaders attempted to institute discussions with a view to forming a representative body which could speak for both East and West Germany, but the SPD leadership refused to participate.[136] Another CDU official attempted to assemble a number of prominent German political leaders from all major parties in Berlin during November 1947 with the purpose of obtaining a joint pledge of support for German unity. But again the SPD leadership opposed this plan and the conference failed to reach a consensus.[137]

In October 1947 Ernst Reuter presented a point of view characteristic of the SPD. He summarized briefly the efforts of the SED to swallow the SPD, and maintained that Berlin's successful struggle to remain free had confirmed and strengthened its moral claim to serve once again as the capital of Germany. There are political elements, he said, which, because of naïvete and also for very transparent selfish reasons, want to write off the east zone of Germany. There are other forces which favor an empire extending from Berlin to Vladivostok. But, he went on, as long as a freedom-loving population in Berlin can prove that it will never allow its ties to the West to be broken, neither the one plan nor the other will be realized. As long as there remains one area in which the idea of German unity is preserved, and in which the bonds between East and West remain so strong, it will not be easy to achieve a final demarcation line through the middle of Germany and through the middle of Europe.[138] The smaller LDP organization tended, in general, to share the SPD attitude.

The points of view of both the CDU and the SPD became increasingly difficult to maintain during the early months of 1948. Soviet measures to choke off Berlin's communications to West Germany, to interfere with the functions of the Magistrat, and to subordinate East Berlin to the Soviet zone administration, as well as the imminence of currency reforms in both East and West Germany, convinced more and more democratic leaders that a "middle position" was no longer possible, and that Berlin would have to throw in its lot with the West.

This was not a sudden transformation. Almost until the time of the full blockade there were powerful elements in both the SPD and the CDU which believed that a reconciliation of viewpoints might be possible and that Berlin could still preserve its four-power character. As late as April 15, 1948, Dr. Suhr expressed the belief that tension among the occupying powers had relaxed, and voiced the hope that this pause would be used "to find a mode of cooperation which would allow a free and unified administration of Berlin, make it possible for German unity to be restored soon and ensure the peace of Europe."[139]

Some of Berlin's "middle-of-the-road" leaders also tried to delay German currency reform in hopes of avoiding a situation where they would have to take sides. At the end of May Deputy Mayor Friedensburg told an American liaison officer that differing currencies in the two parts of Germany would create in Berlin an "economically and politically desperate situation." On June 9, he wrote to the French Military Governor, General Koenig, urging the Allied Control Council to defer currency reform until a proposal could be made for a single solution to the problem in all zones and in Berlin. In a memorandum to General Ganeval, the chairman of the Kommandatura for June, representatives of all three democratic parties expressed their concern about plans for separate currency reforms. These last-minute expressions brought a favorable response only from Soviet Military Governor Sokolovsky, who said cynically that the Soviet Union was in favor of an all-German currency reform, since a separate reform in one or several zones of Germany would mean "a final splitting of Germany, which would not correspond with the interests of the German people and the interests of the peace-loving, democratic peoples of Europe."[140] Some political figures in Berlin advocated that, in the event of separate reforms in East and West Germany, the city adopt a third currency in order to keep Berlin from being tied to the economy of one side or the other.

Similarly, a majority of Berlin's politicians initially opposed the London Recommendations and the idea of forming a West German state. This, they felt, would tend to isolate Berlin and force the city into the arms of the east zone. Representatives of the Magistrat expressed these views at a meeting of West German minister presidents on June 6, 1948, and on June 13 the City Assembly passed a resolution criticizing the London Recommendations and calling for free elections to an all-German national assembly.

Such attitudes toward currency reform and the London Recommendations were understandable. But, in view of the long and completely unsuccessful struggle of the United States and Great Britain to achieve German unity and a quadripartite currency reform, they showed a strong tendency to disregard unpleasant realities. These realities were, however, appreciated by Ernst Reuter and by a few men around him who dimly saw the shape of things to come.

In the spring of 1948 Reuter concluded that the Soviets were intent on dividing Germany and swallowing Berlin, and that the only way for Berlin to maintain her freedom was to associate herself with West Germany's economic development and attempt to secure American aid. The greatest danger to Berlin was that the Western powers might decide it was a liability and withdraw from the city. Therefore, in order to bring as much pressure on the Western powers as possible, Reuter and several other SPD leaders decided to mobilize the people of Berlin in favor of a Western course, and also to try to gain the attention of the free world. If Berlin were to become a recognized symbol of freedom, it would then be more difficult for the democracies to desert it. This strategy was discussed at several meetings of party leaders, and was one reason why several prominent city officials made trips abroad in the spring of 1948. Furthermore, several weeks before the blockade Gustav Klingelhöfer, SPD councilman for economic affairs, urged the Western powers to introduce West German currency into Berlin, since it had become evident that the Soviets would not consent to a currency reform for all Germany except on their own terms.

Some of the SPD leaders were not fully in favor of identification with the Western powers, but they agreed at least to refrain from denouncing the London Recommendations. On one principle, however, all the principal leaders in the SPD, and most of the leaders of the other democratic parties, were unanimous: freedom was worth a fight.

Relations between the Berlin City Government and the Western Powers

Though the pressure of events was forcing Berlin's democratic leaders increasingly to identify their interests with those of the Western powers, their relations with Western military governments in Berlin prior to the blockade were none too good. During most of this period the Allies were still officially committed to searching for ways of cooperating with the Soviets, and were trying hard to preserve four-power harmony. Also, the idea of competing with the Russians for the favor of the Germans was distasteful to many Allied officials, who therefore made a conscious effort to continue regarding the Germans as recently defeated enemies.[141]

As a result, the interests of democratic Berliners were sometimes sacrificed to the ideal of four-power harmony. For instance, the city councilman in charge of education, a Social Democrat, was removed by a quadripartite resolution after he had incurred Soviet displeasure by trying to prevent the use of the schools for communist indoctrination. American spokesmen later acknowledged that U.S. action in this case had been due to lack of knowledge, but the damage was done.[142]

Such instances of the Western powers' willingness to compromise, and their seeming lack of ability to defend their own interests, led Berlin's democratic leaders to feel that they could not count on Western support. In June 1947, shortly after the removal of the city councilman in charge of education, Ernst Reuter referred bitterly to the probable effects of this decision:

> We must expect that the whole structure of our government will be shaken to its foundations by feelings of insecurity and uncertainty, and that the concept of democracy, in the interest of which the victorious powers moved into our city, must suffer serious damage.[143]

Another prominent Social Democrat suggested as a protest measure against this removal that the Magistrat be recognized merely as an executive organ for the occupying powers and not as a body responsible to the City Assembly. This proposal, if it had been accepted, would have played into Soviet hands by gravely weakening the city government.

Western officials probably did not realize how successful they were in hiding from the Germans the basic disagreements between East and West. A high official in the city government stated after the blockade that, until early in 1948, he had believed that four-power harmony had been maintained on essential issues, and that differences between the U.S.S.R. and the Western powers were on matters of detail.

In addition, personal relations between German officials and many Western officials were sometimes far from cordial. Reuter, for example, was distrusted by many French officials because of his strength and independence. A British officer refused to speak to him because he had not been confirmed in office. There were American officials who considered him arrogant and ambitious.

Some occasions for friction between the German democratic leaders and occupation personnel occurred as a result of the confused lines of authority in Berlin's military government. German city officials usually were supervised by a number of different offices in the military governments of the four sectors, as well as by the same military government officials assembled at the four-power level. As city councilman for public utilities and transportation, for instance, Ernst Reuter had to answer to quadripartite committees for electricity and fuel, as well as to numerous offices in each of the four sectors. These various offices and committees often issued conflicting instructions. Furthermore, some military government orders failed to take account of conditions in Berlin and were simply impossible to carry out. For example, a four-power law provided that persons who exceeded their gas quota were subject to a fine amounting to one hundred times the cost of the excess gas, a sum that most offenders were quite incapable of paying. Working under conditions of frequently unenforceable orders and conflicting instructions, German officials who wanted to get their work done were often forced to evade military government controls, obey instructions only partially, and resort to subterfuge. Many military officials understood this predicament and winked at violations, but when they, in turn, were called to account by higher headquarters, they frequently put the blame on the German officials concerned.

There was, however, another side to this picture. While official policies and pronouncements of the Western powers sometimes discouraged the democratic German leaders, a number of officials in the Western military governments individually showed great sympathy and did what they could to help the Berliners in the struggle to preserve their freedoms. Furthermore, West Berliners enjoyed considerable freedom of expression, including the right to criticize actions of military government. For instance, on February 4, 1947, in a speech which was carried over RIAS, Reuter was able to criticize the interference of military government committees in the details of Berlin's administration and to call for broader jurisdiction for German authorities.

This situation, in which Berlin politicians could count on only modest support from the Western powers but were allowed considerable freedom of opinion, was conducive to the development of an independent attitude. Far from having their strategies dictated to them by the West, the German leaders, on the contrary, were constantly pressing the Allies to stand on their rights and prevent the city from falling under communist domination; to cease making concessions to the Soviets and, instead, to face up to the struggle for power. This role of the Berliners in stiffening the policy of the West was alluded to by Ernst Reuter in a newspaper article written shortly before the blockade:

> A struggle for Berlin is going on. It may be that the Berliners will not be able to determine the final decision in this struggle. But without them Berlin would have been written off long ago. The fact that it cannot any longer be written off today, is certainly due to the efforts of freedom-loving Berliners. . . .[144]

And in private conversations Reuter told Allied officials, probably with a view to influencing their decisions, that the Berliners would try and defend themselves, come what may, but that they expected help from the West. One city official remonstrated to an American:

"We don't mind fighting with our backs to the wall, but you are no wall against which we can place ourselves."

Up to the time of currency reform and blockade, the German leaders, on the basis of their previous experience, felt that in a crisis they would not be able to count on Western support, but might be left to their own devices. Nor were they reassured by statements to the effect that the Western powers could bring in enough supplies by air to take care of the needs of their own personnel in Berlin, and that, if the Soviets stopped the overland transportation of food, the responsibility for supplying the civilian population would revert to the Red Army.* This was just what the Berliners did not want, for they knew that Soviet political control would follow closely upon Soviet food.

The gnawing fear that Berlin might be written off by the West was nourished by two events which occurred as late as June 1948. First, Berlin was not mentioned in the London Recommendations. This omission could be interpreted as meaning either that the Western powers had no plans for Berlin, or that the city was secretly being used as a bargaining counter. Next, when the West German currency reform was announced, Berlin was specifically excluded, and this again allowed for disturbing interpretations.

The democratic leaders knew well that, if Berlin were to escape communist domination, it was not enough for the German city government and political parties to stand firm. The Western powers also would have to maintain their authority, but there was no guarantee that they would.[145] Hence, the responsibility of German city officials was great, but their power was limited. The only avenues of action open to them were to urge the Western powers to take a stronger line toward the Soviets, and to try and mobilize public opinion in Berlin to resist communist pressure.

Appeal to the Masses

Much of the struggle for control of Berlin's vital political institutions took place behind the scenes. During 1946 and 1947 the man in the street saw only that all four political parties—including the SED—cooperated in the Berlin government, and that communists and democrats took part jointly in various ceremonial gatherings,

* These statements were made primarily in intra-Allied communications, and reached the German population chiefly in the form of rumors, and through media not intended for German consumption, such as the U.S. Armed Forces newspaper *Stars and Stripes*. They were possibly all the more disturbing because of the manner in which they became known.

such as the traditional May Day exercises. Gradually, however, the masses were drawn into the fight. Their involvement was due partly to the new communist policy developed during 1947, which required mass support for the German People's Congress and the signature campaign on German unity. Another reason was that the democratic leaders, in their efforts to break the communist grip on the trade unions, had to carry the issue directly to the individual union members. Finally, men like Ernst Reuter realized that it would require mass support to defeat the communist bid for domination of the city and to persuade the Western powers to defend its four-power status, and they therefore made a conscious effort to interest the citizens in the struggle.

This mobilization of the masses was a gradual process, and involved much hard and unsung work for the officials of the democratic parties and the independent trade union leaders. There were, however, occasions on which the process could be observed on a large scale. Possibly the most significant of these prior to the blockade was a mass meeting called by the three democratic parties for March 18, 1948 in the square by the ruins of the old Reichstag building. It was the first time since the war that the three democratic parties had conducted a mass event without participation by the Communists.

The decision of the democratic parties to hold an independent mass meeting was, in part, forced by the Communists themselves. Early in February, the SED announced that the People's Congress would meet on March 18, the same day for which a demonstration had been planned to commemorate the one hundredth anniversary of the victory of the liberal movement in Berlin. The Magistrat and the City Assembly requested that another date be chosen for the meeting of the People's Congress. They pointed out that the anniversary demonstration had been planned as a common enterprise, thereby implying that they recognized the People's Congress as a communist instrument. But the only concession the SED would make was to advance the first session of the congress to March 17, with a second session to follow the next day.

Faced with a choice between being swallowed up in a communist-dominated demonstration and arranging an independent affair, the democratic parties chose the latter course, and scheduled their own demonstration for March 18 by the ruins of the old Reichstag building. Their selection of the burned-out Reichstag was a reminder to Germans that, not long before, they had seen their liberties snuffed out by a totalitarian regime. Thus, in several ways, the independent rally became an open challenge to the Communists.

March 18 turned out to be a cold and rainy day, but from sixty to eighty thousand people assembled to hear the democratic leaders. Franz Neumann, chairman of the Berlin SPD, spoke first. The demands made by the workers of Berlin in 1848 are still unfulfilled, he said. Freedom of speech and of the press is not recognized. There are again concentration camps in the east zone, the People's Congress resembles the communist "action committees" in Czechoslovakia, and the rights of man are being trampled underfoot. He concluded: "The cry of free Berlin is heard beyond our city borders, and on beyond the zonal boundaries of Germany. We send our greetings to the Socialists and the freedom-loving peoples of all lands, and to the silent army of the millions in the east zone."

Next spoke Jakob Kaiser, veteran Christian Trade Unionist and a man who, because of his independence, had been removed by the Russians from his post as leader of the CDU in the east zone. If totalitarianism triumphs in Germany, said Kaiser, not only Germany but all Europe will be split in two. If the will to real freedom and democracy prevails, then Berlin will remain united with all parts of Germany. "Berlin is Germany in minature, and Berlin is Europe in miniature, but we want a free Germany and a free Europe."

The third speaker was Karl Hubert Schwennicke, chairman of the Berlin Liberal Democratic Party. Freedom-loving people cannot compromise with communism, he said. In East Germany one can see how the communist process works. It starts with suspicion and denunciation. As soon as the instruments of power have been seized, the gallows follow, as in Prague. Berlin is the last bulwark of German unity, but one cannot sacrifice freedom to gain unity, and, as long as the People's Congress exists, there is no freedom.

Mayor-elect Ernst Reuter closed the meeting. He pointed out that a war of nerves was being waged against Berlin, but that Berliners had shown throughout history that they had strong nerves. Prague had been overrun by the Communists, and Finland was being threatened, "but if one should ask us who will be next, we can answer firmly and confidently: it will never be Berlin." At this point, Reuter was interrupted by applause that lasted for several minutes. He closed with the words: "And if the world knows this, then we will not be abandoned by the world."[146]

The *Tagesspiegel*, then one of West Berlin's most widely-read newspapers, published a picture of the thousands who stood in the rain, and commented:

> . . . it is an inspiring picture, happier than many a spring landscape, for it shows that the fear by which the Communists wanted to rule has been overcome. Those whose political weapon is terror already believed that the Berliners, terrorized by the complete disappearance of so many of their fellow citizens, confused by rumors, and worried by the dark prospects for the future, would apathetically surrender themselves to the fate that had been planned for them. Then came March 18 and broke the ice that had formed around the hearts of many. Berlin not only celebrated a historical holiday; in a deeper sense it celebrated the beginning of spring.[147]

The West Berliners again expressed defiance on May 1, the traditional day for communist and socialist demonstrations. Once more there were two rival mass meetings, one sponsored by the Communist-dominated trade unions in East Berlin, and one called by the independent trade unions in the square by the Reichstag. The latter had as one of their principal speakers a representative of the American Federation of Labor, Henry Rutz. He made headlines when he declared that U.S. troops would stay in Berlin until the troops of all powers had departed. This was just what the Berliners wanted to hear. "AMERICANS TO STAY IN BERLIN," proclaimed the *Tagesspiegel* in black type over its report on the meeting. Another speaker was Ernst Scharnowski, leader of the independent unionists in West Berlin, who vigorously assailed the SED, saying that his forces would not stand idly by and see the trade unions made into an auxiliary of a small political party, which in turn was dependent on a foreign power.[148]

But although the spirit of resistance had been greatly strengthened by the two meetings, many Berliners were still unconvinced that the Western powers would stay in the city if Soviet pressure continued. True, numerous statements by such Western spokesmen as Foreign Secretary Bevin, General Clay, and Under Secretary of State Lovett, to the effect that British and American troops would stay in Berlin come what may, were reported by the Berlin press from January 1948 on. But the earlier Allied concessions to the Soviets, which the Germans remembered, spoke louder than these words.

A few days before the start of the blockade a West German newspaperman, who had just come from Berlin, gave German officials in the U.S. zone a gloomy picture of conditions there.* He wrote: The fatalistic, depressed mood of the Berlin population has been increased by the London Recommendations, which were published on June 8, and failed to mention Berlin. The continuing Soviet measures for cutting off Berlin further add to this fatalism. Nevertheless, there is very little nervousness, except at such places as railway stations and the offices where interzonal passes are issued. Mistrust of the Western powers has increased appreciably, and the fear that they might leave Berlin after all is widely spread, partly as a result of the departure of members of their military staffs, especially Americans. Almost everyone knows of some Americans who have left or are about to leave. Another reason is that the Western powers do not react with deeds to the continuous Soviet provocations. In spite of all this, nobody has opportunistically adopted the communist "line." During the past three years, the people of Berlin have had more opportunity than other Germans to compare Western democracy with Eastern dictatorships, and—in spite of their lack of confidence in the Western powers—the overwhelming majority is thoroughly devoted to freedom and the principles of Western democracy. If another free election were held in Berlin, the SED would probably receive even fewer votes than in 1946.

The reporter then turned his attention to the policies of the Western allies: U.S. Military Government headquarters have changed greatly. Many offices have been dissolved, and others have been moved to Frankfurt and elsewhere in the U.S. zone. The American telephone book shows only about one-third as many names under "OMGUS"† as in the fall of 1947, although there have been no substantial organizational changes in the U.S. sector. American officials say, more emphatically than in previous months, that they are going to stay in Berlin, but they do nothing to relieve the situation. "The 'do-nothing' attitude, which has made Germans so mistrustful, is raised to the status of a policy." The Americans justify this policy in two ways: they say that the Russians will not resort to war, and they believe that the Russians will become more and more unpopular because of their repressive measures and thus weaken their bargaining position. The political goal of staying in

* The following account was made available through the courtesy of officials of the Bundestag in Bonn. It represents a full summary rather than a verbatim translation.

† "Office of Military Government for Germany (US)."

Berlin has taken precedence over the goal of reconstructing the Berlin economy. If worst comes to worst, it is believed that Berlin can be fed by international charitable organizations. The British and French follow the same line as the Americans with respect to Berlin.

The reporter's final observation was that the leaders of the Berlin city government were extremely depressed because of their own inability to do anything to improve the constantly deteriorating conditions.

By the end of June 1948 then, there was a sizable core of Berliners who were determined to resist communist aggression, but others were afflicted by a penetrating fear of the future and by the dry-rot of fatalism and apathy. At this point, the introduction of the West German currency reform touched off a train of events which ultimately forced each West Berliner to decide whether he would cast his lot with the East or with the West.

CHAPTER III

BERLIN IN CRISIS: THE FIRST FOUR WEEKS

THE announcement of currency reform in West Germany on June 18, 1948 inaugurated for Berlin a period in which important events followed each other with breath-taking rapidity. The Soviets attempted to include the whole city in an East German currency reform, but were forestalled by the decision of the Western powers to introduce a limited amount of the Western currency into the three west sectors. The Soviets then closed the overland routes between Berlin and West Germany, and cut off the electric power which entered West Berlin from the east sector and the east zone. The Western powers responded by flying in food and fuel for the civilian population, and continued to expand this means of supply in spite of Soviet protests and veiled threats.

As the Soviet intention to force the Allies out of Berlin gradually became clear, agitated discussions were held in London and Washington, in the headquarters of Western military governments in Berlin, in the city hall, and on the street corners of the former German capital. What should be done? Was there a chance that Soviet pressure on Berlin could be resisted successfully? How much could be flown into the city by the airlift? Would the Western powers try to defend their position, or would they cut their losses and withdraw? Out of these discussions came decisions that determined the policy of nations and the personal behavior of countless individuals.

In order not to become lost in the tangled web of local and international developments, and to recapture some of the atmosphere in which those hurried but far-reaching decisions were made, it is well to consider the events of each day separately. The following pages, accordingly, present a day-by-day account of the Berlin crisis between June 8 and July 15.*

* Because so much of the information about this period is in the form of individual recollections and rather general memoirs, it is sometimes impossible to determine the exact date on which given events occurred. In cases where the time can be narrowed down to a two- or three-day period, the event has been assigned to the day which appears the most probable. Events that proved even more difficult to locate in time will be mentioned in the summary pages at the end of this chapter.

June 18-July 15: A Day-by-Day Account

JUNE 18 (FRIDAY)—CURRENCY REFORM IN WEST GERMANY

Shortly after West German banks had closed for the weekend the text of the First Currency Reform Law, applying to the American, British, and French zones of occupation, was released to the press. It was announced at the same time that this law would become effective in West Germany on June 20, but that it would *not* apply to Berlin. In a reassuring statement to Berliners, Colonel Howley pointed out that the old currency would remain valid in the city, and that delivery of supplies from the west would continue. He added, possibly as a way of warning the Soviets against taking any unilateral action with regard to Berlin's currency, that the city remained under four-power control and was not subject to regulations issued in any one zone.[1] A few hours before plans for currency reform in West Germany were made public, each of the Western military governors informed the Soviet Military Governor of the impending change and expressed willingness to discuss with him a currency policy for Berlin.[2]

The immediate Soviet reaction to the announcement was to impose new traffic restrictions, ostensibly to protect East Germany from a flood of devalued currency. Passenger train travel in and out of the Soviet zone was to cease; all vehicles from the west were to be denied entry into the zone; and even foot traffic into the Soviet zone on passes issued in West Germany was to stop. Freight traffic by rail and canal from West Germany to Berlin could proceed, but only after rigorous inspection of the freight and also of the personal effects of transportation crews and protective personnel.[3]

JUNE 19 (SATURDAY)—THE SOVIETS CLAIM ALL BERLIN

Announcement of currency reform in West Germany was followed, the next day, by a torrent of denunciation in the communist press, and by a statement addressed to the German population from the Soviet Military Governor, Marshal Sokolovsky. This statement aroused particular disquiet in many quarters because it declared Berlin to be a part of the Soviet zone: "Bank notes issued in the western occupation zones of Germany are not being admitted for circulation in the Soviet occupation zone of Germany and in Berlin, which is part of the Soviet occupation zone." Sokolovsky added that Soviet Military Government considered a currency reform for all Germany both necessary and possible.[4]

The Soviet claim that Berlin was to be considered part of the Soviet zone immediately drew indignant or worried reactions from the Western powers, the city government, and the man in the street. General Clay, in a statement to the press, rejected Sokolovsky's view and emphasized that Berlin was an international city. He also said that he would talk with his British and French colleagues about measures for meeting the new Soviet traffic restrictions.[5] An American newspaperman in Berlin reported that worried Germans were stopping U.S. personnel in the streets to ask if Marshal Sokolovsky was correct in linking Berlin and the Soviet zone in his statement.[6]

The City Assembly met on the evening of June 19. It heard a carefully worded statement from Acting Mayor Louise Schroeder, which expressed regret that the four powers had been unable to agree on a currency reform for all Germany, but reassured the population that the functions of the city government would be carried on. Frau Schroeder also appealed directly to the occupying powers to maintain the quadripartite character of the city. Her statement was approved by the democratic majority in the Assembly.[7] The SED, on the other hand, was violently opposed to it, maintaining that currency reform in the West had completed the splitting of Germany, and that the Magistrat should now "draw the political consequences" and take measures to tie Berlin as closely as possible to the economy of the east zone. Earlier in the day, a communist member of the Magistrat had told his colleagues bluntly: "The Soviets have taken Berlin under their protection; four-power administration has gone to the devil."

Although the debate in the City Assembly had been occasioned by news of currency reform in West Germany and Marshal Sokolovsky's statement, it was generally known that currency reform in East Germany also was not far off. Indeed, on the 19th, the president of the East German Central Administration for Finances said that currency reform in the Soviet zone could be expected during the next few days.[8]

JUNE 20 (SUNDAY)—AN UNOFFICIAL SOVIET INVITATION TO NEGOTIATION

An article in the Soviet-published *Tägliche Rundschau* hinted that East-West difficulties could be settled by negotiations among the four powers. This was interpreted in some Western circles as meaning that the Soviets would like to reestablish the Allied Control Council. In a letter to General Clay, Marshal Sokolovsky protested the inauguration of currency reform in West Germany, and again stated that he considered Greater Berlin a part of the Soviet zone economy.[9]

JUNE 21 (MONDAY)—CURRENCY REFORM IN EAST GERMANY IS ANNOUNCED

General Clay replied to Marshal Sokolovsky's letter by inviting him to a quadripartite discussion of the Berlin currency situation in order to develop a solution that would be satisfactory to all four powers.[10] In a statement to the press he added that U.S. forces would stay in Berlin even if land access were denied them, and that it was perfectly possible to supply the 10,000 Americans in the city by air for an indefinite length of time.[11]

Meanwhile, preparations for a Soviet-sponsored currency reform moved ahead rapidly. Heinrich Rau, chairman of the German Economic Commission in the Soviet zone, announced that he had forwarded to Marshal Sokolovsky a plan for currency reform in East Germany and Berlin that he was sure would be approved. Under this plan, the SED, Soviet-controlled enterprises, communist-dominated groups in general, and the officials and functionaries of these organizations as individuals, would be able to exchange their old marks for new ones at a ratio of 1:1. The general public would receive a much less favorable rate of exchange, and private enterprises would be given just enough currency to meet immediate expenses. Funds would not be converted at all for "profiteers" or "fascists," or for persons who had engaged in black-market activities or had manufactured war materials for the Nazis. In practice, this meant that anyone of whom the Communists disapproved could be deprived of his currency holdings.[12]

JUNE 22 (TUESDAY)—ALL BERLIN IS INCLUDED IN SOVIET ZONE REFORM

On Tuesday evening, finance experts from each of the four occupying powers met to discuss the Berlin currency situation. According to an official French statement released several days later, the French representative persuaded his American and British colleagues to agree that the Soviet-sponsored currency should be legal tender for all Berlin. The Soviet representative, however, objected to having the necessary regulations issued under four-power auspices; he insisted that the Soviets alone give the orders, since "Russian legislation must apply to all sectors of Berlin."[13] British and American accounts of the meeting also stressed that it was the

Soviet refusal to recognize the principle of quadripartite government in Berlin which caused the talks to break down.[14] Just before the meeting adjourned, at about 10:00 p.m., a Russian courier arrived, and one of the Allied interpreters heard him whisper to the Soviet delegate that preparations for currency reform in East Germany and Berlin had been completed.* This incident gave rise to the suspicion that the Soviets' principal reason for taking part in the currency talks had been to gain time to prepare their own reform.[15]

At 9:00 p.m., while the currency experts were still in session, Acting Mayor Louise Schroeder was summoned to the city hall by a Soviet liaison officer, Major Otschkin. Deputy Mayor Friedensburg, who accompanied her, wrote in his diary that Otschkin, "with a certain ceremoniousness," handed them three documents: a handwritten note from Soviet Chief of Staff General Lukjantschenko, Order No. 111 of Marshal Sokolovsky dated June 23, and an order of the East German Economic Commission, together with implementing regulations, dated June 21.[16] The note from the Soviet chief of staff explained that these documents provided for currency reform in Berlin, and added: "The Soviet Military Administration does not doubt that the Berlin City Council will carry out its instructions on the introduction of the currency reform. . . ."[17]

After glancing at the documents, Dr. Friedensburg asked Otschkin if Order No. 111 applied to the non-Soviet sectors of Berlin. The Major said it did. "I then asked how this point of view could be reconciled with the provisional constitution of Berlin. Major Otschkin said he couldn't make any statement about this. I finally asked what the Magistrat should do if the other powers specifically made other arrangements for their sectors. Major Otschkin evaded this question by saying he did not think the Western powers would make any conflicting regulations. . . ."[18]

It is unlikely that the higher officials of the Western powers or the city government had much sleep that night. The West was faced with a serious split in its ranks. American and British authorities were convinced that the only way to meet the Soviet move was to introduce Western currency into their own sectors, but the French at first would not agree. Following frantic negotiations, they finally withdrew their objections, but only after advising the other West-

* According to one of the participants, the talks took place on June 23. (Cf. Jack Bennett, "The German Currency Reform," *Annals of the American Academy of Political and Social Science*, January, 1950.)

ern powers in writing that France did not wish to share in the responsibility for the decision to introduce Western currency into Berlin.[19]

JUNE 23 (WEDNESDAY)—CONFLICTING CURRENCY REFORMS AND THE CITY HALL RIOT

When Berliners woke up on Wednesday morning, they were faced with news of two conflicting currency reforms. In response to Marshal Sokolovsky's order that Soviet-sponsored currency was to be introduced in all Berlin, the Western military governors instructed German authorities that the Soviet order applied to East Berlin only. West German marks were to be introduced in the three west sectors, where both west marks and east marks would constitute legal tender. The Soviet move had been anticipated, and measures for introducing Western currency were ready to be announced in Wednesday morning's papers.[20]

Berlin's democratic leaders immediately rallied behind the Western powers. Ernst Reuter greeted the introduction of the west mark and said that this removed any reason for disquiet. Two currencies would circulate in Berlin side by side, and the city administration could continue as before. Professor Landsberg, chairman of the Berlin CDU, denounced as "shocking" the Soviet order to the Magistrat to treat Berlin as part of the Soviet zone. LDP chairman Carl Hubert Schwennicke emphasized that Berliners wanted to continue under four-power rule rather than be attached to any one zone, and said that the introduction of the west mark was the only possible solution. The leaders of Berlin's independent trade unions blamed Marshal Sokolovsky's action for causing the crisis, but thought that the dual currency system could be made to work.[21]

When the Magistrat assembled, the democratic majority formally restated its position that Berlin's constitution, which prescribed four-power rule, must be upheld. An SED councilman is said to have exclaimed: "What the Russians want will be done, whether the Magistrat approves it or not. We should therefore decide to carry out Marshal Sokolovsky's order in the whole city." But the democratic majority, though undoubtedly worried by the implied threat, held firmly to its position.

A special meeting of the City Assembly had been called by Dr. Suhr for 4:00 p.m. But the assemblymen found that obstruction by a communist mob made it almost impossible to convene. An "extra" edition of the *Tagesspiegel,* which went to press just before the meeting was finally called to order, carried the following account:

> The streets before the city hall are crowded with people. Demonstrators, who entered the building about 2:00 o'clock, have forcibly taken possession of the gallery in the Assembly chamber and fill almost the entire upper corridor of the building.
>
> We have heard that Assemblyman Theuner has called for increased police protection. Amid loud protests and threats from the crowd in front of the city hall, Speaker Suhr said that he would not start the meeting until the gallery had been cleared.
>
> More and more people have assembled in front of the building. They are carrying red banners and large slogans. A loudspeaker truck is broadcasting speeches by Otto Grotewohl and Walter Ulbricht.

But police reinforcements never arrived. The city hall was located in the Soviet sector, and the studied inaction of the police made it clear that they were in league with the demonstrators. Order was finally established in the chamber, but only after SED members of the Assembly had given the demonstrators the signal to withdraw.* Observers also credited the cool behavior of Acting Mayor Louise Schroeder with helping to keep the situation in hand.

The meeting was called to order two hours late. In this highly-charged atmosphere, spokesmen for the Magistrat presented their conclusions: Marshal Sokolovsky's Order No. 111 would apply in the Soviet sector only; the other sectors would follow the orders of the Western powers. The fact that two currencies would be circulating side by side would create certain problems for the population, but these problems could be overcome.[22] As City Councilman Klingelhöfer put it, the two currencies would compete with each other to see which was the stronger.

SED speakers polemicised bitterly against the Western countermeasures and the decision of the Magistrat to honor them. One of them accused the Magistrat majority of following orders from New

* An account of the disorders given by noncommunist members at the next meeting of the Assembly made it clear that communist officials had directed the mob. (Cf. Stenographic Minutes of the Berlin City Assembly, I, 75th Session, June 29, 1948.) A TASS report also made this clear in an indirect fashion. "The demonstrators left the hall after Roman Chwalek, chairman of the directing committee of the Free German Trade Union of Greater Berlin [the communist-organized union] had promised to inform the demonstration immediately about any decision of the City Council. . . ." (*Soviet News,* June 24, 1948.)

York and London, of wanting to make Berlin an outpost of Western colonialism. He also threatened those who lived in West Berlin with the loss of their savings:

> The savings accounts of the Berlin population and the social insurance funds are located in the Soviet sector of Berlin. We will never give our consent to sacrificing these funds of the people of Berlin to the monopolistic interests of the Western powers.[23]

In spite of the hostile mob outside the city hall, and the threats of the SED in the meeting chamber, the democratic members of the Assembly voted solidly to uphold the Magistrat. They had soon to pay for their courageous decision. Communist mobsters were waiting for them when they emerged from the city hall, and a number of assemblymen were attacked. Jeanette Wolff, a Social Democratic assemblywoman, was beaten particularly severely. The fact that she had formerly been imprisoned in a concentration camp by the Nazis helped to strengthen a parallel already obvious to many Berliners.

Again the communist police refused to intervene. Some policemen even helped the hoodlums by pointing out particular individuals. "There's the car of that criminal Neumann," one was heard to say, presumably referring to the chairman of the Berlin SPD. An east sector police official, who late that night escorted several assemblymen safely out of the building, was discharged the next day by order of Soviet Military Government.*

A somewhat different picture of these events appeared in the communist press. According to *Neues Deutschland,* the demonstrators were democratic workers and delegates, representing almost one hundred industries and mass organizations, who had convened to petition the Assembly that Berlin adopt the east zone currency as the sole medium of exchange. The banner headline over this story ran for several lines: "THE WORKERS, FURIOUS AT THOSE WHO ARE TRYING TO SPLIT BERLIN, DEMAND STORMILY: ONLY EAST CURRENCY FOR GREATER BERLIN—MAJORITY OF THE MAGISTRAT, AGAINST ALL REASON, FOR DOUBLE CURRENCY AND CUSTOMS BARRIERS IN BERLIN—FOR CHAOS, HUNGER AND UNEMPLOYMENT." The Soviet army publication *Tägliche Rundschau* said that the noncommunist assemblymen had lacked

* This information was contained in a typewritten memorandum protesting Soviet and communist aggressive actions in Berlin which was handed to Western authorities at the Allied Control Council building by a group of government and party officials on September 9, 1948.

the courage to address the crowd, and that therefore the workers had lost patience and taken action against these betrayers of the laboring classes.

An event which shed additional light on the demonstration occurred two days later. A number of workers from one of the east sector shop groups, which allegedly had passed a unanimous resolution opposing the Western currency, called on Dr. Suhr. They told him that the resolution had actually been composed and made public by a few SED members in the shop "in the name of all the workers." The majority of the men, however, were supporters of the noncommunist independent trade unions and had attempted to call a meeting to protest the unauthorized action of the communist minority. This meeting had been forbidden by the Soviet occupation authorities, and the men had been threatened with the loss of their warm noonday meal if they persisted in defying the Communists.[24]

On the night of June 23, after all Assembly members had managed to escape from the city hall, a meeting of the SPD Executive Committee was called to acquaint Erich Ollenhauer, deputy chairman of the SPD in West Germany, with the situation in Berlin. Ollenhauer had just arrived at this critical time, and became a witness to the dramatic events of the following day.

JUNE 24 (THURSDAY)—COMPLETE BLOCKADE

On Thursday Berliners learned that freight traffic between West Germany and Berlin had been stopped and that the west sectors had been deprived of most of the electric current which normally came into the city from East Berlin and the Soviet zone. This information was contained in two short and factual items distributed early in the morning by the East German news agency (ADN), but it was not featured prominently in the communist press or made the subject of any official Soviet announcement. One item, which was printed on the back page of the *Tägliche Rundschau* the following day, announced the stoppage of electric current:

> Berlin, June 24, (ADN). Since Thursday the west sectors of Berlin have been affected by severe shortages of electric current. The cause is a technical difficulty in the Golpa-Tschornewitz power plant, which delivers current to the city. The BEWAG (Berlin Electric Company) has received instructions from Soviet authorities to limit deliveries of current to the west sectors. The power cutoff lasts all day; current can be expected only between 11:00 p.m. and 1:00 a.m.

> Lack of current in the west sectors has already meant that 19 pumps in the sewage disposal system have stopped working. The water supply of the west sectors has also failed in various areas.

The other item, also inconspicuously located in the Soviet organ, dealt with the food supply:

> Berlin, June 24 (ADN). According to informed sources, the technical difficulties on the Berlin-Helmstedt railroad line, which have already been announced, are much more serious than originally believed.
>
> Therefore, it is difficult to say at the present time when the passenger and freight service, which has been suspended in both directions on this stretch, can be resumed. Great apprehension about the food supply for the three western sectors of Berlin has arisen, since they depend for their food on the consignments coming over this line.
>
> The greatest difficulties are expected in the French sector, since in this sector there are no stocks of potatoes, meat, fat or grain. In the U.S. and British sectors, also, food stocks are none too large.

The Soviets further announced that all food brought into Berlin from East Germany would be distributed in the east sector only. This applied principally to fresh vegetables and to the milk which previously had been provided to babies in West Berlin through a special arrangement with Soviet Military Government. Medical supplies were also cut off, and all deposits were blocked in the Berlin *Stadtkontor,* the central bank for the whole city, which was located in the Soviet sector.[25]

The report that the West Berlin water supply was about to fail, which was broadcast over the Soviet-controlled radio, almost succeeded in bringing about the condition it predicted. For Berlin housewives rushed to fill all available containers with water, with the result that the water system almost did break down. However, the U.S. sector radio immediately urged people to use all the water they wanted, explaining that there was plenty of it. At this, the demand subsided, and pressure gradually returned to normal.[26]

Other dire rumors were coursing through the city: the Western powers were planning to leave, epidemics could be expected in view of the sewage problem, Soviet troops were maneuvering outside the city, and so on. To reassure the population Colonel Howley issued a proclamation which was put on the air immediately. It was mainly concerned with the currency reform, and asked confidence in the new issue of west marks; but it also warned against rumors and assured people that food for thirty days was available and that they would not go hungry. Western authorities announced that plenty of powdered whole milk was available to replace the fresh milk supplies which had been cut off, and broadcast instructions to Berlin mothers on how to prepare powdered milk for small babies. Down in Heidelberg, where he was visiting U.S. Army headquarters, General Clay told the press that the only way the Russians could force the United States to abandon Berlin was through war. The Quai d'Orsay issued a statement that the French would stay in Berlin, and General Herbert, the British sector commandant, told the population that steps were being taken to meet the emergency.

At the same time, the Western powers attempted to husband available supplies. They immediately froze all food stocks which were physically located in West Berlin, even though some of these had been designated for use by the Soviets. These Soviet stocks were regarded as "on loan" until the end of the blockade.[27]

In addition, British authorities immediately suspended shipments of coal and steel to the Soviet zone, which had been receiving a million tons of coal and 30,000 tons of steel from the Ruhr each month. This step was presented not as a reprisal, but as necessitated by the fact that the Soviets had neglected to return 16,000 freight cars in which previous shipments had been sent.[28] The U.S.-British Bipartite Economic Commission announced further restrictions on trade with the Soviet zone the following day.[29]

Yet despite these resolute statements and countermeasures, there were indications that confidence did not reign supreme in the Allied camp. A dispatch to the *New York Times* from Frankfurt reported that, in spite of General Clay's statement that nothing but war would drive the United States out of Berlin, the impression was that the Western Allies might leave if the suffering of the Berlin population became too great. "Should the Russians maintain transport restrictions," the dispatch continued, "the city, which requires 2,000 tons of supplies daily, could not be fed by air. In that case a Western allies' decision to leave could be explained as a diplomatic sacrifice in the interest of the Germans."[30]

A mass meeting on Thursday afternoon, however, showed that Berlin's democratic leaders were far from willing to have such a diplomatic sacrifice made in their interest. Thursday morning's edition of the *Tagesspiegel* carried the following notice of the meeting, which had actually been scheduled by the SPD several days before the political situation came to a boil:

> MEN AND WOMEN OF BERLIN: Twice in the past few months you have demonstrated for freedom—on March 18 and May 1—and twice the world has heard your cry and has understood. The SPD has called a mass meeting for this afternoon at 5:30 p.m. . . . , which is to be a third and still louder pledge to freedom. Ernst Reuter will speak on the conditions created by the arbitrary Russian behavior. . . . Communism is trying to bring Berlin into its power by economic pressure. Berliners, whether or not they belong to the SPD, can show by taking part in this meeting that they will not submit to any arbitrary political act.

Some 80,000 Berliners jammed the stadium where the meeting was held.[31] When Acting Mayor Louise Schroeder and Assemblywoman Jeanette Wolff appeared, they were greeted with thunderous applause. Berlin SPD Chairman Franz Neumann opened the meeting: "More than ever the eyes of the world are focused on Berlin. Yesterday the Communists Grotewohl and Pieck, following the model of Hitler and the example of Prague, tried to seize power in Berlin by terror. [His reference was apparently to the city hall riot.] But they miscalculated. . . . Berlin will remain free; it will never become communist."

In the principal address of the meeting, Ernst Reuter again expressed defiance to the Communists. The heart of German democracy beats in Berlin, he said. From now on nobody will doubt that Berlin is again the true capital of Germany. The debates of the City Assembly are heard not only throughout Germany, but throughout the world. In the shadow of Russian imperialism the Communists are trying to carry out a *coup d'état* in Berlin; but we have had enough—we don't want a new dictatorship with its prisons and concentration camps. This coup is being attempted under the pretext of a currency reform and is justified with the sophistry that Berlin lies in the Russian zone. The Communists are trying to use the lash of hunger and the specter of economic blockade to achieve that which they were not able to attain with raw violence in front of the city hall. Under the slogan of "unity" the SED, together with the powers which stand behind it, is waging a war of conquest. But the methods of brutal force necessarily call forth counterviolence.

Freedom is never given to anybody. Finland preserved her freedom because she was determined to preserve it. And the Berliner's fight for freedom will be crowned by victory.

The meeting also heard from Erich Ollenhauer, deputy chairman of the West German SPD. He praised the Berliners for their firm stand, but pointed out that the will to freedom alone could not win the fight, and called on the Western powers to support the city.

Franz Neumann closed the meeting. "We promise you," he said, "that the Assembly and Magistrat will use all the means at their disposal to preserve Berlin's freedom and independence. If Markgraf's police are as passive in the future as they were yesterday, we will call on you to protect your elected representatives yourselves. We must preserve order if the Allies are not able to do so." He also exhorted the Western powers and free men everywhere to come to the assistance of Berlin, saying that the threat had become too great for the Berliners to face alone. The *Telegraf* reported the meeting under the headline: "BERLIN APPEALS TO THE WORLD." Indeed, the words of Berlin's leaders appeared to be directed as much to people outside the city as to the audience before them.

Although the currency reform, blockade measures, and mass meeting constituted the main news of the day, two relatively minor incidents that occurred on Thursday may have been related to projected Soviet moves. First, leaders of the independent trade unions, anticipating an attempt by the communist-led union to call a strike, exhorted workers to refrain from labor stoppages, which would only serve communist political purposes.[32] Second, a barrage balloon was seen flying in the Soviet zone, either in or near one of the air corridors to Berlin. The Royal Air Force lodged a protest, after ordering its pilots to fly at 5,000 feet, and the Soviets lowered the balloon.[33] Appearance of this balloon apparently gave rise to several rumors. According to one, which was picked up by an American news agency, a balloon net had been raised in such a manner as to interfere with landings at the Tempelhof airfield. A West Berlin newspaper editor reported later that, when this news came over the ticker, it gave him a sinking feeling. The decisions in the Magistrat and the City Assembly had been based on the assumption that the Soviets did not want war. Yet barrage balloons, which would interfere with the lifeline of Western occupation personnel,* tended to indicate that the Soviets were not bluffing. An hour later a correction came over the

* The decision to supply the civilian population by air was not made until the following day.

ticker: there was no balloon net east of Tempelhof. The editor heaved a sigh of relief. But on his way home from putting his paper to bed, at dawn on the 25th, he drove by Tempelhof airfield and craned his neck to scan the sky.

JUNE 25 (FRIDAY)—DECISION TO START THE AIRLIFT

On Friday morning the Berlin press carried an appeal from Marshal Sokolovsky to the inhabitants of Berlin, in which the Soviet commander denounced the Western powers for allegedly refusing to agree to reasonable Soviet proposals in the Allied Control Council, for trying to ruin Berlin's economic life by illegally introducing west marks into Berlin, and for trying to split Germany. He did not refer directly to the Soviet blockade of the civilian population, but made it clear that he considered four-power government of Germany ended, and that Soviet Military Government was prepared to assume responsibility for all Berlin:

> Provocateurs are trying to compel the Berlin population to accept the new bank notes of the west zones. In particular, they tell the Berliners that the supply of the population is impossible without the presence of the Western occupation authorities.
>
> Such a view is of very doubtful validity. On the contrary, it is known that even before the entrance of the American, English and French occupation troops the supply of Berlin with all the necessities of life proceeded smoothly. . . .

An ADN dispatch of the same day reported that the British were considering withdrawal from the city. The Attlee government, after hearing a report from Deputy Military Governor Brownjohn, was said to have decided that Great Britain would either have to reach a compromise with the Soviets on the occupation of Berlin, or get out of the city entirely. The communist press reported that Western policies in Berlin were meeting with opposition within Great Britain and the United States. The San Francisco *Chronicle* allegedly denounced General Clay's policies in Germany, while various London papers were said to have opposed the introduction of west marks in Berlin.

If the Western powers had shown any sign of indecision at this point the Soviet design might well have succeeded. Indeed, June 25 and 26 were critical days for the Western powers, and it is unfortunate that more details are not available about the way in which the major decisions were made.

Significantly, however, British aircraft delivered six and one-half tons of supplies for the British garrison in Berlin on June 25.[34] And British officials later revealed that on the same day the British were weighing the problem of supplying Berlin's civilian population by air.

For the United States, the decisions of the day were in the hands of General Clay, and it is largely because he acted rapidly and wisely that June 25 did not turn into a black Friday for the West. Returning from army headquarters in Heidelberg on the evening of the 24th, he found his staff advisors divided: some believed that the Soviets were bluffing or that they could be forced to back down; others felt that the only sensible policy for the United States was to make plans to withdraw. Without a staff recommendation on which to act, he nevertheless had to make a decision.

He proceeded on the basis of the conviction, which he had previously expressed to the Army Department, that it would be politically disastrous for the United States to abandon Berlin. But he knew that it would not be feasible to remain in the city in the face of violent civilian disorders. Somehow, therefore, the Berliners would have to be supplied in spite of the total blockade.

The possibility of at least a partial and temporary airlift for the west sectors had already occurred to General Clay.* It was known that the Allied occupation personnel in Berlin could be maintained by air, and Air Force headquarters in Wiesbaden were already working on plans for increasing the number of cargo flights to Berlin. But two vital questions remained: would the German population be able to hold out in view of the very limited supplies which at best could be made available; and was a greatly expanded airlift technically feasible?

In an effort to answer the first question, General Clay called Ernst Reuter to his office. He told the veteran Social Democrat about his idea of supplying Berlin by air, but emphasized that it would be a minimum supply and that the population would be subjected to severe privations if the blockade extended into the winter. He also pointed out that the airlift could not succeed unless the people of Berlin stood behind the Allies. Reuter replied, without hesitation,

* The idea of starting an airlift appears to have grown up independently in a number of areas. Former Prime Minister Attlee stated later that it was first suggested by a Royal Air Force officer and was subsequently adopted by the United States. (Cf. *The Times*, London, April 15, 1956.) In the opinion of the writer, however, it would be fruitless to attempt to assign exclusive credit for the idea to any one individual or organization in either country.

that the Berliners were prepared to fight for their democratic liberties and would not give in to Soviet demands. But he believed that the Soviets were bluffing, that they did not want war, and that they would lift the blockade if an Allied armored column pushed up the highway from Helmstedt.

Next, General Clay explored the possibility of an expanded airlift to the city, and called General Curtis LeMay at U.S. Air Force headquarters in Wiesbaden.*

A member of General Clay's staff has described the opening passages of this telephone conversation as follows:

"Curt," said General Clay, "can you transport coal by air?"

There was a surprised pause at the other end of the line, and then General LeMay replied: "Excuse me, General, would you mind repeating that question?"

As a result of their conversation, General LeMay mobilized all the available aircraft at his disposal, including those in the pilot proficiency pool at Wiesbaden and some old B-17 bombers, and prepared to lift supplies into Berlin the following day. Since many of these aircraft did not have assigned crews, pilots were detailed from desk jobs and other types of duty.[35]

The transport capability of the United States forces in Europe was then confined largely to C-47 aircraft with only a three-ton capacity, and both General Clay and General LeMay realized that an adequate airlift would require bigger planes. If it could be established that it was feasible to land some 400 flights of C-47 aircraft in Berlin every day, it appeared reasonable that substitution of C-54 aircraft—with a ten-ton capacity—would bring a minimum supply of the city within the limits of possibility. However, there were still many doubts about the practicality of the undertaking. Clay initially mentioned a figure of 500 to 700 tons a day as the maximum in what would be "a very big operation."[36]

General Clay received no marked encouragement from Washington. Indeed, he had to exhort the departments of Army and State to maintain a firm position. In a teletype conference on the afternoon or evening of the 25th, the Army Department suggested that introduction of Western currency in Berlin be slowed down if there were any possibility that it might bring armed conflict. General Clay pointed out that it was too late for this (the exchange of old for new

* General Clay himself gives June 24 as the day he called General LeMay, Other sources fix the date on June 25. The writer does not believe that this possible discrepancy of one day materially affects understanding of the essential events.

currency had started that morning), and also that any indication of a softening of the American attitude would tend to destroy the confidence of Berliners. He went on to explain that the chief danger to the Western position in Berlin was that of a communist-instigated panic among the population: "We do not expect armed conflict. . . . Principal danger is from Russian-planned German Communist groups. . . ." Though the aim of Soviet Military Government apparently was to frighten the Berliners to the point where they would not exchange their old currency for west marks, Clay expressed his belief that the population would support the Western powers:

> Every German leader, except SED leaders, and thousands of Germans have courageously expressed their opposition to Communism. We must not destroy their confidence by any indication of departure from Berlin. . . . If Soviets want war, it will not be because of Berlin currency issue but because they believe this the right time.[37]

General Clay also said once more that he did not believe American dependents should be evacuated.

Meanwhile, the civilian government of Berlin was actively doing its part. In a series of discussions German officials decided that, with careful rationing of supplies, essential services could be maintained for the time being, and that every effort should be made to bring Berlin's plight to the attention of world public opinion. To this latter end they agreed to try and interest the world press in any way possible, and appointed a *Magistrat* committee to draft an appeal to the United Nations.* Surprisingly enough, the SED representatives in the city government cooperated relatively smoothly with their democratic colleagues, although they maintained that the four occupying powers rather than the United Nations should receive the appeal from the Berlin government. The German leaders also decided to press all four military governments to allow both east and west marks to circulate throughout the city.

In Washington, indecision was more marked. Following a Cabinet

* The appeal never reached the United Nations, in part because it was impossible to find any member nation which would officially lay the facts of the Berlin question before the international body. (Cf. *Berliner Schicksal*, 1945-1952, a collection of official documents published by the government of Berlin, 1952, pp. 56-59.) The appeal served a useful purpose, however, since it provided a ray of hope for the city leaders at a time when there seemed to be few means short of war by which to break the Soviet blockade. By the time it became clear that the appeal to the United Nations had failed, the airlift had already reached impressive proportions.

meeting, President Truman met with Secretary of Defense Forrestal, Secretary of the Army Royall, and Under Secretary of State Lovett, to discuss the Berlin situation. Forrestal noted in his diary that the conversation revolved mainly about the legal rights and undertakings of the United States in Berlin. Either Lovett or Royall reported that Stalin had agreed in principle that the United States should have the right to move personnel and supplies into the Berlin area, but that the terms of this agreement had never been worked out in writing. The editor of *The Forrestal Diaries* observes mildly that it was rather striking to find how vague the United States position still was after three months of mounting Soviet pressure against Berlin.[38]

JUNE 26 (SATURDAY)—A SOVIET PROPAGANDA OFFENSIVE

In East Berlin, the big news on Saturday morning was the communiqué from the Warsaw eight-power conference. The banner headline in *Neues Deutschland* ran: "FOR GERMANY—AGAINST THE LONDON 'STEAL'—DEMILITARIZATION, PEACE TREATY, ONE GERMAN GOVERNMENT, WITHDRAWAL OF OCCUPATION TROOPS, FOUR-POWER RUHR CONTROL." Other stories related that British Military Government was blockading Berlin by stopping traffic between the Soviet and British zones, that the Berlin Electric Company had coal for only another ten days, that industry in West Berlin was grinding to a halt, and that food for only thirty days remained in the west sectors. The communist press also reported that the Soviets would not allow Berlin to go hungry, and that "Berlin has decided in favor of the east mark." Soviet-controlled radio stations echoed these themes. Wilhelm Pieck, co-chairman of the SED, told a press conference that the Berlin crisis could be settled only if the Western powers left Berlin.[39]

Press and radio were not the only communist propaganda instruments pressed into service. The *Tagesspiegel* reported that the SED was sending so-called "shock-troop speakers" and "agitation autos" into the west sectors. The speakers would choose busy street corners and there start loud-voiced conversations. As soon as a group had gathered they would attack the Western military governments and quote editorials from the communist press. The "agitation autos" were filled with functionaries and members of the communist Free German Youth organization who drove around distributing leaflets or simply throwing them on the sidewalks.

Meanwhile, Social Democratic leaders laid plans to reassure the Berliners and keep them informed. They decided to call meetings in cooperation with the other democratic parties in all the boroughs of West Berlin, with the borough mayors and other political leaders as speakers. The SPD leaders also discussed the danger that the communist unions might try to call a general strike, thereby discrediting the City Assembly and perhaps giving the Soviets an excuse to intervene with armed force "to restore order." Word was sent out to SPD groups in the factories to be on the alert for any such strike attempts and to nip them in the bud.*

Berliners were encouraged by Saturday's news from England. The Foreign Office, irritated by a communist statement that the British were about to leave Berlin, announced:

> Attention has been called to a report in the *Tägliche Rundschau* which presumes to define the attitude of His Majesty's Government to recent events in Berlin. This report is completely untrue and is very far from representing the Government's real attitude. The statement that we intend to stay in Berlin holds good. The opinion of the whole world will condemn the ruthless attempt by the Soviet Government to create a state of siege in Berlin and so, by starving the helpless civilian population, to secure political advantages at the expense of the other Allied Powers.[40]

And in the Bedfordshire town of Luton, the Conservative Party held a rally to pledge its support to the Labour Government in the Berlin crisis. "There can be no doubt," declared Winston Churchill, "that the Communist Government of Russia has made up its mind to drive us and France and all the other Allies out and turn the Russian zone in Germany into one of its satellite states. . . ."[41]

On Saturday, the U.S. Air Force delivered 80 tons of supplies to Berlin from West German bases. General LeMay continued to scrape together all available U.S. military aircraft in Europe, and cabled Washington for more planes.[42] According to later press reports, additional aircraft took off and headed for Germany within two hours after this cable was received. President Truman ordered that every plane available to the U.S. European Command be pressed into service on the airlift.[43]

As yet, President Truman, and authoritative quarters generally, thought of the airlift as a means of stretching existing rations and gaining more time for diplomatic negotiations.[44] Few believed it

* On the following day (June 27) the *Telegraf* printed an alleged SED order to leading communist officials, telling them to prepare for a general strike.

could supply Berlin very long. Drew Middleton cabled the *New York Times* from Berlin that "the official view" was that West Berlin could be fed for thirty days on existing stocks *plus the goods flown in by air*. He quoted a senior U.S. Military Government officer as predicting that "The situation will become really serious around the end of July." From London, Herbert L. Matthews filed a similar story: "It will be possible to keep Berlin fed, but not for long. . . ." Colonel Howley wrote later: "I couldn't quite visualize how planes could supply 920,000 German families."[45]

JUNE 27 (SUNDAY)—DELIBERATIONS IN WASHINGTON

Communist agitation continued. *Neues Deutschland* carried a small heading: "The Amis are leaving."* *Tägliche Rundschau* reported that in Washington both State and Defense departments were being cautious about saying just how long U.S. occupation forces were to remain in Berlin. This statement was indeed not very wide of the mark. On Sunday afternoon there was an emergency meeting in the office of Secretary of the Army Royall to discuss the Berlin situation. Those present included Secretary of Defense Forrestal, Under Secretary of State Lovett, Navy Secretary Sullivan, Army Chief of Staff General Bradley, and General Norstad from the Air Force. Discussion proceeded on the assumption that present food stocks, plus air-lifted supplies, would last approximately thirty days, and that by introducing dried foods one might be able to feed the Berliners for sixty days. Three possible courses of action were discussed: to decide now to withdraw from Berlin at some appropriate time, to decide to defend the U.S. position in Berlin by all possible means, or to maintain a firm stand in Berlin while postponing the ultimate decision.[46]

Among the arguments advanced in favor of staying in Berlin was that withdrawal would adversely affect U.S. policy in all Europe and promote the spread of communism. Those who argued against remaining in Berlin pointed out that to do so was to expose the United States to repeated crises and humiliation, and that supplying Berlin by force would bring the risk of war. There was also some discussion of possible steps by which to minimize the effects of Western withdrawal from Berlin, if this course should be decided on. Finally, the question was raised whether two B-29 bomber squadrons should proceed to Germany to strengthen the American

* "Ami" was a nickname for "Amerikaner" adopted by German troops during World War II.

position, and whether it would be advisable to base two B-29 groups in England as well.

Among the conclusions reached at the meeting were the following: (1) Forrestal, Royall, and Lovett should meet with the President the next morning and present the major issues involved for his decision, and the departments of Army and State should prepare short statements of the possible alternative courses of action and the arguments for and against each; (2) General Clay's reaction should be obtained on the question of sending two additional B-29 squadrons to Germany; (3) U.S. Ambassador Douglas in England should be asked to explore the possibility of basing two B-29 groups in Great Britain.[47]

The Berlin crisis had been building up for several months and had been acute for about a week. Yet, as far as one can determine the meeting in Secretary Royall's office was the first time Washington had faced squarely the question of counteraction to the Soviet blockade attempt. Even then, relatively little attention was given the airlift, whose potentialities were still not appreciated. But this was not surprising, in view of the skepticism that still prevailed even in U.S. Air Force headquarters in Europe about the degree to which the airlift could be expanded.

JUNE 28 (MONDAY)—PRESIDENT TRUMAN'S DECISION

U.S. policy toward Berlin was clarified as soon as the matter was presented to President Truman. At a White House meeting, Under Secretary of State Lovett recapitulated the details of Sunday's discussion at the Pentagon. When he came to the specific question of whether the United States was to stay in Berlin or not, the President interrupted. There was no discussion on that point, he said. We were going to stay. Period. Secretary Royall expressed "some concern" as to whether the problem had been thought through. He did not think the Americans should be committed to a position under which they might have to fight their way into Berlin, unless this possibility was clearly recognized in advance. The President rejoined that we would have to deal with the situation as it developed, but that "we were in Berlin by terms of an agreement and that the Russians had no right to get us out by either direct or indirect pressure."[48]

At the same meeting President Truman approved sending the B-29 bombers to Germany, a decision in which General Clay concurred in a communication from Berlin. The editor of *The For-*

restal Diaries remarks that, in view of American military weakness at the time, there was nothing else available with which General Clay could be reinforced.[49]

Dispatches from London indicated that the British Foreign Office was likewise prepared to take a firm stand. An official spokesman reiterated Britain's determination to stay in Berlin. A report by the *New York Times* correspondent in London said that "quiet confidence that the Russians will be forced to back down in the Berlin situation appeared to be growing today in official quarters. . . ," and that the British believed one of the best hopes for defeating the designs of the Soviets was to arouse German public opinion against them so strongly that it would be impolitic for Moscow to pursue its blockade policy. "Every effort will continue to be made to impress the Germans with the fact that if the population of Berlin faces starvation, it is the fault of the Soviet Union." At the same time, however, it was reported that the fear of war had for the first time struck the average Londoner and, presumably, people all over England: "Over the week-end . . . one heard talk of war everywhere people were gathered."

In Berlin the Communists maintained their pressure on both the population and the civilian authorities. Soviet Military Government unilaterally instructed the Magistrat that the Berlin post office was not to accept any letters or packages bearing stamps printed on the authority of the Western powers. Western authorities responded by telling the Magistrat that this order was illegal and should be disregarded.[50] The Berlin SED, apparently attempting to offset its increasingly unpopular position, made a public request to Soviet Military Government that milk from the Soviet zone be supplied to sick persons and to children in all Berlin.[51]

At a meeting of the Berlin Magistrat an incident occurred which illustrated the closeness of the ties between the SED and the Soviets. A noncommunist councilman reported that the French were debating whether to present to the United Nations an appeal from the Berlin city government, but they wondered what attitude the Soviets would take toward such a move by France. A communist member of the Magistrat offered to find out. He left the room, presumably to go to the telephone, and returned a moment later with the news that the Soviets would oppose any French move to lay the matter before the United Nations.

The Royal Air Force flew in its first supplies specifically earmarked for the Berlin civilian population. In thirteen flights, the RAF brought in forty-four tons.[52]

JUNE 29 (TUESDAY)—THE AIRLIFT BEGINS TO LOOK HOPEFUL

For the first time, the airlift was recognized by the West Berlin press as something more than an encouraging gesture. Previous news about it had been confined to short items in rather obscure positions. But on the 29th a banner headline of the *Tagesspiegel* ran: "FULL SUPPLIES WILL BE BROUGHT IN BY AIR." This headline was supported by a series of news items. One reported that the U.S. Defense Department had decided to send thirty to forty aircraft, of seven-ton capacity each, to West Germany. Another told how transport planes, in units of thirteen, had left their bases in Alaska and the Caribbean Sea and were heading for Germany. One unit was being held in reserve in Hawaii. From London came the news that at least a hundred Royal Air Force planes had received orders to fly to the British zone and participate in the airlift. The paper observed that, since West Berlin's daily food requirements amounted to 1,100 tons, it was clearly within the realm of possibility that the city could be supplied by air. The *Telegraf*, although somewhat more cautious, also expressed hope that the airlift might be able to supply the city.[53] That afternoon the first four-engine Skymasters roared into Tempelhof.[54]

At Wiesbaden, U.S. Air Force European headquarters continued building up the airlift, although its full potentialities were still unrecognized. Since it was now apparent that the operation would last more than a few days, efforts were made to put it on a routine basis. A special task force had already been organized under the command of Brigadier General Joseph Smith, and to it were assigned all U.S. units taking part in the lift. The probable duration of the operation was estimated at forty-five days.[55]

Major Edward Willerford, who was engaged in working out plans for the operation, has given an informal report of one of the first military staff meetings on the airlift:

> Along about June 29, we had a big staff meeting. I knew the C-54's [Skymasters] were coming in from all over the world. When we got to the point in the meeting where it was necessary to make a forecast on our potential performance, I was ready. General Smith called on me, I stood up and said: "I estimate by July 20 we'll be flying in 1,500 tons every 24 hours.

> I looked around proudly and everyone was studying me in consternation. You could read it all over their faces: "Poor old Willerford is tetched in the head. Grab the strait jacket, boys, before he gets violent." For you see, that day, by straining ourselves black in the face, we'd hauled in 384 tons, and to quadruple that amount in a little over two weeks, looking back now, seemed insane. . . .
>
> Anyway, if you run across anyone in the theater who tells you that he knew we could do it all the time, pass him up. We didn't know all the answers all the time. We kind of astounded ourselves.[56]

Members of the Berlin government and the City Assembly also remained skeptical of the potentialities of the airlift. In the City Assembly, Deputy Mayor Friedensburg said:

> We hear with joy and satisfaction that a certain substitute traffic by air has been introduced, and we shall hope that this emergency traffic will be greatly expanded in the future. But, ladies and gentlemen, in that way—and I want to speak very openly in order to leave no doubt about the seriousness of the situation—in that way at best only a portion of the food supplies can be assured. It is impossible, as far as I am able to judge, to deliver all the necessary food supplies, and it is completely impossible to assure the coal supply by air, so that the other consequences of which I spoke to you—that is, the possibility of cooking and above all the possibility of maintaining the water supply—cannot be assured by air transport measures, no matter how generous.[57]

Convinced that the airlift would not be able to meet all Berlin's requirements, the three democratic parties pushed the appeal to the United Nations all the more vigorously. They were opposed with equal vigor by the SED. In a violent polemic, SED deputy Maron accused them of trying to split Berlin and cause panic among the population. He added:

> One could be amused by this game, if it did not involve the possibility of such serious consequences. Not for those who already sit on their packed bags (laughter from the SPD, CDU and LDP) and think that they can flee in one of the 3000 aircraft which have been ordered—of which possibly each one is to bring an atom bomb to Berlin (renewed laughter from the

SPD, CDU and LDP). But it could be serious for those for whom the individuals who are getting ready for flight have prepared a chaos.[58]

In spite of SED opposition, the Assembly voted to submit to the United Nations the appeal drafted by the Magistrat. Therein it was stated "in bitter earnest" that the intervention of the United Nations would have to come within a month, "if help is not to come too late."[59]

Another stormy sequence ensued when the Assembly debated whether to set up a restricted area around the city hall in order to prevent future attempts to intimidate the Magistrat and Assembly by mob violence. Jeanette Wolff, who had been beaten by the communist mob after the previous meeting, was subjected to particularly severe heckling from the SED side when she told how, at that time, she had overheard members of the mob receiving instructions from SED leaders, including SED assemblymen:

> But, ladies and gentlemen—also of the SED—you can be clear about one thing. I said once that pressure produces counter-pressure. And I say here today—even if you laugh Herr Kessler, for you were back there in the courtyard too—I say here (Assemblyman Mewis [SED]: "no nonsense!")—I will be guilty of no nonsense. I have no fear, my dear Herr Mewis. I was not afraid of the Gestapo which destroyed my family (Shout from the SED: "We are not afraid either"). I kept on working, and gentlemen, I am not afraid of the "consequences" with which you threaten. (Interruptions from the SED). For I have only one life to lose, and this life belongs to freedom. And if it should cost my life on your account, gentlemen, and Berlin could remain free, I declare myself ready for death. (Applause from the SPD.) That, gentlemen, you can take from me. . . .
>
> Ladies and gentlemen. It is necessary to establish a restricted area around the building. ("That's right"—from the SPD.) Not on my account—it is not a matter for one person—but for the sake of the dignity of this parliament. For we do not want to experience again that which we experienced in the years from 1919 to 1933. We want to enlarge the little bit of freedom which we have, and if the occupying powers, who once freed us from the Nazis, do not recognize that the fight for freedom in all Europe is involved in this fight for freedom in Berlin, then

> they will be guilty if the world again is plunged into war. (Lively applause from the SPD.)[60]

Three of the speeches made at this meeting of the Assembly were later brought out in pamphlet form by the Berlin publisher Lothar Blanvalet, and were widely disseminated in Berlin and West Germany.

An event which at the time attracted less attention than the Assembly debates, but may have been equally important in the long run, was a meeting of independent union delegates from various municipal agencies and city-owned enterprises. The independent unionists had elected a majority of delegates to the central conference of this union in April; but the communist leadership had alleged that 23 of the independent delegates had been improperly elected, and continued the old executive committee in office. On June 29 the independent delegates met and founded their own union, the Association of Public Service and Administrative Workers. The bulk of the membership was composed of personnel from the Berlin Electric Company, the Fire Department, and the Police Department, and the rest came from smaller city agencies.[61] The fact that the power of the communist unions over municipal workers was largely broken by the establishment of this new organization was to prove of the greatest significance in the days ahead. Independent delegates from unions representing workers in the food-processing industries also met on June 29 to form their own organization.[62]

As the independent unionists were organizing, word was received that the communist-dominated railway administration was dismissing workers who had become identified with the independents, including the chairman of the railway works council and four other prominent unionists. The railway administration gave various spurious reasons for these dismissals.[63]

W. Averell Harriman, special envoy for the European Recovery Program, arrived in Berlin on Tuesday. He told reporters that his visit had nothing to do with the current situation in the capital, but was connected with reconstruction plans for Germany.[64]

As the airlift began to grow, and Berliners showed no signs of giving in to communist pressure, there were at least two indications that the Soviet attitude might be softening. In a calm and conciliatory letter to General Robertson, Marshal Sokolovsky expressed the "hope" that the railroad from West Germany to Berlin would be reopened before the city's food stocks were exhausted, and maintained that every effort was being made to hasten the repairs. He declared, however, that the "protective measures" against the influx of Western currency would have to remain in force "for the time being," and added: "For my part, I appreciate the measures which . . . are being taken so energetically by British and American authorities to maintain communications with the west zones by air. I hope that the air-safety regulations will be fully and carefully observed."[65] Another Soviet gesture was to allow Germans carrying interzonal passes issued before June 19 to move from the west zones into the Soviet zone. A *New York Times* dispatch observed hopefully: "The break is not a big one, but it marks a definite change in the hitherto adamant Russian attitude toward the blockade."[66]

Less conciliatory were the headlines in the communist press. The SED's *Neues Deutschland* continued to denounce the Western currency reform, the SPD, and the "provocation" of West Berlin newspapers. But it hinted at the terms that would bring an end to the blockade, observing that "the Warsaw foreign ministers' conference shows the way to peace." It also headlined a report that 36,000 tons of Polish coal for Berlin had been delivered, and that more was on the way. Another article assured readers that West Berliners were not eaten alive or dragged away when they came to the Soviet sector, and that they came because they wanted to obtain those good east marks, which were so much better than the Western currency.

JUNE 30 (WEDNESDAY)—THE BRITISH LION ROARS

On Wednesday, there came from the House of Commons in London the strongest official statements about the Berlin crisis that had yet been made by any of the Western powers. Foreign Minister Bevin pledged that Great Britain would maintain her position in Berlin:

> We recognize that, as a result of these decisions, a grave situation might arise. Should such a situation arise, we shall have to ask the House to face it. His Majesty's Government and our western allies can see no alternative between that and surrender, and none of us can accept surrender. . . .[67]

Bevin was cheered, as was Harold Macmillan who, winding up the debate for the Conservative Party, was even more outspoken: "We must, if we are frank with ourselves . . . face the risk of war." The whole House, with the exception of its one communist member, supported the position of the government.

Foreign Minister Bevin also had words of admiration for both the airlift and the Berliners. He said that the results which could be achieved through the airlift had exceeded the original expectations. As for the Berliners, he said:

> We cannot abandon those stouthearted Berlin democrats who are refusing to bow to Soviet pressure. The morale of the large Berlin population is excellent, and their determination to put up with any degree of privation rather than be surrendered to exclusive Russian domination must carry our fullest support.[68]

In Washington, Secretary of State Marshall also issued a firm statement:

> We are in Berlin as a result of agreements between the Governments on the areas of occupation in Germany and we intend to stay. . . . Meanwhile, maximum use of air transport will be made to supply the civilian population. It has been found, after study, that the tonnage of foodstuffs and supplies which can be lifted by air is greater than had at first been assumed.

These words were backed up by news that twenty more B-29 bombers had been dispatched to German bases, raising the total in the U.S. zone to thirty.[69]

At a meeting of the Executive Committee of the West German Social Democratic Party in Hamburg, Berlin SPD Chairman Franz Neumann gave an account of recent events in Berlin. The West German Social Democrats thereupon passed a resolution pledging their support for the Berliners, and proceeded to map out a program which envisaged "save Berlin" mass meetings all over West Germany, as well as campaigns to collect donations from private individuals.[70]

The communist press devoted nearly its entire space to an announcement of a "Two-Year Plan" for East Germany and to a speech by Walter Ulbricht explaining this plan. Ulbricht made it clear that the plan included all of Berlin: "In this plan we have not mentioned Berlin in particular. But we do not conceal the fact that we expect that in the future Berlin will have to be supplied by the [East] German Economic Commission." Berlin's economy belongs to the East, he went on; the representatives of the Western powers are not needed there. The food-supply system of the city functioned smoothly before they arrived, and all they have done is to protect war criminals and split the trade unions. Ulbricht added, by way of cajolery, that the Two-Year Plan would make it possible to increase food rations in Berlin and East Germany by 30 per cent.[71]

JULY 1 (THURSDAY)—THE SOVIETS WITHDRAW FROM THE KOMMANDATURA

Soviet representatives had walked out of the Kommandatura meeting on June 16 but had never officially withdrawn from the fourpower body. On July 1, however, the Soviet chief of staff of the U.S.S.R. delegation to the Kommandatura invited the chiefs of staff of the other powers to a meeting at which he told them that the four-power administration of Berlin no longer existed. He cited the "well-known behavior of Colonel Howley," as well as the unilateral actions of the three Western powers in importing west-zone currency, and declared that a situation had been created in which Kommandatura meetings could no longer take place.[72] It is interesting to note that four-power committees had continued to function up to this time, although the Soviet delegates had not attended all the meetings scheduled. After July 1, however, Soviet committee members no longer appeared at all, Red Army personnel started to remove Russian files from the Kommandatura offices, and the red flag was finally hauled down from in front of the building.[73]

The attitude of the Western powers in the face of the Soviets' official withdrawal from the Kommandatura was that an organization established by four-power agreement could not be dissolved unilaterally.[74] In London there was some feeling that the break was not necessarily final. A spokesman for the British Foreign Office pointed out that, in every one of his moves, Marshal Sokolovsky had left himself an "out." His excuse for stopping road and rail traffic and cutting off electricity, for example, had been "technical difficulties." In no case had he acted with complete finality. The British spokesman expressed the belief that it would therefore be a mistake to make an official protest to Moscow at this point, since that would make it difficult for Marshal Sokolovsky to back down without losing face.[75]

In Berlin communist propaganda continued along familiar lines. The question under discussion is no longer "Will the Western powers leave?" said *Neues Deutschland*, but "*When* will the Western powers leave?" The East Berlin press carried reports of riots in front of west sector food stores. The West Berlin *Telegraf* immediately investigated these reports and found them to be completely unfounded.[76] Both *Neues Deutschland* and *Tägliche Rundschau* reiterated their interpretation of the airlift: since the Western powers can no longer remove their plunder from Berlin by road or rail, they are now calling in planes to do the job.

Communist agitators in West Berlin, having failed to impress the inhabitants by staging streetcorner meetings, were now trying a new technique. These agitators now walked in teams of two or three honest-looking men in work clothes. One of them would strike up a conversation with a stranger. As soon as another stranger joined the discussion, the second Communist would come up; and so on. This was designed to give people the impression that there was at least one Communist for every democrat in West Berlin.[77]

A Hamburg newspaper reported that communist plans for a general strike in Berlin had finally been given up because of popular resistance.[78]

Shortly after the Soviet announcement about withdrawal from the Kommandatura became known, the City Assembly met for its seventy-sixth regular session. In spite of the disquieting news, the assemblymen displayed what the *Telegraf* described as "model behavior," and went about their work without the least sign of nervousness.[79] Much to the amazement of most Berliners, the communist members of the Assembly abstained from the polemics of the previous session and cooperated in disposing of forty-five points on the day's agenda.

More economic help began to arrive from outside Berlin. The SPD Executive Committee reported a telephone call from Stockholm, saying that the Swedish Social Democrats had sent 25,000 Swedish crowns to Hannover with which to buy food for Berlin, and that the Swedes would provide additional assistance in the future. The Finance Committee of the West German *Länderrat* received a recommendation that a credit of twenty million marks be placed at the disposal of the West Berlin government immediately to cover the requirements of the next two weeks.[80]

Mass meetings were held throughout West Berlin on July 1 and 2 to acquaint Berliners with the current situation and strengthen their determination to resist communist pressure. Deputy Mayor Wille of Steglitz spoke to "many thousands" who had gathered in front of the Steglitz borough hall in spite of the rain. "The Communists will never succeed in making a communist citadel of Berlin and thereby of Germany," he declared. "There's one thing all freedom-loving powers should know: we would rather go hungry than become Communists." A mass meeting in Tempelhof heard the mayor of that borough denounce the behavior of the east sector police and the Soviet measures that had deprived 20,000 infants of fresh milk. The mayor declared that it was absolutely necessary for Berlin to be assured of a corridor to the West. The same demand for a neutral corridor was voiced by the independent union leader Ernst Scharnowski, who spoke to an assembly of union officials in the borough of Kreuzberg. Scharnowski also demanded that the studios of the communist Radio Berlin in the British sector be closed down, and that democratic city employees who had been discharged in East Berlin be given the jobs of SED supporters who were occupying positions in West Berlin.[81]

As the spirit of defiance grew, so did administrative problems. West Berlin's leaders began to feel pressures caused by the dual currency. A resolution passed by representatives of all the police units in the U.S. sector asked that the police be paid in west marks. Police authorities from the British and French sectors reported that their men did not want the Soviet-sponsored "wallpaper marks" either. These were only the first in a long series of similar demands that were to be a constant headache for city authorities. While taxes and city services (such as streetcars and post offices) brought in only east marks, all city employees wanted the more valuable west marks in their pay envelopes.[82]

JULY 2 (FRIDAY)—A NEW AIRLIFT GOAL

In Frankfurt, General Smith, the commander of the U.S. element of the airlift, told reporters that a new target had been set: 450 flights to Berlin daily by a fleet of 52 four-engine Skymasters and 100 twin-engine Dakotas. American planes would carry "substantially more than 1,000 tons daily," he predicted.[83] A Berlin reporter was flown from the Berlin Gatow airfield to the R.A.F. base at Wünstorf in West Germany to observe the air-supply operation. Traffic at Gatow, he reported, was worse than the rush hour in the subway. At Wünstorf, he had met a Saxon laborer who was on duty sixty hours at a stretch loading aircraft, and then had thirty-six hours in which to recuperate. "Somewhat exhausting, naturally," remarked the Saxon in his inimitable dialect, "but we are not going to leave the Berliners in the lurch."[84]

At a cabinet meeting in Washington, Secretary of State Marshall discussed the Berlin situation, and read a copy of the message which the State Department proposed to send to Stalin. It recited the moral and legal considerations which justified the Western powers in remaining in Berlin, and reaffirmed their determination to stay. Secretary Marshall also reported that Foreign Minister Bevin had agreed to having two B-29 bomber groups based in England. Somewhat surprisingly, however, the State Department had thereupon instructed Ambassador Douglas to ask Bevin whether he (Bevin) had fully explored and considered the effect that the arrival of these bomber groups would have on British public opinion. Meanwhile, the State Department was weighing the effect which the dispatch of heavy bombers to England would have on the Russians as well as on American public opinion: "He [Secretary Marshall] said the effect on the Russians had to be balanced against the appearance to our own people of what might be construed as a provocative action. . . ."[85]

Two possibly significant statements emerged from a meeting of the communist-dominated German People's Council in East Berlin. The first was by an official of the Berlin SED, Hermann Matern, who reported that Acting Mayor Louise Schroeder had that day been ordered to accept only the commands of Soviet Military Government and to ignore those from the West. He went on to say that it would now be seen whether Berlin was to be torn into pieces or was finally to have a unified administration. As a part of the east zone, Berlin must be drawn into the economic system of this half of Germany, he added. A few hours later, apparently upon a reprimand from higher communist authority, he issued a denial and said that his previous statement had been in error.[86]

The other statement came from Otto Nuschke, an official of the People's Council, who demanded an immediate meeting of the Council of Foreign Ministers to discuss a German peace treaty,[87] a theme that was to be repeated by communist and Soviet sources during the next few days.

The East Berlin police made three raids at the Potsdamer Platz, where the British, American, and Soviet sectors joined. They checked the identity papers of passers-by, and searched brief cases, pockets, and billfolds for west marks. Their victims were taken in trucks to east sector police stations, where their west marks were taken from them and they were threatened with prosecution, only to be released after a few hours. According to one report, the SED police administration had designated thirty-one senior police officials, who were known to be Social Democrats, to conduct these raids. If they did not arrest a sufficient number of people or confiscate enough west marks, they were threatened with the loss of their jobs and even with imprisonment. The *Tagesspiegel* remarked bitterly that these were typical Nazi tactics: causing political opponents to compromise themselves by forcing them to take part in criminal activities.

Defiant mass meetings in West Berlin continued. A Social Democratic speaker told a rally in the French sector that the Soviets' threadbare excuses for their blockade of Berlin showed that they wished to leave the way open for a retreat.[88] At another mass meeting, a Christian Democratic spokesman expressed an idea which was to become more widespread as the blockade went on: "With the modesty which is characteristic of us Berliners, let me say that, just as the Western powers are defending the position of freedom, so we Berliners are defending the international political position of the Western powers."[89] In Charlottenburg, the deputy borough mayor told the crowd that twelve years of Nazi dictatorship had not made the Berliners into Nazis, and that they were not going to become Communists either. And in the borough of Tiergarten, the local mayor exhorted his listeners to keep cool heads, because "in these days each Berliner holds the fate of Berlin in his own hands."[90]

In Hamburg, a mammoth demonstration of sympathy for Berlin was addressed by representatives of Berlin's three democratic parties. Jacob Kaiser of the CDU repeated the demand that a corridor be established between Berlin and the West. He also emphasized the great political significance of the struggle for Berlin:

> More and more the realization is growing that Berlin is the last gate. If communism pours through it, then the revolutionary wave will stream westward. Then the discouragement of all peoples will be so great that every defensive power will be hamstrung. . . .[91]

General Clay, in only slightly different words, had expressed the same idea in his teletype to the Army Department almost three months earlier. It was gaining acceptance in Berlin, but was still not appreciated by many of the most influential leaders in the Western world.

JULY 3 (SATURDAY)—MARSHAL SOKOLOVSKY'S TERMS FOR ENDING THE BLOCKADE

The three Western military governors, in an effort to exhaust all avenues for solving the crisis locally, drove to Marshal Sokolovsky's headquarters near Potsdam. General Robertson acted as spokesman for the group. He expressed concern over the deterioration of relations among the occupying powers and told Sokolovsky that the Western authorities were anxious for an agreement on currency that would make it possible to resume normal traffic arrangements. According to General Clay's account "Sokolovsky interrupted to state blandly that the technical difficulties would continue until we had abandoned our plans for West German government." It was the first time that an official Soviet source had given this as the reason for the blockade. Sokolovsky did not even wish to discuss the currency issue.[92]

JULY 4 (SUNDAY)—COMMUNIST ATTACKS ON THE MAGISTRAT

In an article published in *Neues Deutschland,* the Berlin SED chairman, Hermann Matern, attacked the Magistrat and urged that "all reasonable people" get together to form an orderly administration. The Soviet-sponsored *Tägliche Rundschau* and the communist *Berliner Zeitung* were even more outspoken. An article in *Tägliche Rundschau* denounced the Magistrat as being incapable and not having the interests of the people at heart. The *Berliner Zeitung* demanded the dissolution of the Assembly and the resignation of the Magistrat, and suggested that Berlin be governed instead by an emergency committee nominated by various civic groups.

JULY 5 (MONDAY)—MORE UNOFFICIAL COMMUNIST DEMANDS FOR NEGOTIATION

The East Berlin *Nacht Express* editorialized that, if successful four-power talks were held, the situation in Berlin would be "automatically clarified." It added that the Western powers would have to take up conversations on Germany where they left off at Potsdam.

In a dispatch to the *New York Times* from London, Herbert L. Matthews expressed a forlorn hope which may have been current in some western diplomatic circles. He pointed out that the last recourse on the Berlin level had been exhausted when the three Western military governors visited Marshal Sokolovsky, and added:

> The only remaining hope, therefore, is that the reaction of the Germans in Berlin will be so unfavorable toward the Russians and so favorable toward the Western allies that the Russians will decide it is not worthwhile to keep up their blockade.

JULY 6 (TUESDAY)—WESTERN DIPLOMATIC PROTESTS AND SOVIET AIR INTERFERENCE

Great Britain, France, and the United States delivered similar protest notes to Soviet representatives in London, Paris, and Washington, making it clear that the Western powers regarded the blockade as "a clear violation of existing agreements concerning the administration of Berlin by the four occupying powers." They also stated that the Western powers would be glad to enter into four-power negotiations about any disagreement which might exist with regard to the administration of Berlin, but stressed that such negotiations could take place only after the blockade had been lifted, not as a result of duress.[93] The content of these notes was not made public for several days, so that the Soviet government would have time to study them.

There were several indications that the Soviets might attempt to cripple the airlift. Heavy Soviet fighter activity within the air corridors caused U.S. and British authorities to warn their flyers to stay well within the designated air lanes, and to fly at higher than 5,000 feet. Later in the day, the Soviets disclosed the contents of their reply to an earlier U.S. protest against Soviet interference in the air corridors. In their note, the Soviets alleged that U.S. authorities had decided that the agreed four-power air traffic regulations "would be violated unilaterally and arbitrarily." The note also complained that the Soviet element of the Air Safety Center did not receive sufficient information about American air traffic. An official Soviet protest to the British complained that the Havel Lake, where huge British Sunderland flying-boats had just started landing, was under Soviet control and should not be used. Finally, four Soviet officers appeared at the Berlin Air Safety Center to protest against the "rupture of traffic regulations" by American planes.[94]

The West Berlin morning press reported that the number of U.S. B-29 bombers in Europe would be tripled, and that more fighter aircraft were also on their way.[95]

From West Germany came the news that the state of Nordrhein-Westfalen had decided to make Berlin a gift of 100,000 tons of coal. Sympathy rallies and gifts for the struggling city were reported from all parts of the west zones.[96]

JULY 7 (WEDNESDAY)—COAL BY AIR

The first coal-carrying U.S. Skymaster landed at Tempelhof at 2:30 in the afternoon. It was followed by five others in rapid succession. A high American air force official expressed appreciation for the fine work of approximately five hundred German transport personnel who were working day and night shifts to unload the incoming aircraft.[97]

Soviet-sponsored newspapers continued to call for a four-power meeting. "If peace is desired there is only one solution—negotiation," wrote the *Berliner Zeitung,* and added that the subject of negotiation would have to be not only Berlin but the entire German problem.

JULY 9 (FRIDAY)—THE BLOCKADE'S PINCH IS FELT MORE KEENLY

The airlift had been in operation two weeks, and the results had begun to convince the more optimistic elements in the U.S. Air Force that the blockade could be overcome by air supply.[98] But this optimism was not generally shared. *U.S. News and World Report* editorialized that the showdown in Berlin might be postponed until winter, when the impossibility of flying in enough coal for the Germans would bring on the more serious crisis. It reported further that air evacuation of many of the 24,000 Western personnel in Berlin was probable, and that German leaders who had remained firm against the Soviets might be flown out too.[99] In London, the *New Statesman and Nation* concurred: "But every expert knows that aircraft, despite their immense psychological effect, cannot be relied upon to provision Berlin in the winter months. . . ."[100]

Berliners were beginning to feel the pinch of the blockade. In order to conserve coal and power, the Western authorities announced very stringent electricity and transport cuts. These restrictions were given prominent treatment in the East Berlin press, which used them to strengthen its own political themes. *Neues Deutschland* reported:

> B-MARK* RUINS WEST BERLIN—TRAFFIC IS CURTAILED—FACTORIES CLOSE—"LEAVE" WITHOUT PAY
>
> In agreement with the majority of the Magistrat, and with the express approval of the party leadership of the SPD, CDU, and LPD, the Western occupation powers introduced the separate B-mark. Yesterday, as it was possible to foresee, serious dislocation of the economic life of West Berlin followed. Businesses are being forced to shut down because of arbitrary current stoppages, and it is expected that tens of thousands will become unemployed on Saturday. The effects of the "political" B-mark will be felt in every household. The streetcar and subway will cease to operate during large parts of the day.

* So called by the communist press because it was West German currency with a large "B" (for "Berlin") stamped on each note.

The story continued with a violent denunciation of the Magistrat.

In line with their thesis that the Western powers had no right to remain in Berlin, the Soviets ordered the city treasury to discontinue payments for the occupation costs of the United States, Great Britain, and France. Although the Western commandants protested immediately, their protests were of no avail, since the city treasury was located in the Soviet sector, and they were forced to draw on their zonal budgets for expenses in Berlin. Western military government officials denounced the order as the most bold-faced act yet committed by Russian authorities.[101]

The fact that the city government's funds were banked in the Soviet sector was a constant headache to the German authorities as well. Almost every week they had to plead with Soviet Military Government to release enough east marks to meet the municipal payroll, and on several occasions the pay of many city workers was far in arrears.[102]

JULY 10 (SATURDAY)—WASHINGTON DISAPPROVES ARMORED COLUMN

General Clay again expressed his opinion to Washington that the Soviets did not want war, and suggested that a show of force would break the blockade. His conviction was based on "the care with which the Russians avoided measures which would have been resisted with force." Specifically, his proposal was for American authorities to inform the Soviets that the United States, in accordance with its right to be in Berlin, would, on a given date, move in an armed convoy from West Germany, which would be equipped to overcome the "technical details" that the Soviets appeared unable to solve.[103]

This suggestion was turned down in Washington, on the grounds that it was not justifiable to run the risk of armed conflict until the Berlin issue had been placed before the United Nations. General Clay agreed that there was some risk involved, and stressed that the United States should face frankly the possibility of armed conflict. However, he believed that the chances were small that such a convoy would lead to hostilities. In a cable to Washington a week later, he repeated his belief that determined action by the United States would bring Soviet aggression to a halt without war, and that it might be too late after the next Soviet move: "It [Soviet aggression] can be stopped only if we assume some risk." But official opinion in Washington was opposed to the armored column idea, and action proceeded through diplomatic channels.[104]

Meanwhile, the Soviets continued their efforts to interfere with the airlift. According to the East German news agency, ADN, the chief of staff of Soviet Military Government sent letters to the U.S. and British deputy military governors protesting the failure of U.S. and British flyers to observe "the elementary rules of air safety," and expressing hope that the two commanders would halt "irregular" flights over the Soviet zone immediately. On the same day, the U.S. Air Force was informed that Soviet planes would be flying on instruments at two points along the Frankfurt-Berlin corridor, and that prior announcement to the Berlin Air Safety Center would not take place. Allied air force officers commented that the Russians would be flying in the corridor "at their own risk."[105]

The Soviets also tried to convince people that there really was something wrong with the railway tracks between Berlin and Helmstedt. They announced that, following an investigation, two high-ranking German railway officials had been fired for allowing the right-of-way to fall into a state of disrepair.[106]

JULY 11 (SUNDAY)—BERLIN AS THE CENTER OF WORLD ATTENTION

Under the headline "Center of World Attention," the *Telegraf* reported that Prime Minister Chifley of Australia had arrived in Berlin and that British Air Minister Henderson was expected the following day. Mass sympathy meetings for Berlin were held in the West German cities of Hannover and Essen.[107] At a large rally in Berlin, Ernst Reuter said that the world would support Berlin in its struggle to remain free: "Berliners can be proud that this opposition [to communist aggression] has been kindled by their resolute behavior."[108]

JULY 12 (MONDAY)—CONTINUED DISCRIMINATION AGAINST NONCOMMUNIST WORKERS

A Russian official announced to the Works Council of the Berlin Transit Company (BVG) that the last trade union election, which had returned a majority of independent unionists to the Works Council, had created a new situation. From now on the unrationed noonday meal would be administered by the communist-controlled FDGB. A representative of the FDGB at the Transit Company added that only employees who could show their FDGB membership cards would receive the meal.[109]

JULY 13 (TUESDAY)—COMMUNIST EFFORTS TO CONTROL WEST BERLIN INDUSTRY

The chairman of the executive commitee of the FDGB announced that any West Berlin enterprise which wished to associate itself with the economy of the east zone would be provided with raw materials, and also an opportunity to sell its products, if it applied to the East German Economic Commission.[110] In view of the imminent threat of large-scale unemployment in the west sectors, this new tactic of the FDGB exposed West Berlin's workers and entrepreneurs to serious temptation.

JULY 14 (WEDNESDAY)—THE SOVIET NOTE

Western hopes that the blockade might be lifted as a result of the Allied protest notes of July 6 were dashed by the Soviet reply. The Soviets claimed that the situation in Berlin had resulted from

> . . . violation by the governments of the United States of America, Great Britain, and France of agreed decisions taken by the four powers in regard to Germany and Berlin, which [violation] has found its expression in the carrying out of a separate currency reform, in the introduction of a special currency for the western sectors of Berlin, and in the policy of the dismemberment of Germany.

The note went on to say that the Soviet government did not object to negotiations, but would not accept any preliminary conditions to these negotiations (i.e., would not lift the blockade), and could not agree to limiting them to the question of Berlin, since that question could not be considered apart from the question of Germany as a whole.

Also, the Soviets claimed, "Berlin lies in the center of the Soviet zone and is a part of that zone." And by violating the agreed decisions concerning the administration of Berlin, the Western powers have "reduced to naught" their right to participate in the occupation of the city. The note further stated that the Soviet command had always been concerned for the well-being of Berlin's population, and would, if necessary, provide adequate supplies for all of Greater Berlin.[111]

Even before the Soviet note had actually been received, the Soviet-published *Tägliche Rundschau,* earlier in the day, anticipated the Kremlin's attitude. It dismissed as "laughable" the idea that four-power negotiations could be restricted to Berlin alone, and prescribed as the only sound basis for negotiation the Yalta and Potsdam agreements and the Warsaw communiqué of the Soviet and satellite foreign ministers.

JULY 15 (THURSDAY)—RENEWED FOCUS ON THE AIRLIFT

Possibly as a result of the uncompromising tone of the Soviet note, both British and American authorities stressed the fact that the airlift could be developed still more. British Secretary of State for Air Arthur Henderson, who had just returned from Berlin, told the London press that the R.A.F. had not yet reached peak effort, and assured everyone that the onset of winter weather would not ground the planes.[112] In Frankfurt, General Clay said that the "all-out" airlift had not started, and that, if necessary, Western planes could carry 5,400 tons of supplies to Berlin every day.[113]

Tägliche Rundschau published another article attacking British and American pilots for failing to observe air-safety regulations in the corridors, and cited Soviet air experts as saying that the time had come to settle the problem of the air corridors. The settlement, it was suggested, should take the form of reducing the number of corridors.

Western authorities were worried by the greatly increased activity of Soviet fighter planes in the corridors, and there was some apprehension that the Soviets might raise barrage balloons near the Tempelhof and Gatow airfields. "Reliable sources" reported a Soviet officer as telling a group of editors from the East German press that the Soviets expected to drive the Western powers from Berlin within eight weeks, provided they could cripple the airlift.[114]

Both British and American air force personnel were beginning to feel the strain of operating the lift. Most flyers averaged no more than seven hours' sleep every thirty-two hours. In addition to flying time, they had to put in a great many hours of ground duty. A not unusual schedule would be nine hours of flying and eighteen of ground duty, followed by eight hours of sleep. Toward the end of the first month, during which 68 per cent of his flights had been on instruments, one pilot reported his reaction: "Pretty soon I said to myself, 'Boy, you aren't grouchy. You're just about on the verge of being done in.' "[115]

While the Western pilots were trundling their heavy transports in and out of Gatow and Tempelhof, the National Security Council met in Washington and decided to send sixty B-29 bombers to bases in Britain. Forrestal summarized the reasoning behind this decision as follows: (1) the action would show the American people how seriously the government viewed the Berlin crisis; (2) it would give the U.S. Air Force experience in this type of operation, and would also accustom the British to accommodating Allied forces; (3) once the planes were in Britain, they would become something of an accepted fixture. If the present opportunity for sending them were missed, and the situation in Europe deteriorated thereafter, the British might not be willing to accept the planes later.[116]

That evening Washington announced that the planes would leave the United States on Friday for Royal Air Force bases in Britain. The flight was termed a routine training mission.[117] It led, however, to the establishment of the first U.S. Strategic Air Command base in Great Britain.

The Man in the Street: Anticommunist but Hesitant

Headlines and memoirs do not tell the story of the ordinary West Berliner during the crisis. Yet he was the one who was most affected by conflicting currency reforms and by the blockade. Western nationals could return to their own countries; prominent Germans might be evacuated to West Germany (there were persistent rumors that this would happen); but the man in the street had no place to go.

There is no question that by June 1948 a great majority of Berliners were anticommunist or noncommunist. As early as the municipal elections of 1946 they had given 86.3 per cent of their votes to democratic candidates for the City Assembly. Even earlier, a large majority of the SPD rank-and-file had voted against combining with the Communist Party and against cooperating closely with it. In May 1948 independent labor leaders had gained the votes of a majority of West Berlin union members, in spite of the fact that this was a group which the Communists had made strenuous efforts to win over.

Public opinion surveys conducted prior to the blockade by the Opinion Surveys Branch of the U.S. Office of Military Government also indicated the prevalence of anticommunist attitudes among Berliners. In January 1948, 68 per cent of a cross-section of West Berlin's radio listeners told interviewers that they usually listened to RIAS or the North-West German Radio in preference to the communist-dominated Radio Berlin.[118] The proportion of West Berliners who regularly read a democratic rather than a communist newspaper was apparently even larger.*

The way in which the people of West Berlin reacted to the communist coup in Prague in April 1948 revealed not only their feelings about the Soviet Union but their impression of Soviet strength at that time. Shortly after the coup, the Opinion Surveys Branch asked a cross-section of 260 whether they had heard about the events in Prague.[119] Eighty per cent had heard about the accession of the Czech Communists to power. Of those who were informed, only 14 per cent thought that the change resulted from a free democratic decision, while 80 per cent believed it to be the result of pressure from a foreign power, and 75 per cent said that it was *not* advantageous to the Czech people. The interviewers then asked those who knew of the Czech situation: "Do you believe a change in government following the same pattern as in Czechoslovakia is possible in Berlin?" Forty-four per cent thought that such a change *was* possible in Berlin; 53 per cent said they did not think so; and 3 per cent had no opinion. To judge by this survey, then, most Berliners believed that the consolidation of communist power in Czechoslovakia was the result of Soviet pressure, and a very large minority thought that the same thing might happen in Berlin. Though strongly anticommunist, many Berliners doubted that it would be possible to resist Soviet power.

Individual recollections from this period show that, while nearly all Berliners were anticommunist, their determination to resist Soviet pressure had not yet mounted to the point of defiance. One Western official recalled that a German employee in his office was hesitant about making a radio announcement which was likely to arouse the wrath of the Communists. "If I make this broadcast, can you assure me a place in a plane to West Germany?" the German asked anxiously. The same official reported that later, shortly after the blockade was imposed, this same employee showed almost complete disregard for his own safety. His previous hesitation had been a reflection of the spirit of the time, as shared not only by Germans but by many Allied representatives in Berlin.

* In August, approximately two months after the blockade had started, when asked their newspaper preference, West Berliners mentioned pro-democratic newspapers five times as often as communist papers. According to survey personnel this result merely continued a trend which had started well before the blockade. Cf. "Newspaper Reading in Berlin since Currency Reform and Blockade," Report 138, September 17, 1948, Opinion Surveys Branch, Office of Military Government for Germany (U.S.).

It is clear that, when the blockade came, West Berliners would have voted overwhelmingly in favor of retaining the four-power status of their city and against complete Soviet control. But they were not asked to vote. Instead, they were asked to risk their savings by supporting a new currency, to risk union benefits by joining a new union, and to face possible retribution and almost certain hunger by supporting a democratic order which the Soviets had apparently doomed to destruction.

How did West Berliners behave during these critical weeks in June and July? The historical record gives us a number of general facts. They exchanged a part of their old *Reichsmark* holdings for west marks, as instructed by Allied military governments. (This did not, incidentally, involve an irrevocable decision to throw in their lost with the West, since they were instructed also to exchange a part of their old currency for east marks.) They did not panic or riot. They turned out by the thousands to attend mass meetings sponsored by the democratic parties and the independent trade unions. And, in general, they followed the orders of Western military governments and of the Magistrat.

More detailed information on the attitudes and behavior of Berliners during the crisis has been obtained from a number of specialized sources: In 1951, a Berlin evening newspaper, *Der Abend,* offered prizes for the best essays describing life during the blockade. Over three hundred contestants sent in essays.* Reports of Berlin residents who had been employed by the U.S. Military Government opinion-survey organization about popular attitudes and behavior during the blockade are another excellent source. Finally, in 1951 and 1952 the author conducted interviews with both German leaders and Allied officials who had been in a position to observe popular opinion. To round out the picture of what Berliners were doing and thinking during those critical days, these three sources were supplemented by contemporary descriptions of popular opinion as they appeared in the press, letters to the editors of Berlin newspapers, a small number of opinion surveys, and a few miscellaneous reports from labor unions and political parties.

Berliners Decide to Resist

At the start of the blockade, there was a period when some people were not sure that there was a crisis, and when those who recognized that a crisis existed were not convinced that they were personally

* Additional details concerning this essay contest are given in Appendix A.

involved in it. Many Berliners wondered whether Soviet pressure on West Berlin was another passing incident, or whether this time something more serious was at stake. There was some feeling that this was a dispute among the occupying powers, which did not concern Germans. On the whole, people were far too busy changing their old money into new to worry about the bigger issues.

When it became clear that this time the Soviets were serious in attempting to gobble up the whole city, and that this was a matter of personal concern to every Berliner, there came a period of doubt and hesitation. Would the Western powers resist the Soviet moves? Was there a chance that Berlin could remain free? Would the deprivations induced by the blockade and other forms of Soviet pressure be endurable?

Then, finally, came the time when large numbers of people decided that resistance was possible and that there was hope of avoiding Soviet domination. One after another, they committed themselves to holding out until the blockade was broken. The optimists and the politically-organized among them made their decision somewhat sooner than the pessimists and those not identified with any of the democratic parties. By the end of July those in favor of resistance clearly dominated the West Berlin population, and were able to neutralize the small procommunist element and to control the larger numbers of those who were still politically apathetic.

The chief reason that many were slow to recognize the crisis was the confusion which prevailed in the first few days. It was difficult for the leaders, both German and Allied, to form a clear picture of the situation; for the people at large it was almost impossible. Within a week there had come currency reform in West Germany, two currency reforms in Berlin, blockade of land and water traffic between Berlin and West Germany, stoppage of the bulk of West Berlin's electric power, Soviet threats and protests, Western counter-protests, and the start of the airlift. The currency reforms, in particular, meant that most Berliners had to attend to important personal business, which was bound to take priority over public affairs. A businessman, when asked to describe his experiences of those first days, replied:

> It's difficult to remember the first days of the blockade because they were somewhat overshadowed by the currency reform. Everybody was trading money, trying to get rid of old marks and looking for hard currency or real property. The blockade

and airlift began somehow in the middle of all this, when people were still wondering whether the new currency would command the trust of the population.

A German public-opinion interviewer recalled:

> The news of the total blockade at first was lost in the confusion which the currency reform brought with it. We were all so occupied with questions as to where and how we could change our money, should we also change money in East Berlin, will we have enough money to get along, and so on, that at first the blockade scarcely seemed important. . . . The public mood was very fluid; everything was uncertain and in a state of suspended animation. New money, blockade, the split of Berlin, the beginning of the airlift, the campaigns to support Berlin in West Germany, everything was mixed up. Nobody had an exact picture of the situation. Everything was possible. In my opinion, the popular mood was very similar to that which prevailed just at the start of the second world war.

Speaking to the City Assembly on June 29, Dr. Friedensburg suggested as another important reason for non-recognition of the crisis people's natural reluctance to look an unpleasant situation squarely in the face:

> It may be that our population has not yet appreciated the entire seriousness of the situation. Ladies and gentlemen, I would understand it if even in our own circle we would hesitate to look the Medusa head of this emergency straight in the eye. It is something so unheard-of, something so unthinkable, something so unprecedented, that in peacetime a city, or a large portion of a city, of 2.1 million inhabitants should no longer receive the necessities of life. For this reason an inner sense makes us defend ourselves against such a possibility and we think instinctively that things cannot be so serious, that the threat must somehow be averted, that such a possibility will simply not be tolerated by the world. And so, in conversation with people of our city, you will meet a certain disbelief. And we should be happy that the trust of our people in their fellow-humans has not yet sunk so low that they can seriously consider such a possibility.[120]

A public-opinion interviewer also reported that, for about a week, people just could not believe they were facing a total blockade. They thought at first that the Soviets were merely protecting themselves against a flood of devalued currency from West Germany. Then there were those who felt that this was just another dispute among the occupying powers that did not concern them. Several contributors to the *Abend* essay competition reported that they were at first not particularly concerned by the blockade, knowing that food for thirty days was available and assuming that, before this was exhausted, the occupying powers would have solved their dispute. An official of U.S. Military Government reported that most Berliners at first felt that they were merely objects of policy and did not see that they were personally involved in political developments.

But with every new day, more of the people were jolted out of their concern with day-to-day problems. It was often some particular news report or some personal observation which forced an individual to recognize that he was personally involved in a political crisis. As a chemist wrote in the *Abend* essay contest,

> I cannot forget the impression which the serious faces of the population made on me at the beginning of the blockade. This was particularly striking in the subway stations, when it was announced that the city transit system would run only until 6:00 P.M. in West Berlin starting the next day. That showed how critical the situation really was. . . .

For some, the critical event was the failure of their electricity supply. For many mothers with small children it was the realization that fresh milk for infants would no longer be supplied to West Berlin. The ranks of those who, as Dr. Friedensburg said, refused to look the Medusa head of the situation in the eye, grew thinner as one event followed another in quick succession.

Once having accepted the fact that there was a crisis, people entered the stage of doubt and hesitation, in which they had to decide how they personally were going to behave. In order to arrive at an opinion, they availed themselves of all possible sources of information, including their neighbors, the press and radio, local political leaders, and personal observation. The *Telegraf* reported on June 27 that so many groups were holding discussions in the streets that all Berlin looked like Hyde Park.

Fifteen of the essays in the *Abend* contest refer specifically to this stage in the formation of resistance morale. "Continuing questions, and efforts to foresee the possible consequences of events, composed the subject matter of daily conversations with colleagues and acquaintances," wrote a schoolteacher. "The newspapers were read with nervous haste, and violent discussions about their content took place," wrote a nurse. "Excited groups were debating everyplace," another essay writer remembered.

Expectations about the future were mentioned by sixty-seven of the essay writers. These are summarized in Table 1. While these statistics are not representative of all of West Berlin's population, they give at least an indication of the principal areas of speculation. They also suggest three principal causes of concern: fear of war, fear that the Western powers would desert Berlin, and fear that the airlift would fail to bring in sufficient supplies.

TABLE 1

EXPECTATIONS DURING FIRST FEW DAYS MENTIONED BY 67 ESSAY WRITERS

Expectation	*Number Mentioning**
Expected (or feared) war	19
Did not expect war	32
Feared that Western powers would leave; that Soviets would "just walk in"	16
Expected airlift to succeed	11
Did not expect airlift to succeed	32

* These figures total more than 67 because most essayists mentioned more than one expectation.

Many people were torn between a desire for decisive action to counter the Soviet threat and a desire to avoid additional risks. General Clay's plan to push an armored column through to Berlin touched both of these conflicting tendencies. A public-opinion interviewer reported:

> People whispered about a plan of General Clay to convoy transports with armored vehicles and thus break through to Berlin by force. That was a plan which appealed to many people emotionally because of their rage at the Soviets, but at the same time, when they thought it over, they became worried about the military and political results it might have.

One essayist said that he and his friends greeted the idea of using tanks to break through to Berlin because it would put an end to the terrible uncertainty. An American official, whose work brought him in touch with many sectors of the civilian population, recalled that all over the city Germans and Western occupation personnel were arguing about the possibility of an armored breakthrough. Not infrequently, he said, the same individual would support the idea in one argument and oppose it in the next, depending on whether the fear of war or the dislike of uncertainty was uppermost in his mind at the moment.

The behavioral results of this sense of uncertainty showed clearly in the reluctance of many workers to join the new independent trade unions. A substantial majority of West Berlin's workers had voted in favor of the independent union leaders. But, when it came to tearing up their old union membership books and paying their dues to a new organization, they hesitated. In the West Berlin borough of Wedding, dues collectors for the independent unions systematically asked 6,853 former members of the FDGB: "Do you want to pay your dues to the UGO [the independents] or to the FDGB Executive Committee?" The results were as follows:

For the UGO	29.5%
For the FDGB	19.5
Undecided	51.0
	100.0%

Most people answered: "What does the UGO really intend to do? We would rather wait a while!"[121] Dues collectors in other boroughs and organizers for the independent industrial unions reported similar experiences. Some workers told union interviewers that they wanted to wait until they could see what the independent unions were worth. Others indicated that they did not wish to compromise themselves in case the Soviets were to take over the city. The organizers of the noncommunist Clothing Workers Union reported that their success was dependent "on the confidence with which Berlin clothing workers view the total political situation."[122]

Another area where the behavioral results of uncertainty could be seen was in the city administration. The split into an East Berlin and a West Berlin administration, which started in July, moved ahead with increasing speed during August,* and forced each municipal employee to decide which of the city administrations he would work for.

After the period of doubt, and of reluctance to take any action that would be likely to bring reprisals if the Soviets gained control

* For greater detail, see Chapter IV.

of all Berlin, came the time when most people decided to cast their lot with the West. How soon various individuals or small groups reached that decision depended in large part on how well they were able to combat the fear of war, hunger, and desertion by the Western powers.

The work of the three democratic parties and the independent unions in rallying the population during those critical days was of the greatest importance. Their leaders helped to build resistance morale in at least two ways: By their own steadfast and courageous behavior they inspired confidence in the population at large, and by countless speeches and statements they made sure that all the arguments in favor of resistance were brought to the attention of Berliners. A public-opinion interviewer recalled that, just as people began to be seriously worried about the blockade,

> . . . the population was exposed to a process of very skillful psychological manipulation, which was carried out especially by the three democratic parties, the independent unions, and—to mention one name in particular—by Professor Reuter. His personality and his name, as the elected but unseated mayor, was from a psychological point of view very well adapted to dispel any worries and manifestations of fear, or to redirect them into the "fight for freedom."

The influence of Berlin's democratic leaders was heightened by the fearless behavior of the City Assembly in the face of communist rioters on June 23. This dramatic session had been broadcast by RIAS, and thousands of Berliners thus had personal knowledge of it. One interviewer recalled people saying of the assemblymen: "They certainly conducted themselves very well." And the exhortations of Berlin's leaders at mass meetings in late June and early July were received with greater credence and respect because the democratic politicians had demonstrated that they themselves were willing to stand up for their beliefs.

From the point of view of physical stamina alone, the performance of this relatively small group of democratic leaders is little short of amazing. Some of them addressed several mass meetings a day in both Berlin and West Germany, attended to their administrative tasks, and spent many hours in conferences with occupation officials. Furthermore, they did all this in spite of an inferior diet and in the face of material obstacles of many kinds.

In private, many of the democratic leaders were not so assured or so calm as they appeared in public. For one thing, they knew better than the population at large how many Western officials were in favor of leaving Berlin. But, they realized that to communicate their own doubt and hesitation to the public would be to abandon all hope that Berlin might remain free.

The strongest factor in convincing Berliners that successful resistance was possible was the airlift. For it tended to dispel both the fear that the Western powers would leave, and the fear of hunger. Indeed, since it appeared to be a nonviolent way of breaking the blockade, it also helped to dispel the fear of war. The mere inception of the airlift, long before it became clear that the planes actually could bring in sufficient supplies for the city, convinced many people that the Western powers were serious about remaining in Berlin. A 31-year-old white-collar worker wrote:

> We should also be honest and state that there were very few among us who believed that the Western allies in Berlin would help us. We had too often seen with indignation the way that they had given undue consideration to diplomatic niceties. Therefore, we were all the happier and that much more strengthened in our resolution to hold out when General Clay gave the memorable order to begin the airlift. . . .

In their descriptions of Berlin morale, several public-opinion interviewers stressed that, in the early days of the blockade, the chief significance of the airlift was to prove the good faith of the Allies. As one interviewer said,

> I had the impression that the mood of the population improved tremendously after that day [when the start of the airlift was announced], for everyone had the feeling: they have not disappointed and abandoned us, but are going to help. This stiffened morale greatly, and in my opinion was one of the chief reasons for the resistance to the East. For no one wanted to have anything to do with Russians; the days when they entered Berlin were still too fresh in our memories for that.

A 50-year-old seamstress wrote in her essay that she was terribly anxious at first, but was calmed when she heard that the airlift was to be set up. An actor said that he had been sure of the success of the airlift from the start, because the Western powers had been able to mount such large air raids over Berlin during the war, even in bad weather. Thus, the start of the airlift was proof to many that the Western powers would assist the Berliners with deeds as well as with words, and that there was hope of overcoming the blockade.

Others were more skeptical. The airlift was a fine gesture, but would it be effective? The constantly increasing stream of aircraft landing in the city—the "parade in the heavens," as it was sometimes called—gradually convinced even some of these skeptics that the blockade could be broken. An elderly widow wrote: "One evening I was looking out the window and counted twenty-nine airplanes, one after the other. Then I said to myself: 'Now we certainly don't have to go hungry.'" A resident of Neukölln said that, as the planes became more and more frequent over his part of town, more people began to think that the airlift would succeed.

As with pudding, however, the final proof of the airlift was in the eating. Could the planes really bring in enough food to supply everybody? An unemployed secretary tells the story of how her pessimistically-inclined father was convinced:

> Then came the day [when the airlift started]! Father naturally didn't believe it! Therefore he rode to Tempelhof on his bicycle. He was away a long time. When he came home he said: "They're actually doing it! They're flying food to Berlin. But they won't be able to bring in enough. Think of this huge city with its millions of people!"
>
> The first package of Pom [dried potatoes]. It was like a magic show. Will it really turn into something or will it be all lumpy? Three neighbors watched. They didn't really dare try it. Mother was more resolute. "It's getting thick! Look! It's getting good and thick," cried Frau Schulze, and the first dehydrated potato soup with mother's green vegetables cut up in it tasted wonderful to all of us.

Another essayist wrote:

> In the first few days people were worried that this grandiose undertaking might not succeed. But when people received the first food, thanks to this assistance, they became confident, and finally the roar of the engines became a part of our daily well-being.

When, in addition to food, coal began to arrive in quantity, most of the remaining doubters were won over. One essayist traced in a half-humorous shorthand the process by which he became convinced that the city would be able to hold out:

First day—go to Zehlendorf. Amis still there. Am calmed.
Tenth day—dried potatoes, dried vegetables, tinned meat, egg powder. I'm still calmer.
Thirtieth day—coal from the heavens. Planes like clockwork. Ear plugs by my bed.

It would be a mistake to assume, however, that the will to resist was based exclusively on the belief that the blockade could be broken. There was undoubtedly a substantial minority of Berliners who would have resisted in any case. Just how large this minority was, what forms its resistance would have taken, and how long it would have held out if the situation had proved hopeless, cannot be determined. But the *Abend* essays indicate that it existed. A lady reported that, while waiting in line at the butcher shop, she heard other women say: "Ivan can do what he wants; we are going to hold out whatever happens. Just no more of the Russians." A man wrote that he had heard a woman say in deadly seriousness: "If the Russians come again I am going to hang myself." One writer reported that her father had made some terrible threat about what he would do if the Soviets came into West Berlin again, and that afterward the meat cleaver was missing from the kitchen. Certainly, there was a hard core of those who were prepared to resist Soviet domination with any means available.

The State of Popular Morale In July

As their anxiety lessened, and it became apparent that minimum needs could be met, more and more Berliners became convinced that they could "take it." Several dozen essayists mentioned that Berliners had been toughened by their experiences of the preceding three years and took a certain grim satisfaction in their ability to accept privation. An article in the *Telegraf* in mid-July reflects this mood:

> What does the man in the street say? "This, too, will pass." "His" streetcar line, too, will run again some day. He turns up his coat collar, presses his hat farther down on his forehead and tramps home. It is raining—the way it does every day. A whole caravan tramps through the rain. Worn heels, shoes with holes in them, no raincoats. Nobody complains; everybody grits his teeth. "This, too, will pass. . . . "This expression of the man on the street may be considered characteristic of the behavior of the Berliners during these critical days. They don't

> feel themselves to be heroes at all. That's the way it is, and it must be endured.
>
> "We are accustomed to trouble," says the woman, when she hears the news about the reduction in the gas ration. "We will take anything with good humor. We will even become 'raw-food eaters' if it must be. We get the meat already prepared in cans anyway; it does not need to be cooked. That way one saves gas." Another housewife thinks it will certainly be difficult to get along with the reduced gas ration. She has already thought out what she should do: wash the dishes in cold water and put one pot on top of another when cooking. . . . And once again the people who live alone are hit hardest. For them there is scarcely enough gas to prepare coffee. "I have made an arrangement with my neighbor for us to cook together," says one woman. "My neighbor also lives alone. That way perhaps we'll get along all right. No, I'm far from losing courage on that account."
>
> The same sentiments are expressed by a resident of Neukölln. He is standing at a streetcar stop reading a newspaper. Over him there is the constant sound of aircraft engines. Whenever another plane comes roaring over he stops reading, takes off his glasses and looks up at the sky. Everybody else is doing the same thing. "They are bringing the flour for the white rolls," he says, and smiles. It's seldom that one sees someone smile. . . . There's a ray of light in the midst of power stoppages, transit limitations, and gas restrictions. . . .[123]

A report by U.S. Military Government's Opinion Surveys Branch in July 1948, when the blockade was less than a month old, provides some quantitative information on the attitudes of West Berliners at that time.* It showed, first of all, overwhelming support for the Allied policy of trying to remain in Berlin. Interviewers asked: "Do you believe that the Western powers are right or wrong to stay in Berlin under the present circumstances?" Ninety-eight per cent of the respondents thought the Western powers were right, only 1 per cent thought they were wrong, and 1 per cent were undecided. The airlift itself also received a strong vote of confidence. To the question "Do you believe that at present the airlift supplies Berlin with enough food to maintain the present rations?", 84 per cent

* Sample size is not given in the report, but, according to former military government personnel, a probability sample of from 300 to 600 cases was ordinarily used in Berlin.

of the respondents said they thought it did, 15 per cent thought it did not, and 1 per cent had no opinion.

Regarding the outlook for the coming winter, the respondents were more gloomy. Only 45 per cent of the sample thought that the airlift could bring in enough supplies to maintain Berlin during the winter; 52 per cent thought that it could not; and the rest had no opinion. The survey also showed that people with more than eight years' schooling were less likely to believe that the airlift could supply the city during the winter than were the people with fewer years of education (38 per cent as opposed to 49 per cent).[124] Apparently, the better-educated group in the population was more pessimistic.

Similarly, those among the *Abend* essay writers who were well informed about air transport tended to be more pessimistic than the relatively ignorant. Two of the essayists had had previous personal experience with military airlifts during the war, and on the basis of their prior observations did not believe that the Allied effort could succeed. One wrote: "As a frontline soldier I had seen a body of troops supplied by air and knew to what a catastrophe it must lead. I gave up hope for Berlin." The other, who had participated in the airlift to German troops surrounded in the Stalingrad area, said that he had compared the possibility of supplying Berlin to the experience at Stalingrad, and that the comparison had been unfavorable to Berlin.

Although a majority of Berliners did not believe that the city could successfully be supplied during the winter, this did not alarm them particularly, since most of them (86 per cent of the respondents in the July survey) predicted that the blockade would not last through the winter.

The survey also indicated (Table 2) that, by late July, Berliners were more confident of continued American support than they had been before the blockade.

The figures do not, of course, show how strongly these expectations were held. We may assume, from other information, that at least some of those who replied "will stay" were actually troubled by serious doubts. Nevertheless, the trend toward growing confidence is clear.

By the end of July, therefore, the majority of West Berliners had developed a set of attitudes and expectations which favored resistance to Soviet pressure. Even before the blockade, nearly all of them had been opposed to Soviet domination. This attitude was not

TABLE 2

TREND IN BERLINERS' EXPECTATIONS THAT THE UNITED STATES WOULD STAY IN BERLIN, AS SHOWN BY THREE OPINION SURVEYS

"Do you think the Americans will stay in Berlin as long as they stay in Germany?"

	October 1947	*May 1948*	*July 1948*
Will stay	74%	73%	89%
Will leave	25	12	8
No opinion	1	15	3
	100%	100%	100%

changed by the blockade, but many individuals at first did not see how resistance to the Soviet design was physically possible, especially if the Kremlin should decide to use military force. In the course of three or four weeks, however, a large proportion of the doubters were persuaded that the Soviets did not want war, that the Western powers would not desert Berlin, and that minimum requirements of food and other essentials could be met by the airlift. Wishful thinking undoubtedly played a part in the formation of more hopeful expectations; many Berliners were convinced that the airlift could supply the city long before the British and American Air Forces had proved that this actually was the case. The widespread expectation that the blockade would be over before the winter also must be ascribed, at least in part, to wishful thinking. Certainly, the attitudes that had grown up prior to the blockade contributed to the formation of expectations favorable to resistance. By the time the Soviets launched a new and more intense psychological offensive at the end of July, an effective majority of Berliners were equipped with attitudes and expectations that enabled them to resist this offensive.

A Reconstruction of Soviet Calculations

From the Soviet point of view, Berlin was both a lever and a prize. If the Western powers were subjected to sufficient pressure in Berlin, they might be willing to make substantial concessions in West Germany and accede to the major points of the Soviet program as outlined by the Warsaw communiqué. If, however, they should prove unwilling to meet Soviet terms for West Germany, then all

Berlin could be incorporated in the east zone, a move that would greatly increase the industrial capacity, as well as the military and political value of East Germany to the Soviets.

Of the two alternatives, Moscow probably would have preferred to see the West accept the Warsaw program. This would have meant that the West German military and economic potential would have been effectively denied the democracies, the Soviet Union would have received valuable reparations from current production, and communist prestige throughout Europe would have been greatly enhanced. And even though the Western powers would have been permitted to retain representation in Berlin, the Soviets would have held the whip hand in the city, and Berlin might have served as a useful lever in another connection later on.

Soviet plans for taking over Berlin were well considered. The amazing thing is that they failed. Pressure was to be brought on the Western powers directly, and also indirectly through the civilian government and the citizens. Cautious application of this pressure began several months before the blockade: traffic between Berlin and West Germany was subjected to increasing restrictions; and unilateral orders, hints that the Western powers would leave, and veiled threats were part of the psychological campaign. The blockade, when it came, was merely an intensification of previous policies.

The chronology of events during the first four weeks of the crisis reveals the major Soviet moves aimed, directly or indirectly, at the Western powers.

The first blow was the unilateral currency reform. Had it been successful, this reform would have greatly reduced Western authority in Berlin. For, not only would it have increased the Soviet hold on the city's economy by heavily favoring communist organizations and enterprises, but it would have established Berlin as part of the Soviet economy. A U.S. Military Government official has expressed the opinion that Soviet tactics in this case were based on a maxim of Lenin: "Let me put my hands on the currency and the revolution is mine."[125] It was clear from Soviet conduct, however, that more was desired than the mere introduction of east zone currency into all Berlin. Soviet representatives demanded specific recognition of their right to issue orders of this nature for all Berlin on a unilateral basis, and it was on this rock that the four-power negotiations foundered on June 22.

Within hours after the Western powers had refused to recognize the Soviet claim to economic authority over all Berlin, the Soviets delivered their second blow, aimed at undermining the Western position by bringing pressure against the German authorities. Acting Mayor Louise Schroeder and Deputy Mayor Friedensburg were given firm orders to make arrangements for the introduction of east marks throughout Berlin. This move was followed up by the city hall riot on June 23. To resist the Soviet currency order took considerable courage, since members of Berlin's government knew that their own physical safety was far from assured. If the Magistrat or the Assembly had capitulated, the Western powers would have been in a most precarious position, and faced with the unpleasant alternatives of either assenting to the Soviet move or else trying to administer the west sectors without the cooperation of the German authorities.

When the Western powers announced their intention to introduce west marks into Berlin, and the German authorities refused to accede to unilateral Russian demands, the third blow followed. The Soviets cut off West Berlin's electric power and closed the overland supply routes, thus extending the pressure to the population at large. These moves also must have been prepared in advance, since they followed within hours of the city hall riot.

It is probable that, as a fourth blow, the Soviets had planned a general strike. Rumors of such a strike were prevalent in SPD circles and among military government officials during the first weeks of the blockade, but the Communists were apparently dissuaded from this move by the fact that the independent unionists had already broken the power of the FDGB. Or they may have decided that, rather than resort to a strike which had only slight prospects of success, it would be safer to wait for the blockade to do its work of attrition.

Next, the Soviets began to issue invitations, both official and unofficial, for the Western powers to sit down and negotiate about the future of Germany. These invitations were extended in the columns of the Soviet controlled press, in the Soviet note of July 14, and verbally by Marshal Sokolovsky. All of them stressed that negotiations should not be confined to Berlin but should include the German problem as a whole.

As the Western powers showed no immediate willingness to negotiate on the German problem as a whole, the Soviets kept up their three-pronged pressure, apparently believing that time was on their side. They maintained an unyielding position in the face of Western diplomatic protests, and even went farther in the direction of breaking up four-power government by withdrawing from all Kommandatura activities and removing their files from the Kommandatura building. They stepped up their earlier efforts to limit Allied traffic in the air corridors, and played on war fears in the Western democracies by subjecting the nascent airlift to increasingly annoying harassment. They continued to issue unilateral orders to the German city government and to intervene more and more deeply in the affairs of the municipal administration. German Communists began to denounce the democratic Magistrat as incapable, and to demand its replacement by a group that would cooperate with the Soviets.

Pressure against the civilian population was particularly strong. Prognostications that the Western powers would soon leave became more frequent, as did hints that the blockade would last through the winter and forecasts that conditions in Berlin would become unendurable. Along with these threats, West Berliners were given rosy promises. The SED two-year plan for East Germany promised them greatly increased food rations. Prosperity in East Germany was contrasted with the dire situation which currency reform had brought about in West Germany and West Berlin. West Berliners faced the unpleasant choice between economic stagnation and increasing unemployment, on the one hand, and integration into the east zone economy on the other.

An American journalist, who apparently had informants in East Berlin, has described one version of the Soviet tactical plan as follows: First, there were to be "spontaneous" protest demonstrations in West Berlin against the Allies. Armed Communists were to mix with the crowds and shoot at the civilian police, but not at Allied personnel. This would presumably lead to reprisals from the Western side. In response to such a "massacre," protest demonstrations would be held in East Berlin, at which the people would call for the liberation of the west sectors from the "imperialists." Next morning, East German police would occupy strategic points in the west sectors, but still would not attack Allied personnel. After several days of chaos, the Soviet government would then inform the Western powers that it would have to intervene to restore order in West Berlin.[126]

One reason that this plan, or one similar to it, was never put in operation may have been the Communists' awareness that they could never command even minimum support from West Berliners. Also, the Soviets may have regarded such a plan as too risky. For, although their pressure was relentless, they were careful to apply it in such a way as to keep under control the risk of provoking a war. Interference with Berlin's communications was stepped up gradually, and, in case of strong Western counterpressure, the Soviets could have backed down at any time. When the full blockade was imposed, it was done on the grounds of "technical difficulties." The final withdrawal from the Kommandatura did not take place until a week after the blockade had been imposed. In dealing with Western officials, the Soviets frequently introduced relatively affable statements, which newsmen seized upon as evidence of a "softening" in Moscow's attitude. Marshal Sokolovsky's "friendly" letter to General Robertson on June 29 is probably the outstanding instance of this strategy. Even the behavior of the SED improved periodically, as shown in the Assembly meeting of July 1.

The fact that the heaviest pressure on the Western powers was exercised indirectly, through the Berlin population, was part of this skillful attempt to keep the temperature of the situation below the exploding point. If airlift planes had been shot down, or if a Western soldier had been killed, the political repercussions would have been very strong. But when Soviet officials browbeat German city officials, or leaders of the SED threatened other Berliners, this was unlikely to persuade London and Washington that their vital interests were at stake. Even in bringing pressure to bear on German officials, the Soviets observed a certain moderation. The city hall was located in East Berlin, and the officials who refused to obey Soviet unilateral orders could have been arrested at any time. Yet few of them were, and the most prominent ones were left untouched.

As far as can be determined, the Soviets were confident that their plans would succeed, and that the Western powers would be forced to negotiate on Moscow's terms or else to leave Berlin. A number of the *Abend* essayists, who at the start of the blockade had been in East German concentration camps or in prisoner-of-war camps in Russia, recalled that communist propaganda officials had announced an imminent victory for Soviet diplomacy. The fact that similar statements were made by the Soviets to key officials in the satellite states,[127] suggests that a prediction to this effect may have been distributed through the Soviet propaganda apparatus. Those Germans and Americans who dealt with communist officials in Berlin also received the impression that the Soviets were very confident.

From all indications the airlift did not, at first, affect this confidence. Ambassador Smith in Moscow and Colonel Howley in

Berlin both reported that Soviet officials were quite sure Berlin could not be supplied by air.[128] An American correspondent with contacts in the east sector observed that the Soviets did not even bother to inquire how much coal West Berlin needed, how long the available coal stocks would last, or how long the West Berlin power installations could continue to function, because they apparently were completely convinced that air supply was impossible and that a total economic collapse would result from the blockade.[129]

Such information as the Soviets had with respect to American intentions can only have increased their confidence that the United States would not make a very strong effort to stay in Berlin. A former U.S. Military Government official reported that, shortly before the blockade, one of his German staff members was arrested by communist police in East Berlin and questioned for seventeen hours. The questioning was done by Soviet officers, who said they knew that the United States was not serious about staying in Berlin, in spite of resolute statements by General Clay and Colonel Howley. The American official's comment was that opinion in U.S. Military Government headquarters about the desirability of trying to stay in Berlin under Soviet pressure was indeed divided, and that the Soviet officers seemed to know this. General Clay had already told the Army Department in April that "extension of the blockade to cut food off from the German population in Berlin might succeed in forcing us out. . . ."[130] While the Soviets probably were not aware of this particular statement, they certainly were familiar with the general attitudes among Western officials.

As far as the airlift was concerned, Soviet skepticism was shared by leading figures in the West. There were very few who believed that it could do more than delay the day of departure from Berlin.

The Response in Washington and London

In their public pronouncements, American officials in Berlin and Washington maintained a firm pose regarding Soviet pressure in Germany. But in deliberations among themselves they were deeply split as to the correct course. Both General Clay and President Truman had to take upon themselves the decision to attempt to hold out in Berlin, without the benefit of agreed staff recommendations.* Indeed, staff work in the two centers appears to have been

* It will also be remembered that Mayor Reuter had to make his initial decision—namely, to try and tie Berlin as closely as possible to the West—without the support of a majority in the SPD Executive Committee who favored a more cautious line.

almost paralyzed by an inability to face the situation, and both General Clay and the President were in the strange position of having to convince some of their principal advisors that a decision to hold out was indeed the correct one. Forrestal's account of a cabinet member cautioning President Truman that he should withhold his decision on Berlin because the matter had not been thought through illustrates the dilemma of the principal political leaders. If Washington had temporized long enough to engage in extensive deliberations, it is likely that the United States would have had no position left to defend.

Even after these decisions had been made at the top, indecision at lower levels continued. Within the U.S. Department of Defense, it was pointed out that the Western position in Berlin was militarily unsound. It was also argued that nearly all the available American and British transport planes were being committed to the airlift, and that, in the event of war, the Soviets could shoot down these slow aircraft with the greatest of ease, thereby crippling the entire air transport capacity of the Western democracies. The best course, therefore, would be to get out of Berlin as soon as a face-saving occasion offered itself. One official was quoted as saying: "If you're damned fool enough to let somebody slam a door on your finger, the first thing you do is to pull your finger out."[131] Certainly, the observation that Berlin was militarily indefensible was entirely correct. According to an unofficial source, the United States had 3,000 troops in the city, the British 2,000, and the French 1,500, while the Soviets had 18,000 in the city and 300,000 in the east zone.[132] The National Security Council did not adopt a definitive position on Berlin until some six weeks after the crisis had started.[133]

Indecision within U.S. Military Government headquarters in Berlin was at first at least as great as in Washington. Prior to June 1948 those Americans who believed that Berlin could be held in the event of a Soviet blockade were in the minority. Some offices had drawn up evacuation plans, and prepared lists of Berliners who were to be flown out if possible. And for several weeks after the blockade had started, there were still discussions about the advisability of withdrawing from Berlin.

Another striking aspect of American decision-making during the early days of the Berlin crisis is the fact that the airlift was regarded primarily as a device to gain time for diplomatic negotiations, and its potentialities as a means of breaking the blockade were not recognized. Even after a week of operation, estimates of the maximum that could be brought into Berlin by air were only for about one-fifth of the supplies that were ultimately flown in. As will be shown, this cautiousness in estimating air transport capacity came close to leading the Western powers into a major diplomatic defeat.

Finally, policy-making U.S. officials showed a strong tendency, at first, to interpret the situation in terms of law rather than of power. President Truman's decision was made on the basis that we had a right to be in Berlin and therefore we were going to stay there. The first high-level discussion in Washington on the Berlin question, which was reported by Forrestal on June 25, was also concerned with the "legal rights and undertakings of the United States in Berlin." When asked why the Western powers had reacted more strongly to Soviet interference with the air corridors than with the ground corridors, a senior U.S. official in Berlin replied: "We had a signed agreement on the air corridors, and therefore we had something to defend, but we didn't have anything in writing about the ground routes." This preoccupation with law, while entirely in keeping with the structure and traditions of the American state, probably made it more difficult for the U.S. government to deal effectively with the crisis. It tended to relegate to a secondary place the consideration of power, which clearly determined the calculations of the Soviet Union.

Though less is known about deliberations in London in late June and early July than about those in Washington, it would appear that the initial response of the British government was the more forthright. Officials who were in touch with Foreign Minister Bevin on June 25 and 26 have reported that his position was firm from the outset. The parliamentary debate on June 30 makes it clear that the British recognized their vital interests to be at stake, and faced the prospect that a showdown might lead to war. Even Aneurin Bevan, the fiery Labour Party leader who later became known as an advocate of neutralism, is said to have been in favor of dispatching an armored column up the highway to Berlin. Later, as the war fears of the public apparently communicated themselves to the political leaders, the British approach became more cautious. But at the outset, government and parliament reacted in a manner reminiscent of the days of Palmerston or Disraeli.

CHAPTER IV

JULY–SEPTEMBER: NEGOTIATION UNDER PRESSURE

Although Berlin did not fall, plumlike, into Soviet hands during the first few weeks of the blockade, this did not necessarily mean that communist plans had gone awry. The Soviet note of July 14 had made Moscow's position clear: the Berlin question was a part of the German question. Therefore, if the Western powers wished to discuss Berlin, they would also have to talk about arrangements for Germany as a whole. They would now have to decide whether to proceed with their plans for a West German state or to retain their position in Berlin. It was the communist contention that they could not do both.

In order to hasten a Western decision, the Soviets intensified their three-pronged pressure on Berlin. They subjected the growing airlift to harassing tactics of an increasingly annoying nature, thereby playing on fear of war in the West; they continued measures to intimidate and disrupt the Berlin city government; and they brought new psychological pressures, in the form of threats and promises, to bear on the West Berlin population. Like waves beating on a dam, the Communists sought to find the point of weakness in the Western defenses.

The State of Western Policy in July

The Western powers initially responded to Soviet pressure much in the way that Moscow must have expected, and entered into negotiations at the end of July. Western negotiators did not feel their position to be a very strong one. There were differences of opinion among France, Great Britain, and the United States. Washington itself was sharply divided on the proper course to follow, and confidence in the ability of the airlift to satisfy Berlin's long-term needs was as yet shared by only a minority. Nevertheless, the uneasy consensus was that the Western powers should exhaust every diplomatic recourse to attain lifting of the blockade, and in the meantime improve their bargaining position as much as possible by expanding the airlift and building up Western air strength in Europe.

Differences among the three Western powers were appreciable but not insuperable. France leaned toward withdrawal from Berlin, if a suitable formula could be worked out.[1] The United States tended to take the position that the democracies were in Berlin by right, and that right was not subject to negotiation. The British, their initial determination having weakened somewhat, inclined toward a point of view in between.[2] Reconciliation of the three views required repeated and time-consuming consultations among representatives of the three powers, which prevented the democracies from acting rapidly.[3]

Among American policymakers in both Berlin and Washington there was one group, gloomy and hesitant, composed of those who believed that the Western powers were in a weak position and would have to make concessions. A State Department official recalled that a senior diplomat, returning from Germany in July, had told his colleagues that the United States could hold out in Berlin for only about six more weeks, and that a solution would have to be found before then. Another senior official opposed taking any further economic reprisals against the Soviets for fear of "broadening the conflict." A news dispatch from Washington in July reported the State Department view as being that food could be supplied to West Berlin for a maximum of two more months.[4] Influential writers, such as Walter Lippmann and Sumner Welles, supported the position of this group.

Another American group was in favor of using military or economic force to break the blockade. According to persistent rumors, the plan of sending a three-power armored convoy up the road from West Germany to Berlin was under active consideration.[5] Secretary Forrestal recalls a dinner conversation at which General Clay told him that he still was confident that a convoy could break through without creating a crisis, although the chances would grow slimmer as time went on. The General also stressed his belief that the German people were unequivocally on the side of the West and would do everything in their power to help.[6] In mid-July, Major General William Donovan, at that time not a government official, called for the imposition of world-wide economic sanctions against the Soviets as a reply to the blockade, "even if it means war." General Donovan's statement, though completely unofficial, was broadcast immediately by radio stations in the U.S. and British sectors of Berlin.[7]

One point, however, on which nearly all of official Washington soon came to agree was that the blockade had political implications of the gravest nature. In a meeting with President Truman and high administration officials, Secretary of State Marshall stated grimly that the United States had the alternative of following a firm policy in Berlin or accepting the consequences of failure of the rest of its European policy.[8] General Clay told the President and the National Security Council that departure from Berlin would be a serious, if not disastrous, blow to the maintenance of freedom in Europe.[9]

Nevertheless, Air Force officials still had reservations about the advisability of concentrating the bulk of U.S. air transport capacity in Germany. General Vandenberg pointed out that a maximum airlift would require planes which were intended for emergency use elsewhere. In the event of hostilities, many of these might be destroyed, and the ability of the United States to wage strategic warfare reduced, since it would then be difficult to supply forces at distant bases.[10]

Out of all this discussion there emerged the two decisions that were to govern Western policy during the next few months: to make every effort toward a negotiated settlement with the Soviets while remaining in Berlin; and to strengthen the bargaining power of the Western allies as much as possible short of resorting to measures that might provoke the Soviets to take a stronger stand. On July 19 President Truman, in Forrestal's paraphrase, said that U.S. policy would be to "stay in Berlin until all diplomatic means had been exhausted in order to come to some kind of an accommodation to avoid war. . . ."[11] A similar position emerged from a discussion in the National Security Council three days later, where it was decided to drop the idea of an armed convoy and, instead, to concentrate on expanding the airlift, since the latter course was less likely to provoke war.[12] General Clay, returning to Berlin in late July, told the press that he had been promised a considerable increase in Skymaster aircraft, and that with their help the airlift could be built up to 4,000 tons a day. He added that the expanded airlift would give the Western powers time to approach the problem through all diplomatic methods.[13]

Though the Soviets continued their threats to limit flying in the corridors or to close them entirely, these threats clearly failed in their purpose. When the *Tägliche Rundschau* announced that new measures to regulate the problems of the air corridors were impending, a British spokesman replied that he could not conceive of any changes in the flight regulations unless they were forced by military action.[14] A "responsible officer" said that United States fliers would ignore any Soviet declaration barring flights in the corridors, and added: "The only way they can stop us is to shoot us down."[15] The only effect of the Soviets' threats and minor harassing actions in the corridors was to demonstrate to all concerned that the Western allies were determined to fly in supplies regardless, a determination which tended to cancel out some of the unfavorable impressions created by Western indecision in other areas.

Simultaneously, Western air strength in Europe was augmented. On July 17 sixty U.S. B-29 Superfortresses arrived in Britain.[16] Additional U.S. jet aircraft were dispatched to Germany, and started making familiarization flights over the countryside.[17] The arrival of at least thirty additional Superforts in the British Isles was reported during August.[18]

Finally, in a modest move to tighten the counterblockade, British and American authorities stopped rail traffic across the bizonal area between the Soviet zone and non-German countries. A U.S. spokesman stated sarcastically that this stoppage was due to "technical difficulties."[19] But the political implications of the move were clear.

U.S. policy calculations during this period were strongly affected by two military factors: America's almost desperate weakness in conventional forces, and her monopoly of the atom bomb. Secretary of Defense Forrestal had, on several occasions, pointed out that the nation's total ground reserves amounted to slightly over two divisions, and that only one division could be committed with any speed.[20] With this in mind, an effort to break the blockade with ground forces would look very much like a bluff. And General Clay had stressed that we could not afford to bluff. Consequently, any realistic military gesture would have to be backed by the atomic bomb, but it had not been decided how to turn this gigantic military weapon into diplomatic bargaining power. The bomb was the only real power the United States had, but no one knew under which circumstances it could be used, or indeed whether it could be used at all. Forrestal discussed this problem with a group of high governmental officers at lunch on July 28:

> . . . I said in view of the tensions in the European situation that I felt it was difficult for me to carry out my responsibilities without resolution of the question whether or not we are to use the A-bomb in war. I observed also that it seemed to me that the Secretary of State had a deep interest in this, because, if there were any questions as to the use of this weapon, he was

automatically denied one of the most potent cards in his pack in negotiation.[21]

Forrestal also had several apparently inconclusive conferences with the President on this question during July and August.

This indecision about how atomic energy could be converted into diplomatic potential affected the significance of dispatching the B-29's to England. The B-29's were known as atomic bombers. But did U.S. policy envisage using the bomb if the Berlin crisis became more acute? If the United States were to drop an atomic bomb on Moscow, Soviet troops, in the opinion of many military experts, would immediately push forward to the English channel. General Clay did not believe that "we would have to assume the *immediate* overrunning of France.*" However, he was regarded as optimistic on this score.[22] As has been pointed out above, the U.S. Government found sufficient reason to send the bombers to Britain even without clarifying the question about using atomic weapons.†

Although discussions of atomic policy in Washington were conducted in strictest secrecy, the Soviets must have felt that they could deduce Western policy with considerable accuracy from public statements and with the aid of their intelligence network. They knew that London and especially Paris favored a cautious policy, which would tend to restrain the United States from any adventures that might break up the Western alliance. They also knew that an armored column was being discussed, but that this plan clearly was not about to be put into effect. Consequently, as long as the Western powers shied away from such lesser military undertakings, it was difficult to believe that they would resort to using atom bombs against major Soviet population centers. Finally, Soviet confidence in the superiority of their own ground forces was such as to make them fairly certain that in the event of hostilities they could overrun Europe at least to the Pyrenees. If the United States were to use its atom bomb against a major Soviet center, this would constitute an invitation for the Soviets to take over most of Western Europe. This view, which had been expressed in so many words by the Soviet historian Tarlé the year before,[23] was shared by many Western military authorities. Indeed, the U.S. Secretary of State had already objected to Defense Department statements that emphasized American military weakness in conventional arms. He had pointed out

* Italics added.

† See Chapter III, p. 130.

that repetition of such statements tended to add to the difficulties of our negotiations with Russia and might even delude the Soviets into hasty action.[24]

While the atom bomb was unlikely to be used to break the Berlin blockade, the move of the B-29's to Europe may still have had a very significant meaning to the Soviets. For it represented an increase in the immediate retaliatory power of the West, which the Soviets would have to take into account if they contemplated any new and bolder move. Furthermore, Moscow must have noted that the arrival of the bombers reversed the policy of withdrawing American armed forces from Europe, which the United States had followed since 1945. Since the Soviets definitely did not want war, the presence of the B-29's in England thus may have tended to limit Moscow to measures similar to those which had already been tried and found to be safe. If the Soviets were to make any move designed to give them control of Western Europe, the United States would be in a far stronger position to bomb Moscow. And it would then no longer feel restrained by the fear of seeing Western Europe overrun by the Red Army, for Western Europe would have been lost already. In short, while the location of the B-29 bombers in England probably did not exert any very appreciable influence on the Soviets to change their blockade policy, it may well have helped to set a limit beyond which they felt they could not go without running new and serious risks.

By the end of July, policy-makers in Washington had recognized the serious implications of the Soviet threat to Berlin, but did not feel that an attempt to break the blockade by force was advisable. The airlift was still seen as a device to gain additional time for negotiations. Dispatch of the B-29 bombers to Great Britain was regarded as improving the long-term strategic situation of the Western powers, but not as a solution to the blockade problem. Indeed, Forrestal's summary of the reasons for the move does not mention Berlin at all.[25]

The official American position, as formulated by President Truman, was that the United States would stay in Berlin until all diplomatic means had been exhausted. This was not necessarily a strong stand. Diplomatic means would be exhausted if the Soviets simply said "no" consistently over a period of time. Western counterblockade measures were as yet incomplete. and it was not known whether they added significantly to the bargaining power of the democracies. Various Western statesmen had indicated that they expected public opinion to have a constraining effect on the Soviets, but just how this effect was to be exercised was not made clear. The West thus entered the Moscow negotiations in what appeared to be a weak position. As it later turned out, this position was stronger than originally believed.

*Progress of the Moscow Negotiations**

On July 30, approximately two weeks after receipt of the Soviet note that rejected the original Western protests about the blockade, representatives of the United States, Great Britain, and France in Moscow requested an appointment with Premier Stalin and Foreign Minister Molotov to discuss the Berlin situation. The initial Soviet response made it clear that Moscow was in no hurry to settle the crisis. A spokesman at the Soviet foreign office announced that Mr. Molotov had just started his vacation, and suggested that the Western representatives present the problem to Deputy Foreign Minister Zorin. The delegates persisted however, and after preliminary meetings with Zorin and Molotov on July 30 and 31, they were able to see both Stalin and Molotov on the evening of August 2.[26]

U.S. Ambassador Walter Bedell Smith, as the senior representative of the Western powers in Moscow, acted as spokesman for the democracies. He reported later that the Soviet premier appeared to be in an excellent humor and that, from the Soviet point of view, this good humor was justified; it looked "as if he [Stalin] had confronted us with the flat alternative of getting out of Berlin in ignominious defeat or of staying on under sufferance and abandoning our announced plan of setting up a separate government for Western Germany."[27] At that time, Smith himself had "serious doubts" that it would be possible to feed and supply Berlin by air during the winter months, and he also wondered whether the morale of the German people would stand the strain. He was encouraged, however, by his confidence in General Clay's logistical ability and by the fact that, up to that point, the morale of the blockaded Berliners had remained high. He mentioned in particular the almost daily mass meetings at which they cheered the airlift and defied communism.[28]

As the discussion of August 2 progressed, it seemed to the Western

* A full summary of the Allied-Soviet negotiations during the early stages of the blockade is found in C. H. Pegg, "Die Verhandlungen zwischen Ost und West über die Berliner Blockade von Mai bis September 1948," *Europa Archiv*, January 5, 1957.

negotiators that it might yield results. At first, Stalin and Molotov attempted to obtain concessions in West Germany: they sought to secure a voice in policies governing Ruhr industry and asked that implementation of the London Recommendations be held up. They also asserted that the Western powers no longer had a legal right to retain representation in Berlin. When Smith and his British and French colleagues refused Stalin's demands and insisted on the continued right of their countries to share in the occupation of Berlin, the Soviet dictator moderated his demands and proposed the following formula for ending the blockade: (1) the Soviet zone mark should be introduced throughout Berlin in place of the west mark, and simultaneously all transport restrictions should be removed; (2) the Soviets would no longer ask deferment of the London decisions as a condition for settling the crisis, but this should be recorded as the insistent wish of their government.[29]

Western hopes for a speedy solution on the basis of these general principles were soon dashed. When it came to drawing up a formal written agreement, Molotov proved to be a hard bargainer. He tried on several occasions to make the postponement of a Western German government a precondition for ending the blockade, in spite of Stalin's apparent assurance that this would not be necessary; he interpreted the removal of "all transport restrictions" to mean only those imposed after June 18; and he continued to challenge the right of the Western powers to be in Berlin at all, except on Soviet sufferance. The interpretation on which Molotov insisted was one which, in the opinion of Ambassador Smith, would have enabled the Soviets to control the life of Berlin whether Western troops remained there or not; it would have delayed the establishment of a West German government; and it would have enabled the Soviets to reimpose the blockade at their discretion. To exchange these concessions for a partial lifting of the blockade seemed to the Western representatives too high a price to pay.[30]

Having reached a stalemate with Molotov, Ambassador Smith and his colleagues requested another meeting with Stalin, and this was arranged for August 23. Stalin again seemed in excellent humor and appeared willing to concede a number of points. He agreed verbally that all restrictions of any consequence on Berlin's traffic would be removed, even if they had been imposed before June 18, and also that the east marks used in Berlin would be under the ultimate control of a four-power financial commission. On the other hand, he repeatedly brought up the question of the London Recommendations and expressed his continued desire that the establishment of a West German state be delayed. When Ambassador Smith mentioned the necessity of managing currency matters in Berlin in a way that would give all powers equal control, and when he insisted that the juridical position of the Western powers in the city be respected, Stalin's answer implied that the status of Berlin depended on the abandonment of plans for a West German state:

> Stalin replied that, if German unity were restored by confirming the decisions of previous Four Power conferences, Berlin would remain the capital of Germany and then there would be no objection to the forces and authority of the three Western powers remaining in Berlin and sharing the control of the German government in Berlin with the Soviet Union. If this did not happen, then Berlin would lose its standing as the capital of Germany.[31]

And again, when the question of issuing a four-power communiqué about the discussion came up, Stalin suggested that the following paragraph be included:

> The question of the London decision was also discussed, including the formation of a Western German government. The discussion took place in an atmosphere of mutual understanding.[32]

When the Western representatives refused to accept this paragraph because of its implication of some secret arrangement to abandon plans for West Germany, Ambassador Smith received the impression that Stalin lost interest in the negotiations. Indeed, he left Moscow for a vacation shortly thereafter.[33]

Drafting meetings with Molotov, however, were continued. Although they frequently were acrimonious, agreement was finally reached on the wording of a communiqué and a directive to the four military governors in Berlin. The communiqué announced that traffic restrictions would be lifted, that the east mark would constitute the sole currency in Berlin, and that a four-power meeting would be held in the near future to discuss any outstanding questions regarding Berlin as well as any problems affecting Germany as a whole. The directive to the military governors amounted to a statement of principles, the implementation of which was to be worked out by the four commanders in Berlin. Since this directive became the subject of protracted international negotiations, its most important provisions are here reproduced in full:

> The Governments of France, the United Kingdom, the United States, and the USSR have decided that, subject to agreement being reached among the four military governors in Berlin for their practical implementation, the following steps shall be taken simultaneously:
>
> (A) Restrictions on communications, transport and commerce between Berlin and the Western zones and to and from the Soviet zone of Germany which have recently been imposed shall be lifted;
>
> (B) The German mark of the Soviet zone shall be introduced as the sole currency for Berlin, and the Western mark "B" shall be withdrawn from circulation in Berlin.
>
> In connection with the above you are instructed to consult together with your colleagues so as to make, in the shortest time possible, the detailed arrangements necessary for the implementation of these decisions, and to inform your government not later than September 7 of the results of your discussions, including the exact date on which the measures under (A) and (B) above can be brought into effect. . . .
>
> The regulation of currency circulation in Berlin is to be undertaken by the German Bank of Emission of the Soviet zone through the medium of the credit establishments operating at present in Berlin.
>
> A financial commission of representatives of the four military governors shall be set up to control the practical implementation of the financial arrangements indicated above, involved in the introduction and continued circulation of a single currency in Berlin.[34]

The directive also provided that west marks should be exchanged for east marks at a rate of one for one, that all sectors should have equal treatment as to currency and credit facilities, and that a satisfactory basis for trade between Berlin and the West should be worked out.

Western authorities recognized that this directive left much to be desired. Ambassador Smith reports that he and his associates were eager to produce the document even though it left many questions open, because they felt that only by the acid test of a conference in Berlin could the sincerity of Soviet intentions be determined.[35] His statement implies that the Western negotiators in Moscow felt that they were making certain concessions for the sake of reaching even an unsatisfactory agreement. The State Department in Washington was concerned because the agreement contained no statement about the basic juridical right of the Western powers to be in Berlin.[36] General Clay was dissatisfied for several reasons. He had hoped that the whole process of negotiation could be completed in Moscow, but the directive merely transferred the problem to the four military governors, and he did not see how they could succeed in reaching agreement where they had failed before. Also, he found the wording of the directive ambiguous as to four-power control of Berlin's currency. Despite Stalin's verbal promise of August 23 that the German Bank of Emission of the east zone would be under four-power control in its Berlin activities, the directive gave no assurance of this. General Clay's feeling was "that our acceptance of ambiguous wording just to obtain an agreed directive would lead nowhere."[37] A leading London newspaper commented that the amount of actual agreement reached was very small: All the directive did was to "open a road which may lead to a modus vivendi, provided that everybody wants to use it." But whether the Soviets really wanted to follow this road was very doubtful.[38]

Those who had doubts about the Soviets' good faith found their suspicions confirmed by the events of the summer. Intensified communist pressure on Berliners and on the city government led to new riots at the city hall during the latter part of August and early September.

Communist Pressures on the West Berlin Populace

Before and during the Moscow discussions, the Soviets attempted by threats and cajolery to alienate Berliners from the Western powers and from their own democratic government, and in general to encourage attitudes and behavior that would facilitate communist seizure of power. In this effort they were energetically assisted by the SED.

Berliners were given to understand that their safety depended on their cooperating with the Soviets. *Tägliche Rundschau* proclaimed on August 1 that, since the United States, Great Britain, and France had lost their right to take part in the four-power administration of Berlin, any orders issued by military authorities in the western sectors were invalid. The statement added ominously that all persons or institutions carrying out these illegal orders did so "at their own risk." In commenting on this threat, the London *Times* noted that the former Nazi concentration camps at Sachsenhausen and Buchenwald were being emptied of their inmates, presumably in preparation for a new group of victims. The *Times* added: "The apprehension that what was endured under the Nazis may have to be relived under the Communists weighs heavily on the minds of many. It is an apprehension which the Western democracies cannot ignore."[39]

Threats were supplemented by overt actions. Kidnapings by both communist police and Soviet military personnel were reported frequently. On August 20, for example, a number of Soviet soldiers entered the American sector, kidnaped five policemen, and confiscated their police car. That same day, the chief of the Magistrat's central coal office was taken from his office by east sector police.[40] The following day, Soviet military police entered the American sector and seized two German policemen. When they protested and tried to resist the arrest, they were stabbed and man-handled, and finally dragged into the Russian sector.[41] Nearly every day communist police would stop passers-by at the sector borders and search them for west marks. It seemed that nothing could be done to protect Berliners from these kidnapings, searches, and confiscations.

At the same time, communist propaganda was predicting that the protecting forces of the Western powers would soon be removed. Stories to the effect that General Clay was being recalled appeared in the east sector press. One of these cited as proof the fact that Clay's policies had been attacked by former Under Secretary of State Sumner Welles and also by the well-known columnist Walter Lippmann.[42] A headline in *Neues Deutschland* for August 19 stated baldly: OMGUS IS LEAVING BERLIN. And a few days later, a "reliable source" told the same newspaper that twenty houses near Frankfurt were being prepared for use by the families of leading West Berlin politicians, who were shortly to be evacuated. Soon thereafter, the SED organ alleged that three leading Social Democrats had already taken refuge in West Germany.[43] An interviewer for a public opinion research organization in Berlin recalled that all these reports were reinforced by much more blatant word-of-mouth propaganda, according to which all Berlin would soon be under Soviet control.

The Communists also predicted the failure of the airlift. When, in mid-July, SED Co-chairman Wilhelm Pieck was asked by a correspondent of the *Chicago Tribune* what he thought of the airlift, Pieck replied angrily that it was a propaganda instrument, that it could not supply the west sectors with food, fuel, or raw materials, and that, under the pretext of saving Berlin, an anti-Soviet campaign was being carried on, whose only purpose was to divert attention from the serious damage that was being done by splitting Germany and building up a separate West German state. Pieck added that the cost of the airlift would be loaded on the German people just as occupation costs had been, and that the whole operation would soon fail.[44]

In August, the communist press became more specific about the alleged failure of the airlift. Even General Clay and City Councilman Klingelhöfer, the Magistrat's economic chief, were reported to have admitted a shortage of food and coal. According to one story, grain reserves in the west sectors had shrunk from 30,000 to 8,000 tons, and British Military Government had admitted that only one-third as much food and fuel had come into the west sectors as had arrived in the same period the year before. The West Berlin press publishes figures that show the success of the airlift, continued the article, but these figures cannot be checked. However, the planes that fly back to West Germany are known to be taking raw materials, capital goods, and machinery. At the same time, the city's debt is growing, and Berlin taxpayers will soon discover the other side of the airlift. On August 13 a headline read: "AIRLIFT FIASCO CONFIRMED."[45]

Furthermore, said the Communists, the airlift was senseless because the Western powers, rather than the Soviets, were blockading Berlin. Marshal Sokolovsky had stated that the Russians would not allow the city to starve; it was the West that had cut its sectors off from the east zone. By introducing a new currency, the Western powers had forced Russia to take measures to protect her own zone from economic dislocation. In addition, they had ordered restrictions of their own: they were impeding trade between East and West Berlin, they refused to supply electric current for west sector plants working on Soviet orders, and they prevented necessary materials from coming into the Soviet zone from the west.

Why had the Western powers imposed a blockade? *Neues Deutschland* sought to answer this question in a long article on July 27 under the headline: "IT IS TIME TO MAKE AN END TO THE ANGLO-AMERICAN BLOCKADE OF WEST BERLIN." According to the SED newspaper, the Western powers were attempting: (1) to eliminate the power of West Berlin industry to compete with Anglo-American monopolies; (2) to interfere with the two-year plan in the Soviet zone; and (3) to create in Central Europe a center of unrest where capitalist conspirators could pursue their nefarious aims.

In addition to frightening West Berliners by threats and dire predictions, the Soviets made an attempt to gain their allegiance by promising them food and work. On July 19 the Council of Ministers of the USSR issued a decree that Berlin was to be furnished with sufficient food to meet the existing rations of every citizen.[46] The fact that this food offer was made in the name of such a high Soviet agency, and that it came five days after the Soviets had officially denied the right of the Western powers to remain in Berlin, would tend to indicate that Moscow considered it a major move.

This Soviet move immediately became the basis for a concerted propaganda campaign by the East Berlin press. On July 20 the front-page headline in *Neues Deutschland* ran: "AIRLIFT HAS NO PURPOSE—IN THE FUTURE ALL BERLINERS CAN BUY THEIR RATIONS IN THE EAST SECTOR." The official announcement from the Soviet Military Administration which followed, stated that additional food would be provided from the Soviet Union and that more would be purchased in Poland, Czechoslovakia, and other countries for shipment to Berlin. West Berliners would be able to obtain this food only in east sector stores.

On the following day, the east sector press reported that the workers had greeted the Soviet food offer with wild enthusiasm, while the lazy exploiters had been seized with impotent rage. Interviews with a number of individual west sector citizens provided artistic verisimilitude. But only on July 25 were practical details of the Soviet offer announced. The inhabitants of each west sector borough were instructed to register for food in a designated east sector borough. For example, residents of Reinickendorf, in the French sector, were to register in Soviet-occupied Pankow. On August 1, those registered could start buying food in the Soviet sector.

Throughout August, the communist press emphasized the quality and quantity of these supplies. On August 11 *Neues Deutschland* announced that sufficient provisions had arrived to supply the whole city for forty days. On August 12 a report stated that so much coal had been shipped to East Berlin that there was scarcely enough room to store it all. It was also pointed out that the east sector rations were higher than those in the west, and that the fresh foods being offered were far better for the health than the dried and tinned products that came over the airlift.

The Soviet food offer was supplemented, a few weeks later, by promises of work for unemployed West Berliners, and hints that idle factories in the west sectors could obtain Soviet orders if they made proper application. The work offer was accepted by only a handful of West Berliners and never became the subject of a major propaganda campaign. A few west sector enterprises did accept orders from the Soviets, but both management and labor opposed this practice, and it was later stopped almost entirely by the Western counterblockade.[47]

Public Morale

West Berliners appeared to be relatively little influenced by Soviet threats or promises. One of the major communist goals was to destroy confidence in the west mark. If West Berliners had been persuaded that their future lay with the east zone, it is likely that the value of the west mark would have gone down. Yet, instead of going down, the value of the west mark in relation to the east mark mounted steadily.* At the beginning of August it took 2 east marks to buy 1 west mark in currency exchange offices. By the end of the month it took 3.2.[48]

An even better index of the Berliners' resistance to cajolery or intimidation tactics was their reaction to the Soviet food offer. Both Allied and German leaders in West Berlin were worried by this offer. If a sufficient number of individuals registered in the east, not only would this destroy the solidarity upon which the survival of the democratic island depended, but it would place one of the city's most important administrative functions under Soviet domination and open the door to further inroads. British General Herbert denounced the Soviet move as just another effort to gain control of the west sectors.[49] The noncommunist press cited evidence that the food stocks offered by the Communists were actually coming from East Germany, not from Soviet Russia and the satellite countries, and contrasted the miserable conditions in East Berlin and East Germany with the glowing promises held out to West Berliners.[50] Leaders of all the democratic parties advised people to reject the offer.

As it turned out, instead of drawing a substantial proportion of

* Rates of exchange are available in the official city statistics only from August 2 on. In addition to the licensed exchange offices there were also black-market money changers. Ordinarily, west marks were more expensive on the black-market than in the exchange offices.

the West Berlin population into the sphere of communist authority, the Soviet food offer gave West Berliners an opportunity to demonstrate an impressive degree of solidarity. In spite of all communist efforts to make the offer attractive, only a handful of West Berliners responded. The democratic press reported this with obvious satisfaction. There was little possibility that Berliners would be taken in by such a crude device, wrote the *Tagesspiegel* on July 28, but still it was surprising how few people had registered. At the ration office in Treptow, the report continued, 20 persons from the west sectors have registered, as opposed to the 285,000 who had been invited to do so. In Prenzlauer Berg, there were only 16 registrations, in Pankow 19, and in several offices in Mitte nobody at all had showed up the preceding afternoon. "Apparently even the Communists from West Berlin don't want to register in the eastern paradise," the story concluded, "or else there are so few of them left." Three days later, a borough mayor from East Berlin reported that less than 1 percent of West Berliners had registered for food in East Berlin, and called this response a "secret referendum."[51] By August 4 only 19,000 out of the more than two million persons in the west sectors were on the east sector rolls.[52] The number rose sharply to 56,000 (or 2.2 per cent) during September, but then began to level off.[53] According to the Magistrat, the registrants totaled 85,000 by the end of the year, but it was believed that some persons had registered twice.[54]

The British *Notes on the Blockade of Berlin* attempt to analyze the composition of the east sector registrants. According to this source, the number who registered never exceeded approximately 86,000, or about 4 per cent of the population. Some 11,000 of these lived in areas, on the edge of West Berlin, which Soviet authorities had arbitrarily incorporated into their administrative sphere. Another 15,000 were persons who lived in the west sectors, but who worked in the east sector and continued to buy their rations there, as they had always done, for reasons of convenience. This left a hard core of only 60,000, many of whom had been "persuaded" on political grounds.[55]

In the face of Soviet divisive tactics, the West Berliners' identification with the West continued to mount. Mass meetings sponsored by the city's democratic leaders were well attended; more and more workers started paying their dues to the independent unions; confidence in the west mark increased steadily.

Two incidents help to illustrate the temper of the times. One occurred at a rally sponsored by the Berlin publisher Lothar

Blanvalet and was designed to mobilize the intellectuals to play an active part in the defense of the city's freedom. On July 18 "tens of thousands" responded to this call, and the large square in front of the Schöneberg borough hall could scarcely hold them all.[56] They were addressed by Professor Edwin Redslob and a group of ten writers and artists. Almost at the end of the meeting, sharp-eyed chairman Blanvalet spied Berlin's acting mayor, Louise Schroeder, standing in the crowd. She was on her way from one appointment to another and had stopped for a moment to listen. Seizing the opportunity Blanvalet invited Frau Schroeder to come up to the speaker's platform and say a few words. The crowd parted in the center, and the little gray-haired lady passed through to the rostrum amid almost hysterical applause. An American newspaperman who attended the meeting has called it one of the most impressive displays of emotion and enthusiasm he ever witnessed.

The other event had consequences that were even more moving. On the night of July 24-25, a C-47 aircraft crashed in the Friedenau section of Berlin just prior to landing at Tempelhof airfield. Both members of the two-man crew were killed. Two houses were damaged and set on fire, but none of the residents was fatally injured. German and American rescue workers soon put out the fire and recovered the bodies of the airmen.

The death of the two officers seemed to break down part of the barrier which still existed between Berliners and American occupation forces, and through the breach poured a flood of sympathy, appreciation, and deeds of kindness. The mayors of the six boroughs in the U.S. sector called on Colonel Howley to express their condolences. Berlin's democratic parties sent notes of sympathy to General Clay, and Acting Mayor Louise Schroeder visited American Military Government on the same errand. Dr. Suhr honored the fliers at the next meeting of the City Assembly. A *Tagesspiegel* editorial read:

> An airman who crashes in the course of supplying Berlin is for us more than a transport pilot who has died in an accident: he is a man who has given his life for a free world, for the same world which we choose every day when we put up with discomfort, chicanery, threats, and worse.

The editorial also pointed out that both the officers who were killed had small children. One reader had already sent in 20 marks and had promised to collect 100 more if the newspaper would conduct a campaign to raise funds to support the dependents of the two fliers.[57] A nameless Berliner put a simple plaque at the place of the crash, which read:

> Two American fliers became victims of the Berlin blockade here. You gave your lives for us! The Berliners of the west sectors will never forget you! We stand deeply moved on this spot which has been dedicated by your death. Once we were enemies, and yet you gave your lives for us. We are now doubly obligated to you.[58]

Other unknown Berliners kept the plaque decorated with fresh flowers.

For weeks, contributions and expressions of sympathy continued to pour in from all quarters of West Berlin, and even from East Berlin. An editor of the *Tagesspiegel* said later that the incident had inspired more letters to the editor than any other aspect of the airlift.

In short, during July and August, Soviet efforts to alienate the West Berlin populace from its democratic leaders and from the Western powers were outweighed by influences working in the other direction, and resistance morale improved rather than deteriorated.

Pressure on West Berlin's Leaders

Meanwhile, the Soviets continued their efforts to dominate the central Berlin government or, failing this, to disorganize it completely and drive it out of the east sector. These pressure tactics had started prior to the four-power negotiations in Moscow, and continued with ever-increasing tempo while the negotiations were going on.

A favorite Soviet technique was to subject city officials to endless conferences and interrogations, often late at night. A high official reported later that approximately once a week during this period he was summoned to Soviet headquarters, where he was harangued for hours on end by a succession of Soviet officers about the necessity for cooperating with the SED. During these sessions he was treated "correctly," but was allowed nothing to eat, drink, or smoke. On one occasion, he was detained eleven hours, and his wife concluded that he had been kidnaped.

It was also common practice for Soviet personnel to visit the offices of high city officials and to remain for hours, asking questions and demanding to see documents. This tactic not only prevented the officials from performing their work, but it was quite unnerving to them. Sometimes, as in the case of the food office and the public education office, the Soviets moved their own desks into the working quarters of German officials. Several city administrators were driven close to a nervous breakdown by the constant strain of having Soviet personnel look over their shoulders.

City administrators were in a poor position to counter these tactics. They could not legitimately refuse to confer with representatives of an occupying power. Also their offices were located in the Soviet sector, where they were subject to the authority of the communist German police and the Russian military police. The Western powers were, however, able to offer at least a small measure of protection. When a Soviet officer appeared in one of the city departments, the German authorities would sometimes ask a Western officer to be present as well. Nevertheless, the strain on the leading city officials was very great, and it is remarkable that none of them gave in to the Soviet demands.

Colonel Howley reports that similar tactics were employed in an apparent attempt to unnerve him. He often received strange telephone calls late at night. Sometimes a threatening voice would advise him to get out of Berlin, but more often there was only silence when he picked up the receiver. His doorbell also rang at all hours, but there was no one there when the door was opened. The Soviet-controlled radio kept the air so full of accounts of Colonel Howley's alleged misdeeds that he remarked: "I sometimes wonder how I managed to keep any friends at all in Berlin." Communist media also announced periodically that Mrs. Howley had become panic-stricken and was leaving the city. But she and their four children stayed on.[59]

One victim of Soviet harassment may have been Acting Mayor Louise Schroeder. Toward the end of August she became seriously ill and was flown to a hospital in West Germany. Her health had been poor for some time, and the heavy responsibilities that she carried so stoutly would by themselves have been enough to exhaust the most vigorous executive. In her absence, Dr. Friedensburg (CDU) became acting mayor. He remarked later that he simply "could not afford to get sick," because next in line for the mayor's office was Third Deputy Mayor Acker, a member of the SED. Had the communists been able to break Dr. Friedensburg's health, they would thus have captured the mayor's office, at least temporarily. Fortunately, Dr. Friedensburg proved to have a strong constitution.

Pressure on Departments of the City Government

The police department, which was largely controlled by the Communists already, was the first city department to be split as the result of Soviet efforts to dominate the municipal government. During the spring and early summer of 1948 the Magistrat had made repeated attempts to assert its authority over the police. These were vigorously opposed by the communist police administration, which, in return, made every effort to reduce democratic influence still further. All principal police offices, which had been located in the west sectors, were moved to East Berlin, and Police President Markgraf was reported to have told his subordinates to take orders only from Soviet authorities, and not from the Western powers.[60] The process of weeding out non-communists from higher positions in the department was accelerated, and between July 12 and 25, 590 higher police officials were summarily discharged.[61]

City officials, who had been gravely dissatisfied with the functioning of the police and their apparent complicity in Soviet kidnapings, attempted to take counteraction. Second Deputy Mayor Dr. Friedensburg was the Magistrat member in charge of supervising the police. Although he could not remove Markgraf without four-power approval, he was able to suspend him from office under the provisional Berlin constitution. He did so with the approval of the City Assembly on July 26, and appointed Assistant Police President Dr. Johannes Stumm to take over Markgraf's duties on an acting basis.

The dispute now became the direct concern of the occupying powers. Soviet General Kotikov countered by issuing an order confirming Markgraf in office, reprimanding Dr. Friedensburg, and instructing Acting Mayor Louise Schroeder to dismiss Dr. Stumm. The order was signed "Military Commandant of the City of Berlin," a title that implied, none too subtly, that the authority of the Western powers in the city was no longer recognized.[62] British Military Government, speaking for all the Western powers, replied that Kotikov's order was unilateral and hence had no validity.

In practice, Markgraf retained his authority in the east sector, while Stumm exercised police power in the west sectors. Because the central police headquarters were in the east sector, however, Dr. Stumm was at a disadvantage, especially since Markgraf threatened with reprisals any official who obeyed Stumm's orders. The latter therefore was forced to establish new police headquarters in the west sectors.

Each of the two police headquarters claimed to represent the sole legal authority, and it was up to the individual policeman to decide whom to obey. The results of this "informal referendum" among the guardians of the law were overwhelmingly in favor of Dr. Stumm. Far more than half the personnel from the Soviet sector headquarters moved over to the new building, even many of those whose homes were in the east sector, and in the end Markgraf was left only with SED adherents and a few whose family considerations prevented a shift to the west sectors.[63]

One of the *Abend* essayists, describing the individual attitudes and expectations about the future that played a role in the split of the police headquarters, has illustrated some of the principal trends in West Berlin public opinion at that time:

> In 1948 the political tensions in Berlin reached their highest point. All of us anxiously asked one question: "What will happen to Berlin?" As everywhere, this question was being discussed in our office on the Dircksenstrasse near Alexanderplatz [in the Soviet sector]. Would Berlin be split? Even from external appearances the force could be divided into three groups, which, if one had some experience in judging people, could be distinguished by the facial expression. A happy, expectant face was the mark of a member of the SED or a supporter of the eastern system. By their stern and serious faces the people could be recognized who supported the free world and were willing to lose their jobs rather than bow to the eastern system. Anxious and absent-minded expressions indicated people who were undecided and were asking themselves the fateful question: "What's the best thing for me to do?"
>
> Once again a violent discussion is in progress. An SED member says with a manner of superiority: "In two months at the most Berlin will be ours. The borders are closed and hunger will be painful. Hunger was always the best means of making people obedient and with this instrument the Russians will succeed in Berlin too. One cannot rely on America. The Americans would never start a war over Berlin."—We were all agreed on this last point. Nobody in our broad circle of acquaintance thought there would be a war. The situation looked threatening, but in spite of this those who stood firm put their trust in a miracle.—One day I had a discussion with my chief, Herr X. His expression said clearly that he belonged to the third group.

He described the existing situation as unbearable and expressed the opinion that it was much worse than the situation in 1945 [when Nazi power was overthrown and the Russians entered Berlin]. At that time it had been clear how things would turn out, and so at the right moment he had taken the wise precaution of reporting himself sick and staying away from work. The future had shown how correct this action had been. "After the occupation of Berlin I came out again at the right time," were his words. But what is going to happen now?—On the next morning my chief was absent. His wife notified us that he had been taken seriously ill.

Shortly after this came the appeal of the Police President [for members of the force to follow him to the new headquarters in West Berlin]. Group two and a few undecided men moved into the new headquarters near the airfield. This was a large building with terribly empty rooms. It took considerable courage to start work here. In one room a few abandoned garden chairs and tables were found, and a real fight over these developed. This was our first office equipment. In the air the aircraft engines thundered. Would they be able to supply us with even the most necessary foodstuffs? Days go by; our work proceeds, and the noise of the aircraft becomes louder and louder. In spite of the fact that we had very little bread, dried potatoes, and some tomatoes we had grown ourselves, our mood became more confident every day. The accomplishments of the fliers were witnessed with amazement. It is unbelievable at what short intervals the planes land and take off. . . . After several weeks my chief appears. His first words were: "Where am I working, and which is my office?" He is very confident and hopes to take up his work again in a few days.

The summer goes by and confidence grows, only to fall again as the cold season of the year arrives. My chief, Herr X, finds it uncomfortable in his office and goes home earlier every afternoon. One day he remarked that it was fortunate that he had kept his home in the east sector; there at least one had some fuel to heat with. "And one doesn't need to eat dried potatoes either," someone added ironically.

Now the blockade has been long forgotten. Herr X was one of the first to move into the west sectors. One day I overheard a conversation which he was having with a man who apparently was a former colleague from the east sector. "Yes, my dear fellow," I heard him say, "if we had not been so steadfast at that time and hadn't accepted so many privations, what would have happened to West Berlin?"

As this account suggests, the split in Berlin's police force had the effect of weeding out most communist sympathizers and some undecided persons. What the department lost in experienced personnel it made up by retaining a group of employees who were loyal to the West Berlin administration.

But the existence of dual headquarters did not end the struggle between the rival organizations. When police from the west sectors were sent to the east sector on business, they were often arrested by the communist police for "illegal exercise of authority."[64] Soviet authorities ordered that all messages posted in East Berlin or East Germany, and addressed to the west sector police headquarters, should be intercepted and sent to a special bureau in an east sector post office.[65] As late as November, a comic-opera situation developed when Markgraf refused to allow the new Berlin telephone directory to be distributed in the Soviet sector because it listed Dr. Stumm's office under "Police Headquarters."[66]

Even before the definitive split in the ranks of the police, Soviet Military Government took steps to gain control of the Magistrat's food office, or else force it out of the east sector. When the Soviets made their food offer and arranged for West Berliners to register in East Berlin, they also ordered a new unit of the food office to be set up to administer the program. A certain Paul Letsch was to head this unit and was to take orders directly from the east sector military authorities.[67]

The Magistrat did not contest this arrangement, probably because it did not want to appear as in any way preventing Berliners from taking advantage of the food offer. But the Soviet demands placed the Magistrat's food chief, city councilman Füllsack, in an impossible position. Although nominally responsible for administering the food supply for all Berlin, he actually had no control over Letsch. A week after the new unit had been set up, Füllsack announced stoutly that he would continue the central administration of the city's food supplies,[68] but it soon became clear that the Communists had no intention of permitting this. His office, like most of the Magistrat, was located in the east sector. It had assigned to it a Soviet liaison officer and his staff, who, in collaboration with Letsch, gradually undermined what little authority Füllsack had left. First, Letsch attempted to persuade the majority of food office employees to work directly for his new unit. When this move failed, he requisitioned by name two-thirds of all the personnel of the food office, including nearly all the professionals. His subordinates then proceeded to make decisions regarding the personnel and facilities of the office without consulting Füllsack. Thus, on August 11, they ruled that persons who did not work for Letsch's unit would not be permitted to enter the building. When Füllsack's deputy, Schöpke, attempted to report for work, he was dragged downstairs and thrown out by east sector police. The *Tagesspiegel* commented caustically: "The 'democratic spirit' in East Berlin is not unknown to Schöpke, since he was one of the democratic assemblymen who were manhandled by 'demonstrating workers' following the meeting of the City Assembly on June 23."[69]

As Letsch moved to secure control of Berlin's food office, the German Economic Commission (of the Soviet zone) started to issue orders with respect to the city's rationing system. Deputy Mayor Friedensburg protested this practice in a politely-phrased letter to Chairman Rau of the Economic Commission on August 24, in which he pointed out that no part of the Berlin city government could take orders from an east zone authority.

The reply was a polemical letter in which Rau gave succinct expression to the communist propaganda line. The East Zone Economic Commission, said Rau, was issuing these orders because it had become necessary to rescue the population from the "chaotic and dangerous conditions into which it had been systematically maneuvered by the policies of the present Berlin Magistrat." The commission would have entrusted the Magistrat with carrying out these orders, were it not that the Magistrat did not have the interests of the population at heart and was serving foreign masters instead. "You personally were responsible," Rau continued, "for finally destroying the unity of the Berlin police and thereby bringing about a situation in which the west sector police are protective troops for the black market." The Economic Commission would, therefore, continue to issue orders with respect to Berlin's food supply.

At this, Dr. Friedensburg lost his patience and replied acidly that living conditions in Berlin were actually superior to those in the east zone, as demonstrated by the east zone's own statistics. If the communists really had the public interest at heart, he concluded, they should support elections in Berlin rather than trying to block them.[70]

In spite of communist maneuvers, Füllsack continued to fight a stubborn rear-guard action in his campaign to hold on to the central food administration for Berlin. He opened an office in the British sector, where employees who had been locked out of the east sector building could resume their work, but he kept his own office in the old building. When Letsch and the Soviet liaison personnel continued to contest his authority and made his work all but impossible, he moved to a room in the city hall, still in the east sector. But the Soviet liaison officer followed him to the city hall and persisted in obstructing his activities there. On August 23 Füllsack bowed to the inevitable and officially established his headquarters in the British sector. Another department of the city government had been split.[71]

A third area of the city government over which the Soviets attempted to establish their authority was that of finance. They succeeded in causing serious dislocation not only in the whole city government but in private enterprise as well. On July 30 the Soviet Military Administration instructed the city's central bank, which had its headquarters in East Berlin, to block the accounts of the Magistrat and of all enterprises and organizations in the west sectors.[72] It offered no explanation for this action.[73] As a result, it was impossible at the end of the month to pay the wages of almost 750,000 west sector workers, including firemen, policemen, and transit workers. An American newspaperman called it the "greatest internal economic crisis" West Berlin had faced yet.[74] The London *Times* reported that the Magistrat was frankly anxious lest its activities as an independent administration be brought to a standstill for lack of funds.[75] On August 5, after several days of negotiation with the Magistrat, the Soviets agreed to unblock both private and public accounts. The following day, however, they went back on this agreement and announced that only a limited sum, for specific expenditures, would be available to the Magistrat, and that west sector firms and organizations could have their accounts unblocked only if they promised to carry on all future transactions in Soviet zone currency.[76]

As the economic life of the west sectors staggered under the impact of this blow, the Western powers moved to provide assistance. They offered, first, to meet the payrolls of all industry and commerce in West Berlin.[77] Second, they ordered the Berlin government to stop moving the holdings of west sector branch banks to the central bank, and also to establish a new city treasury in West Berlin.[78] As if to test these orders, the Soviet-controlled central bank shortly thereafter presented a check for over three million marks to its branch in the British sector, saying that the funds were required to pay employees in the Soviet sector. British Military Government refused to allow payment, however, pointing out that the Magistrat's accounts in the east sector were still blocked.[79]

The Soviet authorities made particularly inhumane use of the power of the purse toward the end of the month, when they blocked the accounts of the Berlin Insurance Company, a semipublic agency. This company, on which thousands of elderly or disabled pensioners relied for support, was located in the Soviet sector and had no bank accounts whatsoever in West Berlin. The Soviets agreed to unblock the accounts only if the Western powers made available a portion of the total funds required for pension payments.[80]

Although the Soviet authorities gradually unblocked most of the accounts in question, either partially or entirely, their control of the central bank continued to cause difficulties to the city government. Magistrat funds were released in installments, and only after repeated representations.[81]

Efforts to Undermine the Government as a Whole

Having forced a split in two departments of the city government and caused serious disorganization in others, the Soviets and German Communists moved against the government as a whole. Toward the end of August, just as a purported four-power agreement was being hammered out in Moscow, the communist campaign against the democratic majority in the Magistrat and Assembly was redoubled.

This new assault was preceded by extensive propaganda. A story in *Neues Deutschland* for August 14 was headed "CHAOS IN THE WEST SECTORS IMPERILS ALL BERLIN," and claimed that the "airlift policies" of the Magistrat had led to a new record of more than 100,000 unemployed in the west sectors. The following day, another headline in the same paper trumpeted: "NOT ONE MORE DAY IN OFFICE FOR THIS GOVERNMENT." On the 25th the official SED organ alleged that a "reactionary clique" of Social Democrats was preparing a *Putsch*, with the aim of declaring an emergency, suspending the constitution, and expelling the SED members from the Magistrat. The London *Times* commented that the process of undermining the authority and independence of the popularly-elected city government had already gone dangerously far and might yet go farther, and that it was not unusual for the Communists to accuse their opponent of contemplating the very action they themselves were preparing.[82]

The forebodings of the *Times* were well founded. Already on August 24, at 11 o'clock at night, Dr. Friedensburg had been summoned to the city hall, where a Soviet liaison officer handed him a communication from General Kotikov. In it, Kotikov bitterly assailed the Magistrat for causing "disorganization and division" in the Berlin police force by suspending Markgraf, and also declared all recent decisions of the Magistrat null and void, since they had not been confirmed by the Soviet occupation authorities. City officials who tried to carry out these illegal decisions would be guilty of disturbing public order and injuring the occupation regime.[83] Dr. Friedensburg responded by requesting that he be permitted to comment on this order to General Kotikov personally. The liaison officer said he would forward this request.

The Acting Mayor's comments, in the form of a letter, were couched in diplomatic language, but made it abundantly clear that he had no intention of recognizing the Soviet order. According to Article 26 of Berlin's provisional constitution, he pointed out, only Magistrat decisions of a general or fundamental character required the approval of the occupying powers. It was highly undesirable that regulations which were in force at the time that the four-power Berlin Kommandatura was meeting regularly should now be set aside. Whoever was serious about helping the people of Berlin should endeavor to widen, rather than limit, the power of the city authorities to act. As for Markgraf, Dr. Friedensburg added, he had been suspended only because he had systematically interfered with the constitutional functioning of the Berlin administration. "Disorganization and division" had arisen when the legal regulations of the Magistrat were prevented from coming into force in one sector. By restoring the legal order in the east sector, General Kotikov could end all appearances of division and disorganization in the ranks of the police.[84]

Colonel Howley backed up Dr. Friedensburg in a statement to the press.[85] "Decisions of the representatives who were elected by a majority of the Berlin population will remain in force in the American sector," he said, adding that General Kotikov had no more and no less authority in Berlin than the commandants of the west sectors. The British and French commandants likewise refused to recognize

Kotikov's authority to limit the power of the Magistrat in their sectors.

Next, the Soviets attempted to throttle the City Assembly. The regular eightieth meeting of this body had been scheduled for 2:00 P.M. on August 26. More than an hour before the meeting was to begin, crowds of SED supporters appeared in front of the city hall. As on June 23, they carried banners and placards, some of which urged: "PUT AN END TO THE BANKRUPT MAGISTRAT." Large numbers of demonstrators arrived in Soviet trucks; others marched up to the building in columns. By two o'clock several thousand people were in front of the city hall. A few hundred forced their way into the meeting chamber, where Assemblyman Geschke (SED) told them that the scheduled session would not take place. The chairman of the SED fraction then harangued the crowd, saying that the time for action had come. He also read them a motion he had intended to introduce in the Assembly, which demanded that a special committee, composed of nine assemblymen and nine "citizens," should take over the "chief functions" of the Magistrat. His proposal was obviously designed to shift the authority of the legal Magistrat to a body more sympathetic to the Communists.

While the crowd of demonstrators seethed outside the city hall, Dr. Friedensburg received in his office a ten-man communist delegation, including Berlin's SED Chairman, Karl Maron. After this meeting Maron addressed the crowd from a loudspeaker car outside, saying that his conversation with Dr. Friedensburg had convinced him that the Magistrat was "incapable of working and unwilling to work." "In the next few days," he went on, "decisive things must and will occur in Berlin." And he exhorted his audience to demand the resignation of the Magistrat even more loudly.

As the demonstrators began to disperse, Dr. Friedensburg held a press conference. He explained that the Assembly's Council of Elders had decided to call off the meeting because they feared a repetition of the riot scenes of June 23. An appeal for protection to the east sector police had remained unanswered. Dr. Friedensburg added, however, that the Magistrat was determined to continue its work in the city hall.[86]

According to the SED version, the crowd in front of the city hall on August 26 was composed of 50,000 workers,* who had gathered

* The *Tagesspiegel* (August 28) pointed out with some amusement that the size of the crowd in front of the city hall was reported by east sector newspapers variously as from 10,000 to 55,000: "And so we really need no further proof that

to protest the "sabotage policies" of the Magistrat, and to express their support of the SED program for a unified administration, a uniform food supply, and a single currency. In addition, a total of 250,000 more Berliners were said to have demonstrated against the Magistrat in various districts of the city.[87]

Both the Western powers and Berlin's democrats were quick to react to the demonstration. General Clay made headlines with the statement that no "action committees" would be permitted in Berlin's west sectors. He was supported by statements from official sources in both London and Washington condemning the SED tactics. And only a few hours after the city hall disturbances, 30,000 Berliners attended a protest meeting, sponsored by the three democratic political parties, on the square before the old Reichstag. Ernst Reuter told the crowd: "We Berliners have said 'no' to communism, and we will fight it with all our might as long as there is breath in us. . . . The Magistrat and the City Assembly, together with the freedom-loving Berlin population, will build a dam against which the red tide will beat in vain."[88]

Berlin's assemblymen once again proved a hardy breed. Although the SED demonstration had prevented them from meeting on the 26th, they scheduled another meeting for 10:00 A.M. the next day. In an effort to maintain order, employees of the Magistrat locked the doors of the city hall after the assemblymen had entered, but a crowd of about two thousand persons soon assembled, broke down the iron gate in front of the main door, and tried to force open the door itself. A Soviet liaison officer, who was inside, assisted the mob by demanding that the door be opened for him to go out. Magistrat personnel tried to persuade him to use the back door and, when he refused, told him that the front door key had been lost. He was not satisfied with this explanation, however, and eventually the door was opened. As the Soviet officer went out, a number of the demonstrators pushed their way in.

Meanwhile, an SED assemblyman and a number of east sector police had forced open the back door, and the demonstrators poured in with red banners and placards. Dr. Suhr, the iron-nerved Speaker, had just officially opened the eightieth regular meeting of the Assembly in the chamber. Recognizing that there was no means of preserving order, however, he adjourned it again five minutes later.[89]

---

our numbering system did not originate in Arabia, but in the 'home of all workers.' "

Dr. Suhr then sent a message to General Kotikov, asking whether the Soviet commandant could guarantee the safety of the Assembly members. At midnight on the 27th, two Soviet liaison officers handed him General Kotikov's written answer. "We do not understand clearly what the Assembly Speaker wishes from the Soviet authorities," wrote the General. Did Dr. Suhr want the occupation powers to forbid meetings and demonstrations by the people of Berlin who were opposed to the present policies of the Magistrat? And should this prohibition apply to all Berlin, to the Soviet sector, or only to the central *Bezirk* where the Magistrat building was located? Did Dr. Suhr want the Soviet authorities to interfere with the relations between the Magistrat and the Berlin workers who were not in agreement with the present policies of the Magistrat? Why didn't Dr. Suhr request protection from the German police in the borough where the city hall was located? From what areas of the city should Berlin workers be excluded when they wished to petition members of the City Assembly? "I would like to have answers to these questions as soon as possible," concluded the Soviet commandant, "so that I may take such measures as are within my competence and which reflect the customary democratic practice as it is known in democratic European states."[90]

Although the sarcastic tone of General Kotikov's reply was not encouraging, Dr. Suhr responded to it and again requested the Soviet commandant to provide protection. The east sector press thereupon reported that workers were coming directly from their workbenches to General Kotikov to let him know that they opposed Dr. Suhr's request, and to state also that they were not in favor of new elections in Berlin. When Dr. Suhr and the Assembly's Council of Elders announced that the Assembly would meet on September 3 in the city hall if General Kotikov would assure protection, the *Tagesspiegel* commented bitterly that the Soviet-owned firms in East Berlin still employed a sufficient number of "people's democrats" to see that no meeting would be held.[91]

While Dr. Suhr was vainly requesting General Kotikov to assure protection for the Assembly, the British member of the Western team of negotiators in Moscow, Frank Roberts, was also protesting the disorders in Berlin. On August 27 he called Molotov's attention to the disturbances in the German capital, and suggested that Marshal Sokolovsky be instructed to take measures to preserve a calm atmosphere for the coming deliberations of the military governors. Molotov replied gruffly that Marshal Sokolovsky already had his instructions, and declined to discuss the matter further.[92] There can be little doubt that Soviet policy-makers at the highest level were well aware of the mob scenes at the Berlin city hall, and that these scenes were indeed an integral part of Soviet policy.

Berliners Worry about a Possible Compromise

Soviet pressure on individual German officials, on departments of the city government, and on the government as a whole did not soften the determination of Berlin's leaders to resist the communist assault. Indeed, they seemed to become more defiant as time went on.

There was, however, serious concern about the resolution of the Western powers. If the democracies should abandon their position in Berlin, or even make any appreciable concessions, the Berlin democrats were convinced that they were doomed. Speaking at a mass meeting on July 25, a member of the City Assembly appealed to the Western powers under no circumstances to repeat their Munich policies. In struggles with a dictatorship, he said, democracies must be warlike, if they want to assure world peace and world freedom.[93] At a Party Day Rally of the Berlin SPD on July 31, Erich Ollenhauer expressed similar concern: "We place our entire confidence in the statesmen of the Western powers and trust that they will not enter into four-power negotiations under pressure of the blockade."[94] A few days later, Ernst Reuter warned the Allies against a "rotten compromise," which would vitiate the firm resistance of the Berliners.[95] Similar worried comments could be heard all the time the Moscow negotiations were in progress.

As was pointed out earlier, the fears of the democratic leaders were not wholly imaginary. Among themselves and within themselves the Western powers were divided, and rumors of division reached Berlin. There was always the danger that the forces favoring compromise might gain the upper hand. Furthermore, the reluctance of the Western powers to introduce the west mark as the sole medium of exchange was taken by some German leaders as an indication that such a compromise was in the offing. The very fact that the west marks in Berlin were stamped with a "B" led Berliners to suspect that the Western powers were differentiating the Berlin marks from the West German currency in order to make them easier to withdraw. Colonel Howley remarked in his memoirs that city finances were in a desperate state, but that the Western powers hesitated to take any positive steps to correct the fiscal situation.[96]

Other disturbing rumors concerned evacuation plans. As late as September 7, the Secretary of the Army in Washington said that plans had been drawn up to evacuate actively pro-Western Germans from Berlin in order of priority after the U.S. dependents. He also reported plans for protective measures which would, if possible, be nonprovocative.[97] Measures designed to be nonprovocative often looked like appeasement to the Berliners.

Announcement of the Moscow agreement, on August 31, was greeted with enthusiasm in the German communist press. The West Berlin press was restrained in its response; it clearly viewed with alarm the prospect that west marks were to be withdrawn from circulation. The *Tagesspiegel* expressed editorial concern about the results of a compromise on the currency question, and SPD Chairman Franz Neumann told a mass meeting that, if the Western powers at Moscow had really agreed to the introduction of the east mark, Berliners would regard this as a station on the road to capitulation.[98]

Technical Discussions in Berlin

Under the Moscow agreement, the four military governors in Berlin were to make the necessary technical arrangements for introducing the east mark and removing traffic restrictions, and were to report back to their governments not later than September 7. Accordingly, the four commanders met on August 31 to consider ways of carrying out this directive.

Prospects of agreement on the necessary technical arrangements did not look favorable. For one thing, the communist campaign against the city government and the disturbances at the city hall did not provide an atmosphere conducive to agreement. The disturbances were revived on September 3, and continued until the conclusion of the discussions. It looked as if the Soviets wished to confront the Western military governors with a *fait accompli.*

Secondly, the attitude of the Western military authorities in Berlin was becoming increasingly firm. The view that the airlift could supply the city through the winter, while not yet universal, had gained the upper hand during August. Also the stout resistance of the German leaders and the Berlin populace had made more and more Western officials feel that any compromise would amount to betrayal. Some U.S. Military Government officials were horrified at the written directive from Moscow, which failed to include Stalin's verbal assurances about four-power control of currency, and whose vague wording allowed for an interpretation that would give the Soviets almost complete power over the city. As a junior member of American Military Government said later, "We lost our diplomatic shirt in Moscow." One of General Clay's senior advisers burst out: "Agreement, agreement! Those fellows would do anything to get an agreement." As these statements indicate, the attitude of American officials in Berlin was by then significantly stronger than the attitude in Washington.

Almost as soon as the four military governors met, it became clear that the Soviets had no intention of honoring either the spirit or the letter of the agreement. Indeed, the interpretation placed upon it by Marshal Sokolovsky was so extreme as to antagonize even those French and British delegates who were willing to make very appreciable concessions in order to achieve an end to the blockade.

Briefly, the negotiations broke down on three points: The Soviets rejected the idea that a four-power finance committee should have supervisory power over the issue of east marks by the German Bank of Emission; they insisted on exercising complete control of trade with Berlin; and they demanded restrictions on civil air traffic between West Germany and Berlin. As the discussions wore on, Marshal Sokolovsky showed himself increasingly indifferent to their progress or failure. At the end of the week allotted for negotiation, the military governors had reached no agreement and were unable to submit a report. Marshal Sokolovsky remarked that there was nothing to report.[99] According to "most of the Western Allied experts, including the French," the Soviet proposals would have put the Allies in the status of being in Berlin on Soviet sufferance.[100]

In Washington, news of the failure of discussions was received with gloom. Under Secretary of State Lovett told Forrestal that the "sheer duplicity" of the Soviets in these negotiations was beyond the experience of State Department experts. His only explanation for their extraordinary behavior was that they did not want an agreement. The following day, Lovett reported to the National Security Council that General Sokolovsky had flagrantly ignored the clear directive agreed to in Moscow, and that the situation had been further complicated by Soviet-inspired riots and local troubles.[101] The *New York Times* reported that the political situation in Berlin had been deteriorating so fast under Soviet pressure that many suspected the talks of being no more than a false scent by which to distract the Western powers from the real Soviet objective, the subjugation of Berlin.[102]

The City Assembly Is Forced from the East Sector

While the four military governors were conducting their fruitless talks, communist efforts to gain control of the city government continued. When General Kotikov failed to assure order at the city hall, the Assembly meeting scheduled for September 3 was postponed. Representatives of the SED took advantage of the postponement to meet in the Assembly chamber with individuals purporting to represent the LDP, CDU, and SPD, most of whom, however, were not recognized members of those parties. Under the leadership of the SED, this group formed a "Berlin Democratic Bloc," and delegated four representatives of this bloc to negotiate with the Magistrat.[103] Thus, the nucleus of a communist-dominated city government had been formed, even though it had no legal status whatsoever.

Dr. Suhr and the Council of Elders decided to make still another attempt to meet in the official chamber on September 6. This time the Magistrat deputized some forty volunteers from the West Berlin police force to preserve order in the city hall during the meeting. Their protection proved pitifully inadequate. An hour before the meeting was to begin, demonstrators forced their way into the city hall and occupied the Assembly chamber. Several reporters representing West Berlin newspapers were physically assaulted. The microphone was snatched away from two RIAS reporters, who were also beaten up, as east sector police calmly looked on. The Assembly never had an opportunity even to start its business. Most assemblymen quickly sized up the situation and left.

Communist leaders then took advantage of the fact that they had the Assembly chamber to themselves. At about 2:00 o'clock, Second Deputy Speaker Geschke (SED) called to order an "Assembly meeting" that consisted only of members of the SED and procommunist groups. This rump Assembly quickly voted to put into effect the SED "winter emergency program," and an hour later the demonstrators began to leave the city hall.

By this time, the exits were guarded by east sector police, who examined the identity cards of those going out. Communists were allowed to leave, but others, including two reporters from the British-licensed *Welt* and two from the *Tagesspiegel,* were arrested. The Magistrat's volunteers, who had been detailed to the city hall to maintain order, were a special target of the communist police. Many of them were seized and hustled off to Markgraf's police headquarters. Some, who had attempted to take refuge in the office of the

American liaison officer, were seized at gunpoint by Soviet military police and dragged off in handcuffs. Others had found shelter in the French and British liaison offices.* After these unfortunate men had been confined in their temporary refuge for almost two days, French General Ganeval secured a verbal promise from General Kotikov that they could leave the city hall unmolested. When they filed out of the building, however, they were arrested by Soviet troops and turned over to the east sector police.[104]

At this, Western occupation authorities became infuriated. General Ganeval dispatched a strong letter to General Kotikov, and Colonel Howley added his protest. Soviet authorities tried to justify their actions by asserting that Allied liaison officers had been drunk. The French replied that the strong smell of alcohol in the city hall came from the Soviet offices. General Ganeval's letter stated bitterly: "I can still not yet believe that your personal guarantee should have been broken in such a flagrant way. You have said that my liaison officers were drunk and that this constituted a danger for a building situated in the Soviet sector. You are perfectly aware that this is not true. . . ."[105]

An American observer who witnessed the tumultuous events at the city hall on September 6 reported that they were directed in detail by the Soviets. When the mob occupied the Assembly chamber, a Soviet liaison officer in uniform sat among the demonstrators. Later in the day, he changed into civilian clothes, and could be seen conferring with SED leaders about what to do with the democratic police volunteers. When the mob left the city hall he was again in uniform.

The Communists, of course, interpreted the events at the city hall quite differently: The demonstrators were represented as simple workingmen, who wanted to urge the Assembly to act on the "winter emergency program" of the SED, after the other parties had stubbornly refused to take any measures to relieve the plight of the poor workers. The "Democratic Bloc" had moved to implement this

* In this connection, a former city official recalled that he had been impressed with the speed with which British officials sometimes were able to obtain policy guidance. When Magistrat authorities approached the British liaison officer and asked him to try and protect a number of the men in his office, the officer said he would have to check with higher authority, and called General Robertson. General Robertson, to be certain of his ground, called Foreign Minister Bevin in London. Bevin immediately approved the move, and the liaison officer had his answer within fifteen minutes of the time that Dr. Friedensburg's office had approached him.

program, arranging, as a first step, for support payments to 300,000 pensioners in Berlin and thereby rescuing them from the dire situation into which the neglect of the Magistrat had plunged them. The reason for the antisocial attitude of the noncommunist parties was said to be their desire to split Germany and bring about a *fait accompli* before the four-power Moscow talks could be brought to a successful conclusion.[106]

A later Soviet account, resorting to the lie direct, denied that there had been any disorders in the east sector at all. In a note to the United States Government, dated October 3, 1948, the Soviet Government stated:

> The note of the Governments of the three Powers contains the unsupported assertion that the Soviet authorities in Berlin permitted an attempt on the part of a minority of the population of Berlin to forcibly overthrow the city administration. The fact is that, notwithstanding the dissatisfaction among the Berlin population with the present situation, the Soviet authorities in Berlin have had strict instructions from the Soviet Government to insure a calm atmosphere for the work of the Berlin local bodies, which was confirmed by V. M. Molotov at the meeting of the representatives of the three Governments on August 30. The Soviet Command has unswervingly observed these instructions of the Soviet Government, but the disorders which have disturbed the life of Berlin took place in the part of Berlin which is not under the control of the Soviet Command and for which the military authorities of the three other Powers are responsible.[107]

The allegation of disorders in West Berlin probably referred to the Reichstag mass meeting of September 9, which will be described below.

The Reichstag Mass Meeting—September 9

Berliners had watched the scenes at the city hall between August 26 and September 6 with a mounting sense of indignation. Continued kidnapings and confiscations of west marks by Soviet and German east sector authorities did nothing to allay their ire. West Berlin's democratic leaders decided to hold another protest meeting.

Mass meetings had been an almost daily feature in West Berlin for over two months. Many of them had been held in the square before the burned-out Reichstag building. Yet when Berliners today speak of "the Reichstag meeting"—and they frequently do—they are referring to the gathering that took place on September 9.

This, the mightiest mass meeting of the blockade period, almost did not take place at all. Plans for the rally were announced by the democratic parties and trade unions on September 7. But on the following morning, British Military Government sent word that it considered the Reichstag square too close to the British-Soviet sector line for safety. To have called off the meeting at that point, however, would have been a serious blow to the morale of Berlin's democrats, and the British were finally persuaded not to oppose the plans. Nevertheless, until almost the last minute, the Soviet-controlled radio blared forth the news that the meeting had been forbidden.

The German leaders who were planning the affair were well aware that they themselves might be visited with retribution from the Soviets if they went ahead with their plans. They knew that they could not count on full support from the Western powers in the event of Soviet counteraction. Legend has it that Ernst Reuter and Franz Neumann were discussing who should make the principal address. Neumann thought that it should be Reuter, as the elected—even if unseated—mayor of the city. "Oh, no, Franz," Reuter is said to have replied. "It would be better if you did it. You look much more like a democratic martyr."

In spite of the ambivalence of Western military governments, and of their own awareness of the risks involved, West Berlin's leaders did their best to attract a large audience. The independent trade unions recommended that work stop at 2:00 P.M. on the 9th in order to give people plenty of time to assemble at the Reichstag; they also arranged for the city's transportation system to continue operations after 6 P.M. to take the crowds home. The RIAS radio station carried spot announcements for more than twenty-four hours before the meeting, urging Berliners from both east and west to attend, and telling them the best travel routes.* Special appeals went to women and young people, and instructions on how to avoid trouble with the east sector police, what to do with the baby, and to be sure that the gas was turned off. By five o'clock some 250,000 people were jammed into the square in front of the Reichstag.[108]

Franz Neumann opened the meeting with an appeal for a minute of silence in memory of those who, from 1933 to 1938, had been

* On the following day, RIAS received a worried inquiry from a high official of the Army Department, asking whether it was correct that RIAS had carried "provocative" appeals for attendance.

the victims of totalitarian methods. "These people gave their lives for freedom," cried Neumann. "The concentration camps are still the same, but now the hammer and sickle waves over them instead of the swastika." But Berlin will fight on, he continued, and in this fight we need the help of all countries. "Berlin calls the world."

Ernst Reuter recalled communist outrages of the past few days and exhorted the Western powers not to compromise with the Russians. Berlin cannot become an object of barter in Allied negotiations, he said. He also warned that the appetite of the Russian bear would not be satisfied by Berlin; it would try and swallow West Germany and other areas as well. Whoever would sacrifice this city and its people would be sacrificing himself and the free world. Indignantly, Reuter referred to the fate of the west sector police who had been arrested at the city hall in spite of Soviet promises: "Before the cock crowed three times, the Russian General Kotikov had broken his word of honor." Reuter went on to castigate the SED for its part in the outrage. The SED needs a new symbol to replace that of the clasped hands which it now uses, he said. More appropriate would be a pair of handcuffs—the handcuffs which Germans wore when they were dragged out of the city hall. They would be a fitting symbol for those who "for thirty pieces of silver will sell themselves and their country to a foreign power."

Speakers from the other democratic parties and the independent unions followed. By the time the meeting was over, the crowd was in a ferment. Several thousand persons surged over to the headquarters of the defunct four-power Control Council, where Franz Neumann presented a memorandum to American and British officers detailing Russian excesses in Berlin since 1946.* Others milled around the Brandenburg Gate—the boundary between the British and Soviet sectors—and a young man climbed to the top of this huge stone structure and tore down the Soviet flag. As several members of the crowd started to burn the flag, a number of Russian soldiers rushed up to try and recover it. They fired into the crowd, killing one person and injuring others. A carload of other Russian soldiers appeared and was showered with stones. Vehicles belonging to the east sector police were overturned and some policemen assaulted. Only the presence of mind of a number of British officers and men, who were able to separate the Russians from the crowd, prevented the incident from becoming even more serious. Both sides

* This document is referred to below as the "September 9 Memorandum."

retired, bearing with them their wounded and dead. The east sector police also took a number of prisoners.

The communist version of what went on at the Reichstag was very different. Under the heading "ONCE AGAIN REICHSTAG ARSONISTS," *Neues Deutschland* excoriated those who spoke at the mass meeting:

> Yesterday, in front of the Reichstag ruins, those who are trying to divide Berlin dropped their masks completely. *What they want is a new war.* These criminal fools are now trying belatedly to win Adolf Hitler's war against the Soviet Union, and want to enslave our people under the fascist yoke again. Those who made the principal speeches are fascists, even if they designate themselves as belonging to the CDU, LDP or SPD. At no time since the unconditional surrender of Hitler fascism have such rabble-rousing speeches favoring revenge been made as were heard yesterday. We had already become accustomed to some of this. But now, in their fear of agreement between the Allies, these people scream even louder and involuntarily have let everyone both here and abroad know that *there are again Nazis and open war mongers in Berlin.*[109]

Although this description was neatly turned on its head, *Neues Deutschland* was correct in saying that the democratic forces in Berlin were aroused. Resistance morale in Berlin had matured. West Berliners were ready to face a blockade winter.

The Meaning of Soviet Behavior

Those who, during this period, speculated about the reasons for the Soviets' behavior frequently despaired of arriving at any sensible interpretation. Under Secretary Lovett epitomized a widespread attitude toward the Soviets when he said that it was difficult to deal with someone "whose head is full of bubbles."[110]

There was, however, general agreement on one point: the Soviets were in no hurry to lift the blockade. As General Clay saw it, the airlift had not yet proved itself at the time of the discussions among the four military governors in Berlin, and the Russians remained confident that it would be physically impossible for the Western Allies to maintain their position in Berlin.[111] Secretary Marshall told the National Security Council, on September 9, that time was on the side of the Soviets.[112] Ambassador Smith attributed some of the delays in the Moscow negotiations to the Soviet desire to gain time so that the blockade could do its worst. A similar conclusion was ascribed by a press report to "trained observers" in Paris.[113] The "trained observers" agreed that Premier Stalin had in the blockade a trump card higher than any the Western powers could play at that time, that he could link this advantage to many subjects, and that, consequently, he was in no hurry to abandon it.

With the benefit of hindsight, it is possible to speculate further about the policy which lay behind Soviet behavior during this period. Our original assumption was that the blockade was designed to make the Western powers choose between giving up their plans in West Germany and giving up Berlin. If this was indeed the position of the Soviets, there was no reason for them to abandon it prior to the time of the Moscow conferences, and they do not appear to have done so. Stalin immediately brought up the question of the West German government when the Western representatives talked with him on August 2. When they refused to make concessions, he allowed them to spend the next few weeks in fruitless negotiations. He may have thought that domestic war fears, the blockade, and the mounting pressure on the Berlin population and administration would soon force their governments to give them new instructions. He again brought up the question of West Germany on August 23, when he asked that a reference to amicable discussions on the subject be included in the communiqué. This may have been only an opening wedge. If the Western powers had agreed to this damaging but still relatively modest request, it is possible that further concessions would have been demanded before the blockade was lifted.

The task of the Soviet negotiators was a highly delicate one, and they performed it with great skill. Their proposal about Berlin had to be attractive enough to tempt the Allies to make concessions in West Germany, but at the same time ambiguous enough so that, if the Allies *refused* to make such concessions, they would no longer be able to retain their position in Berlin. Hence, probably, the device of having Stalin give verbal assurances about four-power control of Berlin currency and other matters: If the Western powers "saw the light," these assurances could be put into writing and possibly even implemented. If not, they could be reversed.

When it became clear that the Western powers would not alter their policies in West Germany, the Soviets concentrated on their second objective, which was to obtain control of all Berlin. Molotov turned his attentions to framing the written Moscow agreement in such a manner as to allow for an interpretation that would reduce the authority of the Western powers in Berlin to almost nothing.

Stalin's verbal assurances were omitted, and Smith reports that Molotov wrangled over each word in drafting the directive to the four military governors.[114] Furthermore, by attempting to undermine the authority of the elected Berlin government, the Soviets tried to demonstrate that they wielded final authority in Berlin, and that the democracies would be wise to accept the best agreement they could obtain. On August 27—the same day that apparent agreement on a directive was reached in Moscow—the Communists renewed their large-scale violence against the Berlin Magistrat and City Assembly, and kept it up throughout the talks of the four military governors. At these negotiations Marshal Sokolovsky may have been trying to indicate to the Western powers that they now had a much more limited choice: to stay in Berlin on sufferance, or to withdraw entirely.

This interpretation of Soviet behavior during July and August leaves a number of questions that cannot be answered satisfactorily. One such riddle is the Soviet food offer to the inhabitants of West Berlin. When the blockade was first imposed, many observers assumed that the Soviet strategy was to induce hunger riots in West Berlin and thus force the Allies to withdraw. Yet the food offer was incompatible with the hunger strategy. It was clear that the Soviets gained advantages from the food offer: it provided an answer to charges of inhumanity, it made the airlift "unnecessary," it was designed to bring a large segment of the West Berlin population partly under Soviet administrative control, and it was intended to place one of the most important departments of the Berlin city government under East German authority. It would appear that, when Berlin failed to fall during the first few days of the blockade, the Soviet high command shifted from a strategy of threatening hunger to a strategy of gaining control of the city primarily by taking over its administrative machinery.

If the food offer did in fact represent a change in Soviet policy, was this change brought about by any action of the Western powers? Could the sending of B-29's to England have had anything to do with the abandonment of the hunger strategy? (Announcement that the bombers would leave was made on July 15, and the food offer was decided on by the Soviet Council of Ministers on the 17th.)

Another question is why Kotikov broke his word to General Ganeval so flagrantly. Was he overruled by higher authority, or was the Soviet action in arresting the Magistrat volunteers part of a plan to provoke the Western powers to counteraction? There were those who believed that the Soviets were trying to goad the other powers into sending military police to protect the city hall in the Soviet sector, so that the Soviets might have a precedent for sending their own forces into West Berlin to subdue alleged disturbances there.

In spite of these and other unanswered questions, the main stream of Soviet policy during the period appears to be fairly clear. Having failed to persuade the Western powers to alter their decisions concerning West Germany, the Soviets were proceeding to consolidate their power in East Germany and, if possible, to incorporate Berlin into this area.

Some Western Miscalculations

With the benefit of hindsight it is possible to suggest a number of criticisms of Western policy during July and August.

Above all, it is clear that the Western powers greatly underrated the potentialities of the airlift. Consequently, they believed themselves under greater pressure to come to terms with the Soviets than they in fact were. While estimates of the tonnage that could be lifted into Berlin increased during the period under consideration, they were still considerably below the level it later proved possible to achieve. Because they did not know the capabilities of the weapon at their disposal, the Western diplomats were inclined to settle for a poorer bargain than was necessary.

Second, the Western powers tended to underestimate the full significance of popular morale in Berlin, and it is doubtful whether they realized the extent to which the Moscow agreement could have undermined the support which the Berlin population had given Western policy. That the agreement did so little morale damage was due in part to the fact that its full significance was at first withheld from most Berliners by both German and Western opinion leaders; in part to the communist-led riots, which distracted attention from the Moscow compromise; in part to the resolute attitude maintained by General Clay and Colonel Howley; and, most of all, to the fact that the discussions among the four military governors broke down so quickly.

A possible third criticism of Western policy is that the decision to negotiate with the Soviets was allowed to inhibit positive moves in Berlin. The currency question was maintained in a state of suspended animation, and the Kommandatura was allowed to languish. While the Soviets strove to create a *fait accompli* during negotiations, the Western powers attempted to show their good faith by conducting affairs in Berlin as if they were sure that a compromise solution would be found. Under the circumstances, this procedure would appear to have been unrealistic. For only one side to suspend aggressive action during negotiations may well result in a serious reduction of its bargaining power. That the bargaining power of the West did not deteriorate, but rather increased, was due in part to the temper of the Berlin population and to its able leadership, but even more to the unexpected achievements of the airlift.

Fourth, the West, particularly the United States, seems frequently to have misinterpreted Soviet signals. American newsmen, and also those professionally concerned with the conduct of U.S. foreign policy, tended to greet each affable expression or minor concession by the Soviets as an indication of a basic change in Soviet foreign policy, without asking whether this affability might have some other meaning. This tendency precluded a full and sober assessment of what the Soviets were really trying to accomplish, and it also inhibited any long-term measures by which to offset communist pressure. Again, most newsmen and diplomats interpreted the Soviet use of violence against the Berlin Magistrat during the Moscow and Berlin negotiations as designed to break up negotiations. It would be more reasonable to assume that these attacks were a parallel instrument, used in conjunction with the negotiations, and designed to help achieve the same basic goals.

Finally, there seemed to be a tendency among the Western powers to value agreement for its own sake. It was generally recognized, at least by U.S. policy-makers, that the Moscow agreement was not a very good one, although most experts also conceded that it was probably the best agreement that could have been obtained at the time. True, neither side was irrevocably bound, and there were certain safeguards to the arrangement, such as the fact that its implementation depended on the ability of the four military governors to work out technical details. As it turned out, however, the Western powers would have been in a stronger position if they had left Moscow with no agreement at all instead of an unsatisfactory one. For the documents signed in August returned to plague them in October, November, and December.

CHAPTER V

SEPTEMBER–JANUARY: DIVIDING A CITY

NEITHER side could have been very satisfied with the outcome of the Moscow discussions and the discussions that followed them in Berlin. Western statesmen who had thought that a solution to the crisis was in sight saw the apparent agreement dissolve into a mass of conflicting interpretations. The Soviets, who had offered the Western powers a face-saving way of abandoning their power in Berlin, found that the democracies were still insistent on defending their position.

Under these circumstances, each side returned to the course on which it had embarked prior to the Moscow discussions. The Soviets, having apparently concluded that pressure on Berlin would not be sufficient to obstruct the formation of a West German government, concentrated on consolidating their power in East Germany and East Berlin. They also probably expected still to obtain substantial control of West Berlin, and to this end they clamped the blockade on the three west sectors all the more tightly and invited the Western powers again and again to return to the conference table and make the necessary concessions.

For their part, the Western powers continued to expand the airlift and also to explore every diplomatic avenue that might lead to a solution of the crisis. In October a Combined Airlift Task Force was formed to synchronize the activities of both the British and American elements of the airlift, which hitherto had operated independently. The new headquarters was commanded by Major General William H. Tunner (USAF), with Air Commodore J. W. F. Merer (RAF) as deputy. General Tunner placed increased emphasis on utilizing to the fullest all available capacity and on maintaining a steady, even rhythm, day and night. The constantly rising tonnage of goods flown into Berlin gradually began to inspire Western diplomatic personnel with confidence that the airlift could be more than a stop-gap measure.

Soviet tactics during this period confronted Berlin's democratic leaders with administrative problems of increasing complexity. The authority of the legal Magistrat was more and more curtailed, and at the end of November a separate puppet government was established in the east sector. The Magistrat therefore had no alternative but to move its headquarters from East to West Berlin. There was no question which of the two city governments was supported by the populace. When elections were held in December approximately 85 per cent of the electorate in the west sectors voted for one of the three democratic parties. Indeed, by the time winter arrived the resistance of West Berliners had become so firmly established that the deprivations caused by the blockade proved unable to shake it.

Some of Berlin's leaders, particularly from the ranks of the SPD, were worried by Allied tactics as well as by those of the Soviets. They continued to fear that the diplomatic negotiations, which were occurring half-publicly at a high level during most of this period, might yet lead to a compromise solution that would give the Soviets effective control of the whole city. They therefore pressed the Western powers to abandon the fiction that Berlin could be treated as a unit, and to recognize that the Soviets would agree to reunification of the city only on their own terms. Consequently, they urged that West Berlin be reorganized under three-power control, and that the Allies clearly assume the responsibility of defending it as a part of the Western world.

The Blockade is Tightened

There were some fairly large holes in the blockade during the first few months of its existence. Currency reform stimulated West German farmers to increase their yield to a point where they were interested in trying to retain Berlin as a market. Enterprising truckers managed to evade Soviet controls and spirit produce from West Germany to West Berlin, where it could command slightly higher prices. During the summer there were some days when fresh vegetables smuggled in from the west zones were available at such reasonable prices that the Magistrat was hard pressed to dispose of those marketed through the usual channels.[1]

In addition, throughout the summer West Berliners were able to obtain a limited quantity of food and other supplies from the Soviet zone. Trucks drove out daily into the surrounding countryside and came back with vegetables. Individuals returned by boat, train, subway, or bicycle with wood, coal briquettes, potatoes, and sundries.[2]

In the fall of 1948 the Soviets moved to seal these holes. During October and November new blockade restrictions were announced in the press almost daily. On October 16 German travelers were officially forbidden to bring food and supplies from the surrounding countryside into the west sectors.[3] A few days later, this prohibition was extended to certain raw materials, which West Berlin manufacturers had been able to procure from the Soviet zone.[4] More and more Soviet and East German border guards were brought up to enforce these orders. Controls were extended to the subway lines running between East and West Berlin. By November 10, at least seventy-five control points on the border between the Soviet sector and the three west sectors had been reported. The communist police at these check points not only confiscated food and other goods, but sometimes extended their searches to pocketbooks and wallets and confiscated west marks. They also took the names of "suspicious persons" who carried West Berlin newspapers.[5] During the last two weeks in October, 286 vehicles going to or from West Berlin were said to have been confiscated by the Soviets.[6] The U.S. Military Governor noted that these confiscations and searches further increased the population's antipathy toward the Soviet sector police, and in several cases led to spontaneous attacks on the inspectors.[7]

At the end of October there came a brief, but amusing, break in the blockade. East sector police were withdrawn for a few hours from a railroad station which was usually kept under close supervision, and a train from the west was allowed to arrive without being subjected to the customary controls. Police told an inquiring newspaperman that the reason for this unusual situation was the expected arrival of an international charitable commission, which was to inspect conditions in Berlin.[8] Apparently, other controls also were relaxed on that day. One of the *Abend* essayists recalled that he had learned about this through an "indiscretion" in East Berlin, and had taken advantage of the opportunity to spirit in approximately fifteen tons of supplies from outlying farms. He had placed these at the disposal of his firm, which was thus able to distribute about twenty pounds of potatoes and fresh vegetables to each employee. He concluded: "Since at that time almost nothing but dehydrated potatoes were available, and very few fresh vegetables, jubilation at this break in the blockade was great."

Even after November, a trickle of supplies came into West Berlin by land. The Swedish Red Cross had, since 1947, provided supplementary meals during the winter for approximately 20,000 undernourished children in all four sectors. Food for this program was brought in from Sweden by rail and water. In December, however, the Soviets prohibited the Swedes from transporting any of their supplies into the west sectors, and the program was terminated shortly thereafter. The International Red Cross likewise operated a special feeding project in Berlin. With Soviet permission, food was brought into the city by rail and was used to supply supplementary rations to old and needy persons in Greater Berlin. Ultimately, the Russians ordered that none of these supplies were to go to the west sectors, and the project had to be abandoned in January.[9] Thereafter, the west sectors were almost completely dependent on the airlift and on the supplies produced within their own borders.

Soviet efforts to interfere with Allied air traffic between Berlin and West Germany were intensified during September, October, and November. As before, airlift pilots were subjected to such recurrent annoyances as "buzzing" by Soviet aircraft, bombing or air gunnery practice in or near the corridors, antiaircraft practice, and other types of military exercises, which had the effect of making their backbreaking job even more difficult.[10] Periodically, the Soviets would protest alleged violations of the corridors and of air-safety rules,[11] adding that any aircraft flying outside the corridors and any unmarked aircraft, whether in the corridors or not, would be forced down by Soviet fighters.[12] But British and American authorities simply ignored these Soviet threats and protests, and there is no indication that the airlift was appreciably slowed down.

It should be noted that the Soviets, in order to bring about a critical situation in the west sectors, did not need to stop the airlift altogether. Had they been able to curtail its performance by as little as 10 or 15 per cent, it is likely that essential services and the minimum rations in West Berlin could not have been maintained throughout the winter.

The Soviet government went through violent casuistic contortions in order to find a legal basis for restricting traffic through the air corridors. A communication from Soviet officials to U.S. Air Force representatives in the Berlin Air Safety Center on September 10 alleged that the corridors had been established "by the Soviet command" and not by four-power agreement.[13] Apparently, the Soviets decided that this position was too extreme, however, for they did not refer to it again. On September 18 Molotov handed the Western envoys in Moscow a note which tried to justify Marshal Sokolovsky's attempts to impose restrictions on air traffic at the Berlin negotiations earlier in the month. The note stated that the Soviet Military Governor was merely pointing "to the necessity of the other three Military Governors complying strictly with the regulations imposed by the Control Council's decision of November 30, 1945 on air traffic for the needs of the occupation forces. . . ."[14] Frank Roberts, the British representative, immediately told Molotov that traffic in the corridors had never been limited to supplying the needs of the occupation forces, and that all the occupying powers were free to use the corridors, subject only to the agreed safety regulations.[15]

In another note, delivered in Washington, London, and Paris only a week later, the Soviets used an entirely new process of reasoning to justify restrictions on air traffic: they argued that it was necessary that the air routes should be controlled because the Moscow agreement of August 30 had specified that Berlin's currency and trade would be subject to regulation.[16]

Finally, toward the end of October the Soviets began to deny that there was any agreement on air-safety regulations at all. According to oral and written statements by various Soviet military officials, the air-safety regulations had never been ratified by either the Allied Control Council or its Coordinating Committee and, therefore, were without force. While these facts were substantially correct, the conclusion was erroneous; as Allied spokesmen pointed out, the Control Council in 1945 had delegated to the four-power Air Directorate the power to make safety regulations, and the Directorate had promulgated these on its own authority. At a press conference, General Robertson wondered why, if the regulations were not valid, the Soviets had for months been accusing U.S. and British flyers of having broken them.[17] None of the questions raised by the Soviets about the legal basis of the air corridors or the four-power safety regulations was accepted by the Western powers as having any substance.

In short, while the Soviets sealed off the land routes to West Berlin fairly effectively, they were never able to restrict the airlift itself to any appreciable extent. It is also noteworthy that they never attempted to interfere with the airlift by such direct measures as might have led the Western powers to reply with force. For instance, it would have been technically feasible for the Soviets to jam radio communications in the air corridors, to interfere with the operation of radarscopes, to raise barrage balloons at strategic points, or to take other measures that would have made bad-weather flying highly dangerous or impossible. By doing none of these things, they indicated that they did not want the Berlin crisis to explode into armed conflict.

Consolidation of Communist Control in East Germany

Plans for the formation of an East German state had apparently been prepared before the blockade, and were ready to be put into effect if the Western powers refused to make concessions in West Germany. The resistance of the Western powers and of the embattled Berliners had made it impossible for the Soviets to include all Berlin in these plans, but Moscow nevertheless went ahead with the consolidation of East Germany, although probably more slowly than originally contemplated. According to one leading student of East Germany, provisional appointments to ministerial posts apparently were made during the summer of 1948, and the unofficial People's Council was quietly told to be ready to perform the role of an East German legislature.[18] In addition, the SED two-year plan for East Germany was announced almost simultaneously with the start of the blockade.[19] Efforts to implement this program proceeded from July on, although apparently without notable success.[20]

The next major step was the adoption of a draft constitution for a "German People's Republic" by the communist-dominated People's Council. This move was announced on August 3, just as Soviet and Western representatives were meeting in Moscow, and was believed by some observers to be intended to strengthen the Soviet hand in these negotiations. The constitution was put forward in a context which made it clear that it could apply either to Germany as a whole or to the Soviet zone alone.[21]

During September and October reports about the formation of an east zone government, and in particular about the establishment of armed forces in the east zone, became even more frequent. "Well informed sources" had it that plans for setting up the new government were going ahead rapidly, that Leipzig would be the provisional capital of the new German state, and that the ministries of the new government would be made up of elements from the German Economic Commission, which already was functioning as a provisional government.[22] "Reliable Western intelligence sources" relayed the information that the Soviets and German Communists were organizing a police force of approximately 400,000 in the Soviet zone.[23] Further reports that the Soviets were preparing to transfer control of the east zone to communist officials backed by a police army were received almost daily from East German refugees during October.[24] In the Berlin City Assembly at the end of October, LDP Chairman Karl Hubert Schwennicke denounced the new police force as an organization which, "if one is to judge by its activities of the last few days, does not deserve the name 'People's Police', but is scarcely to be distinguished from the Nazi Elite Guard (SS) of the years 1933-1945."[25]

In the effort to consolidate communist controls in East Germany, anti-Communists or non-Communists were removed from public office, the SED was purged of "unreliable" elements, political forces antagonistic to communism were suppressed, and supervision over the east zone LDP and CDU was tightened.[26] These measures set off an unprecedented wave of refugees to West Berlin and West Germany. During the first weeks of October at least fifty persons a day fled to West Berlin alone.[27] This number may appear modest when compared with the very much larger wave that came several years later, but it must be remembered that in the fall of 1948 Berliners were suffering real privation. Indeed, according to the east zone press, West Berlin was nearing starvation and could have looked attractive as a political haven only to those who were very strongly motivated to flee. The refugees included a number of former Social Democrats who had previously accepted merger with the SED, as well as administrative officials from government and industry and young people who were fleeing forced labor in the uranium mines.[28]

Toward the end of November there were new rumors about an East German government, but this time with Berlin as the probable capital.[29] Whether or not reports such as these constituted accurate indications of Soviet plans, consolidation of communist power in East Germany clearly was moving ahead rapidly in the economic, military, and political spheres.

Communist Consolidation in East Berlin, and the Reaction in West Berlin

In the Soviet zone, consolidation of communist power created no major administrative problems, since the Soviet Union already exercised complete control in that area. In East Berlin, on the other hand, the Soviets were in the difficult position of occupying an area that they could not fully control. The democratic parties and other noncommunist groups were able to conduct political activities in the east sector, although under increasingly severe restrictions. Newspapers published in West Berlin, and many other publications that were annoying to the communists, could be purchased at East Berlin newsstands. There was a continuous flow of persons between the two areas of the city. Worst of all, from the Soviet point of view, vigorous democratic leaders had captured the government of the city and made persistent efforts to exercise their authority in the east as well as the west sectors.

This was a situation that the Soviets could not allow to continue. East Berlin was far larger than any city in East Germany, and its industry represented a substantial proportion of the German industry open to Soviet control. Therefore, if the Soviets were to organize the economy and political structure of their zone without reference to East Berlin, they would be neglecting to exploit one of the most valuable areas under their influence. By the same token, if they allowed the pro-Western Magistrat to assert real authority in East Berlin, the strength of the east sector would tend to redound to the advantage of the West rather than to their own. Therefore, without abandoning their claims to West Berlin, the Soviets moved to bring East Berlin more fully under their control. They removed large numbers of noncommunist officials from the borough administrations, checked the growing power of the independent trade unions, tried to exclude the West Berlin press from the east sector, and in general tightened the controls on the political and cultural life of that area.

These consolidation tactics produced increasingly strong reactions in West Berlin as resistance morale there became ever more firmly anchored. In the government, the trade unions, and the cultural life of the city, the democratic leaders forged ahead to build political and cultural institutions that more nearly reflected their own ideals. The institutions of 1945, either communist-dominated or built on the concept that cooperation with the communists was possible, were abandoned one by one, and new or reconstituted institutions took their place. Thus there emerged more and more clearly the outlines of two cities where one had been before.

Soviet efforts to eliminate the influence of noncommunist individuals and organizations in East Berlin, although cautious at first, had started even before the blockade. The "September 9 Memorandum," which democratic German leaders submitted to Western authorities following the mass meeting before the Reichstag, listed in detail the earlier moves toward consolidation. Large sectors of the East Berlin economy had been arbitrarily removed from the supervision of the city government and entrusted to quasi-public bodies, such as the communist cooperatives and trade unions. The CDU and LDP had been declared illegal by the Soviet sector authorities, and communist-controlled splinter groups bearing the CDU and LDP labels had been recognized instead. Many leading noncommunist borough officials had gradually been removed, as had noncommunist city officials in the police, the schools, the food office, and the labor office.

The SPD was being increasingly handicapped in its activities in East Berlin. The "September 9 Memorandum," in describing the severe restrictions under which the SPD had been operating, illustrates the gradual yet thorough methods used in stamping out noncommunist political influence in East Berlin:

> In the eight boroughs [of the east sector] certain party leaders who are especially well known and respected by the public are not allowed as speakers either at closed party affairs or in public meetings. . . . Discussion of questions which are of particular interest to the public is not permitted. . . .
>
> In the case of public meetings, when permission is given at all, it usually is given at such a late date that it is no longer possible to inform people that the meeting is to take place. . . . Insofar as meetings can be held, they are almost always subject to supervision, even when the most private party affairs are to be discussed. If the [Soviet] borough command does not send one of its personnel to exercise this supervision, a stenographer is usually there. Even meetings of the borough executive committees have been subject to observation in this manner. . . .
>
> Permission for meetings of all kinds is often given only after the third or fourth visit to the local military headquarters. Furthermore, the military authorities demand that applications be delivered and fetched in person by the chairman or secretary of the local group. To have to wait for several hours on several different occasions for permission of this sort has become the rule rather than the exception. And often these visits to the local commands involve being maligned in the most undignified manner.
>
> For example, one party leader had to go to the borough command seven times before he was finally given permission to hold a meeting one hour prior to the time the meeting was scheduled to begin. In this case it meant that a factory worker had to miss 25 working hours in one week. . . . This example could be multiplied. Since almost all local group chairmen serve without

pay, in the long run it would seem that these methods would lead to the end of the party's activity. . . .

> Every leading functionary of the Social Democratic Party in the east sector is continuously being threatened, so that one can no longer speak of free political activity. . . . Even if the will of the functionaries and members to preserve and strengthen the party has not been broken, there is no question that democratic development in the east sector can make no progress, since supervision by the NKVD and the SED has made it impossible for the democratic parties to carry on frank discussions. Numerous reprisals against individuals have led to a state of affairs where even in closed party meetings the discussion must be carried on in the secret language of the oppressed. . . .

Yet, despite all their efforts to undermine democratic processes in East Berlin, the Soviets had to realize that, in the late summer of 1948 the central city administration still exercised a considerable degree of authority in the east sector. There were still borough officials who defied communist dictation, the SPD continued at least some of its political activities, and the West Berlin LDP and CDU, though forbidden to function openly, still exercised an appreciable influence. The impending municipal elections which, under Berlin's provisional constitution, had to be held before the end of the year, threatened to make the situation even more difficult for the communists. It was clear that, if elections were conducted under conditions of even relative freedom, they would sharply reduce the SED's already slight strength in the Assembly, and would reimpose the grip of the Social Democrats on the east sector borough administrations. Furthermore, an electoral defeat would constitute a blow to communist prestige far beyond the city borders.

The desire to prevent elections from taking place in East Berlin and, if possible, in West Berlin as well, may have played a role in the communist decision, at the end of August, not to allow the Assembly to meet again in the city hall. One of the items on the Assembly agenda for August 27 had been the setting of a date for new elections, a decision that the Communists were eager to postpone. Furthermore, by driving the Assembly from the east sector, the SED provided itself with an excuse for not participating in its deliberations, and for arguing later that decisions made at Assembly meetings in West Berlin were invalid.

Throughout the fall of 1948 the removal of democratic officials from the borough administrations of the Soviet sector proceeded at an accelerated pace. On September 20 Dr. Friedensburg told the City Assembly that, up to that time, 16 elected heads of borough administrative offices and 538 borough employees had been discharged in the east sector.[30] By the end of that month the noncommunist personnel chiefs had been removed in all eight boroughs of East Berlin.[31] On October 10 it was reported that the total number of borough officials dismissed by Soviet command exceeded one thousand.[32] By the time the split of the city was completed the total approximated two thousand.[33]

While noncommunist borough employees usually were summarily dismissed, the Soviets were more cautious in their moves against elected officials, especially borough mayors, and ordinarily tried to find a pretext. As of October 25, 1948, five of the eight east sector boroughs still had Social Democratic mayors, one of whom resigned in November because he did not want to work with the "Democratic Bloc."[34] The position of these democratic mayors had been undermined, however, by the fact that a majority of their office chiefs were now members of either the SED or the communist-dominated eastern branches of the CDU and LDP. As a result of the 1946 elections, the east sector boroughs had been staffed with 88 principal officials (nearly all elected), of whom 64 belonged to the three democratic parties and 24 to the SED. As of October 26, 1948, however, there remained only 26 principal officials belonging to the three democratic parties, as against 34 who were members of the SED or of procommunist splinter groups.[35] (Some of the positions from which non-Communists had been removed had not been filled again.)

The dismissal of democratic officials in the east sector caused successive bursts of indignation in West Berlin. While most of the city's leaders tried to hold to a moderate course and to refrain from taking reprisals which might spur the Soviets to even greater excesses, there was constant pressure for retaliation from sources outside the city government. As early as July 22 the *Tagesspiegel* protested editorially that all principal noncommunist postal employees in the Soviet-controlled areas were being fired and replaced by SED members, while no action was being taken against SED members in important postal jobs in the west sectors. At a union meeting in October, the employees of the Wilmersdorf borough administration passed a resolution in which they stated that the Communists, by approving and supporting the inhuman Russian blockade, were to blame for Berlin's hardships. The borough employees therefore said they would refuse to work with such people and would use all the means of organized labor to bring about their dismissal. The *Tagesspiegel* expressed editorial surprise that the responsible officials of Wilmersdorf and most other west sector boroughs had to be told by their employees to take action that West Berliners had been expecting of them for some time.[36] The same report added that the Wedding borough administration had begun to release communist employees in order to make room for noncommunists who had lost jobs in the east sector.

A few days later the borough of Wilmersdorf also began dismissing SED members.[37] By October 14 a total of 547 persons had been discharged or "placed on leave status" from western borough offices (as compared to 1013 non-Communists fired in the east sector).[38] In December, five SED members in the trash-removal section of West Berlin's government had to be dismissed because the other whitewings refused to work with them.[39]

In the end, dismissals and counter-dismissals amounted almost to an exchange of population: Of the roughly two thousand non-Communists thrown out of their jobs in the Soviet sector, nearly all were given government employment in West Berlin.[40] The east sector authorities followed the same policy in reverse,[41] but there were reports that many SED members did not want to accept work in the Soviet sector, since they had become accustomed to the advantages of being paid in west marks.[42]

Soviet moves against democratic officials were accompanied by efforts to maintain communist domination of organized labor in the east sector. Although the old FDGB leadership had refused to surrender control of the union headquarters after its electoral defeat, independent unionists had been able to secure a majority in the works councils of a number of individual industries and shops in the Soviet sector. The communist labor leaders' campaign against these independents, which was intensified during October and November, met with strong resistance from the noncommunist workers. On November 20, for instance, an effort was made to oust the main works council at the Berlin Electric Company, but despite the threats of communist spokesmen and the appearance of east sector police, the works council refused to resign its authority.[43] Nevertheless, democratic labor leaders were fighting a losing battle in the Soviet sector. One by one they were forced out of their jobs, all activities of the independent unions were forbidden, and in many cases workers who had opposed the communist union leadership had to move to West Berlin.[44]

While the East Berlin unions remained instruments of communist power, the independent unions in West Berlin in 1948 could point to substantial achievements. They were gradually growing stronger, but were still faced with two principal problems. One was to find and train a cadre of functionaries to replace the predominantly communist personnel that had run the old FDGB. In the borough of Tempelhof, for example, over 60 per cent of the dues collectors had been Communists, all of whom went over to the Soviet sector unions when the split came.[45]

The other problem was to convince the workers that they should formally transfer their membership from the old to the new unions. In August, for instance, the report of the U.S. Military Governor noted that many west sector workers who wished to join the new organizations were hesitant to do so because they were not sure that the independent unions were financially strong enough to cover benefits to their members.[46] Furthermore, as one independent leader expressed it, many workers first wanted to see what was happening to the "total political situation." Nevertheless, the number of workers formally affiliated with the new unions increased rapidly. In July 1948 the independent leadership was able to collect only 85,000 marks in dues from some 22,000 members. In December the amount collected was 525,000 marks and came from 152,000 members.[47] By the end of the year, though the independent unions had far from completed their organizational work, and their membership was still substantially smaller than that of the FDGB in West Berlin prior to the blockade, they were rapidly outstripping the communist-led unions.

Another device in the Soviet campaign against democratic influences was to stop the circulation of West Berlin newspapers in the east sector. An early four-power agreement had provided for the free circulation in all parts of the city of newspapers produced in the various sectors. At first this agreement was observed with only minor exceptions. But, as the political tension grew, Soviet Military Government violated it more and more frequently, and by September 1948 there were clear indications that western publications would soon be excluded from the Soviet sector entirely.

Characteristically, restrictive measures were indirect. Toward the middle of September a semiofficial distribution agency was formed in East Berlin, and Soviet authorities gave it a monopoly on handling newspaper circulation in that area. Most of the West Berlin papers refused to contract with this new agency, but the French-sponsored *Kurier* and the British-sponsored *Welt* were among those that signed. On September 23 most of the west sector papers that had not signed new distribution contracts were confiscated by east sector police, and their business offices in East Berlin were forcibly closed.[48] On the following day, *Kurier* and *Welt* were also excluded from the Soviet sector, in spite of their arrangements with the East Berlin distribution agency. A representative of the agency stated as the reason that "the workers and employees in Russian sector enterprises had expressed opposition to the Western press."[49]

A particularly important development in the growing division between the cultural institutions of East and West Berlin was the opening of West Berlin's Free University. Even before the blockade, it had become clear that the communist authorities had no intention of allowing freedom of thought at Berlin's old university in the east sector, and a committee to organize a new university in West Berlin had begun its work in June 1948. By fall, the preliminary organizational work had been completed, and lectures at the Free University started on November 15.[50-54]

Other institutions followed suit. By Christmas of 1948 seven trade and professional schools had moved from East to West Berlin, and by Easter of 1949 the number was fifteen.[55]

Even music was affected by sector boundaries. In October the Berlin Philharmonic was ordered by U.S. Military Government not to play for audiences in East Berlin, or broadcast over the communist-controlled Berlin radio, until the blockade had been lifted. In reporting this order, the *Tagesspiegel* expressed the wish that the leaders of the orchestra had made this decision themselves, instead of leaving it to the occupation authorities. It pointed out that the *members* of the Philharmonic had already voted 73:1 (with 7 abstaining) to engage in no further cooperation with the communist radio.[56]

Other cultural and special-interest organizations were gradually divided into those that opposed communism, and whose headquarters were in West Berlin, and those that favored it and were centered in East Berlin or East Germany. Thus, the League of the Victims of the Nazi Regime became an almost exclusively communist group, as did the Association for the Advancement of Culture (*Kulturbund*), while new cultural and political associations grew up in

West Berlin. Individual democrats in the east now had to look to the west sectors for most of their institutional support, while the relatively few communists remaining in West Berlin drew their strength from the Soviet side of the sector boundaries.

Even before the split of the city had become an accomplished fact, some observers recognized that the consolidation of communist power in the east sector had an air of finality about it. The *British Zone Review* of October 15 remarked that ". . . in the Soviet sector a pattern has been created which will not fit, without modification, into the design for a jointly directed city under the terms of previous agreements."

What observers often failed to see was that West Berlin, too, had undergone profound, if less spectacular, changes that precluded any restoration of the earlier pattern. West Berliners, now restive even under the more lenient controls of the Western powers, would never again be satisfied with the limited freedom they had enjoyed under the old four-power rule, or with the inevitable compromises with totalitarianism it entailed. The old formula had worked when people were apathetic and preoccupied chiefly with their private ends. But, since those days, Berliners had tasted some of the fruits of democracy, which they felt they had won by their own efforts. Statesmen and technicians who were conducting international negotiations about Berlin with a view to restoring substantially the situation as it had existed prior to the blockade neglected to take account of the changed mood of the population.

Split of the City Administration

Although the Soviets were gradually able to drive thousands of noncommunist individuals and most noncommunist agencies from East Berlin, they were faced with the fact that the democratic Magistrat and Assembly still had theoretical jurisdiction in all four sectors. Furthermore, the Magistrat attempted to enforce its authority in the east sector insofar as it was able, and could point to some successes. As long as the headquarters of the city government remained in the Soviet sector, the democratic leaders contrived to exercise an influence there of which the Soviets found it difficult to deprive them. Soviet efforts during the summer of 1948 to gain control of Magistrat and Assembly, or to force them to delegate wide powers to communist-dominated groups, had proved unsuccessful. The only alternative, therefore, was to force these bodies out of East Berlin. This was done during the fall, at first gradually and by indirection;

later, more rapidly and crudely. The City Assembly was excluded. Various departments of the city government were split, one by one, and at the end of November a puppet government was set up in the Soviet sector.

A description has already been given of the manner in which Communist mob violence in late August and early September made it impossible for the Assembly to conduct its business in the city hall.* After a final futile attempt to call the Assembly to order in its official chamber on September 6, Speaker Suhr recognized the handwriting on the wall and announced that the next meeting would be held in the British sector.[57] In practice, this resulted in a division of the Assembly into communist and noncommunist components, since SED assemblymen refused to attend meetings in West Berlin.

Having forced the Assembly out of the east sector, the Soviets and German Communists then went through the motions of inviting it back, apparently in an effort to make it look as if the move to West Berlin had been by design of the democratic parties. At the end of September Second Deputy Speaker Ottomar Geschke (SED) called on all members of the Magistrat and of the city and borough assemblies to convene in East Berlin. Assemblymen from the three democratic parties refused to attend this meeting, pointing out that as long as Dr. Suhr and his first deputy were in a position to convene the Assembly, the second deputy had no right to do so.[58]

Several days later Deputy Speaker Dr. Schreiber received a letter from General Kotikov promising in somewhat vague terms that the police would protect the Assembly against mob violence. However, Kotikov refused to agree to the establishment of a restricted zone around the city hall, because, he said, this would be undemocratic. He also observed that Dr. Friedensburg's refusal to see delegations and discuss preparations for winter with them was causing unrest and concern in the population. Kotikov again signed himself "Military Commandant of Berlin and Chief of the Soviet Occupation Forces in Berlin."[59]

The democratic assemblymen did not find these assurances convincing enough to justify a return to the city hall; they observed that General Kotikov had only recently broken his promise to General Ganeval regarding the safe conduct of volunteer Magistrat guards from the east sector, and that presumably a promise to Ger-

* See Chapter IV, pp. 185-187.

man officials was worth even less.[60] The Assembly stayed in West Berlin, and the old meeting chamber in the city hall was used by the communist-dominated "Democratic Bloc."[61]

The communist version of the exodus of the City Assembly from East Berlin is contained in the following official Soviet account:

> At the end of September 1948, the reactionary majority in the City Assembly, following the instructions of the Anglo-American authorities, transferred their activities altogether to the British sector, thereby finally shattering the single municipal administration of Berlin.[62]

One can only speculate about the reason why the move was described as having occurred "at the end of September," when actually it had come at the beginning of the month. Possibly, the Soviets had not given up hope of subverting or overawing the City Assembly on September 6, and had decided to exclude the body from East Berlin only after the mass demonstration of September 9 had fully convinced them of the growing determination of West Berlin's leaders.

The Magistrat offered a more difficult problem for the Soviets than the City Assembly. In spite of the fact that the Police Department and the food office had already been split, the central city government still exercised control over an extensive network of administrative officials with a wide variety of functions. To remove the east sector from the authority of the Magistrat without disrupting essential services, and without taking full responsibility for the split, required more than mob action. Several different techniques were used to split municipal agencies, one after one, into eastern and western components.

Termination of the city's authority over labor affairs in East Berlin was relatively simple, since the municipal Labor Office was already headed by Councilman Waldemar Schmidt, one of the few communists in the Magistrat. By simply disregarding the instructions of the Assembly and the democratic majority of the Magistrat, this official eventually forced his own suspension and the appointment of a successor by the city government. The Soviets refused to recognize the change, and allowed Schmidt to continue in office in East Berlin while the Western powers recognized his successor in West Berlin. This was almost the same pattern that had been followed earlier in the Police Department.

The details of the dispute over the Labor Office are instructive.

Shortly after the start of the blockade, Schmidt's name appeared in the headlines of the Berlin press when he disapproved a number of wage agreements between employers and the noncommunist independent unions. The full Magistrat ordered Schmidt to approve these agreements, since they had been made in the American and British sectors, where the independent unions were the recognized bargaining agents for labor. It also instructed Schmidt to see that the independent unions were represented on the Magistrat's wage committee and other appropriate committees.[63]

Schmidt not only refused to follow these orders, but he defied the city government in other ways as well. He issued a regulation stipulating that policemen who lived in the east sector but worked under the direction of the police headquarters in West Berlin were not to be regarded as members of the police force. This ruling had the effect of depriving these men of their favorable food-ration cards in East Berlin.[64] And the "September 9 Memorandum" relates instances in which Schmidt was able to prevent the payment of unemployment benefits to non-Communists and to make it more difficult for members of the independent unions to secure employment.

Faced with open defiance, the Magistrat resolved to place the matter before the City Assembly. On September 20 the Assembly ordered Schmidt to appear before it and report on matters concerning his office. Schmidt refused to comply, on the grounds that the Assembly's move to West Berlin "was not only illegal but also another fateful step on the road to splitting Berlin." He added that he would be glad to appear before the Assembly in its chamber in the city hall. The Assembly thereupon appointed an investigating committee to examine Schmidt's conduct.[65]

On the strength of the committee's report, the Assembly voted to suspend Schmidt from office. But Schmidt refused to consider himself suspended, and appeared, in his usual place, at the next meeting of the Magistrat in the city hall. When he ignored Acting Mayor Friedensburg's order to leave, the meeting was adjourned and later reconvened in the British sector, because in the Soviet sector Dr. Friedensburg was unable to enforce his orders by police power. Schmidt declined to vacate his office in the city hall, and continued to issue orders which purported to apply to all Berlin. Consequently, the new councilman in charge of labor affairs was constrained to organize a new office in West Berlin, and was denied the use of the files and equipment in the old headquarters.[66]

Thus, another department of the city government had been effectively split, and the Magistrat had been forced to meet in West Berlin. Schmidt's orders affecting labor matters were backed by police power in the east sector, while the new labor chief (Fleischmann) was in control in the west sector. *Neues Deutschland* protested that Schmidt's suspension was another step toward splitting the city, and commented sarcastically:

> Openly acting on the instructions of Reuter, Friedensburg ordered that the headquarters of the Labor Office be moved to another building. He justified this on the pretext that "former Councilman Schmidt would not vacate the present quarters."[67]

The Soviet Deputy Commandant, Colonel Yelisarov, also protested Schmidt's suspension, but Dr. Friedensburg told him firmly that the decision would stand unless reversed by the commandants of all four powers, and that the division of the Labor Office could be ended only if Soviet Military Government withdrew its objection to Schmidt's removal.[68]

Repercussions of the dispute over the central Labor Office were felt in several of the borough labor offices. In Spandau (British sector), the official in charge of labor affairs was a member of the SED, who refused to follow the instructions of the new west sector headquarters and was thereupon removed by the borough mayor. In taking this action, the mayor pointed out that the Spandau labor office had to supply the personnel for work in connection with the airlift.[69]* Much the same thing happened in the British sector borough of Tiergarten.[70]

The other side of the coin was displayed in Prenzlauer Berg (Soviet sector). There the local labor chief was a Social Democrat, who refused to follow the instructions issued by suspended City Councilman Schmidt, and consequently was dismissed by the east sector authorities.[71] Again, when City Councilman Fleischmann, Schmidt's successor, was about to take part in a press conference at the city hall early in November, the Soviet liaison officer forbade him to do so, and threatened him with arrest if he disobeyed. At this, Dr. Friedensburg broke off the scheduled press conference and promised a written protest.[72]

The next city agency to be forced out of East Berlin was the Department of Economics under City Councilman Klingelhöfer, one

* The implication of the mayor's statement, obvious to Berliners at the time, was that this fact would enable a labor office chief to conduct sabotage operations against the airlift.

of the most perceptive of the SPD leaders. Klingelhöfer retained his headquarters in the Soviet sector as long as he was able to preserve some semblance of an orderly administration. But when Soviet and communist interference at all levels became too great, when insubordinate communist employees could not be disciplined, in view of lack of support from the east sector police, and the obstructive tactics of Soviet personnel made operations almost impossible, Klingelhöfer recognized the handwriting on the wall and decided to move his headquarters to West Berlin. One morning, toward the middle of November, he called a meeting of all the personnel in his department, except those who belonged to the SED, and told them that it was no longer possible for the department to administer the economic affairs of Greater Berlin from the Soviet sector. Therefore, he said, it would be necessary to move to West Berlin, and each individual would have to decide whether to come or not. While this meeting was taking place, communist police surrounded the building. When he had concluded his remarks, Klingelhöfer left his headquarters. The police allowed him to pass, and he walked down Unter den Linden, through the Brandenburg Gate, and into the British sector where a car was waiting. A majority of his personnel subsequently joined him at new headquarters in West Berlin.

Meanwhile, other departments had been moving some of their files and personnel more gradually. Ever since October, Ernst Reuter had, little by little, moved essential records and some of the office equipment of his Department of Transportation and Public Services to buildings in West Berlin, and other city agencies attempted to follow his example.

Though Soviet authorities and east sector police did not, as a rule, restrain personnel from moving, they did try to prevent the removal of files and office materials from the east sector. On October 28 the *Tagesspiegel* reported that the Markgraf police had been instructed to guard the Magistrat offices in the east sector in order to see that files were not "smuggled" to the west sectors. Shortly after the middle of November, Soviet Military Government issued an order forbidding the removal of any files, furniture, or other office equipment from government offices in the east sector.[73] Dr. Friedensburg himself was to be responsible for seeing that this order was enforced.[74]

Implicit in these communist tactics was the assumption that an agency could not exercise legal authority if it changed the location of its headquarters. The SED group in the City Assembly made this explicit when it refused to take part in meetings held in the British sector and maintained that any decisions made by the Assembly in that sector were without legal force. Dr. Suhr pointed out in reply that there was nothing in the city constitution or the Assembly rules providing that the Assembly had to meet in any specific place.[75]

By the middle of November the headquarters of most government departments had been forced out of East Berlin, and regular meetings of both the Assembly and the Magistrat were being held in West Berlin. But the Magistrat still claimed authority over the east sector, and Acting Mayor Friedensburg stubbornly retained his office in the city hall.

At this point, possibly with a view to the city elections, which had been set for December 5, the Soviets resorted to more direct means to terminate the authority of the city government in the east sector. On November 15, Soviet Military Government ordered the removal of Ernst Reuter as city councilman in charge of Transportation and Public Services on the grounds that he had shown himself completely incapable of filling the office and had not appeared at his headquarters (presumably those in East Berlin) for three months.[76]

About twenty hours after discharging Reuter, the Soviet Deputy Commandant sent another order to the city hall purporting to remove City Councilman Klingelhöfer from his post in the Department of Economic Affairs. The reason given was that the department's offices had been moved to the west sectors. One of Klingelhöfer's former deputies, a member of the SED, was named temporary head of the department. The *Tagesspiegel,* in reporting this order, also mentioned rumors of the impending dismissal of two other department heads: City Councilman Heinzelmann, in charge of banking and insurance, and Dr. Haas, in charge of finance.[77] A few days later, the Soviets accused Dr. Haas of following an "antidemocratic and antisocial" financial policy, and gave him ten days in which to reform.[78]

All three Western commandants sent formal letters to the acting mayor, declaring that the Soviet orders were invalid as far as the three west sectors were concerned.[79] On November 18 the Magistrat and City Assembly approved a reply to the Soviets signed by Dr. Friedensburg. In it, the acting mayor expressed sorrow and surprise at the orders, and pointed out that under Berlin's provisional constitution, which had been approved by all four powers, heads of departments in the city government could be elected and removed only by the City Assembly. The Soviet orders, said Dr. Friedensburg, could be understood to apply only to the Soviet sector; apparently Soviet Military Government planned to set up separate departments for transportation and for economic affairs, a divisive move against which the Magistrat felt itself obliged to protest.[80]

The final Soviet move to split the administration was a frontal attack on the authority of the acting mayor and the Magistrat. It was preceded by a massive propaganda campaign, which again attempted to place on the West the responsibility for having divided the city.

During the last weeks of November, the East Berlin press fired heavier and heavier salvos at the city administration. "CHAOS IN THE ADMINISTRATION OF BERLIN—THE MAGISTRAT HAS CEASED TO FUNCTION—GROWING INDIGNATION OF THE POPULATION" was the main headline in *Neues Deutschland* on November 20. The story under it began:

> The flight of the irresponsible city councilmen and their immediate staffs continues. Organized theft of files is their last "official action." Insofar as they are not prevented from doing so they are taking autos and furniture as well. The Magistrat has been torn into pieces for weeks; now its dissolution is complete. Berlin is without a central administrative headquarters. Those who have systematically been splitting the city for months want to complete the administrative chaos before December 5.

On the following day the "Democratic Bloc" passed a resolution asserting that the city administration had "ceased to exist." It urged further that the unified administration, which had been split by those trying to divide the city, be immediately restored, and denounced city officials who had "fled from their posts, leaving the people in the lurch at the beginning of winter."[81] During the next few days, mass meetings of workers in East Berlin denounced the "divisive elections" scheduled for West Berlin, and demanded resignation of the Magistrat and free elections for the whole city.[82] On November 29 Second Deputy Speaker Geschke, (SED) declared over the Berlin radio: "The hour is grave. There have been enough fine speeches and promises. There must be action now if Berlin is not to perish."[83]

The Soviet Military Governor joined the chorus. In identical letters to the three Western military governors, dated November 29, Marshal Sokolovsky called attention to "the dangerous actions which are being taken in Berlin's west sectors for the purpose of disorganizing and dividing the German city administration." He accused Western military governments of supporting these divisive actions, and complained that no consideration had been given to Soviet proposals for democratic elections in all Berlin. The separate elections planned for the west sectors, he said, were for the purpose of getting rid of the central city administration and establishing a separate Magistrat. He charged further that in the west sectors democratic organizations were being persecuted by the police, and that conditions for free elections did not exist. Marshal Sokolovsky concluded: "The Soviet command has no intention of showing consideration toward the antidemocratic elements of the Berlin Magistrat that are taking measures to divide the German administrative organs of Berlin. It will continue to strive to preserve the unity of Berlin and to create conditions which will make possible normal activity by all democratic representatives in the organs of Berlin's self-administration."[84]

On Tuesday, November 30, Ottomar Geschke called a "special meeting of the Assembly" in one of East Berlin's large theaters, to which he invited members of the Democratic Bloc and representatives of such communist-dominated mass organizations as the FDGB, the *Kulturbund,* the Free German Youth, and the League of the Victims of the Nazi Regime.[85]

The meeting was attended by 229 representatives of mass organizations, 1151 delegates from various factories, and 236 members of the Democratic Bloc. On the motion of the Democratic Bloc the Magistrat of Berlin was declared deposed. A new "Magistrat" was then elected, and Fritz Ebert, a son of the first chancellor of the Weimar Republic, was designated mayor.[86]

The new "Magistrat" immediately announced that it would carry into effect the emergency program of the Democratic Bloc. This program envisaged fuel for every household, a higher electricity quota for individual users, assurance of more coal and electric power to enable idle factories to resume production, a 30 per cent pay raise for all public employees, increased production, general improvements in the labor situation, and implementation of the SED two-year plan for Greater Berlin, which called for coordinating the Berlin economy with that of the east zone.[87] Indeed, Herr Ebert stated at one point that it was the purpose of his administration to assimilate Berlin into the Soviet zone.[88]

The new "Magistrat" met with speedy and emphatic rejection in the west sectors. The City Assembly convened on December 1, Frau Schroeder leaving her hospital bed in Hamburg to be present for the occasion. In opening the meeting, Dr. Suhr remarked that the *Putsch* in East Berlin could not have achieved success if it had not been supported by an occupation power. The mass meeting that elected the "new Magistrat," he said, was purely a party affair, with no authority to pass resolutions other than those affecting the sponsoring party. If any occupation power should decide that these resolutions had legal force in its sector, the work of splitting Berlin would be complete. Louise Schroeder branded the coup as an attempt by the SED to split the city before Berliners could express their will at the forthcoming elections.

The Assembly unanimously passed two resolutions: to ask all legally elected members of east sector borough administrations to resign, in order not to allow themselves to be misused by the illegal East Berlin government; and to have the Assembly meet daily at 11 a.m. until further notice.[89]

The three military commandants of the west sectors also denounced the communist coup, and made it clear that they continued to recognize the legally-elected Magistrat. They assured West Berliners that they would receive protection and food, and that order would be maintained.[90] French General Ganeval called the move "the most stupid *Putsch* ever made." He characterized the inglorious role of Fritz Ebert by saying that a "nobody" appeared, allowed people to shout at him for a few minutes, and then proclaimed himself mayor.[91]

The Soviet authorities officially recognized the legality of the new "Magistrat" two days after it had been proclaimed. Late at night on December 2, Deputy Commandant Colonel Yelisarov sent a letter to Geschke, saying that the Soviet command recognized the provisional democratic government, which had been elected by the extraordinary Assembly, as the sole legal city administration, and promising the new government all necessary assistance.[92]

An official Soviet account of the event again attempted to place responsibility for the split on the West:

> The disruption of municipal administration and the disorganization of economic life in Berlin by the Western occupation authorities and the reactionary section of the Magistrat that obeys their behests gave rise to large-scale spontaneous actions by wide sections of the population of Berlin against the

anti-people's policy of the Magistrat. On November 30, 1948, the population of Berlin deposed the Magistrat that had betrayed their interests and set up a provisional democratic Magistrat, its mission being to safeguard the genuine interests of the Berlin population.[93]

The morning after the east sector *Putsch,* Acting Mayor Friedensburg, with members of his personal staff, set out for his office in the city hall. When he sought to enter the building, east sector police forcibly restrained him. He returned to West Berlin to conduct the business of the city from there, satisfied that there was now no way in which the communists could slough off responsibility for having split the city's administration.[94] The London *Times* characterized Dr. Friedensburg's appearance at the city hall as a "courageous action."[95]

The Soviets had thus forced the legal city government to abandon its authority in the east sector, which thereafter became an exclusive Soviet preserve. In the months to come, the work of consolidating East Berlin with the Soviet zone proceeded rapidly. At the same time, Moscow continued its efforts to secure control of West Berlin.

Communist Propaganda and the Election Campaign

Under the provisional Berlin constitution, elections for the City Assembly were to take place every two years. The existing Assembly having been elected in October of 1946, new elections had to be held in the fall of 1948. Already in June (i.e., prior to the blockade), the Assembly had voted unanimously to instruct the Magistrat to submit plans for new elections by July 15. The SED, along with the democratic parties, had thus admitted that elections were required.[96]

Between June and August the SED line changed. Communist spokesmen began to assert that new elections were not necessary, and the SED-sponsored disturbances at the city hall prevented the Assembly from discussing election plans. Only after it had moved to the British sector was the Assembly able to approve the plans, and the SED promptly announced that it would boycott the scheduled elections.[97]

The Soviets, too, gave proof that they would oppose elections unless a favorable result for the Communists were a foregone conclusion. In late September, the deputy mayor of Lichtenberg reported that the Soviet command in his borough had ordered him by telephone to stop all preparations for the election. The *Tagesspiegel* commented editorially that Berliners knew enough of Soviet methods to understand that this was not a local, arbitrary action, but a clue to what would happen in the whole Soviet sector.[98]

The following letter from General Kotikov to the city government, dated October 20, made it clear that the conditions under which the Soviets would permit city-wide elections amounted to nothing short of Western capitulation to Soviet demands for control of the whole city:

> The Soviet Berlin Command has examined your letter, in which you request permission to hold Berlin communal elections and also request confirmation of the election procedure, a copy of which was enclosed in your letter.
>
> The Soviet Command is of the opinion that communal elections in Berlin are necessary in the near future, since the promises which the representatives elected to the Assembly in 1946 made to the voters prior to their election have in most cases been seriously violated. The democratization of public life has been prevented. In the western sectors of Berlin militaristic warmongering propaganda is being carried on. Fascist elements are again raising their heads there. The Berlin Magistrat and Assembly have turned themselves into tools of the Anglo-American authorities, who are conducting an antidemocratic policy of splitting Berlin. It is necessary for the city that representatives of the public be elected to its communal organs who are capable of carrying out their promises to the people, enforcing the will of the voters, and assuring democratization of the political, economic, and cultural life in the whole city.
>
> In view of these circumstances, unified, free, democratic elections in Berlin would benefit the Berlin population and would contribute to the improvement of the situation in the city.
>
> Such elections are entirely possible, if in the west sectors of the city the elementary democratic freedoms are restored and if it is assured that the communal organs of the city are unified and that the city's economy is undivided. In view of these considerations the following is necessary:
>
> 1. The democratic organizations which have been illegally forbidden in the west sectors of Berlin are to be permitted once more. These include the Free German Trade Unions, the democratic organization of the intelligentsia—the *Kultur-*

bund, the committees of the German People's Movement for the Unity of Germany and a Just Peace, and other democratic organizations.

2. The persecution of the democratic German organizations and their members is to stop. In particular, those persons are to be released who were arrested for conducting propaganda for the unity of Germany and a just peace. Also to be released are the activists from the unions, the Free German Youth, and the SED, who were thrown into prison because of their democratic political activity.
3. The organizations and formations of a militaristic and fascistic character in Berlin are to be dissolved. Militaristic and fascistic propaganda in the press is to be stopped, and the warmongers are to be stricken from the voting lists.
4. The unity of the city organs of Berlin, and especially the unity of the police, is to be restored, after all fascistic and militaristic elements have been removed. The unity of the budget and of the entire city economy is likewise to be restored.

In this way truly free, democratic elections in all Berlin, the necessity of which is so clear, will be assured. These demands are in accord with the principles of the provisional democratic constitution of Berlin.

The Soviet Berlin Command counts on the Berlin Magistrat to take appropriate measures to ensure that the above preconditions for democratic elections in Berlin are speedily accomplished.

As far as the plan for carrying out the election is concerned, we have some suggestions to make with regard to the further democratization of the procedure—for instance, with regard to lowering the age of the voters. But this is a subsidiary question, the solution of which in our opinion will not cause appreciable difficulties.[99]

West Berlin's reaction to this letter was an angry one. In the City Assembly, Dr. Suhr characterized Kotikov's accusations as "cheap support for SED propaganda."[100] LDP Chairman Karl Hubert Schwennicke said that the General was describing conditions in East Beriln rather than in the west sectors. Dr. Friedensburg stated that he knew of only one fascist-militarist in a leading position and that was Markgraf, the head of the east sector police.[101]

Four days later, after giving the letter further study, Dr. Friedensburg reported on it to the City Assembly on behalf of the Magistrat. He pointed out that Kotikov's conditions were, for the most part, entirely outside the competence of the city administration, and that the letter was based on completely false information regarding conditions in the west sectors. He concluded that the intention of the Soviet commandant had been to make the election impossible in the Soviet sector.[102]

In spite of the Soviet attitude, the Assembly, on October 25, unanimously reaffirmed its resolve to hold elections in December.* If, in individual boroughs, military authorities made it impossible to carry through the election, the present representatives from those boroughs were to continue in the Assembly until their successors could be duly elected. On November 3 the Magistrat took official notice of the fact that election preparations had been stopped in all east sector boroughs.[103]

Soviet Military Government violently denounced the election campaign. On November 27 the deputy military governor told the press that the elections were designed to get rid of Berlin's central administrative organs and to split the city.[104] Two days later Marshal Sokolovsky sent protest letters to the three Western military governors. He accused the West of having ignored Soviet suggestions for city-wide elections, and labeled as undemocratic and divisive the planned elections in the west sectors, whose purpose, he said, was the establishment of a separate Magistrat under Western control.[105]

In the light of later events, Marshal Sokolovsky's letters could be interpreted not only as a last-minute attempt to prevent the elections in West Berlin but also as a preparatory move to the establishment of the new east sector government, which was proclaimed the very next day.†

Undeterred by the Soviets, West Berlin's democratic parties swung into a vigorous election campaign. The SPD, as the majority party, stood mainly on its record of social legislation and resistance to the Communists. The CDU warned against SPD ideas of class struggle and advocated a firm, but less provocative, policy toward the Soviets.

* It will be remembered that the communist deputies were no longer taking part in the meetings of the City Assembly.

† The contents of these letters are summarized in more detail earlier in this chapter in connection with the establishment of a separate east sector government.

The LDP reproached the CDU for a "soft" attitude toward the Soviets and for its indecision in economic questions, and assailed the Marxism of the SPD.[106] For the most part, however, the three democratic parties devoted little time to attacking each other; it was against the SED and the Soviets that most of their verbal darts were directed.*

One of their common campaign themes was that *all* voters who were entitled to vote should do so. A vote not cast would be interpreted as a vote for the SED. Dr. Suhr went so far as to say that every nonvoter would be guilty of high treason, since by failing to cast his ballot he would be helping to sabotage the democratic administration, and thus the freedom, of Berlin.

On the eve of the election, the three parties held a final, joint rally in one of the largest theaters in West Berlin. Ernst Reuter reminded his listeners that the election gave Berliners an opportunity to go down in history. Ferdinand Friedensburg urged everybody to vote, no matter for whom. Karl Hubert Schwennicke asserted that West Berlin could be conquered only by force of arms, and that the Berliners' will to freedom could not be broken.[107]

While the democratic parties made strenuous efforts to persuade all eligible voters to come to the polls, the SED did everything in its power to keep them away. According to the Communists, the elections were a device of American generals who wanted to exacerbate the tension in Berlin; the West wished to retain control of the city in order to exploit the workers; and the SPD had become a tool of the capitalists. To vote on December 5 was to favor the splitting of the city and to approve the deplorable conditions in West Berlin.[108] Besides, the election results would be fraudulent. There was reason to believe, the Berlin SED Chairman declared on November 12, that the returns were already in the files of Allied officers.[109]

One example of SED propaganda was a special appeal to women published in *Neues Deutschland* on November 28:

> HOUSEWIFE IN THE WEST—
>
> Do you want to indicate by voting that you approve of the present conditions? Do you want people to think that you are

* This brief summary of the campaign, based mainly on press notices of election speeches, cannot do justice to the positive programs of the democratic parties. The SPD set forth its stand on principal questions in a booklet entitled *Zwei Jahre Kommunalarbeit in Gross-Berlin*. The CDU likewise published a full program in *Die Politik der Berliner Union*, Berlin, November 1948. The LPD described its program in a series of newspaper advertisements (e.g., *Tagesspiegel*, November 28, 1948).

satisfied with electricity rationing, with the tiny gas ration, with the dark and cold homes into which rain still comes, with the eternal canned food, and with all the difficulties brought on by the west marks? On December 5 get even with those who want to split Berlin: Don't vote.

And on December 3, *Neues Deutschland* published the following jingle:

Don't be lured by promises sweet.
Think of the dried potatoes you've had to eat.
Think of all the cut-down trees
And the dark, cold rooms in which you freeze.
Don't vote for the candidates, like a dunce,
Whose parties already betrayed you once.*

One means of scaring West Berliners away from the polls was to predict that the Russians would occupy West Berlin in any event. On the day before the election, the Soviet army newspaper *Tägliche Rundschau* published the headline: "THE WESTERN POWERS WILL LEAVE BERLIN IN JANUARY." A rumor, possibly spread by the SED, was that it was unsafe to vote because the polling lists would fall into Soviet hands following the evacuation of Berlin by the Western powers.[110] Other rumors, which suggested possible military action by the Soviet Armed Forces or the People's Police, coursed through Berlin during October and November. Berliners who had been arrested in the Soviet zone because their identity cards were stamped with a "B" (as required in West Berlin) gave disturbing accounts of their questioning by Soviet secret police. The Russians seemed particularly interested to know what positions these Berliners had occupied in the former German army, whether they had been members of the Nazi party, and whether they were now enrolled in one of Berlin's three democratic parties. The victims were told that their answers would be checked, and that anyone who had given false information would be punished after Soviet troops had occupied the three west sectors.[111]

Apparently in response to rumors that the Communists might use force, Colonel Howley assured newsmen that there would be no civil war in Berlin, and added that the reports about possible disorders were obviously intended to increase the suffering and fears

* Although this translation may seem crude, it is really not much worse than the original German.

of the Berlin population.[112] A few days later he told the borough mayors of the American sector that there were enough U.S. troops available to protect the sector against the east zone police or any armed mob that might be sent in, and that orderly elections would be assured.[113] *Neues Deutschland*, apparently irritated by this forthright statement, reported it under the headline: "WEAPONS OVER THE AIRLIFT—REMARKABLE ELECTION PREPARATIONS FOR BERLIN'S WEST SECTORS."[114] Howley's statement, said the east sector press, was an attempt to promote civil war in Berlin. Howley replied that he had made the statement because German representatives from the west sectors had told him of their concern over the arming and training of the East Berlin police.[115]

In November, as election day drew closer, reports of military activity in the east zone and sector became more frequent. New Soviet troop contingents with armor and heavy artillery were said to have arrived in the east zone state of Thuringia. Other reports spoke of daily instruction given the east zone German police in the use of pistols, carbines, and machine guns. Two hundred east zone police were said to have moved into the village of Velten, just outside Berlin, and to have been billeted in public halls and schoolrooms. According to an alleged order of the east sector police, all leaves from December 1 had been cancelled, and men were to be taken off desk jobs to serve as patrol reinforcements. A former *Wehrmacht* captain, Woschinski, was reported to be training special groups of east zone and east sector police, his specialty being street-fighting.[116]

At the same time, the SED cited Western sources to support its contention that the Allies would shortly abandon Berlin. British Labourite R. H. S. Crossman was quoted as saying that the Western powers should offer to evacuate by air every Berliner who wished to leave; they would then be in a better position to decide whether their troops should remain in the "Berlin rubble pile" or be concentrated in West Germany. The communist news agency (ADN) added: "In the British capital it is assumed that official circles are behind this proposal of Crossman that Berlin's west sectors be evacuated."[117] The communist press also reported rumors that French Military Governor General Koenig was to be relieved.[118] On December 3 *Neues Deutschland* carried this front-page headline: "WASHINGTON DISSATISFIED WITH GENERAL CLAY—MARSHALL'S 'DIPLOMATIC ILLNESS'—CHANGES IN U.S. MILITARY GOVERNMENT ARE UNAVOIDABLE." The story was that the Senate Foreign Relations Committee was dissatisfied with Clay for breaking off negotiations among the four military governors in

Berlin, and that Secretary of State Marshall's recent physical check-up was a prelude to his impending dismissal.

With considerable ingenuity, the Communists tried to persuade West Berliners to associate themselves with the Eastern economy by buying their food and fuel in East Berlin. *Neues Deutschland,* for instance, printed a series of boxes, captioned "There Is No Blockade," pointing out that West Berliners could obtain all they needed by registering in the east sector. Instructions under the boxes read: "Cut this out and paste it up."[119] Apparently, readers were expected to clip these items and plaster them on walls and hoardings, but there is no indication that many did. Similarly, housewives in the west sectors had received letters addressed "Dear Neighbor," in which they were advised to accept the "generous offer" of the Soviet Military Administration and buy their food in the east sector, and were also told how best to transport the food from East to West Berlin. Moreover, the letter condemned the Magistrat for cutting down Berlin's trees to provide fuel, suggesting that, instead, the Magistrat should arrange with the East German Economic Commission to bring in supplies of coal stored just outside Berlin.[120]

A new dimension in communist propaganda was the antiwarmongering campaign, which seems to have begun, in part, as a Soviet reaction to the mass meeting of September 9. On September 15 General Kotikov sent a letter of protest to General Herbert, whom he addressed as "Chief of the British Garrison in Berlin," while signing himself "Commandant of Berlin." Kotikov reported that a group of criminals had followed up the September 9 meeting by defiling a Soviet war memorial and the Soviet flag in the presence of British military police and west sector police. He called the meeting a demonstration against peace and democracy, and claimed that the "fascist bandits" had shot at Soviet soldiers who were guarding the memorial, and had attacked the Soviet troops and east sector police who attempted to restore order. The inactivity of military and German police in the British sector, said Kotikov, was "taken by the fascist inciters as encouragement for their criminal acts." He therefore asked that the guilty parties be punished and that measures be taken to prevent a recurrence of such incidents. General Herbert replied vigorously, pointing out a number of inaccuracies in Kotikov's letter, and expressing surprise that it had not been written until six days after the incident.[121]

A few days later, Colonel Tulpanov, one of the chief political officers in the Soviet Military Administration, resumed Kotikov's theme. He denounced the men who had spoken at the Reichstag rally, accused them of inciting the crowd to violence, and added that the events following the meeting had been taken "very seriously" in Moscow. He was answered by Dr. Friedensburg, who reminded him that it had not been the speakers who had incited the crowd, but the excesses at the city hall and the mass dismissals of adherents of the democratic parties in the east sector.[122]

Toward the end of October Soviet authorities officially denounced as fascist warmongers six leading officials of the city administration.[123] At about the same time, Colonel Yelisarov sent a letter to Deputy Assembly Speaker Dr. Schreiber, in which he accused members of the city government of making militaristic and fascistic speeches at the Reichstag meeting, with the intent of inciting a riot. This letter occasioned some amusement because it mentioned as one of the objectionable speakers an SPD leader who had not taken part in the meeting. It presumably was addressed to Dr. Schreiber instead of Dr. Suhr, because the latter was among those accused.[124]

All these Soviet protests were accompanied by a barrage of propaganda in the SED press. One device by which the leaders in West Berlin were made to appear as Nazis or fascists was to print excerpts from the *Tagesspiegel* or *Telegraf* that had some verbal similarity to passages in the Nazi press under the Hitler regime. Another tactic was to dig into the past of Berlin politicians for incidents which, taken out of context, would make it appear that they favored Hitlerism. When the communist press had no material available with which to defame an individual, it would publish his name and picture and invite readers to send in any derogatory information they might have about his background.[125] The West Berlin press was referred to as the "warmongering press," and quotations from it were taken out of context to support the charge.[126]

On October 21 representatives of East Berlin's press, political parties, and mass organizations founded a "Committee against Warmongering." A week later, this Committee sponsored a mass meeting, which went through the motions of passing a resolution charging that certain warmongers in the German capital were methodically engaged in fascist propaganda and were abusing the democratic freedom of the press. The meeting specifically condemned Reuter, Suhr, Neumann, Friedensburg, and several others for warmongering and fascist excesses at many meetings, especially the Reichstag rally of September 9.[127]

But the Communists did not stop at propaganda; they did their best to disorganize the election campaigns of the three democratic parties, often by violent means. An SPD party worker, who was putting up posters in the French sector, was kidnaped by east sector police who had slipped into West Berlin, dragged back to the Soviet sector border, and delivered to two waiting Russian soldiers. At numerous election rallies, SED activists engaged in cat-calls, hurled stink bombs, chanted communist slogans in unison, and created general disturbances. They were temporarily able to stop an SPD meeting in Neukölln, but were finally thrown out of the hall. When Theodor Heuss tried to address an election rally, communist interruptions prevented him from speaking for several minutes. He refused to abandon the rostrum, and his hecklers finally left the hall singing the "Internationale," but not before some blows had been exchanged. In another case, 250 communist sympathizers occupied a hall where an election rally was scheduled to be held, and the meeting had to be transfered to another hall. In many places, SED "pasting groups" covered democratic election posters with stickers urging people to stay away from the polls. In others, posters were simply torn down.[128]

But this Communist violence did not go unchallenged. The SPD organized a number of heavy-muscled young trade unionists to eject SED hecklers from their meetings. On at least one occasion, the Social Democrats set up a first-aid station outside a meeting hall, where the hecklers were treated after their ejection.[129]

The Communist authorities took special measures in East Berlin to make access to the polls difficult for those who lived in West Berlin but worked in the east. Thus, a mass meeting of SED functionaries unanimously adopted a young worker's suggestion (allegedly spontaneous) that election Sunday, December 5, be made a "reconstruction day," on which all workers would be expected to appear at their jobs.[130] According to reports that reached the West Berlin press, West Berliners employed by the German railroads were to be assigned to work that day at very distant points, and the time necessary for them to commute to and from their jobs would thus make it impossible for them to go to the polls either before or after work.[131] There was also a rumor that service on the elevated railroad would be interrupted on December 5, so that West Berliners working in the east would not be able to get home before the polls closed.[132]

West Berlin authorities did their best to counteract such measures. It was announced that those who were forced to work on election

Sunday could apply for a certificate which would enable them to vote at any polling place on their way to or from their jobs. At the last minute, the independent trade unions took a leaf out of the communist book and announced that the elevated and subway systems would not be operated until 10:00 A.M. on Sunday. People working in the east sector would thus find it physically impossible to leave West Berlin before they had had an opportunity to vote.[133]

When election day dawned, there was some apprehension in West Berlin that the East German police or even Soviet troops might intervene at the last minute. The armed forces of the Western powers were held in readiness, and reinforced west sector police patrolled the city. But, as it turned out, such incidents as occurred were minor. A few armed Russian soldiers and officers appeared in outlying polling places, but were persuaded to leave by German police and Western military authorities.[134] At several polling stations, SED members started to note down the names of voters, but the police promptly intervened. In Neukölln, Communists went from house to house warning people not to vote, "as the Russians will be coming soon."[135]

Despite all attempts at intimidation, West Berliners went to the polls in unexpectedly large numbers and handed the Communists a major political defeat. Of the approximately 1,500,000 eligible voters, 83.9 per cent cast their ballots for nominees of one of the three democratic parties, 2.4 per cent cast invalid ballots, and 13.7 per cent did not vote. It cannot be assumed, however, that all those who did not vote were communist sympathizers, since in the 1946 elections, in which the SED also put up candidates, voter participation was only 6 per cent higher (89.7%), and 8.6 per cent of all eligible voters failed to vote. This suggests that, in 1948, only 5 to 6 per cent of the electorate demonstrated their sympathy for communism by staying away from the polls.[136] U.S. Military Government calculated that the strength of the SED in West Berlin had shrunk from 14 per cent in 1946 to under 5 per cent at the end of 1948.[137]

Problems of City Administration

In retrospect, it is amazing that the forcible division of the city by the Communists did not bring about a collapse of orderly administration in the west sectors. Members of the SED in the Magistrat and other branches of the city government did not surrender their positions until the final split of the city. Until that moment, therefore, the democratic members of the Magistrat were never able to discuss in official meetings any move that they did not wish to have immediately reported to SED headquarters and to the Soviets. Such confidential moves as those involved in planning airlift requirements had to be discussed in informal meetings from which SED officials were excluded.

Also, as in the case of City Councilman Schmidt, SED officials sometimes simply refused to carry out the orders of their superiors. For instance, Councilman Füllsack instructed a key official of the accounting section in his city food office, who was a member of the SED, to keep records of certain costs in west marks, because most supplies had to be bought and paid for in West Germany. The employee pointed out in a threatening manner that west marks were illegal in Berlin by order of the Soviet command and therefore should not appear on the books of the city government. Füllsack was ultimately forced to set up a separate accounting office in West Berlin where those accounts were thereafter kept.

Another consequence of the city division was the loss of records. The Communists were most insistent that official files remain in East Berlin, and officials who had been compelled to move their offices to West Berlin found it extremely difficult to compile adequate statistics for use in rationing, distribution, and the framing of airlift requirements. East Berlin authorities were also successful in preventing the removal of much of the office equipment on which orderly administration depended. Before the split, for instance, the city administration had had some 2,000 typewriters and 360 calculating machines. At the end of 1948, the west sector offices had only 990 typewriters and 104 calculating machines (and 273 of the typewriters and 58 of the calculating machines were rented).[138]

Finally, there was the problem of turnover in personnel. The city administrative offices, especially the key positions, had been heavily stocked with Communists, who now had to be replaced with employees whose loyalty to the legal city government was assured. That the administration of West Berlin remained as orderly as it did is a tribute to the energy and resourcefulness of the Berlin democrats.

An area of particular confusion was that of finance. The Soviets used their control over the central banking facilities to cripple the movement of funds needed for the payment of municipal expenses, as well as those of private industry, and the result was a money famine. The slightest error in the distribution of cash or credits would render firms unable to meet their current expenses.[139] The city government was kept solvent only by periodic injections of west marks from the Western powers.

Because the orderly functioning of the German administration was inhibited by the division of the city, as well as by direct communist interference, there was often no legal basis for governmental action. For instance, when the mobs at the city hall prevented the Assembly from meeting at the end of August, the government was unable to obtain an extension of its authority to pay unemployment benefits. Yet these benefits clearly had to be paid.

Administrative problems were compounded by complicated political relations among the democratic parties. To begin with, there was the anomalous situation of an administration headed by a member of a minority party. Dr. Friedensburg, acting mayor because of the illness of Louise Schroeder, was a member of the CDU, whereas by far the largest party in the Assembly was the SPD. Although stoutly opposed to Soviet domination, Dr. Friedensburg apparently still believed that the future of Berlin, and indeed of all Germany, lay in taking a middle position between the Soviets and the Western powers. This "bridge-building" philosophy differed strongly from the belief of Professor Reuter and many other SPD leaders that Berlin's only hope was to become firmly established as a part of the West.* Moreover, the Reuter group reasoned, if German officials were to strive for a middle position, this might provide an excuse for the Western powers if they should ever seek a way to escape their responsibility for defending Berlin.

Occasionally these differences between Friedensburg and the SPD leadership rose to the point of open conflict. The SPD, for example, was in favor of moving essential city services to West Berlin before the Soviets disorganized them entirely or drove them out by force; Dr. Friedensburg wanted the central government to stay in the city hall just as long as possible, so that the blame for the ultimate split could be laid squarely at the door of the Communists. Another serious issue arose over the elections, when the SPD accused Dr. Friedensburg of delaying election preparations in order to perpetuate himself in office. CDU leaders rejoined that the delays were not excessive, and were designed only to avoid further division of the city.[140] At an SPD rally, Dr. Suhr went so far as to state that he con-

* Dr. Friedensburg's views on this question are summarized in his *Berlin-Schicksal und Aufgabe*, Pädagogischer Verlag Berthold Schulz, Berlin, 1953, p. 38. A good statement of Reuter's views is contained in the latter's Introduction to *Berlin 1949*, the Magistrat's annual report for 1949.

sidered Dr. Friedensburg unfit to serve as acting mayor, and that, in the absence of Louise Schroeder, Ernst Reuter should head the city government. Dr. Suhr added that the division of central offices of the Magistrat between East and West Berlin was an untenable improvisation.[141]

City government and Western occupation officials, although they worked together more smoothly than before the blockade, still had a variety of problems in their mutual relationships. Since the Kommandatura had ceased to exist, there was no machinery for assuring uniformity in the measures taken in the several west sectors. Furthermore, so many military committees and authorities were involved in the operation of the west sectors that the German officials often did not know to whom to turn. A proposal of the city administration might be accepted by one occupation authority and rejected by another. Certain German recommendations about the operation of the airlift, for instance, were accepted by military government and then turned down by the U.S. Air Force for technical reasons. Also, there was a marked lack of consistency in the degree of authority allowed German agencies. Sometimes they would be given full responsibility for major programs; at other times, Allied authorities would interfere in minute details. Occasionally, as in the case of the first currency reform, the German officials were left ignorant of a major Allied decision until shortly before it went into effect.

Raised, as they were, in different cultural patterns, German personnel and Western occupation officials often saw the same facts in an entirely different light. To Americans, for example, the loss of airlift goods through wastage and thievery was very small; to Germans it was shockingly large. When City Councilman Füllsack made a personal inspection of one of the Berlin airfields and objected to some of the procedures for handling supplies, he was promptly arrested by suspicious military police, and it was three hours before he could be extricated. Another misunderstanding arose over the felling of trees for fuel. A British officer ordered a city official to cut down more trees than the Germans were willing to part with. The argument became bitter, the Englishman drew his revolver, and it was several days before the matter was settled with apologies on both sides. In spite of incidents such as these, however, team work improved steadily. Mayor Reuter could justly say that the world had seldom witnessed such cooperation between victors and vanquished so soon after a great war. And British Sector Commandant General

Herbert, a gruff man not given to diplomatic expression, could say to Reuter: "I have seen in this city the rebirth of a great nation."

Another stumbling block to efficient collaboration was a basic policy difference between the Western powers and the majority of city government officials. The Western powers, still committed to the principle of negotiation, hesitated to take steps to regularize the administration of the west sectors, whereas most of the German democratic leaders favored this. The SPD and the LDP demanded an integrated city administration in West Berlin and the establishment of the west mark as the sole valid currency. The fact that two currencies were circulating concurrently not only caused financial chaos; it also brought severe suffering to a large number of people who were paid in east marks but had to pay west marks for many necessities.

West Berlin's leaders were deeply troubled by the continuing negotiations between the Soviets and the Western powers, and the fear that these might end in some compromise that would betray the Berliners. Councilman Klingelhöfer, in a speech on November 20, attacked the "United Nations illusionists," who still hoped to see the blockade lifted on the basis of four-power control of east currency. They do not understand, he said, that the currency question is just a blind to hide the Soviet intention of mobilizing East Germany and Berlin in the fight against the Marshall Plan. He predicted that, before the United Nations ended its "slow-paced deliberations," the east sector would have become completely Sovietized and incorporated in the east zone.[142]

Most industrial and labor leaders shared this attitude, and bombarded military government authorities with requests to oppose any compromise that would foist the Soviet-sponsored currency on the city.* For example, on October 26 a committee representing German industry in the U.S. sector wrote to the Economics Division of U.S. Military Government:

> It would be disastrous for the economy of West Berlin if the Western powers were to decide to introduce eastern currency as the sole legal tender in Berlin. That would mean, sooner or later, the end of economic freedom in West Berlin. Therefore, the Industry Committee requests U.S. Military Government to

* Some of the smaller merchants, on the other hand, were in favor of retaining the dual-currency system. Many of this group supported the CDU, and this may help explain why the CDU was relatively cool to the suggestion that the west mark be established as the sole currency.

> oppose the introduction of the east mark. In this connection we would like to point out also that the effect of introducing the east mark would have most unfavorable psychological and political effects on the population. The man in the street would not understand it if he were given the less valuable east mark instead of the good west mark. His trust in the Western allies would be shaken. The fight for the freedom of Europe would be made considerably more difficult if Berlin were to be lost first economically and then also politically.

In point of fact, many military government officials personally shared this point of view, but the policy of their governments did not allow them to express their agreement in more than qualified tones.

Despite chaotic administrative conditions, and despite friction among various factions of the German government and between military government and German officials, the affairs of the city were conducted with an efficiency that was little short of amazing. Everyone in West Berlin received his rations. The city's economic requirements were worked out in great detail, and lists of necessary supplies were submitted to those in charge of the airlift. Social services and relief work functioned more smoothly during the fall and winter months than anyone had a right to expect, and coordination between the Berlin government and the Western powers was somehow achieved.

The city functioned, in defiance of all the laws of administration and bureaucracy, chiefly because West Berliners, as a group, were so widely agreed on the principal goals of the struggle that each person was able to direct his own activities toward their attainment. Governmental officials were able to act even when they lacked legal authority, because they were conscious of serving the people, and there was no question what the people wanted. An American scholar and observer of this period has described the situation as follows:

> Thus it was often up to individuals with authority to do what they felt necessary without specific mandate. Actually, what they were doing was as illegal as it was arbitrary. . . .
>
> *Ad hoc* authority for such action was given whenever possible by the City Assembly or by the majority of the Magistrat, but often such approval came after the historical development had verified the wisdom of the action. The authorization with which the actors reckoned was anticipation of and a sense of security

> about the popular response. In terms of German culture and traditions of authority, this can be considered revolutionary.[143]

When a country is at war, the individual tends to judge a given action by asking: "Will it help to win the war?" Similarly, in Berlin, it was possible to measure each action by the question: "Will it help to break the blockade and preserve freedom in the west sectors?"

This atmosphere of spontaneity was favored by two developments. One was the decimation of the ranks of old German officialdom by the war and its aftermath. City offices now were full of new civil servants, who were less imbued with the tradition that there must be specific authority for every action. The second development was the increasing identification of government workers with the independent unionists.[144]

The fact that this spirit of resistance was frequently shared by Western officials helped to grease the wheels of Allied-German cooperation. Some of the imaginative improvisation of the airlift seemed to communicate itself to military government offices, and the emphasis came to rest more and more on getting things done rather than on doing them according to the book. In the absence of coordinating machinery, both German and Allied elements were willing to work together informally. German administrative records of the time refer to innumerable informal conversations with Allied officials, up to the military governors. In this connection, the mutual respect which seems to have prevailed between General Clay and Ernst Reuter deserves special mention. When all else failed, Reuter would go to see Clay, and the problem in question usually would be solved.

Following the establishment of a separate government in East Berlin, and the December 5 elections, there came a reorganization of West Berlin's government—both military and civilian. The Kommandatura was revived on a three-power basis, in part as a result of German pressure. Ernst Reuter was again elected mayor by the City Assembly, and this time he was duly approved by the Western powers. The administrative provisions governing the three west sectors were made uniform, and the Magistrat appointed a "blockade committee" to act as a clearinghouse for the requirements of the German economy.[145] By the end of January 1949, many of the city's major administrative problems had been solved. Others, such as the problem of the dual currency, remained. But the period of greatest administrative chaos had been survived.

Tegel and Stolpe

The results of the December 5 elections gave West Berlin's democrats strength and confidence. When the City Assembly met on December 7, Dr. Suhr characterized the vote as the citizens' overwhelming expression of devotion to freedom and also as an indication of popular support for the policies of the city government.[146] Ernst Reuter, the twice-elected mayor, declared that he would do his best to serve as spokesman for the whole city and would endeavor to lead Berlin on the way to becoming a unified and free city and the capital of the German Federal Republic.[147]

This mood of hopeful defiance was heightened when, on December 16, the tower of the Soviet-controlled Radio Berlin in the French sector was blown up by order of General Ganeval, because it constituted a hazard for airlift planes coming in to the newly-opened Tegel airfield. West Berliners were delighted. Not only was the unpopular radio station temporarily silenced, but the French commandant had tweaked the bear's tail in a manner calculated to provide, as a report of the U.S. Military Governor put it, a "tremendous uplift to west sector morale."

From Soviet Military Government headquarters came the "strongest possible protests."[148] Under its main headline, "BERLIN INDIGNANT OVER ACT OF VIOLENCE," *Neues Deutschland* characterized the destruction of the tower as "cultural barbarism" carried out at American command, and as a disgrace to France.[149]

A few days later, French Military Government handed over to the Soviets the village of Stolpe, which up to that point had been administered as a part of the French sector.[150] No connection between the destruction of the tower and the surrender of Stolpe was officially admitted, but Berliners generally assumed that this was the price exacted by the Soviets for acquiescing in the French action. Actually, Stolpe might have had to be turned over to the Russians in any case, since it had originally been taken out from under the Soviet zone administration and added to the French sector on the grounds that the French needed the space for construction of an airfield. With the completion of the Tegel airfield (in the French sector), the original justification for French administration of Stolpe had been removed.

Whatever the legal virtues of the case, the surrender of Stolpe produced indignation and nervousness in West Berlin. In a meeting of the steering committee of the City Assembly, to which representatives of the press were invited, several assemblymen expressed apprehension that the action of the French authorities in the case of Stolpe might portend further concessions by the Western powers. The aspect of the incident that was resented most bitterly was that it involved the surrender of human beings. It was pointed out that the eligible voters in Stolpe, 93 per cent of whom had defied the Communists by participating in the recent elections, would now be exposed to reprisals.[151]

Rumors to the effect that other outlying areas of West Berlin would be turned over to Soviet administration were reflected in a flood of letters to West Berlin newspapers and radio stations. An anonymous Berliner, reporting such a rumor about his section of the city in a letter to the U.S.-operated RIAS radio, added plaintively: "Would the Ami really do anything like that to us? We want to preserve our freedom." Rumors continued to circulate during the first three months of 1949, and U.S. and British military governments had to issue several public denials and assure Berliners that no further transfers of territory were contemplated.[152]

Destruction of the radio tower and the return of Stolpe were almost the last in the series of dramatic incidents that had punctuated the political history of Berlin in the opening months of the blockade. The remainder of the blockade period was marked by the reconstruction of a more orderly political and economic life in West Berlin.

International Negotiations

While the Soviets were sealing off East Berlin from Western influence and tightening the blockade, diplomatic activity proceeded at a furious pace. Aides-mémoire were exchanged in Moscow, notes circulated among the four governments involved, the United Nations Security Council was brought into the dispute, and diplomats from nations not directly concerned tried their hand at finding a solution.

The Soviet purpose during these negotiations was apparently to keep the Western powers at the conference table until the blockade of West Berlin forced them to make appreciable concessions. Moscow's spokesmen tried increasingly to blame the West for the breakup of the Berlin discussions of the military governors in September, and insisted that the Soviet Union was willing at any time to settle the Berlin question on the basis of the Moscow Agreement.

The Western powers, for their part, still insisted on their legal right to remain in Berlin, and refused to make the concessions demanded by the Soviets. Instead, they strengthened the airlift, took additional counterblockade measures, and continued to seek a solution through diplomatic channels which would not compromise their position in Berlin. But at the same time, the Allies' unwillingness to make the west mark the sole currency in West Berlin, and their hesitation about reorganizing the Berlin Kommandatura on a three-power basis, may have encouraged the Soviets to believe that Western concessions might yet be forthcoming.

Although they were ordinarily able to maintain a firm diplomatic front in public, the Western allies sometimes found it difficult to agree among themselves on a common course of action. Also, there were serious differences of opinion within each of the three nations. In Washington, though there was now almost universal agreement that to abandon Berlin would be a major mistake, some officials remained hesitant, while others believed that time was now on the side of the West. As airlift performance improved, the more optimistic group grew in strength.

These general developments were reflected in negotiations on the Berlin question between September 1948, and February 1949. A brief description of these negotiations follows.

Breakdown of the Berlin discussions among the four military governors in September had put the West back in the situation it had faced in August, and many of the diplomatic personnel felt tired and dispirited. Secretary Marshall reported at a cabinet meeting on September 10 that all persons concerned with the Berlin negotiations were close to exhaustion. Officials in Washington had been conferring with the U.S. Embassy in London by transatlantic teletype until 2:00 A.M. the night before, and had resumed their talks at 8:30 in the morning. Negotiations were greatly hampered by the fact that, at that moment, there was no responsible government in France.[153]

On September 14 the Western representatives in Moscow delivered a new aide-mémoire to Stalin and Molotov, which reviewed the three main points at issue during the Berlin discussions of military governors: traffic restrictions between Berlin and West Germany, four-power supervision over Berlin's currency, and control of Berlin's trade. The document demonstrated that on each point the Soviet Military Governor had deviated from the understanding reached earlier in Moscow.[154]

Stalin was still on vacation, and Molotov appeared in no hurry to reply to this note. Rather than exchange communications on a governmental level, he said, he was in favor of referring the questions back to the military governors in Berlin for a report. When the Western representatives pointed out that the four commanders had already found it impossible to agree, Molotov reluctantly agreed to present the matter to his government.[155] But, according to news stories, he referred the Western memorandum to Marshal Sokolovsky anyway.[156] Dr. Philip C. Jessup, who later was to present the U.S. position at the United Nations, characterized these negotiations by saying: "We discovered that the talks we were holding were serving as an excuse to prolong the blockade rather than as a method of removing it."[157]

On September 18, an official Soviet reply to the Western memorandum denied that Sokolovsky had deviated from the Moscow Agreement and accused the Western powers of interpreting the Moscow directive in a "unilateral manner." The note maintained that Marshal Sokolovsky, in demanding restrictions on air traffic to and from Berlin, was merely pointing to the necessity of observing regulations that had been imposed by Control Council agreement in 1945.[158] With regard to four-power currency controls, the Soviet memorandum alleged that the Allies' proposal would enable the Western occupation powers to exert undue influence on the whole Soviet zone. Moscow defended Marshal Sokolovsky's position on the trade issue, and supported his demand that the Soviets have the final authority to issue licenses for the traffic of goods in and out of Berlin.[159]

The Western powers were prepared for this negative Soviet reaction. On September 22 they delivered identical notes to the Soviet embassies in Washington, London, and Paris, which asserted that Soviet unwillingness to accept previous agreements was still preventing a settlement, and outlined the "final position" of the three governments. This position was that no restrictions on Berlin's air traffic could be accepted, that a four-power finance commission would have to exert effective control over the introduction and use of the east mark in Berlin, and that trade between Berlin and the west zones would have to be under true four-power control. The notes concluded by asking bluntly whether, in order to create conditions that would permit further discussions, the Soviets were prepared to remove the blockade.[160]

Up to this time negotiations among the four powers had been conducted in secrecy, but now there came a series of leaks from the Soviet side. On September 22 the Prague newspaper *Svobodne Slovo* published a story blaming the Western powers for the breakup of the Berlin discussions. The story was attributed to "well-informed journalistic quarters in Paris," and was picked up by the Soviet-controlled German press on the following day. The causes of dissent were said to have been "artificially created" by the American, British, and French commanders, who had deviated from the precise instructions contained in the Moscow Agreement and had tried to secure four-power control over the circulation of currency in the Soviet zone as well as in Berlin.

The British Foreign Office unofficially denounced these reports as a "gross distortion of facts," and there was a flurry of indignation in Washington as well. The London *Times* expressed the opinion that the leakage was officially inspired.[161]

Close on the heels of these press reports came an official Soviet reply to the Western notes of September 22. In notes delivered in Washington, London, and Paris on September 25, the Soviets reiterated that the Berlin problem was a result of Western currency reform, and accused the Western powers of introducing their own currency into Berlin in order "to dislocate the economy of the eastern zone of Germany and, ultimately, to force the U.S.S.R. to withdraw therefrom."[162] They insisted on their previous position regarding Berlin's finances, and repeated their demand that the air corridors, as well as other avenues to Berlin, should be controlled, arguing that air-traffic control was a necessary prerequisite to four-power control over currency and trade. The notes did, however, state that the Soviets would be willing to agree to four-power control of Berlin's trade, provided agreement were reached on other points. In subsequent discussions, Russian spokesmen frequently referred to this concession on trade as evidence of the Soviets' sincere interest in reaching an agreement.

The day after the Soviet notes had been delivered, a statement from the official Soviet news agency, TASS, reproached Western spokesmen for not giving a true picture of the Berlin situation, and asserted that the Berlin negotiations had collapsed because the three Western commanders had referred certain questions back to a governmental level instead of settling them on the spot. The tone of the TASS statement was considerably milder than that of the earlier Czech and German newspaper stories, and the last paragraph expressed the Soviets' desire to reopen negotiations.[163]

If the offer of concessions on Berlin's trade was intended to bring the Western powers back to the conference table, it failed in its purpose. On September 26 the Western powers replied to Moscow that the "illegal and coercive" blockade of Berlin made further negotiations impossible, that the Soviets had created "a threat to international peace and security," and that the democracies therefore found themselves "obliged to refer the action of the Soviet Government to the Security Council of the United Nations."[164]

Accordingly, on September 29, the British, U.S., and French governments sent identical letters to the Secretary General of the United Nations, asking that the Security Council consider "at the earliest opportunity" the threat to the peace (within the meaning of Chapter VII of the United Nations Charter) that had arisen in Berlin.[165]

The Western decision to refer the Berlin matter to the United Nations had been debated among the Allies for several weeks, and serious differences of opinion had become evident. The British and French would have preferred to ask Stalin for new discussions.[166] Also, neither Britain nor France was willing to frame diplomatic communications to the Soviets in as firm a language as the United States desired. On September 13 Secretary Marshall told the cabinet that Bevin had sent him a personal cable expressing the hope that a break in negotiations with the Soviets could be avoided and that it would not be necessary to send the issue to the United Nations. The cabinet then discussed the war-weariness of the British, and their hesitation to make crucial decisions because "they were in the front line."[167]

Washington's evaluation of British attitudes may, however, have been unduly pessimistic. When Bevin discussed the Berlin situation in Parliament a few days later, he made it clear that the British position had not softened. The London *Times* reported that there was a weary bitterness about the way he denounced the "dastardly scheme" of the Soviets. Berlin, he said, stood out now as a symbol of resistance. When the blockade was imposed, a great choice had had to be made: It was either to stand firm or to face another Munich. The British had chosen to stand firm.[168]

In bringing the Berlin question before the United Nations, the Western powers were appealing to world public opinion. A press report from Paris on September 23 cited "officials in close touch with the Moscow negotiations" as saying that the latest diplomatic notes to the Kremlin were chiefly for the record, so that the Western public might know that every effort had been made to bridge the gap between the Soviet Union and the democracies; if, as expected, the Berlin issue was carried to the United Nations, it would be for the same purpose.[169] Another report, a day later, indicated that neither American nor British officials expected an appeal to the United Nations to do more than transfer the Berlin issue from the realm of ultra-secret diplomacy to the court of world opinion.[170] On September 26, the Department of State, in the same endeavor to put the issues before the people, published an official account of negotiations on Berlin up to that time,[171] and the British Foreign Office issued an almost identical report on October 11.[172]

Some observers predicted that the appeal to the United Nations would lead to a Soviet walk-out.[173] As expected, the Communists were prompt to denounce the Western action. Articles in the Soviet-controlled Berlin press called it an attempt to "torpedo the United Nations." A front-page editorial in *Neues Deutschland* on September 30 charged General Clay personally with responsibility for breaking off the Berlin negotiations. In a 5,000-word statement to the East German press on October 2, Marshal Sokolovsky presented the Soviet version of the Berlin events. He charged that the Western powers were using the Berlin issue to build up an aggressive military bloc against the Soviet Union, that they were splitting Germany and Berlin, that the "so-called airlift" was a purely propagandistic measure, which placed an unnecessary burden on the Germans, and that the three Western military governors, by their unwillingness to honor the Moscow Agreement, had caused the breakdown of the Berlin discussions. The Soviet government, said Sokolovsky, had already informed the West that it was prepared to continue the Berlin talks on the basis of the Moscow Agreement, and the solution of the problem therefore depended on the United States, Great Britain, and France.[174]

The next day, October 3, the Soviet government replied officially to the Western notes of September 26. The Soviet diplomatic note covered much the same ground as Marshal Sokolovsky's statement. It denied that the Berlin dispute could properly be referred to the United Nations, and charged the democracies with sabotaging the Berlin discussions and using the United Nations for their own aggressive aims. It proposed that the Moscow Agreement be recognized as the basis on which to regulate the Berlin situation, and asked that the Council of Foreign Ministers be convened to consider the question of Germany as a whole.[175]

Over the violent objections of Soviet delegate Vyshinsky, who maintained that the Berlin question should be referred to the

Council of Foreign Ministers, the United Nations Security Council voted on October 5 to include the dispute on its agenda. Vyshinsky thereupon announced that the Soviet delegation would take no part in the discussions.[176] Soviet representatives did, however, sit in and listen while Dr. Philip C. Jessup for the United States, Sir Alexander Cadogan for Great Britain, and Alexandre Parodi for France asserted the right of the Western powers to remain in Berlin, denounced the Soviet blockade, and appealed to the Council for action. The three spokesmen did not suggest what this action should be, but, as Cadogan expressed it, were content to place themselves in the hands of the Council.[177]

Those not directly involved in the Berlin dispute, the six "neutral members" of the Security Council, were clearly worried by the danger to world peace that was posed by the Berlin situation. Under the leadership of Argentine Foreign Minister Juan Bramuglia, they immediately approached Soviet and Allied representatives in hopes of finding a mutually satisfactory formula.[178] In the course of these informal conferences, Dr. Bramuglia asked each of the four powers to reply to certain questions, such as what was the extent of the traffic restrictions, and why were the military governors unable to carry out the Moscow Agreement. The Western powers agreed to provide the information, but Vyshinsky insisted that the Soviets would stand by their decision to boycott the discussion, and told the Security Council on October 15: "You ask questions and attempt to get replies, and thus put the Soviet delegation into the position of embarking upon consideration of them. . . . It is useless to think we will bite this bait."[179]

The six "neutrals" nevertheless continued their efforts and, on October 22, presented a resolution to the Security Council which, they hoped, would provide a basis for ending the blockade. All traffic restrictions were to be called off immediately, and the four military governors were then to meet and arrange for unification of currency in Berlin on the basis of the east mark in accordance with the Moscow Agreement. Finally, there was to be a meeting of the four foreign ministers to discuss problems affecting Germany as a whole.

The Western powers agreed to support the resolution, but the Soviet Union vetoed it on October 25 because, as Vyshinsky said, it did not provide for introduction of the east mark simultaneously with the removal of transport restrictions.[180]

Once again, the Soviets attempted to place the blame for the breakdown on the West. In a statement given to *Pravda* on October 29, Stalin asserted that Vyshinsky and Bramuglia had reached agreement on a solution to the Berlin question. And he implied that the Western powers had at first accepted this agreement, but had then gone back on their word.[181] The *Pravda* reporter asked dutifully: "What is the matter then? Could you explain?" Stalin's reply is an excellent sample of the Soviet prose of the period:

> The thing is that those in the U.S.A. and Great Britain who inspire an aggressive policy do not consider themselves interested in agreement and in cooperation with the U.S.S.R. What they want is not agreement and cooperation, but talk about agreement and cooperation so as to put the blame on the U.S.S.R., because a policy of concord with the U.S.S.R. undermines the position of the instigators of war and deprives the aggressive policy of these gentlemen of any purpose. It is for this reason that they disrupt agreements that have already been reached, disavow their representatives who have drawn up such agreements together with the U.S.S.R., and, in violation of the United Nations Charter, refer the question to the Security Council, where they have a guaranteed majority and where they can "prove" whatever they like. All this is done to "show" that cooperation with the U.S.S.R. is impossible, to "show" the necessity for a new war, and thus to prepare the ground for the unleashing of war.
>
> The policy of the present leaders of the U.S.A. and Great Britain is a policy of aggression, a policy of unleashing a new war.[182]

In Paris, where the Security Council was meeting, Dr. Jessup told the press tartly, in answer to questions about Stalin's statement, that "no . . . agreement [between the Western powers and the neutrals] existed and therefore there was no question of any violation of such an agreement."[183]

When the Soviets published the agreement that the West was alleged to have rejected, it became clear that it differed on only one major point from the resolution Vyshinsky had vetoed. The Soviet version provided that the blockade was to be lifted simultaneously with the actual introduction of the east mark as the sole currency in all Berlin. [184] The proposal of the neutrals had been that the blockade was to be lifted first, and that the four military governors were then to make arrangements for the currency adjustment. In effect, the Soviet proposal meant that, unless the Western military governors accepted the Soviet interpretation of four-power currency control, the blockade would remain.

Though discouraged by the Soviet veto, the neutrals as well as United Nations staff personnel did not give up hope. The day after the veto, U.N. Secretary General Trygve Lie began an attempt to use the facilities of his office toward a solution of the Berlin problem. Briefly, his plan was that the senior Soviet and U.S. members of his staff at the United Nations should act as intermediaries between the principal parties involved, and thus help to work out a settlement without the formal negotiations in which both East and West were then unwilling to participate.

Mr. Lie's plan at first received only slight encouragement from the Western powers and a distinctly cold reception from the Soviets. Mr. Feller, a senior American member of the U.N. staff, agreed that intervention by the Secretary General would be "worth a try." Mr. Sobolev, senior Soviet staff member, expressed doubt that anything would emerge from such consultations, but agreed to arrange a talk between Lie and Vyshinsky for the evening of October 28. At this conversation, Vyshinsky was distinctly discouraging. He did not believe, he said, that the Americans and British really wanted a settlement, and in any case he lacked authority to comment on the Secretary General's plan.[185]

Lie's persistence was rewarded when, on October 30, Vyshinsky asked to discuss the matter with him again. The marked change in Vyshinsky's attitude at the second meeting led Lie to conclude that the Soviet diplomat had meanwhile been instructed by Moscow to support the new, indirect negotiations.[186]

When the British Foreign Office was informed of Lie's plans, however, it objected that the proposed procedure would, in fact, constitute negotiation between the Soviets and the Western powers, and that the British, for their part, would not enter into negotiations as long as the blockade continued. Instead, London suggested, the neutrals should resume their efforts, with all possible assistance from the four powers. The other Western powers promptly agreed to the British proposal, and Dr. Bramuglia took up his efforts again in November.[187]

In two respects, the new attempt differed from the previous one. First, the Soviets this time collaborated with the mediators. Second, it was decided that a U.N. committee of experts from the six neutrals would try and work out all the necessary technical details regarding the introduction of the east mark as the sole Berlin currency. Thus, the matter would not have to be referred to the four military governors, and it would become possible for the lifting of the blockade and the new currency regulations to go into effect simultaneously. Secretary General Lie appointed Dr. Gunnar Myrdal, the Swedish Executive Secretary of the United Nations Economic Commission for Europe, as his representative to the committee, and Dr. N. Kaldor, a member of the Economic Commission staff, as secretary. Lie remarked later that, as is often the case, especially in technical questions, the secretary did much of the work.[188]

While waiting for the other members of the committee of experts to be appointed, Dr. Bramuglia sent out a new questionnaire to the four disputants. The Soviet answer came back almost immediately and, in general, reiterated the Soviet position on the basis of the Moscow Agreement, but without demands for control of air traffic and with a modified stand on trade.[189] The reply of the Western powers, received toward the end of November, stated that the situation had changed considerably since August 30, that four-power control of currency might not be sufficient to meet the needs of a city administration that was rapidly being split in two, and that it would be necessary to arrange four-power control of the Soviet zone bank of issue insofar as its operations extended to Berlin.[190]

Just as the neutral committee was starting its work, the Soviets finally split the Berlin government completely by setting up the east sector "Magistrat" on November 30. This caused the Western powers to modify their position still further. A State Department spokesman observed that the Soviet action made solution of the Berlin crisis much more difficult, and might make it impossible.[191] In a statement to Dr. Bramuglia, the Western powers pointed out that the Soviet action had created a situation in which it was no longer possible for them to agree in advance to whatever recommendations the Security Council might make. They would continue to cooperate with the committee of neutrals, but they could not be bound to submit to all Soviet measures "which add to and intensify the Soviet blockade" while the Soviets remained wholly uncommitted to any restraint.[192] In London, diplomatic quarters regarded the Soviet decision to split the city government as a blow that might be fatal to the efforts of the neutrals.[193] A few days later the Western powers issued, for the information of the neutrals, a review of

Soviet actions in Berlin, in which they said that any agreement on currency was rapidly being rendered inapplicable by the division of the city's administration. Ernest Bevin voiced a similar opinion in the House of Commons.[194]

Privately, some Western officials expressed themselves even more gloomily. General Clay wrote later that, in his opinion, the deliberations of the neutral committee had "no reality from the day it was established."[195] He felt that the currency problem could be resolved only if quadripartite government were restored in Berlin, and that this could not happen unless either the Soviets backed down or the West sacrificed the German political leaders who had chosen to stand for freedom. American financial experts who took part in the currency discussions later expressed the opinion that a fair solution on the basis of the Moscow Agreement would have been difficult, if not impossible, even if Berlin had remained intact. One of them remarked that the agreement of August 30 came close to handing financial control of Berlin over to the Soviets. There were, however, political specialists in the State Department who took the more hopeful view that an equitable arrangement with the Soviets could yet be worked out without sacrifice of basic freedoms.

In spite of the dominant attitude of skepticism on the part of Western experts, the neutral commission proceeded with its endeavors, and the Soviets appeared even more cooperative than before the split of Berlin. On December 4, TASS published a lengthy series of clarifications to the material already turned over to Bramuglia.[196] The clarifications once again stressed Soviet eagerness to arrange a settlement on the basis of the Moscow Agreement, but made no mention of the split of Berlin. This omission was not surprising. According to the official Soviet interpretation, the city government had not been split at all: the legal Magistrat simply had been deposed and replaced by another government.

Shortly before Christmas, the neutral experts produced a plan for a settlement of the Berlin dispute based on the Moscow Agreement. This led to a temporary difference of opinion among the Allies. American experts regarded the plan as inherently unworkable, while the British and French, along with the Soviets, were willing to accept it as a basis for discussion. The American position was made more difficult by the attitude of staff members of the U.N. Economic Commission for Europe, who provided most of the research and consulting facilities required by the neutral experts. Dr. Myrdal and Dr. Kaldor were both brilliant and persuasive men.

But their opinions, in the eyes of U.S. financial experts, were closer to the Soviet than the American viewpoint. As one U.S. observer phrased it, "they took the 'neutralist' position that East and West were equally to blame for the situation in Berlin, and they were always trying to shove east marks down our throat." Another American official remarked that during this period the United States was fighting an uphill propaganda battle, brought on by its unwise acceptance of the Moscow Agreement in August.

When currency experts of the four powers returned to Paris in January, the United States submitted a counterproposal to the effect that the Soviet mark should be introduced throughout the city, but should be under exclusively Western control in the west sectors. The Soviets rejected this plan as not in accordance with the Moscow Agreement, and Great Britain and France, though not enthusiastic about the new U.S. proposal, thereupon agreed to reject the plan of the neutral committee.[197]

Whether the Soviet Union would actually have accepted the formula proposed by the neutral committee is open to question. A U.S. observer noted that, when the committee's draft was first issued, there was a great deal of jockeying to see who would comment on it first. The Soviets insisted on waiting for the U.S. reaction. After the United States had rejected the proposal, the Soviets could safely say that they accepted the draft in principle. Even so, their acceptance was so hedged with reservations that it also could have been interpreted as a rejection. The British government later stated that Soviet acceptance of the draft had been subject to major amendments "designed to increase the degree of Soviet interference in the day-to-day administration of currency and trade in the western sectors and to twist the committee's plan to enable the Soviet authorities to gain a stranglehold on the economic life of these sectors.[198]

Having already implied that the Moscow Agreement had been overtaken by new developments, the United States in January restated its position more formally. It demanded that the west mark continue to circulate in the west sectors until a unified city administration could be restored, and was supported on this point by England and France. On February 3 the *New York Times* reported that Washington now wished to lay aside the Moscow Agreement entirely, and on February 11 the committee of neutrals advised the President of the Security Council that "the present positions of the experts of the Four Occupying Powers are so far apart in this matter that further work by the Committee, at this stage, does not appear useful.[199]

Although the Berlin question formally remained on the agenda of the Security Council until the end of the blockade, diplomatic action shifted away from this arena in February 1949, and representatives of the four powers resumed conversations directly and in secret.

The Development of Western Policy

Western policy during this period moved in the manner of the pilgrim who takes two steps forward and one backward. But, little by little, the stand of the West became more firm.

Already in September and October of 1948, there were leading American officials who believed that the Soviets could be forced to back down without concessions on the part of the West. At a high-level conference in Paris in late September, General Clay stated that the airlift could support Berlin indefinitely and that the European Recovery Program would eventually build up Western Europe to a point where it could exert, rather than absorb, pressure. This power of Western Europe, he felt, was the force that could be counted on to bring the blockade to an end.[200] Clay's analysis of the situation was shared by Mayor Reuter and some of Reuter's associates in the Berlin SPD. Ambassador Smith, on the other hand, said at the same conference that Berlin was a liability to be disposed of at the first auspicious moment, even though for the time being it was necessary to defend the Western position in the city.[201] Only a few days before, Secretary Marshall had expressed the opinion that time was working in favor of the Soviets,[202] and James Reston made a similar evaluation in the *New York Times* on September 28. Trygve Lie has noted in his memoirs that Americans in Berlin were more inclined toward a firm stand than was Washington.[203]

There is no question that the ever-increasing success of the airlift helped to stiffen Western resolve. On October 1, the London *Times* suggested that time was working in favor of the West, when it reported that stocks in Berlin were now actually more plentiful than before the blockade. Lie notes that, by the end of October, United Nations circles were largely convinced that the success of the airlift had rendered the West less willing to make concessions. As a case in point, he mentions Professor Jessup, who, he thought, had become more hopeful about finding a solution to the blockade problem as a result of a visit to Berlin in the fall of 1948, where he had seen the airlift in operation.[204] General Clay told the National Security Council on October 22 that the airlift was no longer an experiment, and that it could supply Berlin even under adverse weather conditions.[205]

Nevertheless, some indecision remained. Colonel Howley tells of his indignation at learning, after the split of the city government, that the State Department had not ruled out a compromise solution to the blockade.[206] The fact that the Western powers still allowed the east mark to circulate in West Berlin and differentiated the west marks in Berlin from those in West Germany by stamping the former with a "B" also suggested the continued possibility of compromise. Press reports early in December indicated that the west mark would be made sole legal tender on January 1,[207] but the day came and went with no change in the currency situation.

In spite of this element of indecision, which was not disposed of until early in 1949, the West was gradually building up the two chief instruments with which it was able to oppose the blockade directly: the airlift and the counterblockade. British and American air forces continued to add aircraft to the lift during September, and to make more efficient use of those already at their disposal. On October 15, the Combined Airlift Task Force was established, under the command of General William H. Tunner, to direct the gigantic operation on a joint Anglo-American basis. A week later, General Clay flew to Washington and, in twenty-four hours, secured authorization from President Truman and the National Security Council for adding sixty-six more C-54 transports to the airlift, thereby increasing its capacity by approximately one-third.[208] Construction of the big Tegel airfield and other facilities continued in Berlin, and Tegel was opened for traffic on December 1.

The counterblockade was built up more cautiously. Normal commercial traffic from West Germany to the Soviet zone had been stopped on June 24, but the zonal frontiers had never actually been closed by the West, and substantial quantities of materials were still passing back and forth. Soviet and East German purchasers also were able to obtain some items in West Berlin. On September 22 the London *Times* reported that unspecified "new measures" were being taken to stop this leakage. A few days later, U.S. military authorities in Berlin issued orders to the German police to crack down on smugglers who were removing goods from the American sector. The German police gleefully seized upon this order as a stick with which to beat the Communists, and in a single day stopped more than fifty trucks on their way from the Soviet zone to the Soviet sector, confiscating dozens of tons of coal and food.[209] The other Western powers did not immediately follow the American example. Even trade between East and West Germany was not brought to a complete halt. On January 5, 1949, the London *Times* reported that British authorities were concerned about smuggling from the British zone to East Germany. A proposal to station 5,000 lightly-armed police at the border had not yet been adopted, and east zone industry was still obtaining substantial quantities of raw materials from the west.

The most important programs of the Western powers in Europe during this period were the Marshall Plan, the establishment of a West German government, and the formation of defensive alliances. Though not specifically directed against the blockade, they probably played a much more important part in bringing it to an end than did the counterblockade. Beginning in September 1948, representatives of the eleven West German states met as a "Parliamentary Council" in Bonn to draft a basic law, or constitution, for West Germany. At the same time, the Western powers were working out the terms of an occupation statute, which was to define the authority of the occupying powers when the West German government came into being. They also concluded an agreement, together with the Benelux nations, on the establishment of an international authority to supervise Ruhr industry.[210] By the spring of 1949, these preparations for the creation of a West German government were completed. Meanwhile, the effects of the Marshall Plan had become apparent. Along with currency reform and the vigorous enterprise of the Germans, it was transforming West Germany from an economic desert into a thriving and productive society. Some phases of the program in Germany were 20 per cent completed by October, 1948,[211] and economic activity was increasing in other Western European lands as well. By March 1949, nearly five billion dollars had been authorized for the purchase of goods needed in Europe.[212]

Finally, the democracies were rallying for military defense. Talks that were to lead to the establishment of the North Atlantic Treaty Organization were in progress all during the latter half of 1948, and a common military organization for the defense of Western Europe was announced by Great Britain, France, and the Benelux powers at the end of September. The balance of power in Europe appeared to be shifting in favor of the West.

The Impact of Events on Soviet Diplomatic Behavior

Events went against the Soviets in the fall of 1948. The remarkable achievements of the airlift breathed new confidence into the statesmen of the Western powers. Far from being intimidated by Russian threats of violence and hunger, West Berliners and their leaders were becoming ever more defiant, and their shouts before the Reichstag on September 9 must have been heard within the walls of the Kremlin. In spite of the onrushing winter, the likelihood of either a supply or a morale crisis in Berlin became more and more remote.

At the Berlin conference of military governors early in September, the Soviets tested the resolution of the democracies. But the Western military governors realized then that, if they accepted Marshal Sokolovsky's interpretation of the Moscow Agreement, economic control of the whole city would go to the Soviets, and the democracies would remain in Berlin only on sufferance. The Soviet proposals were therefore rejected out of hand by all the Western military governors.

Simultaneously, the Soviets were subjecting the democratic city government to one last severe test. Communist efforts to intimidate the City Assembly and supplant the Magistrat during the last days of August would, if successful, have placed the German civilian government under the control of Moscow, leaving the Western powers no more than a token voice in the affairs of the city. But the Berlin government emerged from this test more resolute than before.

Having started the blockade with the intention of imposing a difficult choice on the West, the Soviets themselves were now faced with a dilemma: Should they continue to pursue the rapidly fading hopes of securing control over all Berlin? Or should they concentrate on consolidating communist controls in East Berlin with a view to making this area an integral part of East Germany?

As far as can be determined, they chose to take the bird in the hand, but without giving up entirely the hope of capturing the bird in the bush. They speeded up the process of eliminating all opposition to communism in the east sector, thus making it an exclusive Soviet preserve. At the same time, they tightened the blockade on the chance that the Western powers might yet find themselves forced to surrender all or part of their power in the city.

This dual policy was not without its dangers for Moscow. As long as Berlin was a single city with a democratic government, the

Soviets could not afford to accept any settlement that left them with less than full, or nearly-full, control. They were not willing, therefore, to trade complete domination of East Berlin for a compromise solution in the whole city. They wanted full control in East Berlin, or else a preeminent position in all Berlin. This, presumably, was why Vyshinsky, on October 25, vetoed the first proposal of the neutral members of the Security Council, even though, superficially, it seemed to offer more favorable terms than the Soviets later secured in the final settlement. The proposal would have allowed the east mark to become the exclusive currency in all Berlin, and this in itself would have given a tremendous boost to Soviet prestige throughout Germany. But the plan also would have enabled the Western powers to insist on genuine four-power control of the currency in the whole city, and this the Soviets were not prepared to accept. Moscow's unsuccessful counterproposal, by which the blockade would not be lifted until the currency question had been settled, would have left the way open for Soviet economic domination of the whole city.

Following establishment of the separate east sector "Magistrat," the Soviets were in a slightly stronger negotiating position. Whatever the currency arrangement, it would not be likely to impair their authority in East Berlin, since it would be administered by compliant communist authorities. Adoption of the Soviet zone mark in West Berlin, on the other hand, would be a major blow to the prestige of the democracies. If, therefore, the Soviets seemed eager to secure another proposal from the neutral committee in December and January, after they had swallowed East Berlin, they probably were motivated not only by the desire for a propaganda advantage, but also by the calculation that whatever concessions could be extracted from the West at this date would represent pure gain.

But Washington's repudiation of the Moscow Agreement, in January of 1949 reduced almost to zero the possibility that the Soviets might profit from further currency negotiations. Furthermore, spring was coming, and the greatest days of the airlift lay ahead.

CHAPTER VI
LIFTING THE BLOCKADE

IN JANUARY 1949 there were a number of indications that the Soviets had decided to investigate the possibility of removing traffic restrictions without demanding appreciable concessions from the West. They were, however, in no apparent hurry to bring the crisis to an end. Their aggressive policies in Berlin were pursued with undiminished vigor, and the city remained dependent on air supply for several more months. Meanwhile, life in the blockaded city gradually became more normal, the airlift—after struggling through several critical winter weeks—mounted from triumph to triumph, and the Western powers began to tighten the counterblockade to the point where only an insignificant trickle of supplies reached the Soviets from West Germany or West Berlin. By the time the blockade was lifted in May of 1949, a communist peace campaign was in full swing, and a new phase in Soviet foreign policy had begun.

The Beginning of the End

On the last day of January 1949, Premier Stalin replied to a number of questions that had been put to him on January 27 by J. Kingsbury Smith, European manager of the International News Service. One of these questions was directly related to Berlin, and question and answer ran as follows:

> *Question:* If the Governments of the United States of America, the United Kingdom and France agreed to postpone the establishment of a separate Western German state, pending a meeting of the Council of Foreign Ministers to consider the German problem as a whole, would the Government of the U.S.S.R. be prepared to remove the restrictions which the Soviet authorities have imposed on communications between Berlin and the Western zones of Germany?
>
> *Answer:* Provided the United States of America, Great Britain and France observe the conditions set forth in the third question, the Soviet Government see no obstacles to lifting transport restrictions, on the understanding, however, that transport and trade restrictions introduced by the three powers should be lifted simultaneously.

Another question, related only indirectly to the Berlin situation, was whether Stalin would be in favor of a meeting between President Truman and himself. The Soviet leader replied that, as he had already stated, there would be no objection to such a meeting from his side.[1] His reference to a meeting with President Truman initially aroused more discussion than his statement about a possible end to the blockade. Such a meeting had previously been advocated by the leftist Progressive Party in the United States, and had been enthusiastically greeted by the Moscow press,[2] but President Truman and Secretary Acheson had immediately thrown cold water on the proposal. Acheson, who had been sworn in as Secretary of State on January 21, said cautiously that discussions with the Soviet Union could be resumed only after the Berlin question had been solved and the blockade lifted. And he added that the United States did not propose to exclude other interested nations from these discussions. President Truman remarked that he would be glad to receive Stalin if the latter wished to come to Washington, but that the U.S. government would not enter into bilateral negotiations with the Soviets.[3]

The Soviet premier's statement about Berlin, although less noted at first, ultimately resulted in the reopening of U.S.-Soviet negotiations. In Washington, State Department specialists surmised that Stalin's failure to mention the currency problem might indicate his willingness to abandon the Moscow Agreement as a basis for settling the Berlin dispute. Accordingly, on February 15, Ambassador Jessup informally inquired from the Soviet representative on the Security Council, Jacob Malik, whether Stalin's omission of any reference to the currency question had been accidental. One month later, on March 15, Malik informed Jessup that the omission was "not accidental."[4] From that point on, negotiations progressed rapidly.

Meanwhile, there had been other developments that might well have portended a change in Soviet policy. On January 28, the press reported three events of possible significance, all of which were connected with an SED party congress then being held in East Berlin. The first was the suppression of a speech that Colonel Tulpanov, chief of Soviet Military Government's Information Division, had made at the congress. The London *Times* reported that the action had been preceded by telephone conversations between Soviet Military Government headquarters and the Kremlin, and interpreted it as a censure of Tulpanov's strong anti-Western stand at a time when Moscow was seeking to achieve a certain relaxation in international tension.[5]

Next, a press conference, which was to have been given on January 27 by delegates from the sixteen nations represented at the SED congress, was canceled, ostensibly because the Czech and some other delegates had had to leave unexpectedly. And a meeting of the East Berlin "Magistrat," scheduled for the same day, was also called off.[6]

Finally, Walter Ulbricht, probably the most powerful man in the SED, was reported to have said in a speech that day: "We do not consider Berlin a Soviet zone city, but the German capital." He also added that Berlin would not be incorporated into the Soviet zone. Previously, communist speakers had always taken the line that Berlin was an integral part of the east zone.[7]

In keeping with these developments was an unusually conciliatory gesture on the part of the East Berlin police. In November of 1948, Marshal Sokolovsky had ordered the introduction of new personal identity cards for the city of Berlin and the Soviet zone. Since the West Berlin authorities did not recognize the right of the Soviets to legislate for the entire city, no arrangements had been made to issue these cards in the west sectors. This raised the possibility that West Berliners who traveled into the east zone or sector might face arrest for not carrying valid identification, and the introduction of the new identity cards was awaited with considerable apprehension. On January 29, however, East Berlin police headquarters told the DENA news agency that the old identity cards of West Berliners would continue to be recognized as valid.[8] Thus, a weapon that might have caused West Berliners a great deal of additional harassment was voluntarily abandoned.

There is no proof that the foregoing events and statements were, in fact, reflections of a change in Soviet policy toward Berlin, but in the light of later events it seems probable that they were. At the time, they were overshadowed by indications that the Soviets were planning to continue and intensify the blockade.

Soviet Policy in Berlin: January to April

Between December 1948, and the following May, Soviet and East German political behavior remained outwardly unchanged. The Communists solidified their power in East Berlin, and continued their efforts to gain authority in West Berlin. The Soviets found ways of tightening the already efficient blockade. Arrests and kidnapings of west sector personnel by east sector police were still quite frequent, and most of the communist propaganda themes remained unchanged.

To complete their grip on the east sector, the Communists reintroduced the system of "house wardens."[9] Devised by the Nazis and continued by the Soviets after the fall of Berlin, this system had finally been abolished at the insistence of the Western powers. It provided for a network of minor officials, each of whom had responsibility for a very small area—a single apartment house or a group of detached houses. The house warden assisted in such matters as the distribution of ration cards and certain welfare functions, but his most important duty was to observe any signs of political dissatisfaction or activity directed against the regime and to report these to his superiors. The revival of this institution did not go unchallenged, even in East Berlin. Preaching in the Soviet sector, Bishop Dibelius told Berliners that for any house warden to betray his fellow men to the authorities was "the work of the devil." In spite of immediate threats from the Communists, the hardy Lutheran held his ground.[10]

The system of house wardens was complemented by a Soviet decree providing imprisonment or even death for sabotage of, or agitation intended to interfere with, the economic measures of East German authorities.[11] Since it was up to the communist authorities to decide what constituted sabotage or harmful agitation, this measure represented a legal device by which almost any citizen could be eliminated.

At the same time, a number of persons who lived in the east sector but displeased the East Berlin authorities were expelled from their homes. Thus, the house of Karl Hubert Schwennicke, chairman of the Liberal Democratic Party, was seized early in February, ostensibly because the building was needed as a club house for the communist Free German Youth.[12] A few days later, the *Tagesspiegel* angrily observed that forty families who had been expelled from their homes in the east sector had been waiting vainly for housing in West Berlin, while officials of the East Berlin government were still permitted to occupy space in west sector apartment buildings. Reprinting the eviction notice that was being sent to east sector residents, the paper suggested sarcastically that the West Berlin authorities save labor by using the same notice to evict communist officials.[13]

Blockade restrictions were still enforced vigorously. Early in January, Soviet authorities turned back fifteen freightcar loads of gift packages from America which had come to Germany by way of Sweden.[14] West Berliners who crossed into Soviet-controlled territory were still subject to search and confiscation of their west marks.[15] In February, new barriers were constructed by the Soviets along the West Berlin borders, and all traffic was funneled through a smaller number of check points.[16] Additional police barriers at the sector boundaries were established as late as April.

Also in April, the Soviets tightened the blockade through several completely new measures. They rerouted all telephone circuits that had previously linked the long-distance telephone office in West Berlin with the Soviet zone, and thereby deprived the western postal authorities of about 20 million marks in annual revenues.[17] In addition, Soviet troops made several attempts to occupy the locks in certain waterways in the British sector and to stop all vessels not registered by the East German authorities. In one instance, the Russian soldiers were withdrawn after a British protest; in another, it was necessary for the British to call up their troops to isolate the Soviet contingent.[18] On the last day of April, more than fifty east sector police raided a farm just inside the British sector. They cut the telephone lines, drove all the cattle into the Soviet zone, and were gone before British troops and West Berlin police arrived on the scene.[19]

Kidnapings and arbitrary arrests continued to cause disquiet. In many cases, the victims simply disappeared. On February 9, for instance, it was reported that a dues collector for the independent trade unions had been missing since January 31, presumably having been lured into the east sector and kidnaped. At the beginning of March, three members of the Soviet zone police in civilian clothes were caught in the act of abducting a former east zone resident who had moved to West Berlin. The following day brought the discovery that an SPD assemblyman had been arrested in his east sector residence six days previously, with no official reason for the arrest.[20] How Berliners succeeded in remaining calm in spite of the constant threat to their freedom is one of the mysteries of the blockade.

In various ways, east sector authorities tried to promote the fiction that their jurisdiction extended over the entire city. Early in 1949, placards in the elevated railroad stations of West Berlin instructed all children of school age to register in certain east sector schools. They were signed: "Education Section, Magistrat of Greater Berlin." West Berlin newspapers pointed out that these placards were the work of the "City Soviet," and urged their readers to pay no attention to them. The East Berlin labor office sent safety inspectors to factories in the west sectors, apparently in an effort to assert its authority there. Similarly, the East Berlin government attempted to persuade victims of the Nazi regime to register in the east sector, and set up a number of "social commissions" in West Berlin to establish contact with these people. Those who refused to register were threatened with severe disadvantages. The West Berlin authorities responded by instructing police to keep sharp watch over these activities.[21]

Early in January, the Communists even made an audacious attempt to take over the administration of one west sector borough. The *Tägliche Rundschau* announced a mass meeting in a railway station in the borough of Kreuzberg "to elect a mayor and other officials." West Berlin police took over the station, however, and the meeting was never held.[22]

In the East Berlin press, Soviet-controlled Germany continued to be represented as an area of progress and prosperity, while the west zones and sectors appeared as hotbeds of imperialism, fascism, and misery. The airlift was shown as an instrument of economic exploitation which would ultimately beggar West Berlin and West Germany. There were renewed suggestions that General Clay would be removed from his post, and that Secretary of State Marshall also would be forced to go. When General Clay finally did indicate that he might ask to be relieved, the communist press was triumphant, and described the West Berlin press as "dumbfounded." *Neues Deutschland* saw General Clay's impending resignation as confirming the bankruptcy of his policies.[23]

The virulence of communist propaganda during this period is illustrated by the following excerpt from a broadcast over the Soviet-controlled Radio Berlin,* which was reprinted in the *Tagesspiegel* on April 24:

> What has American imperialism to offer us in the way of culture? Is it the boogie-woogie culture and the sensational and immoral films which appeal to the lowest instincts? Is it poisoning of our youth by the dirty fantasy of a Henry Miller and the dirty hands of a Jean Paul Sartre! Is it the shameless exploitation of the poverty of our young women which makes them into soldiers' prostitutes and infects our girls with American syphilis at the price of a bar of chocolate and a few Camels!

* Probably by Wilhelm Girnus, the deputy chief of Radio Berlin.

There was thus little to indicate that Moscow's policies with respect to West Berlin were in the process of changing. Only one propaganda development may, in the light of later events, have been significant: the East Berlin press was giving increased emphasis to the communist peace campaign.

One facet of this campaign that received particular attention was a petition circulated by the communist-dominated German Democratic Women's Organization, asking that the atom bomb be outlawed. On February 15 *Neues Deutschland* reported that this petition, with five million signatures, would be displayed at a mass meeting the following day and would then be sent to the United Nations. Another aspect of the peace campaign concerned the previously established Committee against Warmongers. During the early months of 1949, this committee appealed to the public to provide information about the activities, since 1933, of "Warmonger Erik Reger" (publisher of the *Tagesspiegel*) and a number of other prominent West Berliners.[24] Those who were exposed to communist propaganda must occasionally have wondered how long the Soviets could maintain both a blockade and a peace campaign.

Reconstruction in West Berlin

Political and economic life in West Berlin was recovering rapidly in spite of the blockade. The reestablished Allied Kommandatura, free from the Soviet veto, was able to act vigorously and effectively. The same was true of the reorganized city government under the able leadership of Ernst Reuter. A uniform system for rationing in all three west sectors was agreed upon, trade associations were revived, cooperative associations were organized, and for the first time the three west sectors functioned as an economic unit.[25]

Just as West Berlin's outlook for the future seemed so much improved, the airlift experienced a serious crisis, which almost led to the breakdown of the city's vital services. In November 1948, weather conditions on fifteen out of thirty days had made flying almost impossible, and the weather during December was not much better. The result was an acute shortage of coal. By January, fuel stocks were sufficient to maintain the city's vital services for only slightly more than a week, as against the fourteen-day minimum that military authorities regarded as essential. Since food stocks, on the other hand, were relatively ample, those in charge of planning airlift requirements took a calculated risk: they reduced the amount of food to be flown in and devoted more space to coal. Fortunately, the weather improved, and it was possible to build up coal stocks again before the food supply was exhausted. The airlift had succeeded in surmounting the obstacles of winter, but only barely.[26]

After this setback, the tonnage flown into West Berlin increased steadily, rising to almost 200,000 tons in March, and more than 235,000 tons in April.[27] April 16 marked an all-time record, when 12,490 tons were airlifted in a 24-hour period. This, said General Clay, would show the Soviets that aircraft could deliver supplies to Berlin on the same scale as preblockade land transport.[28] Even higher praise was given involuntarily by the Soviet officer at the Berlin Air Safety Center, who complained that there were so many British and American planes in the corridors that he could not keep track of them.[29]

The airlift also carried increasing quantities of commercial exports from the city. Valued at less than one-half million west marks in January, these had more than doubled by March.[30] Professor Landsberg, at that time leader of the CDU fraction in the City Assembly, went so far as to say that the expansion of the airlift as planned by the Western powers would provide Berlin with enough raw materials to enable the city to exploit its full economic potential and would thus enable it to become self-supporting.[31]

A variety of other measures were designed to increase West Berlin's self-sufficiency. Lack of facilities for generating electric power had been one of the chief economic problems in the west sectors, since the Russians had dismantled the largest power plant before the arrival of the Western powers in 1945. Strenuous efforts now went into making the plant operative once again. In January 1949, it was announced that 5,000 tons of machinery would have to be brought in by air, and, in the months following, bulky pieces of generating equipment were flown in, to the amazement and satisfaction of the Berliners.[32] Efforts were also made to exploit deposits of coal which had been discovered within the city limits. In February, when the Assembly was working on a law to govern mining operations, Dr. Friedensburg brought with him a briefcase full of coal that had been dug in the French sector.[33] The blockade was over, however, before coal digging had passed the exploratory stage.

By far the most important economic measure of this period was a second currency reform, which made the west mark the sole legal currency for most purposes. When the west mark was first introduced, in June of 1948, military government regulations provided that it was to circulate alongside the Soviet-sponsored east mark, and that both currencies were to be legal tender for essential purchases and payments. This provision was intended to facilitate reunification of the city's economy in the event that the Soviets agreed on four-power currency control. The arrangement, while politically justifiable, was catastrophic in its economic effects. Although legally the east mark was the equivalent of the west mark, its real value rarely exceeded 30 per cent of that of the western money. The resulting situation was described by City Councilman Klingelhöfer in the report of the Magistrat for the year 1948:

> The incomplete currency reform of June 1948 had disastrous consequences. While it provided that the east mark would be legal tender for all vital purchases, it did not provide for an orderly system of banking, for an established relationship between the two currencies, or for the equal apportioning of the two currencies in sales and incomes. The weaker currency (the east mark) became a Soviet instrument for plundering the West Berlin economy and population. The stronger west mark was used for hoarding and as a vehicle for the flight of capital from the city and from the city's taxes. To the same degree that the west mark became rare and the east mark plentiful, the economy and the population were impoverished. Goods offered for sale increasingly required payment in west marks, and necessary purchases had to be made on the black market at high prices. Whether a person prospered and lived comfortably came more and more to depend on where and by whom he was employed, or where his wares were sold, and whether his employer was able to obtain west marks and was required to change east for west marks at parity. Although the courts held that each person had a right to receive 25 per cent of his income in west marks, a survey made by the independent labor unions (UGO) showed that the actual figure, on the average was nearer 10 to 12 per cent. No black market, however bad, under normal currency conditions could have wreaked such havoc in the sense of justice and in economic morality as was inevitably done by this currency dualism.[34]

In short, people in West Berlin wanted to be paid in west marks, but they tried to spend only east marks. Manufacturers and tradesmen complained that their income was largely in east marks while their expenses had to be paid mainly in west marks, and there was widespread agitation in favor of making the west mark the exclusive currency. As early as November 3, the Magistrat passed a resolution that the west mark be made the basis for the city's economy.[35]

Despite such pressure, the Western powers took no steps to abandon the dual currency system until it was abundantly clear that the technical committee of the Security Council would not be able to work out an acceptable plan for a single currency. After its initial proposal had been rejected by the United States, and later by Britain and France, the technical committee reported in February that it was impossible to find a solution, but this verdict was not made public until March 16.[36] It was the signal for the Western powers to introduce a second currency reform, which put an end to the dual-currency status.[37]

Sunday, March 20, marked the official shift from dual currency to the exclusive use of the west mark. At next day's Assembly meeting, Mayor Reuter said that the fact that the Western powers had taken this step was more important than a whole sheaf of declarations that they were "going to stay here." It meant, he said, the definite recognition that Berlin belonged to the West ideologically and politically, and that it must be bound to the West economically.[38]

While the second currency reform created a number of new problems—especially for those who worked in East Berlin but lived in the west sectors—it was greeted with enthusiasm by a large majority of Berliners. When U.S. Military Government's Opinion Surveys Branch asked a cross-section of West Berliners whether they considered the reform "basically necessary," 81 per cent of the respondents replied that they did. Only 17 per cent thought it was not necessary, and the rest had no opinion.[39]

As was to be expected, the second currency reform was vigorously denounced in the SED press. *Neues Deutschland* called it a move to plunder the west sectors, and said that it increased the danger of war. Denying that it was a reform at all, the paper described it as a sly *Putsch* engineered by the speculators and gangsters who governed West Berlin.[40] The SED called for a mass protest meeting, and *Neues Deutschland* claimed that half a million persons attended this gathering in East Berlin on March 26. After listening to a speech by SED Chairman Hans Jendretzky, those present resolved unanimously (by show of hands) that the new reform tended to split Berlin even further and that it increased the danger of war. Other communist speakers at the meeting emphasized that the value of the east mark was firm and that no new currency reform was planned in the east zone.[41]

The reaction of Soviet Military Government, by comparison, was surprisingly mild. The day after the reform, Colonel Yelisarov, deputy commandant of the Soviet sector, said that no countermeasures would be taken in East Berlin. Soviet Military Government was anxious to help the people of West Berlin, he added, and it therefore would place no difficulties in their way if they wished to use east marks in the Soviet sector or Soviet zone.[42]

Currency reform, airlift, and institutional reorganization thus enabled West Berlin to start out on the slow road to recovery even before the blockade was lifted. With the coming of spring, an air of hopefulness could be detected in the battered city. Some of Berlin's leaders, Councilman Klingelhöfer among them, looked forward to full economic and political union between West Berlin and West Germany. Klingelhöfer wrote in March that such a union was to be expected soon, and would "bring the economic and political changes in the structure of Berlin to a final conclusion for the foreseeable future."[43]

The West on the Offensive

With the new year, the political initiative appeared to be passing from the East to the West. The Western powers introduced a more effective counterblockade, West Berliners began to strike back more frequently and vigorously at their communist tormentors, plans for a West German government moved ahead, and signs of the military and economic recovery of Western Europe in general became visible.

The Western counterblockade had, up to this time, been of a partial and sporadic nature. Anyone had been free to purchase unrationed commodities in the French and British sectors and carry them into Soviet-controlled territory without hindrance. What restrictions had been introduced in the U.S. sector had not been fully effective. The flow of supplies from West Germany to East Germany had been reduced but not halted.

In January and February of 1949, the counterblockade was tightened. Early in February, vehicles bound either to or from the Soviet zone were forbidden to cross the U.S. and British zones, regardless of their point of origin or their destination.[44] Later in the month, controls at the zonal borders were sharpened to stop the transport of freight by foot, the reason being that some international transport firms had been driving trucks up to the western side of the zonal border, carrying the freight over the line by hand, and then loading it into other trucks on the Soviet side.[45]

The shipment of goods from West Berlin to Soviet-controlled territory also was subjected to increasingly severe restrictions. Some goods (mainly manufactures) could not be shipped at all; others could be exported under license from Western military government only if sufficiently valuable items were obtained in return. Military authorities in the west sectors were not concerned about the effect of these measures on employment, because the airlift had now grown to a point where it could support fairly extensive trade between Berlin and West Germany.[46] On the first day that the new controls were enforced, early in February, West Berlin police seized such items as 320 kilograms of printers' lead, three boxes of machine parts, a truckload of chemicals and medicines, and a typewriter.[47] No one knows the precise extent to which the sharpened counterblockade hampered the East German economy, but reports in the West Berlin press mentioned a number of factories that had been forced to lay off workers or curtail their working hours because of it.[48]

While the Western powers were thus tightening economic restrictions, West Berliners showed increasing defiance of communist police power. For example, when a policeman tried to search the baggage of a woman traveling by subway across the east-west sector borders, she boxed his ears, and was then protected by twenty to thirty other passengers from being arrested by a second policeman.[49] In another instance, a policeman in the Soviet sector was forced to flee, after a crowd of angry Berliners had threatened him for trying to seize the contents of a shopping bag.[50] The *Tagesspiegel* added to the pressure by blacklisting the officers involved in such incidents through the prominent display of notices such as the following:

ERWIN WOLF, POLICE SERGEANT
at the 11th Police Precinct, Magazinstrasse,
who lives on Grosse Hamburgerstrasse, Berlin N4,
is stealing baggage at the Neanderstrasse subway station.[51]

Successful defiance remained the exception rather than the rule, and the communist system of controls at the sector boundaries, on the whole, was not seriously impaired. More and more often, however, the east sector police found it necessary to use firearms, and reports of shootings increased. Many of these bullets were directed at blockade-running trucks, which tried to crash through the barriers into West Berlin without stopping.

There were still other signs that West Berliners were adopting a more offensive posture. A new organization, which called itself Fighting Group to Oppose Inhumanity (*Kampfgruppe gegen Unmenschlichkeit*), received frequent attention in the West Berlin press. The group assembled information about conditions in East Germany, and gave advice and all possible assistance to individuals and groups that were being persecuted in the east zone and sector. Also, West Berlin's democratic parties—in particular the Social Democrats—were establishing or reestablishing contacts with their former members or sympathizers in the Soviet-controlled areas of Germany.

For the first time, the Magistrat began to limit the activities of the Communists in the west sectors. The SED had always been permitted to operate freely in West Berlin and had, in fact, held more public meetings than any of the other parties, except the SPD.* At the beginning of February, however, the Magistrat forbade SED meetings in schoolrooms or other public buildings until such time as restrictions on the activities of the three democratic parties in East Berlin were removed.[52] Shortly thereafter, Mayor Reuter ordered that no space on public billboards be given to announcements or advertisements of the communist radio station or any east sector organization which was subordinate to, or under the influence of, the Soviet Military Administration, the East German Economic Commission, or the "City Soviet" (as the east sector "Magistrat" was called).[53]

News from the Soviet-controlled areas made life in the blockaded city seem preferable by contrast. In February, an average of 92 persons a day, mostly from the Soviet zone, were reporting to the registration office for political refugees.[54] In East Berlin, lack of confidence in the east mark came close to creating a financial panic. Officially-licensed exchange offices in the west sectors tried to hold to the rate of somewhat over four to one, but they limited the amount that could be exchanged to two marks per person. Unlicensed money-changers were asking as much as nine east marks for one west mark. Merchants in the east sector began to take goods off their shelves and to restrict the sales of unrationed goods.[55] After a few critical days, the east mark once more became relatively stable, but its value thereafter rarely rose above one-quarter of the west mark.

* According to a report by the West Berlin police, the SPD held 199 meetings between August and December of 1948, the SED held 79, the CDU 78, and the LDP 36. (*Berlin 1948*, annual report by the Magistrat of Greater Berlin, Kulturbuch-Verlag, Berlin, 1950, p. 161.)

The behavior of the personnel of Soviet-controlled Radio Berlin also did little to bolster the prestige of the East German regime. Two of the favorite themes of Radio Berlin were that the east mark was more valuable than the west mark and that the food in West Berlin was of poor quality. In January, radio artists were reported to have asked that their wages be paid at least partly in west marks. Their request was refused by the Soviet authorities, and the performers had to be content with a 50 per cent wage increase and periodic food packages. A few days later, it was learned that several of the leading officials of Radio Berlin were buying their food in the west sectors. The *Tagesspiegel* commented that they were probably eating the "horrible tinned meat, the unhealthful dried potatoes, and the maggot-infested raisins" in order to try and use up the "vanishing" food stocks in West Berlin.[56]

Berliners were heartened by the warm recognition their firm stand against communist encroachment was receiving in West Germany and the rest of the Western world. At the German Conference of Mayors in Berlin, in February, all speakers paid tribute to the city's magnificent record of resistance, and representatives of Frankfurt and Stuttgart said that they continued to recognize Berlin as the German capital.[57] A visit by Premier Attlee in March, and a message from President Truman complimenting Berliners on their behavior, showed that the blockaded city continued to enjoy world attention.[58] Mayor Reuter visited France, Great Britain, and the United States early in the new year, and all the West Berlin papers noted with great satisfaction the details of his enthusiastic reception in Western capitals. On his return from the United States, in April, Reuter gave a glowing account of his trip to the Assembly.[59] The following passage from the annual report of the Magistrat for 1949 bears witness to the meaning and importance that Berlin attributed to Reuter's trip:

> The visit to the United States publicly demonstrated the fact that Berlin had in the meantime become a symbol of the will to freedom for the whole world. The warm and enthusiastic reception which was given the city's chief official in Washington, New York, and many other American cities constituted a recognition of the behavior of the Berlin population. This recognition could not have been shown more impressively.[60]

The efforts of the Western powers to achieve European economic recovery moved ahead rapidly during this period. The effects of the Marshall Plan on the West European economy were becoming more and more apparent. A North Atlantic Treaty was signed by representatives of the United States, Canada, Denmark, France, Iceland, Italy, Norway, Portugal, the United Kingdom, and the Benelux countries on April 4. This development was hastened, in the opinion of President Truman, by Soviet truculence in Berlin.[61] On April 7, the five defense ministers of the Western Union nations met and approved a plan for West European Defense. April 8 saw agreement among the United States, Great Britain, and France on an occupation statute for West Germany.[62] Western Europe seemed to be nearing the point at which, as General Clay had predicted, it would itself be able to exert pressure, not only absorb it.

Moscow's New Line

The Soviets had long insisted that the blockade, if it existed at all, was a creation of the Western powers. Communist propaganda, therefore, devoted relatively little attention to Soviet traffic restrictions between Berlin and West Germany. As the end of the blockade drew closer, the avowed interests of the Soviets and German Communists became more and more firmly focused on three other issues, which were only indirectly related to the Berlin crisis: trade between East and West Germany, German unity, and world peace.

Already in January, Soviet officials had approached their opposite numbers among the Western powers to request that certain goods be allowed to pass through West Germany into East Germany. The West, in refusing, had pointed out that Berlin was still blockaded.[63] In March the Soviets again expressed interest in resuming interzonal trade. Indeed, an East German economic plan released at that time was based on the expectation that materials from West Germany would be available. Drew Middleton, in a dispatch to the *New York Times,* observed that these expressions of interest in trade might, in actuality, be a face-saving device, which would permit the Soviets to lift the Berlin blockade "in the interests of the Germans," and not under Allied pressure.[64]

During April there was a veritable flood of requests for interzonal trade from the Soviets and East Germans. The German Economic Commission of the east zone announced that permission had been granted enterprises in Soviet-controlled areas to establish commercial ties with concerns in West Berlin, and Mayor Ebert of East Berlin made a public proposal that firms in East and West Berlin resume trade contacts. Mayor Reuter replied that the blockade would have to be lifted before there could be talk of restoring free trade. A few days later East German officials approached West German economic authorities in Frankfurt with the request that trade be resumed as soon as possible.[65] Reports reached the British-sponsored *Welt* on April 17 that a former Soviet ambassador to Germany was even then in Berlin advising the Soviet Military Administration on the resumption of interzonal traffic. On April 19 Western newsmen learned that the Soviets had directed the East German Railways to include an interzonal train in their summer timetables, and also that Soviet officials had made a new approach to Mayor Reuter with an offer to trade potatoes for steel products.[66]

The second communist policy line during this period concerned German unity and the evacuation of occupation troops. Toward the end of February, West German Communists advanced a plan, allegedly backed by the Soviet Union, whereby troops of all the occupying powers would be withdrawn to the edges of Germany.[67] In March the People's Council of the Soviet zone invited West German leaders to confer on means of avoiding a division of Germany between East and West. Western leaders indignantly refused on the grounds that this would only confuse the issue.[68] A few days later, the People's Council called for the election of an All-German People's Congress to ratify a previously-drafted communist-sponsored constitution that purported to apply to all four zones of Germany.[69] The proposal was denounced in West Germany. An American spokesman declared that the communist-dominated People's Council had no status in West Germany and would not be allowed to carry through balloting there.[70] Communist agitation for troop withdrawal and East-West negotiations on German unity continued throughout April and into May.[71]

All the while the Communists were expanding their peace campaign, not only in Germany but throughout the world. Speaking in Leipzig on March 7, SED Chairman Wilhelm Pieck announced that the new People's Congress, when elected, would organize the fight against the new war which, he alleged, the Western powers were plotting in their zones of occupation.[72] Election propaganda embodied standard peace slogans. On April 19 East German authorities announced that elaborate plans had been made to "demonstrate the will for peace of the Germans of the eastern zone" on the occasion of the "peace congress," which was to open in Paris the following day. Factories, public buildings, and trains were to be decorated with flags and slogans. In large towns, all traffic would observe a short pause to mark the significance of the day. Church bells would be rung, and, along the zonal border, beacons would be kindled to "summon the people of the western zones to the common fight for peace."[73]

The campaign also involved a series of international meetings. The Cultural and Scientific Conference for World Peace met in New York late in March and included a Soviet delegation of twenty-three, among them the composer Dmitri Shostakovich. The meeting, and the controversies it aroused, received wide attention.[74] Even before the echoes of this conference had died away, another was held in Paris. Billed as the World Congress for Peace, it provided a forum for attacks on the North Atlantic Pact and other Western policies.[75] Again, Shostakovich was present, together with a large U.S.S.R. delegation. According to the Moscow radio, delegates to this congress had been elected by three hundred million persons.[76] Simultaneously with the Paris conference, another Congress for Peace was held in Prague, for those delegates who had been refused French visas and consequently could not take part in the Paris affair.

These, however, were only the beginnings of the communist peace campaign. It was to become much louder after the blockade, rising to a crescendo at the time of the Stockholm Peace Conference in 1950.

The Blockade Is Lifted

In the third week of March the Jessup-Malik negotiations led to a tentative agreement for lifting the blockade and counterblockade. The discussions, slow at first, had progressed more rapidly since March 15, when Malik told Jessup that Stalin's failure to mention Berlin's currency in his statement had not been accidental, and that the currency question could be discussed at a meeting of the Council of Foreign Ministers, if such a meeting could be arranged to review the whole German problem. Dr. Jessup then asked whether the Soviet government was contemplating a meeting while the blockade was in progress, or whether the blockade would be lifted in order to permit the meeting to take place. Mr. Malik said he would refer back to Moscow, and, on March 21, came back with the answer that, if a definite date were set for the meeting of the Council of Foreign Ministers, the restrictions on trade and transportation in Berlin could be lifted reciprocally, and in advance of the meeting.[77] Details were then discussed jointly with French and British representatives, and, on May 5, an official statement issued in Washington, London, Moscow, and Paris announced that the blockade would end on May 12:

> The Governments of France, the Union of Soviet Socialist Republics, the United Kingdom, and the United States have reached the following agreement:
>
> 1. All the restrictions imposed since March 1, 1948, by the Government of the Union of Soviet Socialist Republics on communications, transportation, and trade between Berlin and the Western zones of Germany and between the Eastern zone and the Western zones will be removed on May 12, 1949.
>
> 2. All the restrictions imposed since March 1, 1948, by the Governments of France, the United Kingdom, and the United States, or any one of them, on communications, transportation, and trade between Berlin and the Eastern zone and between the Western and Eastern zones of Germany will also be removed on May 12, 1949.
>
> 3. Eleven days subsequent to the removal of the restrictions referred to in paragraphs one and two, namely, on May 23, 1949, a meeting of the Council of Foreign Ministers will be convened in Paris to consider questions relating to Germany and problems arising out of the situation in Berlin, including also the question of currency in Berlin.[78]

The agreement did not cover all the blockade restrictions. General Howley (who had been promoted in March) pointed out that the statement failed to mention the restoration of West Berlin's electricity supply. He expressed the hope that the Soviets would allow current to flow "in the spirit of the agreement," as in fact they did. Also, the Soviet zone railways announced that 4,000 freight cars would be returned to West Germany "as a sign of good will."[79]

Discussions between Jessup and Malik had at first been conducted in the strictest secrecy. Even General Clay knew nothing about them, and, in press interviews in mid-April, he discounted all rumors that the blockade would shortly be lifted.[80] He later said that he first learned about the Jessup-Malik discussions from the newspapers, and that France and Britain also were not drawn into the discussions until they had been in progress for some time.[81] Newspaper stories—at first unconfirmed—began to appear on April 20. On April 26, TASS issued an account of the discussions, and this was followed immediately by an official release from the Western powers.

One event which, with the benefit of hindsight, may be called an indicator of the impending agreement was the reassignment of Marshal Sokolovsky, whose name had been so closely associated with the blockade. On March 29 the Moscow radio announced that he would be replaced by General Chuikov. Sokolovsky does not appear to have been in disgrace, however, since he became First Deputy Minister of the Soviet Armed Forces.[82]

The manner in which *Neues Deutschland* presented the end of the blockade allows a minor case study of the treatment of unfavorable news in a communist organ. On May 4 a one-column story, under the small heading "REGARDING THE JESSUP-MALIK CONVERSATIONS," reported that American diplomats were trying to resume the talks they themselves had previously broken off. Were the Americans really serious this time? Perhaps they were, said *Neues Deutschland,* because their policies in Germany had suffered such a fiasco that they might be ready to try something else.

On May 5, the day of the official four-power statement, the paper said that the very fact of the negotiations showed the success of the world-wide peace forces, and especially of the unchangeable peace policy of the Soviet Union. Having thus attempted to turn the failure of the Soviet blockade into an advantage by crediting the end of the blockade to the communist peace campaign, *Neues Deutschland* went on to another familiar theme: Now that the great powers were meeting to discuss the German question, it was important that the voice of the German people be heard, and that everyone participate in the elections for a new People's Congress, to be held on May 15 and 16. The four-power communiqué was reported on May 6 under the headline: "THE POLICY OF PEACE IS SUCCESSFUL—TEXT OF THE COMMUNIQUE OF THE FOUR GREAT POWERS—GENERAL CLAY IS STRUCK DUMB." An editorial went on to say that the airlift, like Hitler, had killed itself with victories.

On May 11 and 12, when West Berlin papers could find space for little besides news of the end of the blockade, *Neues Deutschland* devoted its front page to a communist plan for a meeting of "all democratic mass organizations in Germany," and to speeches by communist officials. Only a small item on May 12 noted that interzonal trade had been resumed and that unemployed persons would welcome this news.

The barriers between Berlin and the Soviet zone fell at midnight of May 11, and May 12 was a day of jubilation for West Berlin. School classes were dismissed after brief sessions in which teachers pointed out the significance of the event. The City Assembly held a special, ceremonial meeting, which was attended by the western military governors and by German dignitaries from the west zones. This was followed by a mass meeting addressed by leaders of the three democratic parties. The first trucks and trains to arrive in the city were decked with flowers. Private and public celebrations dominated the west sectors.

A note of sadness was introduced by those who recalled the lives that had been lost in the course of the airlift. The *Tagesspiegel* devoted a large portion of its front page to a picture of a wrecked aircraft and reminded its readers that seven British and seventeen American planes had suffered accidents, and forty-eight men had been killed:

> The lives of forty-eight men weigh heavily in the scales of freedom, and when in a few days the foreign ministers meet in Paris, they will not be permitted to forget these men who made the supreme sacrifice in the battle for democratic rights.

Mayor Reuter, at the special meeting of the City Assembly, also referred to the pilots who had lost their lives, and all those present rose to their feet. At the same meeting, Franz Neumann read the names of those who had been killed, and submitted a resolution that the square in front of the Tempelhof airport be named "Platz der Luftbrücke" (Airlift Square) in commemoration. The resolution was passed unanimously.

The airmen were not the only foreigners who were honored at this festive meeting of the Assembly. Mayor Reuter singled out General Clay for words of praise, the like of which have rarely, if ever, been heard by a military governor from an elected representative of a conquered people:

> In our great demonstrations in the summer of the past year, we called on the world for help. The world heard our cry. We are happy to have here in our midst as a guest the man who, together with his two colleagues, took the initiative in organizing the airlift in the summer of last year. The memory of General Clay will never fade in Berlin. We know for what we have to thank this man [prolonged stormy applause], and we take advantage of this hour in which he bids farewell to Berliners to say that we will never forget what he has done for us.[83]

Dr. Suhr also extended formal thanks to General Clay, not only, he said, because of the American military governor's part in organizing the airlift, but also for his contribution to the economic support of Western Europe and to the prospects for a new governmental order in Germany: "As the representative of a victorious power you have understood how to work for peace. That, I think, is the highest praise that can be given a soldier. For that the men and women of Berlin thank you."

Konrad Adenauer, as the principal representative of West Germany at the Assembly meeting, was also greeted enthusiastically. His visit, said Dr. Suhr, was to Berliners a sign of the solidarity of all Germans. When the future West German chancellor promised that West Germany would maintain its ties with Berlin, come what may, he was answered with cries of "bravo" and thunderous applause. The various speakers' references to West German assistance during the blockade, and to the fact that Berlin representatives were taking part in the work of the Parliamentary Council in Bonn, produced the same enthusiastic response. The lifting of the blockade seemed to presage the reunification of Germany.

At the mass meeting that followed, the speakers expressed many of the same ideas, praising the steadfastness of Berliners, the help of the Western powers, and the solidarity of all Germans. Dr. Adenauer alluded to the steadfastness of Berliners as an inspiration to the writers of the West German constitution. Carlo Schmid, for the SPD, expressed the belief that West Germany, and indeed the whole Western world, had drawn moral strength from the behavior of the Berliners. Mayor Reuter, in conclusion, spoke hopefully of the future, of the day when trains would be running on double tracks from Berlin to the cities of East and West Germany, and when Berlin would once again be self-supporting. He then called for a democratic offensive in East Berlin.

Everybody applauded the mayor's remarks, including a little grey-haired woman near the rostrum. Only then did the crowd notice Louise Schroeder. Although the meeting had already been formally closed, people refused to leave until she also had spoken. And so she said a few words extemporaneously, just as she had when called upon unexpectedly at another mass meeting, the year before. She spoke primarily to the women of Berlin, who had borne so many of the privations brought on by the blockade. They could be happy, she said, for they had displayed the greatest virtue—faithfulness to a good cause.[84]

Berlin's troubles were by no means over. The end of the blockade was followed by a dispute between the city's railroad workers and Soviet Military Government, over the latter's insistence that railroad workers who lived in West Berlin be paid in east marks. This led to a strike, which delayed recovery by another six weeks. Soviet and East German authorities continued to impose periodic restrictions on Berlin's trade, thereby hampering economic reconstruction and causing unemployment to rise. Above all, there was the nagging feeling of insecurity brought on by the continuing East-West tension. Nevertheless, Berlin managed to rise above these problems and to remain an oasis of freedom and democracy in a totalitarian desert.

Behind the Blockade Settlement

The Soviet decision to lift the blockade has usually been ascribed to a combination of factors. Ambassador Smith wrote that it was based in part on the fact that the counterblockade was hurting the East far more than the blockade was hurting the West.[85] J. P. Nettl, a student of the east zone economy, also maintained that East Germany suffered more severely from the economic effects of the crisis than did West Germany.[86] General Clay expressed the opinion that it was not only pressure on the East German economy but also the revival in West Germany that led the Soviets to change their plans.[87]

Others, in seeking to explain the Soviet action, have placed the stress elsewhere. U.N. Secretary General Trygve Lie believed that the propaganda effects of the triumphant airlift, possibly combined with the force of world public opinion, played a large role, in addition to the counterblockade. He also pointed to the fact that the blockade had led to a tremendous increase of Allied air power in Western Europe.[88] British and American diplomatic officials have added the theory that the Soviets, feeling themselves excluded from all means by which they might influence developments in Western Europe, had wanted to rejoin the "diplomatic club" and had therefore proposed the meeting of the Council of Foreign Ministers. Another factor that was believed to have prompted the Soviet decision was the loss of prestige to communist parties throughout Europe, caused in part by the dramatic success of the airlift.

All these considerations probably entered into the Soviet decision. In the light of broader Soviet policies, however, Moscow's reasons for ending the crisis when it did appear in a somewhat different perspective. The blockade had been imposed originally as one phase of an effort to ensure the continuance of a European balance of power favorable to the Soviets. At first, the Soviets demanded that the Western powers either sacrifice all of Berlin (and with it much of their prestige in Europe) or else give up their plans for a West German government. When the airlift showed that the Allies would do neither, the Soviets decided to consolidate their position in East Berlin. Having completed that process, they found that what advantages could thenceforth be derived from the continuation of the blockade were relatively modest. One advantage was that the airlift constituted an appreciable financial drain on Germany and the Western powers; another, that it effectively tied up the bulk of Western military air transport in Berlin.*

The disadvantages of continuing the blockade, on the other hand, were substantial. Far from weighting the balance of power in favor of the Soviets, it was producing the opposite effect. The Western powers were united in their stand on Berlin. So were the West German states. As long as the Soviets were cast in the aggressive role of blockaders of more than two million civilians, they were in a poor position to interfere with the formation of the North Atlantic Treaty Organization, the functioning of the Marshall Plan, and the establishment of a West German government. Local communists in West Germany and West Europe were equally hampered in their opposition to these Western moves. The blockade was thus furthering the very developments in Western Europe that it had been intended to block.

In casting about for some other instrument with which to oppose Western consolidation, the Soviets, it appears, decided to promote the growth of a "peace" or "neutralist" sentiment in Western Europe. By this tactic, they hoped to encourage divisions among the Western powers that would prevent their forming an effective military counterweight to Soviet power. France, in particular, had

* Some observers of international relations have advanced the thesis that one purpose of the Berlin blockade was to occupy the attention of the Western powers in Europe while Chinese communist armies were advancing in Asia. The communist conquest of China proceeded during much of the Berlin blockade, and Shanghai was occupied on May 25.

The writer is not inclined to include this "diversion of attention" tactic among the causes of the blockade. All the available information indicates that the Soviets at first expected the blockade to be concluded successfully in a relatively short space of time, and that they certainly did not foresee the massive airlift. Nevertheless, the possibility cannot be completely discounted that Soviet delay in lifting the blockade was due in part to the war in China. By ensuring that Western air transport was fully occupied in Germany, Stalin could guard against the possibility that last-minute logistic aid might be extended to Chiang Kai-shek.

already shown herself extremely suspicious of plans for a West German state, and might be pried loose from the Western alliance, once the Berlin tension had been eased. Through the campaign for German unity and withdrawal of occupation troops, the Soviets also hoped to promote divisions of opinion within West Germany. Even if these might not be sufficient to stop the creation of a government, perhaps they would at least prevent the new government from cooperating in Western defense.

Viewed in this broader perspective, then, the blockade can be said to have been withdrawn in order to clear the way for other tactics: a peace offensive and a campaign for German unity. The end of the blockade signified a change in Soviet strategy, but not in Soviet aims.

In this interpretation, the counterblockade assumes only very limited importance. For one thing, its full effects were not felt until February or March of 1949, by which time the Soviets must have made at least a tentative decision to restore land communications to Berlin. For another, though the counterblockade caused definite hardships to certain branches of East German industry by depriving them of critical materials, it did not affect a very large volume of trade. Soviet efforts, all along, had been directed toward making the Eastern bloc economically independent of the West. Before World War II, according to a study of the Economic Commission for Europe, the annual interchange of goods between what are now East and West Germany was valued at some 2.7 billion marks. In 1947 the value of this trade was calculated at 496 million marks. During 1948 and 1949, both of which years were affected by the blockade, the value dropped to 357 and 432 million marks, respectively. In 1950 the figure jumped to 807 million "payment units,"* but it sank again to 365 million payment units in 1951 and 293 in 1952.[89] Despite the obvious difficulties of comparing values expressed in different kinds of marks and in payment units, it is clear that postwar trade between East and West Germany was relatively small, irrespective of the blockade. The *Deutschland-Jahrbuch* for 1949 observed that in 1947, the last "normal" year before the blockade, trade between East and West Germany amounted to scarcely the volume of one of the larger prewar department stores.[90] It is difficult to believe, therefore, that economic considerations played more than a minor role in the Soviet decision to lift the blockade.†

* A device used because of the difference in value between east and west marks.

† As far as the author could determine, no Allied agency ever attempted a sys-

The Soviets themselves seemed anxious to have their action ascribed to economic motives. This was pointed out by newsmen at the time. The repeated communist requests to West German and West Berlin authorities, in early 1949, for a reopening of interzonal trade were certainly made in the knowledge that they would be rejected as long as the blockade continued. The purpose of these overtures, therefore, must have been chiefly propagandistic. They not only put the Western authorities in the position of saying "no" to a suggestion that seemed to favor the economy in both East and West Germany, but they also made it appear that the Soviets were taking the interests of the Germans into account when they decided to lift the blockade.

Moscow's desire for a meeting of the Council of Foreign Ministers also seems to have been an excuse, rather than a reason, for lifting the blockade. The meeting, which convened in Paris on May 23, settled nothing. Indeed, a leading student of the period observed that this session "produced no clear-cut indication of what the U.S.S.R. was driving at: If Soviet policy was a mystery . . . on May 23, it was scarcely less so when the conference adjourned four weeks later."[91] The major Soviet political moves during this period were made not in diplomatic discussions but at the peace congresses in New York and Paris.

Whether Western tactics during the negotiations that led to the lifting of the blockade had any effect on Soviet behavior is impossible to determine. Certainly, Western behavior at the time of these negotiations was very different from what it had been during the previous, unfruitful talks. Whereas in 1948 the Western powers had been willing to bargain, and anxious not to provoke the Soviets and thereby prejudice the situation, they now adopted a "take it or leave it" attitude. Some diplomatic officials have ascribed this to the Allies' thorough disillusionment as a result of the previous negotiations, which made them inclined to sit back and wait for the Soviets to show evidence of good faith.

While this may have been part of it, there were additional reasons for the Allied attitude. As newsmen repeatedly pointed out at the time, many Western diplomats felt that the blockade was working in favor of the West. On March 30 a *New York Times* report from Frankfurt described Allied officials as believing that new negotia-

---

tematic study of the actual or potential effects of the counterblockade while it was in progress or after it was over. Data are consequently extremely fragmentary.

tions with the Soviets should be undertaken only after the bargaining position of the democracies had been strengthened by the signing of the North Atlantic Pact and the establishment of a West German government. A few weeks later Drew Middleton reported from Berlin that "most United States and British officials in Berlin" believed that the German impetus to form a West German state would be lost if the blockade were lifted.[92] Two days after that the *New York Herald-Tribune* described officials in Washington as apprehensive that a softening in the Soviet attitude might delay both the ratification of the North Atlantic Pact and West Germany's acceptance of the proposed occupation statute.[93] Once it was fairly certain that the Soviets were serious, Western officials pushed ahead with negotiations to end the blockade, but they did so without any sense of urgency or anxiety.

There is no way of determining whether the changed Western attitude hastened or retarded the negotiations. It was during the time of these final discussions that Allied policy in Germany was becoming noticeably firmer, as shown by the intensified airlift and counterblockade, and the second currency reform. The Soviets must have assumed that this posture was adopted in full knowledge of the Jessup-Malik talks, for they could not have known that Western military authorities were, in fact, unaware of the discussions. It may be significant that negotiations nevertheless did not break down.

There remains one puzzling question: Why did more than a month elapse between Stalin's famous statement to Kingsbury Smith and Malik's reply to Jessup that Stalin's failure to mention the currency question was "not accidental"?

There are various explanations, all of them conjectural. The idea that Stalin, on second thought, may have wished to keep Western air transport tied up in Germany until China had been overrun by communist armies has already been mentioned. There is also the possibility that the Soviets were waiting to see how the weather in Germany developed, before committing themselves to lifting the blockade. A period of very bad weather or intense cold during February might well have weakened the Western bargaining position. Then again, Stalin may have hoped to resume negotiations about Berlin in direct conference with President Truman, and may have had to recast his plans when the United States government turned down his proposal for a high-level conference.

Another possible explanation for the delay is that the Soviets did not wish to abandon their pressure on Berlin until they had developed a new form of pressure to take its place, and that they needed more time to prepare their peace campaign. The staff work for the New York and Paris peace congresses may have taken longer than originally expected.

A final possible interpretation is that it was a basic principle of Soviet diplomatic behavior always to have negotiations of one type or another in progress. Stalin's January 31 statement may have been indicative, at the time it was made, not of any serious wish to end the blockade, but only of a desire to ensure continuous negotiations.* It was by then clear that the efforts of the technical committee were about to break down, and Moscow may have been looking toward the establishment of a new forum for discussions.

Whatever the specific reasons that prompted the Soviets to end restrictions on traffic between Berlin and West Germany just when they did, it is clear that behind their decision to raise the blockade was the fact that it showed no prospect of achieving either of the gains to which they had apparently aspired in June 1948: incorporation of West Berlin into the Soviet zone, or further delay in the recovery of West Germany.

The course of events in West Germany, in particular, must have weighed heavily in convincing Stalin that the blockade was a liability and that a new policy was necessary if the balance of power were not to shift to the disadvantage of the Soviet Union. Indeed, one can say with a large measure of justice that the blockade was defeated in West Germany as much as in Berlin. The following chapter is accordingly devoted to a review of reactions to the blockade in the three west zones.

* One small shred of evidence tends to support this view. The TASS account of the Jessup-Malik conversations represents Jessup's question about Stalin's statement and Malik's reply as having occurred on the same day—February 15. In actuality, Malik's reply was not received until March 15. This change in date might mean that the Soviets wished to show that they were serious about entering into new negotiations one month earlier than they actually were. Or, it may simply have been an error. (Cf. The London *Times*, April 27, 1949.)

CHAPTER VII

THE SOVIET DEFEAT IN WEST GERMANY

THE blockade's failure to achieve Soviet aims in West Germany was less dramatic than its failure in Berlin, but it was if anything even more crushing. At best, the Soviets had hoped to hamper West Germany's recovery, to forestall its alignment with the West, to prevent formation of a West German state, and possibly to destroy confidence in the new West German currency; at the least, the blockade could be expected to lower the prestige of the Allies, to weaken any government formed under their auspices, to demonstrate Soviet power and to show all Germans that the economic and political future of their country lay with the East.

As we have seen, the blockade accomplished none of these ends. Its effect, combined with that of the airlift, was to raise Western prestige and reduce Soviet influence in West Germany, thereby promoting the identification of that area with the West and helping to create the conditions for a sound, Western-orientated economy, and the establishment of a viable West German state. At the same time, the position of communism in West Germany deteriorated rapidly, and organizational ties grew up that established Berlin as an outpost of West Germany behind the iron curtain, thereby indirectly weakening the hold of communism on the east zone as well.

The Berlin Issue and the West German State

A reciprocal relationship existed between the Berlin blockade and formation of a West German state. On the one hand, a viable West German government probably would have been impossible to form if Berlin had fallen. On the other hand, creation of the Federal Republic helped to bring about the end of the blockade.

The threat that the blockade posed to Allied policy in West Germany was recognized immediately by political observers on the spot. As General Clay had said in a communication to the Army Department at the start of the blockade, "When Berlin falls, Western Germany will be next. If we mean . . . to hold Europe against communism, we must not budge."[1] Similarly, the *New York Times* cited the opinion of "most German officials of the Bizonal Economic Administration" to the effect that a retreat from Berlin would cause uneasiness in the rest of Germany and make it difficult to gain the support necessary for the projected government.[2] Also, "reliable German political observers" were quoted as saying that the success of the Allied proposals for a West German government rested with the success of the West's efforts to break the blockade: if Berlin were forsaken, there would be no guarantee that a West German government might not be set adrift also.[3]

Another reason for German insistence on a free Berlin as a precondition for a West German government was the dedication of many of the democratic leaders to the idea of Berlin as the center and capital of the new Germany, and their determination not to take part in any West German government in which Berlin had no representation.[4] Reports of the U.S. Military Governor during the blockade emphasized the growing insistence of West German officials and political parties that Berlin be included in the projected federal state.[5] Had Berlin been lost, there would no doubt have been vigorous resistance to the idea of a West German government.

In retrospect, several West German newspapermen and political leaders mentioned still another threat that the Soviet blockade had posed to Allied plans. They believed that, if the Western powers had capitulated in Berlin, people in West Germany would have felt the need of a nationalist, authoritarian leader to protect them against the communist menace. Though West Germany would not have gone communist, it might well have experienced a neo-Nazi revival, and the Allies would hardly have been likely to turn over wide authority to a government of ultranationalist tendencies. According to this theory, the West's successful resistance to the blockade was thus a major factor in making possible a stable West German government based on middle-of-the-road parties.

However, at the same time that the Soviet blockade of Berlin threatened Allied plans for a West German state, resistance to the blockade by the Western powers and the Berliners also unleashed forces favoring the formation of the Federal Republic. The Allied airlift awakened the admiration of West German leaders, mitigated their strictures of certain aspects of Western policy, and caused them to cooperate with Western military government. The blockade itself intensified existing anti-Soviet attitudes, and helped convince German democrats that cooperation with the Soviet Union was not feasible. Perhaps even more important was the degree to which Berliners, and especially Ernst Reuter himself, were able to strengthen the proponents of a West German state and neutralize the opponents of the plan.

To understand the effect of the blockade and airlift on Allied-German relationships, it must be remembered that the Berlin crisis came just on the heels of the London Recommendations, which embodied the Allies' policies toward Germany. The autonomy granted to West Germany under these recommendations was considerable, but it fell far short of complete independence. Products of the Ruhr were to be distributed in accordance with the rulings of a three-power authority; there were to be minor border modifications in favor of Holland and Belgium; and military government retained veto power over large segments of West Germany's political and economic life. On July 1, the Western military governors authorized the minister presidents of the West German states to call a constitutional convention, but at the same time specified the powers to be reserved to military government under an occupation statute.[6]

Neither the London Recommendations nor the military governors' steps toward their implementation were greeted with enthusiasm in West Germany. The minister president of Bavaria was quoted in the press as saying that the Western proposal for an occupation statute was "bitter evidence of the defeat and the weakness of Germany."[7] Konrad Adenauer, as leader of the Christian Democratic Union, criticized the Recommendations as unclear and unjust, and foresaw that the Germans would have no choice but to "preserve their honor before posterity" by refusing to cooperate with the Western powers.[8] A Social Democratic speaker in Schleswig-Holstein observed caustically that, if the Western powers had intended to give the west zones the greatest possible degree of unity and freedom, they had magnificently succeeded in phrasing the London Recommendations in such a manner as to conceal this intention from the German people.[9] A U.S. Military Government editorial roundup showed that the initial German press reaction to Allied proposals for a West German government was strongly negative.[10] If the London Recommendations had been the only major issue in June and July of 1948, the Western powers would have faced a group of sullen parliaments and a recalcitrant Economic Council in West Germany.

The West's firm stand in Berlin, together with the airlift, helped to counterbalance the unfavorable reactions engendered by the London Recommendations. The juxtaposition of the two issues was made clear by a Christian Democratic deputy in the Nordrhein-Westfalen parliament:

> Yesterday and today there have been many justified, but harsh, words said in criticism of military government and international politics—words which were not easy for everyone to say. I believe it is necessary that a friendly word as well be said to the Allied powers, and that it may be formulated as follows: We recognize, and we are happy, that the attempt of Russia to conquer Berlin in this way has been thwarted by your resistance—we hope for ever. (Cries of "bravo.")[11]

Speakers of all the noncommunist parties in the various parliaments expressed their recognition of the Allied stand. A Social Democratic member of the Württemberg-Hohenzollern government characterized the airlift as an "amazing accomplishment," and added that those Germans who considered the fight of the Berliners to be right and necessary ought to be thankful for the achievements of the Allies.[12]

The press joined in the chorus of recognition. Munich's *Süddeutsche Zeitung* wrote that the airlift was not only the largest operation in the history of aviation but also the most humane, for it kept two million people from perishing as innocent victims of the East-West conflict; it was a bridge between peoples who were supporting each other in the fight against terror and slavery.[13] Similar statements could be found in many other papers, both liberal and conservative.

A CDU leader who was interviewed in 1952 stressed the importance of the airlift in convincing people that the Western powers really meant to stay in Berlin:

> Two factors assisted particularly in awakening West Germany to the significance of the Berlin struggle. One was the steadfastness and courage of the Berliners. The other was the airlift. I cannot emphasize too strongly the tremendous psychological importance of the airlift. The Germans are accustomed to brush off many things as propaganda gestures, but it was not possible to do that with the airlift. This was the most important move taken by the United States since the start of the occupation. . . . And then the fact that lives were lost on the airlift removed it from any suspicion of propaganda.

There are indications that the stationing of additional United States military aircraft in Europe as a result of the blockade crisis also helped to demonstrate the strength of the Western powers and to reassure West Germans in the face of the Soviet threat. The *Rheinische Zeitung* in Cologne wrote:

> Molotov . . . is not likely to forget that the 90 Superfortresses stationed in Germany, when loaded with atom bombs, represent a destructive force which is four times as great as the entire Air Force of the United States in the Second World War. It is a disgrace for present-day humanity that such arguments, scarcely three years after the most terrible war, appear to be the strongest props of peace.[14]

Throughout the blockade, the movement of U.S. Air Force units to Europe received good coverage in the West German press.

Partially as a result of the situation brought about by the blockade, many West German leaders now saw the relationship between West Germany and the Allies as one of mutual dependence. As the *Süddeutsche Zeitung* put it,

> The fight for Berlin has created an unusual political situation. The Western Allies can fight this battle only with the determined help of the Germans, whose fate, in turn, depends on the powerful and continuous support of these Allies. . . .[15]

A Christian Democrat in the Nordrhein-Westfalen parliament said that, if the Allies had not come to the assistance of Berlin, they would have forfeited the trust of the Germans.[16] Their support of Berlin, in turn, was repaid by a growing sense of obligation among West German leaders to help the Western powers. This was reflected in a statement issued by SPD headquarters in Hannover in the early days of the blockade:

> We must show the Berliners that we comprehend the importance of their struggle. But we must also make it clear that the Western powers, by their actions in Berlin, are defending the interests of all Germans. For we should not forget that Berlin's fate is also ours.[17]

Not all criticism of Allied policies was stilled in this new atmosphere of cordiality. Objections to the London Recommendations and other proposals continued to be voiced, although in more moderate tones, and the Western powers had to make a number of modifications in these proposals before they were finally accepted. On the whole, however, the blockade redounded to the benefit of Western policy in Germany. The airlift, in particular, was and remained a positive symbol. An American, who had been a liaison official with the German Parliamentary Council in Bonn during the blockade, recalled later that the airlift was the one subject on which all those present could talk with good feeling. In his opinion, it was the most graphic proof of the power and determination of the United States. There was no question, he thought, that the blockade crisis and the airlift helped push through plans for a West German government, and that they strengthened the Western coalition at a time when the support of West German leaders might well have proved difficult to secure, and when France and England showed signs of going their separate ways.

General Clay came to a similar conclusion. On October 22 he told the National Security Council that, as a result of Allied action in Berlin, the German people had closed ranks and applied themselves to the tasks of reconstruction with new vigor. Germany had been waiting passively to see where she should cast her lot for the future, but was now veering toward the cause of the Western nations.[18]

While the blockade situation raised the Western powers in the eyes of the German leaders, and thus facilitated the formation of a West German state, it severely prejudiced German attitudes toward the Soviets. In the minds of many, the Soviets had made themselves eligible to replace the Nazis as the lowest internationally-recognized form of political life, and this tended to remove some of the stigma that Hitler had fastened on the whole nation. West Germans echoed the Berliners in speaking of the blockade as a crime against humanity; they recalled the Nürnberg trials at which Nazis had been condemned for similar crimes; and they stressed the parallel between Soviet and Nazi methods.

Spokesmen of all the noncommunist parties were agreed that the Soviet action in Berlin was something akin to a war crime. When the president of the Hamburg parliament, in reading a resolution in support of Berlin, came to the words "We see the hunger blockade against Berlin as a crime against humanity," he was interrupted by applause.[19] The Council of Elders of the Niedersachsen parliament condemned the "hunger blockade against women and children" as a "striking instance of a crime against humanity."[20] Speakers in parliaments and city councils throughout West Germany used similar terms, and many made reference to the Nürnberg trials. Said one CDU deputy:

> I think that these days there is probably no German whose thoughts do not turn to the Nürnberg court which again and again, as a foundation for a new international law, raised the accusation of crimes against humanity. . . .[21]

Many West Germans drew parallels between Soviet and Nazi methods. The chairman of the Frankfurt City Council, for instance, in describing the communist attacks on democratic city council members before the Berlin city hall, pointed out that such "spontaneous" actions were known from the time of the Nazis.[22] A Christian Democratic deputy denounced Soviet methods in Berlin as "cursed similar to National Socialist methods."[23] And a Social Democrat argued that the West Germans should assist the victims of the Soviets for the same humanitarian reasons that people assisted the victims of the Nazis: ". . . for it is all the same, ladies and gentlemen, under which symbol or under which political ideology misery appears. Fear is fear, terror is terror, hunger is hunger, concentration camp is concentration camp, whether it appears under this or that political label."[24]

Several observers felt that the Soviet blockade policy, in addition to causing a general deterioration in attitudes toward the Soviets, played a direct part in bringing West Germany's political leaders to support the idea of a West German state. According to *New York Times* correspondent Drew Middleton, the minister presidents of the West German *Länder*, who had been lukewarm, and even hostile, to the idea as long as they saw any opportunity for the reunification of Germany, now were convinced by the blockade that the Soviet Union would never agree to unification except on its own, unacceptable terms. Hence, these men became more receptive to the London Recommendations after the summer of 1948 than they had been at first.[25]

That the influence and example of the blockaded Berliners also contributed to West Germany's cooperation with the Allies, and thus indirectly to the establishment of the Federal Republic, can be inferred from numerous remarks of West German leaders. A Social Democratic spokesman pointed out that Berliners had shown in the December elections that they stood firmly behind the Western Allies.[26] Parliamentarians who tried to refute the argument that East and West were equally responsible for the blockade often pointed to Berlin's solid support of the West. The reasoning was something akin to a political syllogism: Berliners support the Western powers; West Germans must support their fellow nationals in Berlin; therefore, West Germans should support the Western powers.

Furthermore, the Berliners, projected by the blockade into national and even international prominence, tended to be intolerant of West German criticism of Allied policies. When Dr. Adenauer attacked the London Recommendations and spoke of the "forced labor of the Ruhr coal miners," he was immediately called to account by the Berlin *Tagesspiegel*, which accused him of involuntarily playing into the hands of Soviet-directed propaganda. If he really wanted to know what slave labor was, said the paper, he should look at the uranium mines of the east zone.[27] With Berlin so solidly behind the Western powers, it was more difficult than ever for West German leaders to oppose the Allies.

Ernst Reuter's personal influence was a powerful factor in the creation of a West German state. Early in the blockade there was still some fear even in Berlin that such a government might serve to perpetuate the division of Germany and isolate Berlin behind the iron curtain—a view which found support in the councils of the Berlin Social Democratic Party itself. However, Reuter and a number of his colleagues became convinced that a strong West Germany was necessary to support a free Berlin, and they came out strongly in favor of a West German state, which, they felt, should incorporate Berlin.

In July and August Reuter presented his views forcefully to both Allied and West German leaders. He attended conferences with the minister presidents of the West German *Länder* and, according to some observers, was influential in framing the compromise between Allied military governments and the minister presidents which led to the founding of the Federal Republic in its present form. Indeed, a *New York Times* dispatch on July 23, 1948 reported that a big factor in the German decision to push ahead with the building of a government was the fact that Mayor Reuter had come out publicly for the formation of a West German state. A former member of the U.S. Military Government staff recalled that Reuter had taken part in a number of three-power discussions of the subject, and had exercised a substantial influence on Allied policies. Since British and French officials did not feel that he ought to join them directly in top-level conferences, he had been invited to be available immediately outside the conference rooms and had been frequently consulted.

The degree to which the crisis as a whole tended to advance plans for a federal republic was further indicated by the apprehension about the future of these plans following the first rumors, in the spring of 1949, that the blockade might be lifted. A *New York Times* dispatch on April 17 cited "most United States and British officials in Berlin" as believing that the impetus among the Germans for the formation of a West German state would be lost with the lifting of the blockade. Two days later, Homer Bigart reported to the *New York Herald-Tribune* that "any hint of a possible settlement might also delay acceptance by the Western Germans of the tripartite occupation statute which has been proposed. . . ." That U.S. Military Government was worried about this possibility is clear from the choice and wording of a question that the Opinion Surveys Branch asked in three cities during the spring of 1949: "If the Berlin blockade should be lifted, do you think plans for the establishment of a Western German government should be dropped, or should be carried through?"[28] (In Frankfurt, to cite one example of the results, a quarter of the respondents thought plans should be dropped, slightly more than half were in favor of carrying them forward, and the rest were undecided.)

Successful resistance to the Soviet blockade thus came close to being a prerequisite for the establishment of a stable West German state, and the blockade situation itself helped pave the way toward the formation of the Bonn government. The Soviet blockade, one of the purposes of which had been to interfere with Allied plans for West Germany, had actually worked in their favor.

Communist Influence Decreases

The West German Communist Party apparently had had no advance warning of the Soviet plan for a full blockade. Scattered reports of communist reaction in various localities indicate that at least the lower leaders of the party did not know what position to take. In the small town of Melsungen in the north of Hessen, the communist fraction in the county assembly voted along with the noncommunist parties in favor of a sympathy rally for Berlin. (The deputies reversed their position a short time later, apparently in response to objections from higher communist headquarters.)[29] At a meeting of the budget committee of the Economic Council on July 6, 1948, the communist spokesman on the committee joined with representatives of the other parties in voting a credit of 20 million marks for Berlin;[30] he later became a bitter opponent of financial aid to Berlin. In the Wiesbaden City Assembly, the four communist deputies voted in favor of a resolution expressing sympathy and support for the people of Berlin, but they did oppose another resolution, which condemned the Berlin Communists specifically.[31] In the discussion following a political mass meeting in Düsseldorf, a Communist Party member (who was not identified) was reported as saying that the policies of his party amounted to a betrayal of the German people.[32]

Confusion within the party did not last long. By the middle of July communist deputies in West German legislative bodies apparently had been briefed on what line to take in their speeches. From then on all of them advanced almost identical arguments. The motions introduced by communist deputies also appear to have been framed at a central point for use by party members in the various parliaments.[33]

The West German communist line with regard to Berlin was vigorously aggressive:[34] The other parties were using the Berlin crisis as a screen behind which to hide the catastrophic results of the West German currency reform, which in turn had been designed to split Germany. Berlin was in trouble because the Western powers had violated the Potsdam Agreement, and it was therefore up to them to find a solution for the difficulties they had caused. West Germany had no business assisting Berlin so long as it had within its borders thousands of expellees and refugees who were without the basic necessities of life. The Special Berlin Tax,* by which West Germany was raising money to support Berlin, was one of the "material and ideological preparations for war," and in supporting it, the noncommunist parties were simply acting as flunkeys for the warmongering Western powers.

The Communists also used every opportunity to mention the high cost of the airlift, and either to imply or to state outright that the costs of this huge operation would be borne by the German taxpayer. They referred to the airlift contemptuously as the American "flying sport" or "air acrobatics," and suggested that the Americans should pay for such luxuries themselves. Unemployment in West Germany, said the communist speakers, was rising as a result of restrictions imposed by the Western powers, and German workers were violently opposed to extra taxes and deductions from their pay

* *Gesetz zur Erhebung einer Abgabe "Notopfer Berlin."* The author has been unable to find a completely satisfactory translation for this title. The present one is only an approximation.

envelopes that would only finance the political ambitions of the West.

In the West German parliaments, the Communists opposed all measures for the support of Berlin in general and the Special Berlin Tax in particular, and made every effort to show that the Berlin Tax was a levy aimed at the workers and sparing the wealthy. Communist deputies in several of the parliaments proposed measures for special assistance to the needy within the West German states, rather than to Berlin. In Hessen, for example, the Communists introduced a bill to provide funds to all families with an income of less than 140 marks a month, so that they might buy coal and potatoes during the winter, and most speeches in support of this measure took the form of attacks on the Special Berlin Tax.[35]

When other parties moved to express sympathy with Berlin or introduced legislation to provide support for the city, the Communists attempted to tack amendments on to these motions to the effect that the Western powers were responsible for the plight of Berlin. In the Hessian parliament, for instance, the SPD and CDU submitted a joint resolution, which ended with the parliament's expression of "its recognition to the Berlin population for the presence of mind and determination which the Berliners have shown." The communist fraction thereupon moved to add the words: ". . . , after the West attempted to subject the German capital to a separate currency reform."[36] But the amendment was rejected by the other parties.

Communist propaganda throughout West Germany echoed the refrain of communist parliamentarians. In addition, party workers promoted expressions of discontent in trade-union groups and other organizations, and many of these groups did indeed pass resolutions against the Special Berlin Tax. A veteran West German union official described the situation as follows:

> They [the Communists] took advantage of the fact that workers don't like to have deductions made from their wages—no matter what the reason is, they naturally don't like it. This does not mean that they were against Berlin; they were just against *any* new tax, and still are. Therefore, the Communists were able to get quite a few West German labor organizations to pass resolutions opposing the Special Berlin Tax.

One Social Democrat explained that it was part of communist tactics to include the Special Berlin Tax on any list of grievances that was drawn up by the unions. Politically inexperienced union leaders then would sometimes approve the whole list without scrutiny of the individual items on it. As soon as SPD officials pointed out the political stratagem by which the Communists had introduced the Special Berlin Tax into a list of legitimate grievances, most of the duped union leaders immediately tried to revise the list or at least to submit the various items to the membership for separate votes. In the few unions where Communists had gained control of the administrative machinery, the union executive committee usually passed resolutions without consulting the membership at all.

One cannot fail to be impressed by the resourcefulness, and the excellent preparation, of communist deputies in the various state parliaments, as well as by the energy of the publicists and agitators who spread the party line throughout West Germany. Communist deputies were almost invariably armed with quotations and statistics when they rose to make what appeared to be carefully prepared speeches in West German legislatures. Occasionally, they would make skillful use of rhetorical tricks. For example, a deputy in the Economic Council quoted a passage which, he alleged, had been written by Major Reuter of Berlin. When Social Democratic deputies expressed approval, the Communist revealed that the quotation actually came from former Nazi Propaganda Minister Goebbels.[37] It was apparent that, for the communist deputies, politics was their chief concern and a full-time job. By contrast, many of the other deputies, though quite often the better orators, appeared to speak without the benefit of much advance preparation.

In spite of the conscientious efforts of communist deputies and the perseverance of party propagandists, the communist cause suffered seriously in West Germany during the period under consideration. There were at least three reasons for these political setbacks. First, the communist line with regard to Berlin was so far removed from the facts of the matter—and these facts were easily available to every German—that it became practically indefensible; communist propagandists were forced to make suicide stands in untenable positions. Second, East Germany was a serious liability to West German Communists. No matter how glowing the pictures of a workers' paradise they painted, the news that trickled through into West Germany from the other side of the Elbe made it abundantly clear that conditions there were not such as to make communist rule attractive. Third, communist deputies and propagandists, while clever and hard-working, were frequently boorish and insulting. For the sake of some slight propaganda advantage they would often sacrifice the mutual confidence that was necessary if they were to take part in the democratic process.

The attitude of noncommunist deputies toward the communist propaganda line on Berlin is illustrated by the reaction to an attempt by a communist deputy to expound the communist line in the Economic Council. The speaker was met with laughter from all sides of the house, and an SPD deputy interjected: "Do you happen to live on the moon?"[38] The Communists fared no better in the various state parliaments whenever they attempted to present the Soviet position.

Soviet policy in Berlin and East Germany provided democratic deputies with a ready weapon for use against communist advocates. For example, when military government in the American zone suspended certain sections of a law governing works councils, which had been passed by the German authorities, a communist deputy in the Hessian parliament used this as a peg on which to hang a vigorous denunciation of both the United States and the noncommunist parties. In reply, a Social Democratic deputy, without endorsing the action of military government, cast considerable doubt on the good faith of the communist orator:

> I have not heard that Herr Müller [the communist speaker] has protested against the policy of the occupation power which is presently delivering millions of Germans in Berlin to hunger. (Cries of "that's a good one!" from the SPD and CDU.) I have heard no protest from Herr Müller and know of no exceptions taken by him to the disgraceful verdicts which have been handed down by military courts in [the Soviet sector of] Berlin. (Cries of "very good" from the SPD and CDU.) And I would have been happy if Herr Müller had protested and demanded that Lord Mayor Professor Reuter, who was elected in a democratic fashion by a huge majority, finally be installed in his office. I would have been happy to see Herr Müller come out in favor of allowing the democratic parties in the east zone to conduct their activities in a free and democratic manner. As long as the Communists do not do this they have no right and no cause to accuse others of kowtowing to the occupation powers.[39]

In Württemberg-Hohenzollern, a communist deputy assailed the law which instituted the Special Berlin Tax as a "law for the preparation of war." A conservative (DVP) deputy replied: "I don't entirely understand Deputy Zeeb. . . . I recommend that some time he take a look at the east zone police, as I was able to do, then he will know what preparations for war really are."[40] When a Communist in Nordrhein-Westfalen accused the democratic parties of trying to split Germany, a Social Democratic heckler cried: "Just look at Berlin."[41] And so it went in every West German legislature, and in many public meetings.

Perhaps it was the very hopelessness of their political position that made the Communists in West German parliaments more aggressive than usual during the blockade. In the Economic Council, a communist deputy characterized the Special Berlin Tax as "a new way of robbing the workers and the poorest people among us, the refugees and the returnees." The presiding officer interrupted him and requested that he take back the term "robbery," because it went beyond the bounds of permissible language, but the communist deputy refused to take back the objectionable word.[42] There was similar trouble between the communist fraction and the chair in almost every parliament because of interjections from the floor. German parliamentary custom permits any deputy to make comments while another deputy is speaking, so long as these interjections do not make it impossible for others in the chamber to follow the speaker's remarks. Communist hecklers, however, frequently startled their fellow deputies with interpolations of such length and volume as to disorganize the proceedings, and bring reprimands from presiding officers. And at times, communist deputies indulged in personalities that must have made their relations with the other lawmakers most difficult. To cite only one blatant example, a Communist who had been irritated by a conservative deputy's description of conditions in East Germany shouted at him: "Don't make yourself ridiculous. You surely are not more stupid than you look."[43]

In their exposed position, and as a result of their own tactics, the Communists in West German legislatures became more and more isolated. A resolution adopted by the West German SPD shortly after the start of the blockade contained the phrase: "In the west zones, the political consequences should be drawn from the fact that the Communists have given active assistance to the terror measures in Berlin.[44] When the president of the Nordrhein-Westfalen parliament called for a standing vote on a motion to express solidarity with Berlin and present the city with 100,000 tons of coal, only the Communists stayed in their seats, and were booed by the other deputies.[45] In Hamburg, the City Assembly voted "no confidence" in a communist member of the city government because he opposed certain relief measures for Berlin.[46] In some of the parliaments, and also in the Economic Council, it became the custom for most of the noncommunist deputies simply to leave the chamber whenever a Communist rose to speak.[47] This progressive isolation of the communist parliamentarians was, of course, due to a great many factors, and had begun even before the Berlin blockade. But the communist position on the blockade greatly accelerated it. Whereas previously the Communists had cooperated with other parties on certain types of legislation and had thereby managed to exert a modicum of influence on the legislative process, such cooperation and influence became almost nonexistent during the blockade.

Communist influence among the West German public suffered a similar decline. While many West Germans grumbled about the Special Berlin Tax and showed little interest in other measures for the support of Berlin, this did not mean that they endorsed the communist position. From the latter part of 1948 on, the Communists lost heavily in most West German state and local elections.[48] In the densely populated state of Nordrhein-Westfalen, where they had received 14 per cent of the votes cast in the state legislature elections of April 1947, their share of the vote dropped to 7.8 per cent in the local elections of October 17, 1948. The U.S. zone had no state elections during the blockade, but the federal elections of August 14, 1949 showed that the Communist Party had lost strength in every area.

A number of observers on the spot attributed this decline in the communist vote at least in part to the party's stand on the Berlin question. As a Social Democratic deputy said to a communist colleague who had just expounded the party position,

> During the past months the German people have decided about this in all the elections which have taken place. Your party . . . has paid the cost of that point of view which you have just made known.[49]

In an analogous situation in the Economic Council, another Social Democrat replied to a communist spokesman:

> In answer to the criticism which the previous speaker made of this proposal [the Special Berlin Tax] and the basic ideas behind this proposal, my friends and I can only join with the

voters of Nordrhein-Westfalen, who last Sunday gave the Communist Party their answer with respect to the policies which have been followed in the east zone and in Berlin.[50]

During 1946 and 1947 many West German voters had seen the Communists merely as one of the anti-Nazi political parties. By 1949, however, the Communist Party was recognized as an arm of Soviet policy; stories told by refugees from East Germany, as well as news reports, had thoroughly discredited the Soviets; and the blockade had played its part in educating the West German voters about the methods of the Soviets and the functions of their German auxiliaries. From a powerful political force the West German Communist Party was reduced to a small splinter group.

Berlin Becomes a West German Outpost

When the two currency reforms and blockade plunged Berlin into an economic crisis the Magistrat immediately turned to the West German Economic Council for aid. This plea for assistance speeded up a process that had already begun. On April 22, 1948 the bizonal Economic Council had voted to establish a committee to promote economic cooperation with Berlin.[51] Then, on June 19, the Berlin Magistrat sent an urgent call for assistance to the president of the Economic Council and the chairman of the Council's Executive Committee. According to this note, West German currency reform (which at that time did not include Berlin) meant that the city would no longer be able to pay for vital imports from the three west zones. The Berlin Magistrat was therefore forced to request credit. This request was considered by the Executive Committee in its meeting on June 23, and the sum of 45 million marks was thereupon placed at the disposal of two bizonal agencies (the Administrations for Food, Agriculture and Forestry, and the Administration for Economics), with instructions that West Berlin be supplied with necessary goods from West Germany.[52]

This West German assistance to Berlin was granted prior to the full blockade. When the blockade became total, and the Soviets froze the bank accounts of the Magistrat in East Berlin, the city's financial situation became even more urgent. The Magistrat then appealed for an additional credit of 20 million marks on an emergency basis. This was approved by the budget committee of the Economic Council on July 6.[53] Shortly thereafter, Acting Mayor Louise Schroeder revealed that she would ask for a further credit of

100 million marks "with which to carry on the battle for Berlin" when the minister presidents from the West German states met on July 11. At her request, a memorandum already had gone from the bizonal authorities to the finance ministers of the West German states, apparently in order to guard against the possibility that the West Germans might dismiss the financial problems of Berlin as concerning only the occupying powers. Part of this memorandum read:

> In support of her request Frau Schroeder said that everything must be done from the German side to prevent the defense of Berlin from collapsing before the diplomatic actions of the Western powers could take effect. She also said that, while the fate of Berlin in this dispute between East and West could not be decided by the Berliners and the Germans, nevertheless the Germans must not neglect to use every means [to support Berlin] until the dispute has been settled, in order to ensure that in the event of an unfavorable result the Germans will not be held responsible for not having made sufficient effort.[54]

The conference of minister presidents at Koblenz, in which Louise Schroeder took part,* supported her request in principle, but did not settle the problem of how to raise the money. One proposal was that the funds be raised by withholding part of the new money which was being distributed to each person in West Germany under the currency reform. West Germans had already received one installment of twenty marks per head in the new currency, and were due to receive another payment in the same amount. This proposal, to the effect that two marks of the second twenty be withheld for the benefit of Berlin, was voted down in a meeting of bizonal finance authorities on July 16. One high official felt that it would burden the West Germans too heavily. Another objected that the money to be raised would serve to finance the political actions of the Americans against the Russians, and he considered it inappropriate for German authorities to promote the policies of a foreign power. From a humanitarian point of view, however, he saw the necessity of assisting the Berliners, and the only way to do so,

* Former Minister President Arnold of Nordrhein-Westfalen testified to the deep impression that Louise Schroeder made on the West German officials present: "I shall never forget with what inner emotion the chief official of the so oppressed city of Berlin, Acting Mayor Louise Schroeder, took part in these meetings. . . ." (*Stenographischer Bericht über die 49. Sitzung des Landtages Nordrhein-Westfalen*, July 14, 1948, p. 631.)

he thought, was to issue an appeal for contributions from the public.[55]

When the outcome of the meeting became known in Berlin, it brought a peppery letter from a representative of the Magistrat to the bizonal Administration for Finance. Granted that the Berlin question was highly political, wrote the Berliner, and that a final solution could be found only through negotiation among the occupying powers, it was an important *German* question too. If German authorities neglected to take financial action and simply referred the matter to the Allies, the latter were bound to say: "What are *you* doing?" The best thing would be to go ahead and vote the money and then turn to the Allies for help, if necessary. The Magistrat official also felt that withholding part of the second allotment of new money would be a good idea, even if only one mark were withheld instead of two. This measure recommended itself by its very crudity: it would show the world public what a sacrifice the West German population was actually making. "Complicated and adjusted taxes could scarcely be expected to achieve the same political effect."[56]

However, West German authorities apparently still regarded the withholding idea as politically unwise. On July 29, 1948 the finance ministers of the West German states decided that 75 million marks should be provided by the newly established *Bank deutscher Länder* and guaranteed by the states of the three west zones. The bank, however, did not regard this security as adequate, and refused to provide the funds. In the end, the necessary amounts were scraped together from a variety of sources. Military government provided some from income on German exports, the bizonal administration succeeded in borrowing 45 million marks from the *Bank deutscher Länder*, and smaller sums were borrowed from the Central Bank of Hamburg and the state of Nordrhein-Westfalen. Altogether, by September 20, 120 million marks from West German sources had been placed at the disposal of Berlin.[57]

By early fall, it had become apparent that the blockade might last a considerable length of time, and that funds for the support of Berlin would have to be raised by other than emergency expedients. Accordingly, the Berlin Committee of the Economic Council, on September 22, requested the Executive Committee to draft a law which would provide for a regular source of funds for the assistance of Berlin. The committee suggested that the possibility of new taxes be examined, that the post office issue special stamps to be sold for the benefit of Berlin, or that the interest on frozen bank accounts be placed at the disposal of Berlin.[58]

The draft legislation, which was submitted to the Economic Council on October 19, 1948, was entitled: "Law for the Collection of a Special Contribution to Relieve Distress in Berlin" (this has been referred to as the "Special Berlin Tax").[59] As finally adopted, the law provided that special 2-pfennig stamps should be affixed to every domestic letter, and that the revenue from these stamps should be used for the benefit of Berlin. It also called for a very small graduated surcharge on individual incomes, and a tax on corporations. All told, these taxes were designed to raise 25 million marks per month.[60]

From then on, the Berlin problem was frequently before the Economic Council. The Special Berlin Tax law required periodic renewal, and several committees of the Council were in constant touch with the affairs of the beleaguered city. The three states of the French zone, which were not under the authority of the Economic Council, also passed laws providing for special assistance to Berlin, and then renewed them as necessary.

These new administrative ties between Berlin and the west zones led to ever more frequent personal meetings between officials from the two areas. Members of the Magistrat took part in the committee work preparatory to drafting the Special Berlin Tax law.[61] Berlin's food and economic officials were in constant touch with bizonal agencies in connection with airlifted supplies, representatives of Berlin came to Bonn to assist the Parliamentary Council in drafting a provisional constitution for West Germany, and so it went.[62] As a result of all these contacts, West German officials received first-hand information on the Berlin scene from some of the men best qualified to give it.

When, today, one enters the meeting chamber of the German federal parliament in Bonn, one sees behind the speaker's table the coat of arms of the city of Berlin along with those of the West German states. A parliamentary staff assistant explained this to the author by saying: "Although West Berlin is not a member of the West German Union *de jure*, it is *de facto*, because of the close financial and administrative relationships which grew up during the blockade."

By entering into these relationships, the West German states accepted a part of the responsibility for the support of West Berlin as an island of freedom in the Soviet zone. They were thus formally aligned with Western policy and placed in a position of opposing Soviet aggression even before the airlift had demonstrated that Berlin could be sustained throughout the winter.

The Struggle for West German Public Opinion

While West German leaders became almost unanimous in their conviction that West Germany should help support Berlin, they sometimes had difficulty in carrying their constituents with them. Immediately after the imposition of the blockade the public had shown appreciable enthusiasm about the resistance of the former capital to Soviet aggression. People attended mass meetings in large numbers and applauded speakers from Berlin. They even made appreciable cash contributions to the various campaigns to assist Berlin. But as time went on their enthusiasm waned, being replaced in most cases by apathy, but in some cases even by opposition.

The problem with respect to West German public opinion was to prevent apathy and opposition from mounting to a point where political leaders would no longer find it possible to unite behind measures in support of Berlin. Any wavering on the part of official bodies in West Germany would have had serious repercussions in Allied capitals. For, if the Western powers had become convinced that their position in West Germany would not be weakened if they gave up Berlin, and might even become stronger, the hand of those in favor of giving in to at least some of the Soviet demands would have been greatly strengthened. And if the Western powers had abandoned their steadfast opposition to the Soviets in Berlin, the prospects of forming a viable West German state would have been dim indeed. Adverse developments in West German public opinion could thus have started a disastrous chain reaction.

A Berlin newspaperman who visited Bavaria during the early phase of the blockade testified to the interested, and even enthusiastic, attitude toward Berlin. He reported that he was deluged with questions, and that the inhuman plans of the Soviets—including the starvation of nursing infants—had aroused broad circles in West Germany from their lethargy. He concluded that the people of West Germany had abandoned Berlin just as little as had the Berliners themselves.[63]

Similarly, the polls conducted by U.S. Military Government's Opinion Surveys Branch in the U.S. zone during July and August revealed a high degree of support for the Allies' Berlin policy. For the most part, U.S. zone residents shared the opinions of West Berliners, but there was a higher percentage of "undecided" or "no opinion" responses. For instance, in August, cross-sections in West Berlin and in the U.S. zone both were asked: "Do you believe the Western powers are right or wrong to stay in Berlin under the present circumstances?"* To this, 97 per cent of the Berlin respondents replied that the Western powers were right, as compared to 89 per cent in the U.S. zone sample. In Berlin, 2 per cent thought the Western powers were wrong, and 1 per cent were undecided; in the U.S. zone, 3 per cent thought the Western powers were wrong, and 8 per cent were undecided.[64]

As time went on this enthusiasm for Berlin began to cool. Appreciable popular opposition to the Special Berlin Tax was revealed in some of the parliamentary discussions that preceded its passage. Lawmakers in the Economic Council who voted the Special Berlin Tax for the British and American zones did not feel the pressure of public opinion directly, since they were elected by their respective state parliaments. The debates of the Economic Council, therefore, do not contain extensive discussions of the state of public opinion with regard to the Berlin situation.† In the French zone, however, it was necessary for the three state parliaments individually to pass the law providing for the Berlin Tax, and the deputies were very directly concerned with public opinion about it. When the question of renewing the law came up for discussion in the parliament of Württemberg-Hohenzollern (French zone) in March 1949, deputies of the noncommunist parties recognized that there was considerable popular opposition to it, but ascribed this to the public's lack of understanding. A Christian Democratic deputy explained:

> It is correct that there is opposition [to this law] in the state. But the necessary educational work with regard to it has not been done by the newspapers and the labor unions. One shouldn't blow the same horn, but should tell the people—as I have—simply and plainly that this sacrifice is necessary. (Remark from the floor: "They can't do that for political reasons.") One can maintain this point of view very well as a trade union member. I am also a trade union member, and have expressed

* A sample of 511 was used in West Berlin, and a sample of 3000 in the U.S. zone.

† In the course of the discussion preceding original passage of the law, a Christian Democratic deputy did refer to resolutions from various workers' bodies which opposed it, but he ascribed this opposition to communist agitation. (Cf. Economic Council, *23. Vollversammlung*, October 19, 1948, p. 1053.)

> this point of view to my fellow members. One must have courage to look at things as they really are.[65]

A Social Democratic deputy echoed his words, saying that the press and the functionaries of the various parties should give a fuller explanation of why the parliament had voted as it did. "If more [educational work] had been done with regard to the Special Berlin Tax, I am convinced that this argument would not have arisen."[66] And the Minister of the Interior added that the parliamentary deputy should lead, rather than follow, public opinion:

> Now for the other objection [of the communist speaker]. The workers oppose this Special Berlin Tax. I will not deny that. . . . In itself it is correct to say that every deduction these days is felt by the worker and ever deduction—no matter how small—means a sacrifice for him. But it depends what position one takes with regard to this state of opinion. One can fan the flames or one can try and put them out by informing the people. (Remark from the floor: "That's right.")[67]

Another indication that popular enthusiasm for supporting Berlin was waning rapidly was the relatively modest success of the campaigns for voluntary relief contributions. A communist deputy in Württemberg-Hohenzollern asserted that the campaign in that area was able to raise an amount sufficient only to cover the costs of collection.[68] Other parts of West Germany seem to have raised somewhat larger amounts, but the total must have been disappointing to those who organized the campaigns.

One of the essayists in the *Abend* competition, a Berliner who had left the city about a year before the blockade and settled as a mason in Bavaria, gave a description of opinion on the Berlin question in his new community:

> Then the blockade came. I did everything I could to supply my relatives with food and medicines. I helped every way that I could. . . . Every Friday I went to the movies. When the newsreel came on, showing pictures of the airlift, there were loud protests. People laughed, whistled, stamped their feet, and yelled. It became worse and worse. . . . I thought at first this must be a communist propaganda campaign, but soon was taught better. That was a sad chapter, very sad. I had many discussions at my place of employment and found again and again that there was a certain antipathy against Berlin and

> against this whole business. The workers who were in the SPD were interested in this battle for freedom and accordingly conducted themselves decently. That was understandable because the SPD in Berlin was leading the fight and because the workers had interest in political matters. But my landlord called the Berliners "lousy dogs," and only his poor physical condition prevented me from beating him up. The SPD called upon people to make a modest gift of 200 grams of bread and 40 grams of sugar. Coupons for these amounts were held back when ration cards were given out, since a voluntary collection would hardly have gotten anything. Then the communists started the slogan: "Go and get your coupons back." So everybody hurried down and got their coupons back. The Berliners and the refugees watched all this with deep disgust. . . . In addition came the many complaints and the groaning about the Special Berlin Tax with its 2-pfennig stamps and payroll deduction. . . . Agreeable conversations with decent Bavarians provided a ray of light in this darkness, but these did not occur very often.

An almost equally dark picture emerges from an opinion study undertaken by a West German advertising agency in the spring of 1949.* According to the agency's report, which was made available to the Berlin authorities, popular sympathy for Berlin had been very great in the first few months after imposition of the blockade, but had gradually turned into almost complete apathy. Most people, said the reports, were now convinced that Berlin was lost, and that the Western powers were only looking for a chance to abandon the city gracefully. The popular attitude was expressed by the slogan: "Whoever supports Berlin throws good money after bad."

New York Times correspondent Drew Middleton made a similar observation. He reported that Berlin's resistance to the blockade had at first been greeted approvingly in West Germany, but that, by the spring of 1949, the blockade had become an expensive bore to large sections of the population. The prevailing sentiment was: "Let the Russians and the Americans worry about it."[69]

Six West German newspapermen, who were consulted three years after the blockade, agreed substantially on the following picture of West German attitudes during the latter part of the blockade and

* This study was based on interviews in six West German cities. The manner in which respondents were selected, and the total number of respondents, are not given.

airlift: The Soviet action in blockading Berlin was reprehensible, and the Allies were to be commended for their action in starting the airlift. People grumbled about the Special Berlin Tax, but for the most part their grumbling was not serious. ("When you give some people a ham they will complain that it's not a whole pig.") They were willing that West Germany should help support the Berliners if absolutely necessary, but would have preferred to see the Western powers do the whole job by themselves. ("Berlin's all very well—but to pay money for it!") The attention of most West Germans was focused on the acquisition of sufficient stocks of the new currency, currency with which one could actually buy almost any commodity ("Now every pfennig means something"), and there was little time left to worry about Berlin. Without question, the professional politicians recognized the importance of the Berlin issue far more clearly than did the masses.

And yet, there was enough popular support for the Special Berlin Tax and other aid proposals to enable the noncommunist deputies to pass these measures in the various parliaments without experiencing political reprisals. Appeals to nationalism, humanitarianism, justice, and the desire for reunification, certainly influenced politically conscious members of the public. Such appeals were frequent in the West German press and radio, in the speeches of political leaders, and in letters from friends and relatives in Berlin and the east zone.

Personal experience with communism was another important factor. Over one million former residents of Berlin or the east zone had entered West Germany before the blockade, thus comprising about 2½ per cent of the population.[70] The blockade itself brought about 100,000 more from Berlin alone.* Expellees from the eastern territories totalled nearly seven million, or about 17 per cent of the West German population.[71] Former Berliners and those who had lived under Soviet occupation were more likely than other Germans to take a strong stand against communism, and consequently to approve of the support of West Berlin as a bulwark against Soviet expansion.

A newspaperman suggested that former Berliners played a significant political role in West Germany by exposing Communists in public argument. He reported that one propaganda device of the

* In 1952, 6,500 of Wiesbaden's 230,000 inhabitants were former Berliners. (*Wiesbadener Kurier*, March 8, 1952.) Naturally this proportion cannot be projected to apply to the Federal Republic as a whole.

West German Communists was to send representatives to meetings of all kinds—singing groups, cultural meetings, political gatherings, and so on—where they would seize any opportunity to make political speeches. As it happened, however, Berliners also liked to attend meetings, and most of them were politically well informed. No sooner would a communist agitator start a political speech than a former Berliner would jump up and contradict him.

Public opinion in favor of supporting Berlin was also strengthened by the airlift. Not only did the airlift arouse enthusiasm because of its technical achievements, but it gave a substantial number of West Germans an economic interest in Berlin. A large labor force was required to maintain West German airfields, to load and unload airlift planes, and to operate ancillary transportation services. Although some of this labor force was composed of Allied military personnel, and some of displaced persons, airlift officials estimated that over three-quarters of it was made up of Germans. West German business, as well as labor, was heavily involved in processing and transporting supplies required, directly and indirectly, by the airlift.

All these factors tending to influence public opinion in the direction of supporting Berlin were not sufficient to sustain a high pitch of popular enthusiasm throughout the blockade. They did, however, keep apathy, neutralism or communist agitation from undermining the position of political leaders who favored the West. West German public opinion never reached a point where political leaders were forced to withdraw their support of Allied policies.

In another sense, the struggle for West German public opinion was won by the West when the blockade failed to undermine confidence in the new currency, or to inhibit the individual's efforts to improve his economic situation by making him uncertain about the future. When the Soviets cut the overland routes to Berlin in June 1948, military government and press observers noted signs of nervousness among certain elements of the population. In some cases people who lived near the borders of the Soviet zone began to move property to areas they considered safer. A journalist recalled hearing businessmen say during the first few days of the blockade that they regarded West Germany as a poor place for investments because of the probability that it would fall more and more under Soviet influence. Public opinion polls indicated that about half the population thought communism would spread westward if Berlin fell.[72]

But nervousness never became widespread and had no opportunity to grow into panic or defeatism. Indeed, outward indications of disquiet were of such a transient nature that they were quickly forgotten and few references to them remain. Confidence in the new currency developed rapidly. People felt sufficiently secure to make plans for the future and to work furiously to turn these plans into reality. The resistance that the Western powers and Berliners offered to Soviet pressure served as a wall behind which a state of mind favorable to the economic revival was able to flourish.

The Soviet device of blockading Berlin, combined with the response to it by the Berliners and the Allies, thus helped to align almost the entire political leadership of West Germany on the side of the West. Representatives of all major parties were able to agree on the formation of a West German state, on adoption of Berlin as a West German outpost, and on a Western orientation in other respects. Meanwhile, individual West Germans turned their full energy and attention to economic reconstruction. These developments amounted to a major defeat for the Soviets, who saw the economic—and ultimately the military—weight of Germany gravitating toward the democracies. To arrest this process, Moscow shifted its emphasis to a peace campaign and a campaign for German unity. One aspect of this new communist approach was removal of the blockade.

CHAPTER VIII

WHY BERLINERS RESISTED

IN CONTRAST to the situation in West Germany, where politics remained the concern of political leaders and the masses were preoccupied with their personal economic problems, Berlin's population as a whole took keen interest in political developments. For the blockade directly affected the daily life of every West Berliner.

The way individual Berliners made their decision to try and hold out when the blockade came has been described in a previous chapter, in which it was pointed out that even though nearly everybody wanted to resist, most people hesitated to cast their lot with the West until they were sure there was some hope of success.* The present chapter will summarize briefly the pressures to which the population was subjected during the crisis and will then discuss the reasons *why* Berliners wanted to resist, and why such good morale was maintained in the city as a whole during the long period it was cut off.

Briefly, the thesis presented below is that Berliners wanted to resist because as a group they were tough-minded and politically sophisticated, because prior experience had left most of them with strong anti-Soviet and pro-Western attitudes, because they received a number of psychological gratifications from resistance, and because they anticipated certain material benefits after the blockade had been broken. Good morale was maintained over such a long period because a social mechanism for controlling those who showed signs of yielding to Soviet pressure developed and because the course of events during the blockade provided periodic stimuli to morale. But before discussing these subjects further, it may be useful to define more precisely the types of behavior which resistance involved.

A Definition of Resistance

By "resistance" is meant the sum total of those actions by which Berliners expressed their aversion to communist or Soviet domination and their allegiance to the Western world or the legally-elected Berlin government. Some of these actions were open to any member of the West Berlin public; they included refusal to join in commu-

* See Chapter III, pp. 132-44.

nist-led demonstrations, refusal to register for food or other supplies in East Berlin, voting for democratic candidates at the city elections in December of 1948, attending mass demonstrations called by Berlin's democratic leaders, and using west marks in preference to east marks. Numerous less specific actions also could be taken by any Berliner: putting up with hardships of all kinds without undue complaint, expressing approval of the city's noncommunist leaders, and following the instructions of the city government and the Western military governments.

Other types of resistance could be displayed only by certain specific groups. Municipal employees are a case in point. Because of the confusion attendant on the split of East Berlin from the rest of the city, and the blurring of lines of authority that this often entailed, civil servants sometimes had to choose whether they would work for the Communists or for the legal government; they occasionally had to exercise discretionary authority when no clear instructions were available, and many of them showed a devotion to duty beyond that ordinarily required of civil servants. The men of the West Berlin police deserve special mention. Although constantly exposed to kidnaping and other forms of violence at the hands of the Communists, most of them performed their functions in an exemplary manner.

Berlin's labor force was another group whose resistance was especially significant. By withdrawing majority support from the communist-led FDGB and giving it to the independent unions, the workers made it difficult for the Communists to dislocate the delicate economic machinery in West Berlin. Furthermore, members of the labor force as a whole showed great understanding in the face of their almost impossible working conditions, and refrained from protest activities that would have weakened West Berlin's ability to hold out.

Employers, large and small, also did their part. By the exercise of great ingenuity, they managed to avoid laying off workers and thereby contributing to unemployment. A British official who was concerned with the economic administration of Berlin during the blockade remarked later that the employers managed to make these difficult adjustments for the most part without direction from any authority; they simply understood the problem and met it as best they could.

Another large group that has often been singled out by observers of the blockade was composed of the housewives. Faced with new and difficult problems of home economics, the housewives managed somehow to feed their families, raise their children, and maintain conditions in the home which made life bearable, if not pleasant.

Different individuals engaged in resistance to varying degrees. There were a few in every group who failed to oppose the Soviets in any way. Other individuals displayed resistance behavior on some occasions and not on others. On the whole, however, resistance was the rule rather than the exception.

Psychological and Material Pressures on the Population

Berliners resisted in the face of strong psychological and material pressures to give in to Soviet demands. Soviet propaganda sought in a variety of ways to induce people to throw in their lot with the East, or at least to withdraw their support from the West. It argued that Berlin was situated in the center of the Soviet zone and had no alternative but to become integrated in this zone. It sought to take advantage of the Berliners' desire for a better life by giving glowing accounts of conditions in the east zone, and predicting economic chaos in West Germany. The SED promised Berliners more food, electricity and fuel right away if they would throw in their lot with the East.

More insidious were the communist appeals to fear: fear of war, fear of retribution if the Western powers departed, fear that those who displayed an anticommunist attitude would be kidnaped, fear of material privation, fear that Soviet forces or the East German police would invade the west sectors.

Fear found a fertile soil. Berliners knew that, in a military sense, the Soviets had Berlin at their mercy. Many of them were constantly apprehensive that the Russians "might just walk in." Although considerably allayed by Allied reassurances, such fears persisted in the back of the minds of most Berliners to the very end of the blockade. Communist propaganda contributed to keeping this apprehension alive by constantly threatening West Berliners that they would be punished for anticommunist actions after the Soviets had assumed control of all Berlin.

Fear of war was also widespread. In the fall of 1948, a U.S. Military Government opinion survey found that approximately half the West Berlin population expected a war in the relatively near future.[1] Similar results had been obtained in August by a UNESCO-sponsored poll, in which Berliners were asked whether they thought it was likely that all countries would be able to live together in peace.[2] A substantial number of *Abend* essayists also mentioned that they had expected or feared a war at the outset of the blockade. Communist charges of "warmongering" in West Berlin may have been intended to exploit these fears.

Fear of being abandoned by the Western powers probably was the most immediate cause of anxiety for Berliners. It was particularly strong during the Moscow negotiations in August 1948, and could be detected both in public expressions at the time and in the subsequent observations of essayists. This fear was nourished by the Communists, who emphasized every sign of indecision on the part of the Western powers, and cited domestic criticism of governmental policy in the United States, Great Britain, and France.

Apprehension of cold, hunger, unemployment, and other privations, although partially dispelled by the growing success of the airlift, was present during much of the blockade. U.S. Military Government's Opinion Surveys Branch periodically asked West Berliners whether they thought it would be possible for the airlift to maintain life in Berlin all through the winter. In July, 52 per cent of the respondents did *not* think it possible. By September, however, the proportion of respondents who took this gloomy view had sunk to only 11 per cent.[3] Of the *Abend* essayists who mentioned the subject, over one-third said that, at the outset of the blockade, they had not expected the airlift to succeed. A public opinion interviewer recalled that, in the fall of 1948, many people had wondered how they would manage during the winter: how they would cook their food, and whether life in unheated homes would be bearable.

Much of the fear that plagued Berliners was an undefined foreboding that they might be betrayed from within. In the words of an American observer who was in close touch with political opinion in Berlin at the time,

> The fear that hung like a phantom over the city took concrete forms in the neighborhood, office, and shop: the known communist neighbor or colleague, and the unidentifiable *Spitzel* [informer] or *agent provocateur*, and more frequently the uncanny recognition—after Nazi experience—that weak characters would change like salamanders were the Russians to come. . . .[4]

Many Berliners were tormented also by a feeling of being trapped. If Russian troops came into West Berlin, the ordinary citizen would have no place to go. As the Communists constantly predicted, Berlin's leaders probably would be "taken care of," for the Western powers would certainly try to remove prominent government and party officials by air. But the man in the street would have to pay the price for Berlin's resistance.

None of these fears was based on imaginary dangers. Communist propaganda could point to indisputable facts, and, at times, the Western powers themselves inadvertently lent further substance to these fears, as, for example, when they allowed evacuation plans to become known.

The ordinary Berliner thus lived under great psychological pressure and, at the same time, was exposed to severe temptations. The Soviet authorities offered him food, fuel, and employment, if he would allow himself to be administered in part by Soviet agencies. Or, he could put an end to the gnawing uncertainty by moving to East Berlin. Conditions under Soviet rule might not be attractive, but at least they seemed more predictable than in West Berlin.

People reacted to these psychological pressures in different ways, and some were exposed to them more than others. Among the most vulnerable were those who lived in West Berlin but worked in the Soviet zone or sector—some 10 per cent of the population.[5] Their peculiar difficulties during the blockade are well described by one of the *Abend* essayists, the wife of a skilled worker who was employed in Soviet-occupied Potsdam:

> The first difficulty concerned buying food in West Berlin at the time of the blockade. My husband was ordered to buy in the east. His objection that it was impossible because he worked such long hours was not accepted. He was told that his wife must do it—or else! We both considered this demand to be nonsense, as good work on the job had nothing to do with where one bought groceries. But I was ordered to appear in person and explain. Determined, I obtained a medical certificate saying that I was too sick to appear and that any exertions would be dangerous, so I couldn't go to buy groceries in the east. We thought the episode was closed, but it wasn't.
>
> In the shop [in Potsdam] there were generous special distributions made at very low prices to workers who lived in West Berlin but worked in the east. These were valuable, scarce items—meat, butter, potatoes, coal, and even real coffee. There were often cash bonuses too. But my husband was not allowed to share in any of these things. He was disobedient. We bought our food in West Berlin, he was told. . . . Now my husband was

> in constant trouble. The management was suddenly dissatisfied with the man they had previously considered a good worker. He was mistrusted; his work was bad; he was reprimanded for carelessness, and so on. We thought he would be discharged any day. But my husband could not quit his job. There was none for him here in the west, and in such an event he would receive no compensation. Then we couldn't have existed. So there was nothing to do but try and hold out.

As expected, this man eventually was discharged, but he managed to obtain part-time work in West Berlin. Characteristically, his wife in her essay did not explain why she and her husband were willing to risk their livelihood merely to avoid buying their groceries in the east. To her, as to other West Berliners, the reasons were self-evident.

Besides living in a state of constant apprehension, inhabitants of the west sectors had to endure material conditions even worse than those of the immediate postwar years. The nature of these physical hardships, and the degree to which people were conscious of them, were revealed by a poll taken in October 1948 (see Table 1), when

TABLE 1

PRINCIPAL HARDSHIPS OF THE BLOCKADE AS MENTIONED BY A CROSS-SECTION OF WEST BERLINERS IN OCTOBER[6]

Hardship	*Percentage Mentioning**
Lack of gas and solid fuels	42
Power shortage	35
Food	23
Business troubles	9
Financial troubles; not enough west marks, etc.	9
Unemployment; anxiety about unemployment	7
Transportation difficulties	7
General helplessness about the quarrel of the big powers	4
Other; lack of clothing, medicine, shoes	5
No troubles	5

* Replies total more than 100 per cent since some persons mentioned more than one hardship.

a cross-section was asked: "In which way are you personally most affected by the Berlin blockade?"

It is apparent from this tabulation that problems of heating, lighting, and eating were felt most keenly at that time. The *Abend* essays reveal a similar pattern (see Table 2), although they mention the electricity shortage slightly more frequently than the lack of gas and solid fuels.

TABLE 2

PRINCIPAL HARDSHIPS OF THE BLOCKADE AS RECALLED BY ESSAY WRITERS

Hardship	*Number Mentioning**
Lack of electricity, mainly for lighting	72
Lack of fuel, mainly for heating	69
Lack of food, or dullness of food	35
Unemployment	18
Transportation difficulties	12

* These are absolute numbers, not percentages.

None of these material hardships alone was such as to threaten the physical existence of Berliners; added together, they made life difficult in the extreme. Furthermore, they continued month after month.

However, the blockade failed completely to reduce significantly the caloric intake of most Berliners. In the spring of 1948 inhabitants of the U.S. and British sectors were receiving an average of 1,779 calories per day per person.[7] Table 3 shows the actual amounts of food contained, for example, in the daily rations of heavy workers and "other adults."

These rations were maintained, with some substitutions, until November 1, when the average ration was increased to 1,998 calories. This was, of course, still far below the average consumption in economies where food was freely available. Also on November 1, some high-value foodstuffs, including cheese, were introduced into the West Berlin diet, to most people for the first time in many years. Later there even were limited quantities of such coveted items as jam and real chocolate.

On the debit side of the gastronomical ledger was the fact that the available food became extremely monotonous. Fresh vegetables

TABLE 3

RATIONS IN THE U.S. AND BRITISH SECTORS OF BERLIN AT THE OUTSET OF THE BLOCKADE[8]
(grams per day)

	Heavy Workers	*"Other Adults"*
Bread	600	400
Other cereals	80	40
Potatoes	400	400
Fat	30	10
Sugar	25	20
Meat	100	40
Coffee Substitute	150	150

or fresh milk could not be brought in by plane, and, during most of the blockade period, supplies from other sources were far from sufficient to meet the demand. In order to reduce bulk and weight, the airlift brought in dehydrated foods wherever possible, and dried potatoes, dried milk, and dried eggs became unpleasant symbols of the blockade. Lack of fuel for cooking made it difficult to prepare these foods in the most palatable manner, and some babies were unable to digest the powdered milk. Families with that particular difficulty were usually able to obtain fresh milk from the 3,468 milk cows which were blockaded along with the two million people.[9]

Conditions would have been far worse had not the airlift rations occasionally been supplemented with other foods. During the first few months of the blockade, it was possible to smuggle in fresh vegetables and other supplies from the Soviet zone and West Germany. Even after these sources were cut off, some vegetables and other fresh foods were grown within the city limits. Urban farmers contributed sufficient vegetables to provide each person with over one pound of fresh vegetables per month, and those who cultivated tiny garden plots were allowed to keep what they grew for their own use.[10] These amounts were, of course, pitifully small, but they helped to alleviate the uniformity of the diet.

The airlift was not able to take care of West Berlin's fuel and power requirements as well as it took care of the city's food supplies. At the outset, a thirty-day supply of coal was available,[11] but it was impossible to bring in by plane enough stocks to allow consumption to continue as before. Coal for space-heating in homes and most other buildings was ruled out almost entirely. A total ration of twenty-five pounds of coal was allotted each normal family unit for the entire winter; homes with small children and very old people received a somewhat larger allocation. This slender ration was supplemented by wood cut from the parks and tree-lined avenues of the city. Most Berliners were able, at the most, to heat one room, and that only spasmodically.

Cooking also was restricted. Prior to the blockade, 90 per cent of domestic cooking had been done by gas, and the shortage of coal now sharply curtailed the available gas supply. During the first five months of the blockade, consumers were limited to half of their previous gas consumption, which in practice permitted them only one hot meal per day. On December 1, this ration was raised to 75 per cent of the pre-blockade figure, and the careful housewife could once more cook full rations for her family.[12]

As for electricity, each user was normally permitted four hours per day, usually in two periods of two hours each. These periods came at different times of day in different sections of the city, and not infrequently people had to rise at odd hours in order to take advantage of the available current. Those who did their cooking by electricity sometimes had their big meal of the day shortly after midnight.[13]

As a result of these restrictions, many Berlin homes were both cold and dark during the long winter evenings. In October 1948, Opinion Surveys Branch asked a cross-section of West Berliners whether they were able to light their homes at all during the time the current was off. Almost one-third replied that they were unable to do so. Approximately one-quarter of the respondents reported that they had neither heat nor light at those times. Most of the others said they relied on lamps or candles to provide a minimum of light.[14]

The electricity shortage, due not only to lack of coal but also to the limited generating capacity in West Berlin, had severe repercussions on transportation. Subway service was suspended between 6:00 P.M. and 6:00 A.M., and streetcar service was greatly curtailed. Buses could be used only very sparingly because of limited gasoline stocks. Nevertheless, transportation services were maintained to a surprising degree. An official British estimate put them at almost two-thirds of their former capacity.[15] The fact that the East Berlin authorities continued to operate the elevated railroad through the west sectors was of great assistance to the footsore citizens. The reason they did so was probably that discontinuation of the service would have hampered them more than the West Berliners.

Berlin's workers often found themselves ground between transportation restrictions and electric power stoppages. Small businesses that required electric current for their operations had no choice but to operate when this was available, even if at four o'clock in the morning. More often than not, their employees had to get to work on foot. The schedule of almost every household represented a strenuous attempt to reconcile the hours when transportation was available with the time that employment was available, not to mention the limited hours when there was electricity for domestic use.

In view of the limits on raw materials for most industries and the short supply of electricity and fuel, there was, at the outset of the blockade, a justified fear of disastrous unemployment. Yet the ingenuity of Berlin's employers, and the labor requirements of the airlift, made it possible to keep the number of the totally unemployed to a surprisingly low figure. Much of this employment was, of course, uneconomic, and the value of industrial output per man employed declined sharply after the imposition of the blockade. The number of persons employed in West Berlin's industry, which had been 183,696 in June of 1948, was still at 165,196 in April 1949. The gross value of West Berlin's industrial production, however, sank from 136 million marks to 74 million marks during the same period.[16]

The employment picture was actually gloomier than these figures would make it appear, since many industrial workers were employed only part time. Furthermore, as the blockade continued, nonindustrial employment receded even more than employment in industry. The precise extent of unemployment is difficult to compute, since the laws governing unemployment registration and benefits were changed during the blockade. According to West Berlin's official statistics, the total number of unemployed at the end of June 1948, was 46,920 (or 5 per cent of the labor force), and increased steadily thereafter; by April 1949, it had reached 156,320 (or 17 per cent of the labor force).[17]

A British analysis, at the end of 1948, ascribed the relatively low incidence of unemployment in West Berlin during the blockade to the following four factors, listing them in the order of their importance.

1. Resourcefulness of individual firms in Berlin in maintaining production. No military government or city plan could have taken care of so complex an upheaval as this; the greatest credit must go to private employers, with cooperation from their employees.
2. A turn-over to rehabilitation of factory buildings and layouts.
3. "Unseen" employment, where employers pay for little work rather than risk losing services. This especially in view of continuous efforts from the Soviet sector to divert skilled labor to that sector.
4. Alternative employment. Three western airfields employ 15,000. An additional 12,000 are employed on rubble clearance. More could and should be employed, but for currency difficulties.[18]

Spokesmen for U.S. as well as British Military Government also paid tribute to the resourcefulness of employers in maintaining employment at a relatively high level.[19]

Unemployment relief, on the whole, was handled in an orderly fashion and at least assured recipients of a living. Indeed, jokes circulating at the time compared the lot of the unemployed worker in West Berlin with that of the employed worker in East Germany to the advantage of the former.

Perhaps the most unsettling element in the life of West Berliners stemmed not directly from the blockade but from the fact that east and west marks were circulating side by side. A survey conducted by the Opinion Surveys Branch in October 1948 revealed that most West Berliners believed they had enough east marks, but that nobody was satisfied with the number of west marks he was receiving. Over one-third of the respondents said that they had no west marks in their incomes at all.[20] Employed persons usually received at least a part of their wages in west marks, but pensioners, during part of the blockade, received their stipends in east marks only.

One pensioner wrote the *Tagesspiegel* that he received his allotment in east marks, but that only his baker and butcher were forced to accept this currency for rationed purchases. He also pointed out that he could not afford to exchange three east marks for one west mark (the exchange rate at that time), and continued: "I can figure out with mathematical accuracy when I must die. One shouldn't blame us old people if in our desperation we register for food in the east sector, where only east money may be used."[21] Another letter-writer complained that east marks would not buy a piece of soap or a glass of beer in West Berlin.[22] A landlord protested against the regulation which permitted tenants to pay rent in east marks, leaving landlords unable to discharge those obligations which had to be met with west marks.[23] An official report of the Berlin city government characterized the currency situation in the early months of the blockade as disastrous.[24] Some of the inequities were gradually corrected, but the problem of the dual currency remained acute until March 1949, when the second currency reform took place.

Despite dull food, fuel shortages, electricity stoppages, unemployment, and dual currency, the basic functions of life continued much as they had before the blockade. Any serious social or economic dislocation would undoubtedly have been reflected in changed rates for marriages, births, divorce, sickness, crime, and so on. But, with minor exceptions, there were no appreciable statistical changes. Marriages in West Berlin averaged 8.87 per thousand during the blockade and 8.94 in the remaining thirteen months of the 1948–1950 period, a difference so slight as to be attributable to chance.[25] The birth rate in West Berlin dropped very slightly during the period starting nine months after the imposition of the blockade and ending nine months after it was lifted, but the decline was too small to have any statistical significance. The divorce curve also remained relatively undisturbed during the blockade period, although here the administrative difficulties which attended the splitting of the judicial system make it impossible to form more than an impression from the statistics available.

Paucity of data does not permit a direct comparison of the incidence of crime during the blockade with that in non-blockade months. But, according to a British source, the state of law and order, at least during the last six months of 1948, compared favorably with pre-blockade conditions:

> Although street lighting has been reduced 87 per cent compared with that used this time last year, and lack of domestic lighting aids the burglar, statistics for robbery and housebreaking for the months of October, November and December compare favorably with figures for the corresponding period of 1947.
>
> Numerous black market checks have produced results similar to before the blockade. . . .

> Only in cases of fraud is there any increase. This is no doubt connected with the currency situation.[26]

An American newspaperman, citing Berlin's police authorities and "outside experts," reported that crime in West Berlin during the blockade was less than in any other population group of that size in the Western world.[27]

Disease, as measured by the number of persons in hospitals and nursing homes, also failed to increase markedly. The incidence of serious diseases, such as tuberculosis, diphtheria, typhoid, continued to decline during the blockade. Only the death rate showed a moderate but significant increase, especially among the very young.

From all this one can conclude that the conditions of life in West Berlin during the blockade, although hard, were not unbearable. People were depressed by the drabness of existence, the darkness, and the cold, but they were able to obtain the basic necessities. The economic and social fabric of the city never was strained to the breaking point.

On the other hand, one should not minimize the extent of the suffering caused by the combination of physical and psychological pressures. A parliamentary deputy from the South German state of Württemberg-Hohenzollern told his colleagues after a visit to Berlin:

> One receives a tremendous impression when one comes into besieged Berlin. The population suffers terribly. You must imagine what it means now in winter for the western part of this gigantic city, most of which is destroyed and lies in ruins. It is without light, and 70 to 80 per cent of the households have no heat. A doctor told me what effect this has: today already small children are freezing, infants in their swaddling clothes freeze to death in cold apartments. One must have experienced it himself to know how oppressive it is to be enclosed, without any possibility to get out of the city into the surrounding zone or into the free western zones. And in spite of all this, the population holds with complete firmness and determination to that which they consider right from a political and human point of view. . . . They have not let themselves be led into temptation by all those things which have been promised them, not even by the lights which burn in the east sector of Berlin, and not by the higher food rations, for they know the way it looks in the east zone as a whole.[28]

General Howley, too, reported considerable suffering among the 920,000 families in West Berlin. Every household function, which ordinarily would have been routine, became a problem to be surmounted. Even those who did not suffer acutely were oppressed by the continual, dreary darkness which prevented them from reading or relaxing in other ways during the long winter evenings, and most people went to bed early, exhausted by their grim existence.[29] The understatement of the year came from British diplomat Harold Nicolson, who revisited Berlin at the end of September after an absence of nineteen years. Nicolson said: "The change was marked." To him, the city seemed "black and dumb and flattened as the Tiergarten."[30] Not all people were exposed to physical hardships to the same degree, but there were few who did not feel both the material and psychological pressures of life in the blockaded city.

Forces Favoring Resistance: The "Berlin Character"

For most West Berliners, those psychological and physical pressures were offset by even stronger forces working in the opposite direction. First of all, they had become inured to hardships. The years before the blockade had been characterized by cold, darkness, and hunger. To be sure, the blockade intensified these hardships, but it was not as if the population had suddenly been forced to abandon a comfortable standard of living for a period of acute privation.

Another, though indefinable, factor was the character of the people. Berliners have long been known for a certain toughmindedness, combined with an ability to joke about their misfortunes. Harold Nicolson observed after his visit:

> The character of the Berliners had not altered. There was the same grim humor, the same sense of detachment, the same skepticism, the same dogged obstinacy. It may well be that Germany will regain her confidence through the persistence of the curious character, sardonic and yet individual, which that huge, amorphous Babylon has evolved for itself within the space of sixty years.[31]

A discussion of Berlin's blockade humor could easily fill a volume. Lowell Bennett, one of the chroniclers of the blockade, has collected some of the stories and sayings that circulated in Berlin. A typical quip went:

> God knows, even the best blockade is no bargain. But if there must be a blockade, then it's better to be blockaded by the Soviets and fed by the Americans. Just imagine if it were the other way around.[32]

Berlin humor at its best is typified by the work of Günter Neumann, an outstanding writer and political satirist, who gained an enormous following during the blockade. His radio program, "Die Insulaner" (the island dwellers), was carried weekly over RIAS, and its meaty, topical observations—usually kindly, sometimes bitter, but always trenchant—kept people chuckling until the following week. He also published a periodical, *Der Insulaner,* which somewhat resembled *The New Yorker.* His portrayals of the economic problems presented by east and west marks, of cultural life during the blockade, of Soviet and Allied foibles, and of many other aspects of the situation probably constitute some of the most incisive commentary on life during the period. Unfortunately, most of his work is untranslatable, depending for its effect both on the Berlin dialect and on a very detailed knowledge of day-to-day events. But his genius was such that he could turn the Soviet from a terrible into a ridiculous figure. He also struck out at the remnants of Nazi sentiment. Nor were the Western powers spared, although witticisms at their expense never questioned the basic community of interest between them and the Berliners. Neumann's moral is clear: no matter how bad conditions are, as long as you can laugh at them they are not unbearable. The ability to laugh stood Berliners in good stead during the long months of the blockade.

Another salient aspect of the Berlin character is an interest in politics. This interest was temporarily dulled during the immediate postwar period, but revived by the beginning of the blockade, and was stimulated still further by the long crisis that followed. Political considerations came to play a more and more important part in determining the behavior of individuals.

Nearly everybody in West Berlin had an opinion on the major political questions. In public opinion polls conducted just before and during the blockade, Berliners gave "don't know" or "no opinion" responses to political questions far less frequently than did their cousins in West Germany. On some questions less than 1 per cent of the respondents in Berlin failed to express an opinion. The *Abend* prize competition essays reveal this same high degree of political interest. Half a dozen writers remarked that they and their friends read the newspapers and listened to the radio more carefully during this period than they had before. Several families subscribed for the first time to both an evening and a morning newspaper.

The essays show also that political matters not only were followed with more attention than before, but had a growing effect on attitudes and behavior. A housewife observed that her fourteen-year-old son ate his dehydrated food without complaint because he understood that Berlin's political situation made it necessary. Another woman said that people put up with the lack of coal for heating their houses because they understood that nearly all the coal that could be flown in had to be used for industrial purposes. Still another essayist wrote: "Now those who previously had been uninterested in politics became interested, and the reaction against the unfair means which the East used in the form of the blockade led to political opposition, to the unqualified will to hold out." A 51-year old unskilled laborer remarked: "I realized then for the first time that democracy can be more than a slogan."

Public opinion interviewers also noted this increased political awareness. One of them wrote that people now saw politics as the key to everything:

> Even housewives who previously had read only the serialized novels in the newspapers began to take an interest in the first page, where the political news appeared. And they didn't do that only because the paper shortage had eliminated or reduced the space for the continued stories; they did it because politics was now something that concerned them. For even the menu was determined by the political situation.

Another observed that the morale of the unemployed in Berlin during the blockade was not as poor as one might have expected, because nearly all those without jobs knew *why* they were unemployed and *whom* they had to blame for this. Their resentment was focused on the Communists, and besides, they had hope for the future. According to a *Tagesspiegel* editorial, people who had grumbled about unreliable transportation and electric stoppages during 1946 and 1947 accepted the much more rigorous curtailment during the blockade, because they understood its purpose.[33]

As the Berliner's traditional interest in politics revived, the sphere of politics broadened. Not only were more people interested in political events, but more events and activities were seen as related to politics. Choices which previously had been determined by nonpolitical considerations came to be made more often on the basis of political attitudes. For example, a person's political beliefs might determine whether he went to the theater in the Soviet sector, or they might dictate his choice of food. In short, they came to play an even larger part in molding his general behavior.

Attitudes toward the Soviet Union

In addition to a resilient personality and political sophistication, most Berliners had a set of attitudes predisposing them to resist communist demands and hold out in the face of the hardships that accompanied the blockade. The most prominent of these attitudes was one of opposition to the Soviet Union; indeed, it overshadowed all other political attitudes in Berlin during the blockade period.

Anti-Soviet feeling had existed among broad circles of the German population even before the war and had been stimulated by the Nazi authorities.* It was heightened by the war, and was greatly intensified by the conduct of the Soviet troops that entered Berlin in 1945. Affairs in the Soviet zone did nothing to counter this feeling; on the contrary, the economic depredations and political persecution which Berliners observed from their democratic island only strengthened their anti-Soviet attitudes still more. Finally, the blockade, and the high-handed measures that went with it, reduced the supporters of Soviet policy in Berlin to a few communist diehards and a somewhat larger group of opportunists who identified their material well-being with a seat on the Soviet bandwagon. Berliners might differ in their social and political philosophies and in their attitudes toward the several Western powers, but they were united by an almost universal opposition to Soviet encroachment in Berlin and to its German instrumentality, the SED.

Directly or indirectly, nearly all the *Abend* essays, and all the reports about the blockade by public-opinion interviewers, mention this strong anti-Soviet feeling. About one out of every four essayists explained his attitude on the subject by reference to his own previous experience with the Soviets. The specific experiences cited are broken down in Table 4.

* It is dangerous, however, to assign too much weight to the role of Nazi indoctrination in the formation of anti-Soviet attitudes in Berlin. Berliners as a whole were among the groups within Germany which resisted National Socialism most successfully, and their tendency was to condemn both the Nazis and the Soviets as two manifestations of the same basic phenomenon.

TABLE 4

EXPERIENCES MENTIONED BY ESSAY WRITERS AS REASONS FOR AN ANTI-SOVIET ATTITUDE

Experiences	*Number of Mentions*
Experiences during the Soviet entry in 1945	25
Experiences in connection with the blockade	47
Experiences in connection with the Soviet zone	11
General experiences with the Soviets	12

References to the entry of Soviet troops in 1945 are almost exclusively concerned with assault, robbery, rape, and murder. Five essay-writers recalled that the phrase "Lieber Pom als Frau komm"* became popular during the blockade. Some were more specific. A retired white-collar worker wrote:

> I remember with pain that time, from May until July 1945, in which Berlin was conquered and brutally plundered by the Soviet Russians. It is unpleasant to remember the theft of machinery from Berlin's industry, the destruction of the West Berlin power plant, and the thoroughgoing dismantling of our gigantic telephone office in the Winterfeldstrasse. So much for the technical equipment. Mentally, I live through this terrible time again. I hear the terrified cries for help from the women in the neighborhood who were being violated by drunken Soviet troops, I see the columns of miserable men who had been arrested and driven east like cattle. . . . And then finally the Allied occupation troops arrive—Americans, British, and French!

"What we went through in the weeks of Berlin's liberation and in the years after that made us reject the idea of giving in of our own free will," wrote a 44-year-old housewife. Memories of 1945 probably lingered in the minds of those essay-writers who did not specifically refer to them.

Most frequently mentioned among the reasons for anti-Soviet attitudes was the blockade itself, or specific aspects of it. A 32-year-old

* A free translation would be: "I'd rather eat dehydrated potatoes than have the women raped again." "Pom" was a brand name for dehydrated potatoes. "Frau komm" (woman, come here) was the phrase often used by Russian troops to announce their amorous intentions.

housewife wrote that the blockade, though not the first piece of chicanery organized by the East, was the most monstrously malicious. Several essayists remarked that the blockade had unmasked the Soviets and shown them in their true colors. Apparently, the single most irritating aspect of the blockade was the confiscation of fuel and foodstuffs by east zone or East Berlin police. A streetcar conductor devoted his entire essay to describing a pathetic incident, in which one of his passengers had been arrested in East Berlin on Christmas Eve for trying to take a small bag of coal to his family in the French sector.

A third group of writers based their attitudes on experiences in the east zone, either their own or those reported to them by friends or relatives who lived there. A businessman who had left his factory in East Germany and fled to West Berlin before the blockade told of the experiences with Soviet control officers which had led him to take this step.* A housewife wrote that, prior to the blockade, she used to see hungry women from the east zone come to West Berlin to forage for food. The suggestion that inhabitants of Soviet-dominated areas were in many respects worse off than the blockaded residents of West Berlin was confirmed by other essayists. As a retired schoolteacher put it, "All those who knew conditions in the east zone said we must hold out."†

And some of the writers, in explaining their hostility toward the Soviets, simply limited themselves to such general remarks as "we knew the Russians well," or "Berliners have good memories."

The adjectives used by the essayists to describe the Soviets or their conduct were in themselves revealing: "inhuman," "malicious," "hypocritical," "arbitrary," and "cruel" were the terms most often used. Eight persons compared the Soviets to the Nazis; as one put it, "A wolf remains a wolf, whatever you call him."

The fact that the existing anti-Soviet feeling was intensified by

* According to Berlin's official statistics, over 61,000 persons moved from the Soviet zone to West Berlin between March 1948, and October 1949. In addition, more than 32,000 persons arrived from war prisons and internment camps (mostly in Soviet-controlled areas) during that period. Thus there was in West Berlin during the blockade a substantial number of persons who had had recent experience in Soviet-controlled areas. Cf. *Berliner Statistik,* Jahrgang 1949, Heft 12, p. 291.

† According to officials of RIAS, this radio station received a substantial number of letters from listeners in the east zone and east sector just prior to the West Berlin elections of December 5, 1948. Many of these letters described the unbearable conditions in Soviet-controlled areas and exhorted West Berliners to vote for one of the democratic parties.

the blockade is confirmed by answers to a question which U.S. Military Government's Opinion Surveys Branch put to a cross-section of West Berliners in July 1948: "How do you think the Germans regard the Russians as a result of the recent developments in Berlin—better, worse, or the same as before?"[34] Eighty per cent of the respondents thought that German opinion about the Russians had deteriorated, 16 per cent saw no change, and only 1 per cent thought that the feeling had improved. The rest did not commit themselves.

The following month, a UNESCO-sponsored poll asked a sample of 644 West Berliners: "Which foreign people do you feel least friendly toward?" Seventy-nine per cent of the respondents named the Russians, 3 per cent mentioned the Poles, 3 per cent scattered their replies among several other peoples, and 15 per cent had no opinion.[35]

Negative attitudes toward the Soviets were directly related to behavior, and often went to explain specific actions. Thus, a locksmith who hated corn and had sworn never to eat it again (he thought it made his skin yellow) wrote: "But to give in to the Russians? No! Never! I'd rather eat corn until I end up yellow as a mummy." Even dehydrated potatoes came to be accepted as a lesser evil.

In themselves, these anti-Soviet attitudes are not enough to account for the resistance of West Berlin. But, in conjunction with other attitudes, expectations, gratifications, and pressures, they go far toward explaining why Berliners behaved as they did during the blockade.

*Attitudes toward the Western Allies Prior to the Blockade**

In rejecting the Soviets, West Berliners were implicitly making a choice in favor of the Allies. In their eyes, the Western powers benefited from comparison with the Soviets, and the choice in most cases was automatic and received little discussion.

Prior to the blockade, the Berliners' attitudes toward the Western powers, especially Great Britain and the United States, were based largely on their experience during three distinct periods of the recent past. The first period was the time of heavy bombing in the

* Berliners regarded each of the Western powers with a slightly different set of attitudes. The available material, however, does not permit one to compare the attitudes toward the French and British with those toward the United States. Most essayists either referred to the Western powers collectively, or else referred only to the United States as the most prominent among the Western powers.

closing years of World War II, of thousand-plane attacks, and nights spent in air-raid shelters. Among the *Abend* essayists, more than twenty recalled the bombing of Berlin during the war, and almost twice as many mentioned that the Western powers had previously been the enemies of Germany.

The negative attitudes toward the West that the war and heavy bombings had inevitably aroused were somewhat modified by the relief at the arrival of Western troops in 1945. After the ravages of the Russian soldiery and the plundering of the city by Soviet authorities, West Berliners were inclined to greet the French, British, and Americans as liberators. Eleven of the essayists alluded to the favorable attitudes engendered by the comparison between the Soviets and the Western powers in 1945. These attitudes were, of course, relative: if Soviet troops had never entered Germany, it is improbable that the Western powers would have won any popularity contests.

A third way in which West Berliners came to know the Western powers and to form attitudes about them was by observing Allied behavior in Berlin and West Germany between 1945 and 1948. Strikingly enough, the *Abend* essayists almost never commented on Allied policy during this period. While several of them expressed disapproval of Soviet policy in East Germany, not a single one said anything specific—either approvingly or otherwise—about Allied policy in West Germany before the currency reform. Among the more general statements on Allied policy, the only favorable comment was by a policeman, who observed: "General Clay's policy was not to hit a fellow when he's down, and the Germans appreciated this." By contrast, there were fifteen unfavorable mentions, most of them reproaches to the Western powers for their "soft" policy toward the Soviet Union, or their weak and vacillating policy in general. As a hospital nurse wrote, "The angelic patience which was shown by the Americans, British, and French was simply incomprehensible to most of us."

Studies by the Opinion Surveys Branch of U.S. Military Government confirm that Berliners' attitudes toward the United States up to the time of the blockade were relatively favorable but far from uncritical. Immediately after the breakup of the London conference, in December of 1947, interviewers asked 188 Berliners* why they thought the conference had failed. Only 1 per cent blamed the

* The small size of the sample, and the fact that interviewing was done in the streets, suggest the possibility of a large margin of error.

United States exclusively, and 40 per cent blamed the Soviets; on the other hand, 42 per cent thought that both sides were partially responsible. The rest had no opinion.[36] A few months later, in the spring of 1948, cross-sections of respondents in Berlin and major cities of the U.S. zone were presented with a list of adjectives, and asked to indicate those which best described Americans. Their responses are given in Table 5.

TABLE 5

ADJECTIVES CHOSEN BY CROSS-SECTIONS IN WEST BERLIN AND U.S. ZONE CITIES TO DESCRIBE AMERICANS[37]

Adjective	*In Berlin*	*In U.S. Zone Cities*
Friendly	59%	57%
Cultured	46	15
Generous	37	31
Natural	39	33
Intelligent	33	15
Presumptuous	6	8
Wasteful	9	13
Bureaucratic	7	6
Calculating	20	27
Undisciplined	6	2

Thus, attitudes toward the United States appear to have been slightly more favorable in Berlin than in the U.S. zone, but Berliners by no means indicated blanket indorsement of American conduct.

Effect of the Airlift on Attitudes toward the West

The airlift and, to a lesser extent, the complex of events leading up to it, greatly increased the frequency and intensity of pro-Western attitudes. Several of the *Abend* essayists said that they had been greatly encouraged by the Western stand on currency reform, since it was the first occasion on which the Allies had not given in to the Soviets.* A dozen mentioned how surprised and pleased they had

* On August 8, 1948, a letter-writer to the *Tagesspiegel* noted first that the Western powers had been on the defensive for three years and had made many mistakes; then he added: "The fact that the Western powers did not allow themselves to be dissuaded from their plans for currency reform in West Germany and Berlin seems to me to show that their own position has become clear to them. . . ."

been when the airlift was started. As one man wrote, "I could not believe that America would recognize the resolution of the Berlin population. She must have seen the hope with which Berlin looked to the West." The same writer observed later in his essay: "But things turned out in a way that nobody could easily believe. The enemies of yesterday became the friends of today." A stonemason wrote: "People who for a long time had been opposed to us in battle suddenly stood at our sides as if they were our own brothers."

With the start of the airlift, the United States, Great Britain, and France ceased to be viewed principally as a lesser evil, but were seen as having certain virtues in their own right. The airlift neutralized many of the unfavorable attitudes toward the United States and Britain which were left over from the days of the air war; it atoned in part for what Berliners had previously regarded as Allied "softness" toward the Soviets; and it led the people of Berlin to credit the West with more positive characteristics than before.

Ten of the *Abend* essayists mentioned that attitudes they had entertained as the result of wartime bombing had been altered by the airlift. A 45-year-old stenographer wrote: "I was thankful to those who had created the airlift and forgot somewhat the severity of their warfare which had caused us such physical anguish." Or, in the words of a 50-year-old watchman, "In spite of all the suffering and sorrow which the nights of bombing had caused us, no hate or reproach for our former enemies could be felt. On the contrary there developed in me and in others a feeling of the greatest respect for the tireless pilots of the airlift." A 65-year-old professional man spoke of his changed attitude toward Allied fliers:

> When the first victims of the combined airlift were reported, we grieved about these young men as much as if they had been our own. Nobody wanted to mention that perhaps it had been the same boy who had presented us with a quite different variety of cargo a few years before, and whom we then quietly cursed when he, without animus but only trying to strike home, released his 1,000-pound virgin over the target area. When such a flier dropped his dangerous baby in our vicinity and at the very least tore open once more the windows which we had with such labor covered with wood and paper, then our powerless,

---

He went on to urge Berliners not to criticize minor aspects of Western policy but to concentrate on resisting the Soviet offensive.

imprisoned spirits railed passionately against the aviators and against all those who might be responsible for the misery of war.

For such people as these, the airlift tended not only to wipe out past bitterness, but led them to see air power as an instrument of humanitarianism and peace as well as of war.*

The airlift also impressed the essayists with certain specific traits and achievements of the Western powers, particularly the United States. Most frequently mentioned was the speed with which the operation was mounted. This inspired a growing faith in the ability of the Western powers to take quick and forceful action: "In the West they didn't talk; they acted." Or, as another essayist put it, "Now was the time for action, and action was taken. The Western occupying powers did not spend time in long deliberations."

Other essayists recalled how the strength of the West had been emphasized by the airlift. A 31-year-old skilled mechanic wrote:

> It was a machine that ran like clockwork, conceived on a grand scale and yet planned down to the smallest detail, and what power and strength of the Allies it revealed! That which I and who-knows-how-many people had not considered possible became a reality. And even those who had immediately believed in it were extremely surprised when the airlift broke its own records month after month.

According to a 42-year-old housewife, it was easier to hold out after one had personally gone down to the airfields to watch the airlift in operation, and had formed an idea of Western strength for oneself. The Berliners' trust in the strength of the Western powers, said another essayist, had increased with every ton of supplies that was unloaded.

Whether because of the impression made by the airlift, or because of other factors, most Berliners believed that in the last analysis the strength of the West was greater than that of the East. In the fall of 1948, U.S. Military Government's Opinion Surveys Branch asked a cross-section: "If there should be a war, who do you

* On July 5, 1948, the *Telegraf* wrote with respect to airlift planes: "They are no longer a cause for anxiety. No, quite the contrary. Their roar is deep, good, and has a quieting effect, when one knows that from the bellies of these aircraft there come raisins, canned goods, and white flour. Only a few years ago the sound of aircraft engines had a distinctly unpleasant undertone, and it was advisable to take cover as rapidly as possible. . . ."

think is more likely to win?" Eighty-three per cent of the respondents assumed that the West would win; only 4 per cent thought the East would win; and 13 per cent had no opinion.[38]

For some people, the airlift demonstrated the devotion of the Western powers to the highest values—peace, freedom, humanity, charity. A 15-year-old girl wrote that the airlift showed how brute force could be conquered by peaceful means. Speaking of the Allied and German casualties of the airlift, she said: "Their sacrifice reminds us that in this world there are higher things than national egoism—namely, humanity and the existence of all peoples in human dignity." Several essayists referred to the noise of aircraft engines as "a symphony of freedom." Others, possibly with reference to the Soviet peace campaign, said that the airlift was "the greatest peace demonstration of all time." After several months of blockade, Mayor Reuter attempted to sum up what the airlift meant to Berliners:

> The thunder of the aircraft motors . . . has preserved our trust in the great moral strength of the world—a strength which has guaranteed to us that one day we will win our freedom and independence. The flying personnel are for us harbingers of peace and friendship. The pilots who have sacrificed their lives in this difficult service will never be forgotten. We know that from this common experience of freedom-loving peoples there will arise a better world than from the bloody war, which was the terrible result of a power-hungry dictatorship. We know that the superior moral, technical, and economic power of the new world will preserve our city from the fate which was planned for it. We will show our gratitude for this help by redoubling our own efforts.[39]

In short, the airlift won over some of those who had been cool toward their wartime opponents, and it strengthened the respect and good will of the many who already were partisans of the West.

Residual Friction with the Western Powers

There remained, however, those who, despite the airlift, still bore resentment toward the Western powers. A housewife reported:

> There were also people who had been made hard and bitter by what they had been through and said: "Well, they're just trying to get rid of all the stuff they can't sell over there and now they will charge us stiff prices for it."

A bookdealer wrote that many people originally believed the airlift to be a device to provide work for people in the United States who were being laid off because of reductions in the American arms program.

Some of the resentment appears to have been caused by the relatively high standard of living of the Allies. Public opinion interviewers recalled that many people were worried by what they believed to be a "business-as-usual" attitude on the part of the occupying personnel. Allied nationals were thought to waste too much food, to consume more than their fair share of airlift supplies, to be careless about turning off electric lights, and to occupy more housing space than they really needed.* When, during the winter, members of the occupying forces opened the windows of their houses at night, this caused considerable comment. The military transportation system throughout West Berlin also drew criticism because its buses sometimes ran without a full load. However, observations of this type apparently were made more in sorrow than in anger, and did not appreciably affect basic attitudes toward the Western powers.

More serious were the criticisms of those who believed that the Allies should have taken an even stronger stand against the Soviets and should have broken the blockade by force. A popular saying, which was still remembered three years later, was: "Allies, have no fear; the Berliners will protect you." Many Berliners felt that France, in particular, was not doing her fair share in maintaining the freedom of the city.

Those dissatisfied with the Allied effort constituted a fairly large group, as indicated by responses to the following question, which the Opinion Surveys Branch asked periodically during the blockade: "Do you think the Western powers are doing their utmost to relieve distressed conditions in Berlin, or could they do more?" In July of 1948, 77 per cent of the respondents thought that the Western powers were doing their utmost, 22 per cent thought they could do more, and 1 per cent were undecided.[40] When asked, several months later, what further action the Western powers should take to break the blockade, 58 per cent said they favored using more force, 13 per cent advocated seeking agreement with the Russians

* In point of fact, the occupying powers did make stringent efforts to economize on their consumption and these efforts were reported in the press. *Cf. Tagesspiegel*, June 29, July 11, and September 2. Nevertheless, the per capita consumption of food, electricity and fuel was still much larger for Allied than for German personnel.

by peaceful means, 7 per cent thought the Western powers should simply stay in Berlin and remain firm, 5 per cent wanted all four powers to leave Berlin, and another 5 per cent suggested various other actions.[41]

Motives Attributed to the Western Powers

Though Berliners were inclined to criticize Allied policy on a number of points, they were almost 100 per cent agreed that the Western powers were right in trying to stay in Berlin.[42] When asked, however, "Why do you think the Western powers should stay?" they tended to differ. A poll conducted in July of 1948 shows that answers to this question bore a direct relation to the respondents' educational background (see Table 6).

TABLE 6

REASONS WHY THE WESTERN POWERS SHOULD STAY AS GIVEN BY A CROSS-SECTION OF WEST BERLINERS (BY EDUCATION)[43]

		Education	
Reasons	*Total Sample*	*8 Years or Less*	*9 Years or More*
They cannot deliver us to the Russians–they are our protectors–otherwise Berlin would starve–the Western powers must keep their promises.	58%	65%	40%
Otherwise communism would absorb all Berlin (or Germany, or Europe).	20	17	29
They have to do so in order not to lose prestige.	13	9	25
Otherwise democracy and freedom would be endangered.	5	3	9
	96%*	94%*	103%*

* Answers total more or less than 100 per cent because some respondents could not give any reason why the Western powers should stay, while other gave more than one reason.

The better-educated tended to see the blockade as a struggle in which vital political interests of the Western powers were involved, while those with less education were inclined to view the airlift as a relief action. This was evident also from answers to the question (Table 7) "Are the Americans more interested in the welfare of the Berliners or in strengthening their power?"

TABLE 7

U.S. MOTIVATIONS FOR STAYING IN BERLIN AS SEEN BY A CROSS-SECTION OF WEST BERLINERS (BY EDUCATION)[44]

		Education	
	Total	*8 Years or Less*	*9 Years or More*
Welfare of Berliners	34%	42%	14%
Strengthening Their Power	43	34	67
Both	18	19	14
No Opinion	5	5	5
	100%	100%	100%

One might be tempted to conclude that those who thought the Americans were chiefly interested in "strengthening their power" entertained attitudes unfavorable to the United States. But there are reasons to believe that this was not necessarily so, and that indeed the opposite may have been true. Berliners were tormented by the thought that the West might decide to write off Berlin. Consequently, the belief that the Allies were taking action in their own interest as well as in the interest of the Berliners was a reassuring one. As a 52-year-old actor wrote in the *Abend* competition,

> I will freely admit that I occasionally became doubtful and shared the opinions of many Berliners that, if the affair became too "serious," the Americans would desert us and forego any real attempt to break the blockade. But reason said to me: to overcome the blockade would mean at the same time a victory for the Americans over their previous allies—and therefore they *had to fight,* not *only* for our sake. This realization did not diminish the thanks due them for coming to our rescue.

Even though the Allies were widely believed to be acting largely in their own interest, the expressions of appreciation and gratitude to them were many, both during and after the blockade. The impressive tribute paid to the fliers who lost their lives in the airlift has already been mentioned. Not uncommon were statements like the following, which appeared in a letter to the *Tagesspiegel*:

> With admiration we Berliners see the help of the three Western military governments and also the West German states. They can be sure of the thanks of the Berliners for this. . . . To the aircraft personnel and to all those who are taking part in this deed of true humanitarianism belong our special thanks.[45]

Similar letters were received by other West Berlin newspapers and by RIAS. Nearly all the *Abend* essayists, directly or indirectly, expressed some of the same spirit.

If there were any doubt that the blockade experience left West Berliners with predominantly favorable attitudes toward the Western powers, this would be dispelled by their reactions to General Clay, the primary symbol of the Allies in Germany. Clay's name was mentioned in thirty-two of the *Abend* essays, and always favorably. Next among Allied figures was General Howley with six mentions. No other Allied official was mentioned in more than two essays.

General Clay thus stood out clearly as the chief representative of the Western powers in Germany, and the compliments showered upon him by the essayists, three years after the blockade, are indeed impressive: "General Clay and his work will live forever in the hearts of the Germans, and especially in the hearts of the population of Berlin"; "The airlift was a stroke of genius of General Clay"; "We were enthusiastic about this man and his lightening-swift decisions"; "My trust in this man was unbounded"; "It must be said that he was the best thing that Truman could have sent us at that time." And so it went. A Lutheran pastor told of coming out of his parish house, a year after the blockade, and seeing a large and enthusiastic crowd in what looked at first glance like an organized demonstration. Then he noticed that most of the people were from his own parish. Word had spread that General Clay, back in Berlin for the dedication of the Freedom Bell, was to pass that way, and these people had spontaneously assembled to welcome him. "Furthermore," added the pastor, "I was cheering too." Dr. Friedensburg wrote later that he regarded the popularity of General Clay as an indication of the changed attitude of Berliners toward the Allied occupation forces.[46]

The Concept of Partnership

The blockade situation brought a change, not only of attitude, but in the actual relationship between Berliners and the Allies. Several public opinion interviewers commented on this development: "Wherever Germans and personnel of the Western powers came together," wrote one, "whether at work at the airfields or in discussions, everywhere one could perceive a new tone." Another recalled: "A more cordial relationship developed. There was no longer the crass difference between the occupiers and the occupied, which one often had been able to feel up to that time. During the blockade there grew up a friendly attitude similar to the one between acquaintances or neighbors."

Other observers also noted this new relationship. Mayor Reuter wrote, shortly after the end of the blockade, that the mutual trust which had grown up between the German administration and the Allied authorities in Berlin was regarded as remarkable throughout the world.[47] Dr. Friedensburg said later that fighting a joint battle during the blockade had completely changed the relationship between the Berliners (citizens as well as officials) and the occupation authorities: Berliners had come to regard the occupation less as a control authority than as protection and assistance against the common danger.[48] An American newspaperman reported that Germans and Allies, who before the blockade had formed two clearly separate social groups, had become merged after just a few weeks: "They all were in the same boat. . . . From this situation there grew mutual understanding and cooperation which—so recently after a bitter war—is unique in history."[49]

More than twenty of the *Abend* essayists referred to the new German-Allied relationship as a "partnership," and many of them made clear that this sense of partnership with the West contributed to their will to resist. "The Western powers did everything that was in their power," wrote a 30-year-old housewife, "therefore we had to show them how resolutely we could hold out." Others spoke of their emotional commitment to the crews of the airlift planes: The American and British fliers were risking their lives to bring in supplies, hence Berliners could not betray them by yielding to Soviet blandishments. In the words of one essayist:

> We did not think that our behavior was so remarkable. It was a matter of course to us that we had to hold out. Only in that way could we force those who were blockading us to change

their tune. *Or did one think that we should betray the airlift pilots, who were helping us without interruption, trusting in our steadfast behavior!* (Italics supplied.)

Sometimes this concept of partnership with the Allies was made even more explicit. Thus we read in the annual report of one of the independent unions: "The agricultural and forest workers consider themselves a pillar of the airlift in this critical time. . . ."[50]

The subtle interrelationship between the behavior of West Berliners and their attitudes toward the democracies was described by a professional man, whose work brought him in frequent contact with people of all social and economic groups:

> The West Berliners felt pride in the performance of the Allies, but also in their own performance. They said: "The Amis have accomplished something and we have accomplished something." All this led to a greater and greater feeling of solidarity and more and more contempt for those who were faint-hearted or gave in to the Communists at any point. Because the Allies took action the Berliners took action—they resisted. Then they interpreted further Allied actions as resulting in part from their own behavior. One could hear such phrases as: "They wouldn't have sent so many airplanes if we had not held up our end so well," or "If they don't send more planes, then we'll go and demonstrate in front of the Reichstag again."

The idea of interdependence between Berlin and the West also helped to change Berliners' thinking about their own role in political affairs. Several observers noted that people who formerly had thought of themselves as playthings in the hands of the occupation powers now realized that they could exercise an influence on their own future, that they were, as one essayist put it, "masters of their fate." An interviewer wrote: "*Above all* the feeling now disappeared that we were a football for the occupying powers." And a *Telegraf* editorial early in the blockade expressed the opinion that the Western powers were dependent on the Berliners, just as the Berliners were dependent on the Western powers.[51] The people of West Berlin thus suddenly found themselves in partnership with nations that they considered both admirable and powerful. This partnership gave resistance a new importance. Furthermore, in the popular evaluation, the Allies had certain vital interests at stake in the blockade and had to depend on the Berliners to hold up one end of the partnership. It was therefore less likely that the city would be deserted and the Berliners left to their fate. This relationship, combined with the prevalent opinion that the West was more powerful than the East, helped to neutralize—although it could never completely banish—the fear that the blockade brought with it.

Gratifications of Resistance: A Sense of Virtue

Many of the *Abend* essayists were conscious of having done something important for Germany and for the world when they resisted Soviet encroachment. A professional author was one of those who felt that resistance had served to drive away the cloud under which the Nazis had placed his country:

> Berlin became the symbol of a new Germany in the whole free world. The city in the shadow of Stalin showed that the German is better than his reputation; that he knows how to fight stubbornly and well for a cause when he is convinced of the righteousness of his task.

Others remarked that freedom in West Berlin had to be preserved for the sake of the East Germans, if they were not to lose all hope of eventual liberation. Several of those who had lived in East Berlin or the Soviet zone during the blockade recalled that they exhorted friends or relatives in West Berlin to hold out. Such appeals must have confirmed West Berliners in the feeling that, in trying to maintain the freedom of their city, they were acting not only for themselves but for other Germans.

To some people, however, resistance was not only a matter of service to the nation; it was, in addition, a service to humanity and its highest ideals. Ten of the *Abend* essayists believed that the resistance of their fellow citizens had redounded to the defense of all Europe, to the benefit of the whole noncommunist world, or to the furtherance of freedom and justice. A 51-year-old woman remembering her difficulties in trying to cook meals in an unlighted and unheated house, wrote:

> One wished that it were possible to escape from this oppressive atmosphere and go somewhere where there was light and freedom. Only the thought that all sorrows have to have an end and that the resistance of the Berliners was important for the future of Europe restored inner tranquility.

In the opinion of a 31-year-old master-mechanic, Berliners felt that it depended on them whether Germany, and perhaps Europe and the whole world, would live in freedom or slavery. And an unemployed white-collar worker said:

> The inhabitants of East Germany saw the situation in precisely the same way as we who lived here in free Berlin—it is not a question of a half-city or of a country, but of the future of all freedom-loving humanity. To protect this, no sacrifice is too large and no difficulty too great.

The results of a question asked by U.S. Military Government's public opinion research staff in West Berlin on three separate occasions in 1948 (see Table 8) indicate that devotion to the concept of freedom grew stronger in the course of the blockade.

TABLE 8

TRENDS IN OPINIONS REGARDING THE RELATIVE IMPORTANCE OF FREEDOM AND ECONOMIC SECURITY, AS SHOWN BY THREE CROSS-SECTION SURVEYS DURING 1948[52]

"Which of these two kinds of government would you personally prefer?" (Here the interviewer shows the respondent a card with the following alternatives: (a) "a government which provides the people with economic security and good employment opportunities," or— (b) "a government which assures free elections, free speech, a free press, and freedom of religion.")

	April 1948	*June 1948*	*Nov. 1948*
Economic Security	58%	61%	40%
Freedom	38	34	54
No Answer or No Opinion	4	5	6
	100%	100%	100%

While these figures indicate that freedom became an increasingly popular symbol, they also remind us that, after several months of blockade, and under the imminent threat of the loss of democratic freedoms, almost half of the population still felt that economic security was more important.*

* The analysts of the Opinion Surveys Branch noted that somewhat fewer respondents would vote for "freedom" when they were unaware of the fact that

Ideas about the wider significance of resistance for Germany and for the world were worked out and publicized by Berlin's leaders both before and during the blockade.[53] At mass meetings, in the press, and through the radio Berliners heard that they had an historic mission, that Berlin was fated to play a decisive role in the course of world events, that steadfast conduct on the part of the population would promote the reunification and rehabilitation of Germany, and—as Mayor Reuter put it—that Berliners were responsible for defending "those great traditions on which our whole material and spiritual existence is based."[54] These ideas were a comfort to the man who could feel the wet pavement through the holes in his shoes as he walked two miles to work, to the woman trying to get her family's clothes clean in ice-cold water, and to the child faced once again with a meal of dehydrated potatoes and powdered eggs.

Acceptance and Recognition

The airlift played an important part in convincing Berliners that they had been, as it were, readmitted to the Western world, a fact that was brought out by many of the essayists. To some, the airlift was a common experience and a common effort with the West. To others, it was the helping hand of the West, which told them that Berliners were still considered part of Western culture. A 49-year-old housewife wrote that the airlift "suddenly was the intermediary between us and the rest of the Western world, which with interest and sympathy followed the developments in the Berlin question." And a 42-year-old musician compared the airlift to a rainbow: "At one end stand the opponents of yesterday; at the other end we Germans—not only the Berliners—and with measured steps we approach each other."

Also important were the admiring editorials in foreign newspapers, which were freely quoted by the Berlin press; the visits to Berlin by important men from many lands; the messages from presidents and prime ministers, and the enthusiastic reception given Berliners who travelled abroad. All these forms of recognition assured Berliners both that they were once again accepted and that the eyes of the world were upon them.

Again and again, there appears in the *Abend* essays the phrase "We were not abandoned." (More than thirty essayists used these

---

Military Government was sponsoring the poll, but that the *trend* shown in the series of polls was thought to be entirely valid.

words or their equivalent.) The surprise, and even the wonder, implicit in such exclamations can be traced largely to feelings of rejection that had been aroused by a lost war, by the collective-guilt doctrine, by three years of cold and hunger in a destroyed city, and by the occupation policies of austerity, dismantling, and de-nazification. Then, almost overnight, the Berliners ceased to feel and be treated as a conquered people. Their erstwhile enemies not only showered them with high praises; they came to their aid in a manner that was all the more impressive because it entailed great expense and even loss of life. To many Berliners, the hardships of the blockade were more than compensated for by the recognition, acceptance, and solicitude of the outside world.

Several of the essayists were quite explicit in their descriptions of this gratifying experience. One housewife found herself almost embarrassed by it:

> Since the Western powers up until the time of the blockade had treated us Berliners, and all other Germans, as third or even fourth-class citizens, I was convinced that for the sake of Berlin they would never engage in open conflict. I was greatly surprised that they kept up the airlift, with which they responded to the blockade, for such a long time. But I was even more amazed at the almost affectionate recognition they gave to the behavior of us Berliners during the blockade. This recognition was a little embarrassing to me, since I did not regard myself at all as a heroine, but much rather as a miserable, half-starved little "sausage," for whom in this situation there was no other choice but to hold out.

Another housewife said that Berliners had been having a hard time all along, "but now people in the whole world paid attention to us. We were important." A third woman explained how the knowledge of being noticed and admired ennobled even the most routine tasks:

> The world, the press, the speeches of our city fathers, letters from outside Berlin—they all spoke of the bravery of our conduct. The Berlin housewives were accorded particularly high praise. Many times I have had to do things that were unpleasant, and I have often had to do my part of difficult tasks, but unfortunately there was rarely anybody there to bestow appropriate admiration on me. But now, even if together with a large group, I was given this satisfaction. I was a heroine! A

> Berlin housewife who kept her ears stiff as iron, who did her duty as a matter of course. Of course I was not entirely at ease when all this recognition came my way. Things were made so easy for us. We just felt ourselves to be a part of the West and acted accordingly. Nevertheless, this extra praise helped to give a stiff backbone, and I walked proudly through the streets. I was helping to write a proud page in the history of Berlin's housewives.

A public opinion interviewer described the mixed feelings with which Berliners received the plaudits of the outside world:

> Berliners themselves made fun of the boastfulness which, to some degree, was implicit in their own behavior. They smiled when some leading personality of the West spoke over the radio and praised the courage and steadfastness of the Berliners. But in this smile there was something akin to embarrassment and pride. We didn't know whether we were really "heroes" or not. And if we are "heroes," it isn't because we have done so much. In the last analysis we are heroes because we are afraid of the Soviets and because we happen to live in Berlin.

"The world is watching us," "the world respects us," "the world cares about us," "the world is fighting for us"—these ideas appear again and again in descriptions of life during the blockade.

The Berliners' intense local pride fed on the high praise they were receiving. Traditionally, the inhabitants of Berlin, like those of nearly every metropolis, have tended to think of themselves as a little more intelligent, a little more enterprising and resourceful, than the people in less-favored parts of the nation. The experience of the blockade justified and reinforced this flattering image. Said a 30-year-old housewife: "The will to freedom and democracy of two million people was to be broken by hunger, cold, and darkness. That this experiment did not succeed can be explained only by the fact that it was tried in Berlin." "A Berliner can't be fooled so easily," wrote a tailor; "This breed is much too smart for that." "I am proud to be a Berliner," observed a small businessman, who had been forced into bankruptcy by the blockade. The very privations of the blockade made people feel that they were upholding the proud traditions of their city, and thus served also to renew their pride in the image of their collective selves.

Individually and as members of the West Berlin community, Berliners felt gratified in a way that had direct implications for resistance behavior. Plaudits from the outside world made dehydrated foods more palatable, and cold, dark homes more bearable. Furthermore, in order to retain the attention and approval of the outside world, Berliners had to continue to hold out, no matter what the pressures. They could no more give up than could a football-player, faced with a stadium full of admiring fans, suddenly drop the ball and leave the field.

Hopes for a Better Economic Future with the West

Some of the gratifications that resistance brought with it were in the present; others were in the form of hopes for the future. Knowing how currency reform had transformed West Germany, as if by magic, Berliners hoped ultimately to share in this West German prosperity. Only a week after the start of the blockade, the *Tagesspiegel* published a full page of pictures showing West German stores piled high with consumer goods—silk stockings, quality foods, wine, and other items that had been scarce for so long.[55] As two of the public opinion interviewers pointed out, the blockade had dashed the Berliners' hopes that the currency reform might bring them the kind of prosperity they were witnessing in West Germany, but by the same token people now had one more thing to fight for. As one interviewer said, "Hope of a life similar to the one which developed in West Germany shortly after the currency reform held the Berliner steadfast." Three of the *Abend* essayists expressed similar opinions. "I know no Berliner," wrote an unemployed girl of twenty-two, "who did not regard all these hardships as necessary in order one day to enjoy the kind of normal life which was already developing in West Germany." An older housewife reported that people interpreted the Western powers' impressive effort to supply the city as an indication that they would take an active part in economic reconstruction, once the blockade was over.

That these sentiments were shared by large numbers of Berliners is underscored by a memorandum, written in August of 1948, in which the three democratic parties and the independent trade unions asked Western military governments to designate the West mark as the only valid currency in West Berlin, and stated that the population wished to be associated with the West's policy of improved living standards.

Foreign newspapermen who were in Berlin at the time made similar observations: the Berliners wanted to live a normal life again, and saw a victory of the West as offering the only possibility of achieving it; if the East were to triumph, "normalcy" would be gone for good.

Delicacies from the West that arrived by way of the airlift during the blockade gave promise of a better life to come. The necessity of flying in foods with both a low avoirdupois and high caloric value, which for the most part caused the substitution of dehydrated for fresh foods, also added a few choice items to the diet. A refugee from the east zone, who moved to West Berlin during the blockade, wrote:

> When we received our first food ration, we sat at the table speechless with amazement. There was butter—genuine, good butter—which we had not seen for months, white rolls, and tinned meat. . . .

Clearly, these rations, beyond their dietary value, had a political meaning to at least some of the recipients. By holding out, rather than giving in to the more immediate but less elegant rewards offered by the East, they could hope ultimately to share fully in the riches of the West.

The Role of Solidarity

Berliners who turn their memories back to the time of the blockade frequently recall the sense of solidarity they experienced during the months when their city was cut off from the outside world. First, there was the solidarity of the individual with all his fellow Berliners—his local pride. Second was the growth in primary-group solidarity: many Berliners found that their ties with neighbors and family members became stronger during the blockade.

Each kind of solidarity served its own, important function. The civic *esprit* reduced corrosive factionalism and contributed toward the smooth functioning of the city's administration. The solidarity of the primary group tended to heighten the coercive force which such groups always exert on the behavior of their members; the small, tightly-knit groups provided a mechanism for controlling those who showed procommunist tendencies or in other ways departed from group standards. And the knowledge of his group membership, whether in West Berlin's citizenry as a whole or in the primary group, added to the individual's pride and inner security, giving him a feeling of warmth and belonging.

Nine essayists referred specifically to the sense of solidarity among all the citizens of West Berlin. "Everyone knew," wrote an engineer, "that withstanding the blockade would depend on the steadfastness of each individual." A 42-year-old white-collar worker observed that after the start of the blockade "the Berliners showed their true metal. They all joined together and felt themselves as one in the time of difficulties and threats." And here is a passage from the essay of a 31-year-old administrative assistant:

> . . . it has really not been a long time since the pressure of circumstances, the hardship of the times, forged us West Berliners into a single community. . . . There was only one resolution in the city and that simply and clearly was: We will stand together, the Soviets will not overcome us, their devilish plan will shatter on our determination. . . . Then, in the time of the airlift, there was a single will in Berlin—the will to freedom, the will to resist the totalitarian danger . . . a divided city, cut off from the surrounding world and supplied only by the brave fliers of the Western powers, stood together as one man.

Some of these essayists spoke of particular manifestations of this feeling of solidarity. "All party disputes seem to have been put aside," said one. Another reported that people were ready to help each other to an unprecedented extent. A policeman, having described how thousands of Berliners spent their spare time searching for fuel in Berlin's parks and tree-lined avenues, went on to recount the following touching incident, which took place in his precinct:

> We contacted our local park supervisor and he gave us permission to take a few dead trees to use in our stove in the station house. But after we had all worked to cut them down, our chief raised the question of whether we wanted to burn the wood or give it to old and feeble persons who couldn't get any for themselves. All of us decided for the latter course. After duty hours there was vigorous sawing and chopping, and in a few days the wood was in small pieces. Then, with a truck that we borrowed from the fire department, we drove to the homes of needy old people who were known to live in our police precinct. The joy of these people gave us strength to bear the cold nights on the streets and the hours that we spent at the cold station house.

One of the public opinion interviewers mentioned the thoughtfulness and politeness of people; especially in the crowded transportation vehicles, it was apparent that nearly everyone had more than the usual consideration for his "fellow-sardines."

Thus, many Berliners were keenly aware of their interdependence with one another, and their actions reflected an unprecedented degree of sympathy, understanding, and responsibility toward their fellow-citizens.

The essays and other reports about life during the blockade period are full of indications that primary group ties were strengthened also. For one thing, there were few opportunities for a person to spend time away from his family or neighborhood unit. Most transportation ended at six o'clock in the evening. The neighborhood bars were cold and dark, and, besides, they had little to sell. Motion-picture theatres were plagued by the electricity and fuel shortages.

In August 1948, U.S. Military Government's Opinion Surveys Branch asked a cross-section of West Berliners: "Have you personally—as a result of the blockade—less opportunity than before to divert yourself and participate in any amusements?"[56] More than a third of the respondents replied that they had "much less" or "somewhat less" opportunity. When the respondents were divided, however, into those with less than nine years of schooling and those with nine years or more, it was found that almost exactly one-half of the latter reported less opportunity for recreation. This led the survey analysts to conclude that, of the two groups, the better-educated were more likely to be affected by blockade conditions because they were more accustomed to go to the theatre or cinema before transportation and currency difficulties interrupted these habits. We can assume that in the months following this survey, as evenings began to grow longer and colder, even fewer people were able to find entertainment outside their family or neighborhood circle. This restriction, of course, was true not only of amusements. Several public opinion interviewers mentioned that people's circles of acquaintance became reduced to those friends who either lived or worked in the same area.

Not only did transportation and other shortages tend to keep people in the neighborhood, but the scarcity of electricity and fuel forced them to herd together. Almost a dozen essayists mentioned that, in their homes, the kitchen was the only room that could be heated, and hence became the center of all activities during the long winter evenings. If one household had fuel while a neighbor's did not, the neighbor quite naturally would be invited over to get warm. One man wrote somewhat testily: "There were parliaments of nine women in my kitchen, which was so small that it was crowded when only two people were in it." Similarly, those who received more electric current than their friends, or who had some other source of light, were likely to find themselves very popular. A lady who lived near the Tempelhof elevated station, and whose electric system was connected with the transit power lines, had light all the time, to the benefit of her entire neighborhood:

> So, every evening, my lamp served all our acquaintances and neighbors. This source of light helped to solve those countless problems which, especially for those with jobs, the blockade with its electricity stoppages made it almost impossible to overcome. For one came running from the office into a dark apartment. By candlelight one could get something to eat all right, but to darn stockings was almost impossible—although it was even more impossible to wear stockings with holes in them to the office. . . . So people wrote political articles, did their school work, knitted clothes for the baby—everyone who needed light came to see me.

More than ten of the *Abend* essayists who spoke of the enforced sociability of the blockade period indicated that these small family or neighborhood groups felt bound together by stronger ties than ever before. A 61-year-old professional man wrote:

> How was it then during the time of the Berlin blockade? In the evening we sat together in a group with several people who lived in the same building . . . and talked over what had happened during the day and in the previous few weeks. There were thick clouds of smoke from half-filled pipes or from homemade cigarettes made from tobacco we had grown ourselves, glasses of thin beer or some artificial mixture, and now and again the inevitable corn liquor from some dark source. In the middle of the circle was a very old candle or taper of tremendous size, with a thick, lumpy wick. . . . Jokes and songs always came into their own, and the airlift planes roaring through the night sang the bass in perfect time. . . . The unity among those who lived in the building often reminded one of the sociability in the air-raid shelters several years before, but

> without the terribly oppressive worry about the family members in battle far away and about one's own danger in the emergency bunkers. We would stay together cheerfully until almost 11:00 o'clock. The tiny light in the radio, which was already turned on, lighted up punctually [as the current came on] and all sharpened their ears to hear the evening news broadcast. The electric light shone wonderfully bright, even though we had only half the bulbs on for the sake of economy. The candle, of which we were so proud, was blown out with huge puffs, and the evening magic was over. We quickly parted, in order to make preparations for the next day, and immediately went to bed, since electricity had to be saved for the even more necessary cooking purposes.

Another essayist paints a less cheerful picture:

> Old people froze to death in their beds, but many were saved by the help of their neighbors. . . . After the day's work I was not in a position to prepare an evening meal because of the lack of gas and electricity. But this difficulty was overcome with the help of friendly neighbors. We sat together in one room, which we all helped to heat, by the light of a carbide lamp. . . . Insofar as he could, everyone helped everyone else.

Several writers mentioned the feeling of solidarity that developed at their places of work. Especially in smaller enterprises, employer and employees were drawn into a closer relationship. People who worked together were faced by common difficulties. The threat from without gave a common meeting ground to even the most diverse personalities, and the limitations on the individual's social contacts usually led him to cultivate more deeply those available to him.

As one result of the increasing solidarity of Berliners and the greater intimacy of personal relationships, the community was able to exert considerable pressure on individuals susceptible to Soviet demands or weak enough to accede to them. Fourteen essayists and several of the public opinion interviewers pointed out that people who accepted the Soviet food offer, who left Berlin without compelling reasons, or who spoke favorably of the Communists were subjected to some form of social pressure. A 31-year-old housewife wrote:

> Of course there were a few who followed the siren notes of the Communists, but for the most part these people were already known as SED supporters, and their behavior caused no surprise. Besides, the small number of people of this type, in comparison with the masses of those who behaved otherwise, made them of little importance. We simply avoided them, while all others made up a great community.

The situation of one essayist, a retired white-collar worker, was not so simple. His wife wanted to register for food in the Soviet sector, but he would not let her. "With that," he reported, "the peace and quiet in our household was gone." A 49-year-old professional woman spoke scathingly of those who deserted Berlin:

> There were also in West Berlin people who were dissatisfied with everything. They didn't want to submit to the blockade restrictions; they wanted to get out of Berlin. That was possible, but only with the help of the airlift. We didn't want to have any gripers among us and were glad when they left. But this was only a very small group.

The solidarity of those who remained was thus reinforced by the feeling that they could look down on the ones who had left.*

A public opinion interviewer, having described how persons opposed to Western democracy lost the respect of their fellow-citizens, commented:

> Of course there were a few people who were trouble-makers and grumblers for ideological reasons, and who should be distinguished from the larger numbers who will always find something to grumble about. But even these weren't important, and everybody else tried to keep these people under control so they wouldn't do any damage.

He reported also that those who registered for food in the east sector were considered "traitors," and that there was some discussion of measures that might be taken to exclude these people

* This was not entirely fair to the majority of the roughly fifty thousand Berliners who left the city during the blockade, since many of them did so for their own or their children's health, or for some other compelling reason. Yet the contempt for those who left the city became so well established that even a publication of the Magistrat referred to "opportunist actors who left Berlin to join other theaters." (Cf. *Luftbrücke Berlin*, a pictorial report published by the Magistrat of Greater Berlin, Arani Verlag, Berlin, 1949, pp. 81-82.)

from the community of West Berliners. Another interviewer observed that, with the exception of SED adherents, nobody wanted "to expose himself to the danger of being thought to sympathize with the East." Several of the essayists said that they took it upon themselves to buck up those among their acquaintances who showed signs of weakening. It is clear that any member of a "kitchen group" would immediately have been called to account, had it become known that he or she entertained ideas, or engaged in action, which the group as a whole regarded as subversive.

In some respects, this social pressure took the place of official regulation. Since, for instance, the Berlin city government took the position that it would not interfere with anyone who wished to register for food in the east sector, those who were tempted by Soviet blandishments could be controlled only through informal mechanisms. Indeed, at one point the informal mechanisms may have operated at cross-purposes with the formal ones. At the beginning of 1949 the city government announced that persons who had at one time registered for food in the east sector might now, if they wished, come back and re-register in the west, and a substantial number accepted this invitation. To judge by the many indignant letters to West Berlin newspapers and radio stations, however, these lost sheep were greeted on their return with something less than enthusiasm. As one lady wrote to RIAS,

> Why must two million people be cold, why must all the world have light except for us? We have no potatoes, and not enough possessions to get some by barter, and yet we support democracy and, in spite of promises of coal, potatoes, and all sorts of things, don't register in the east sector, since we stand up for our principles. But what happens to us? We are stabbed in the back, inasmuch as one now appeals to those who registered in the east sector to come back. All that's lacking now is that these people should be given the contributions which were made for Berlin, after they have already received coal, potatoes, and other comforts in the Russian sector, while we sit freezing in the dark by the cold stove, and puzzle over the injustice. . . .

In the month of February, RIAS received more letters along these lines than on any other political subject.

In trying to explain the stalwart behavior of Berliners, it may be relevant to note that the city's democratic political institutions, the civic *esprit*, and the small primary groups tended to supplement one another. The ideals enunciated by civic leaders, those shared by the public in general, and those of the small social groups were all essentially the same. Had the "official" ideology of the city fathers been different from the point of view that governed the discussions in the heated kitchens, it is unlikely that resistance could have been sustained as successfully as it was.

In spite of the impressive degree of social cohesion in the city, Berliners could not take their solidarity for granted. Many people were clearly worried whether others really shared their attitudes. They required constant reassurance that they were not being betrayed by their fellow-men. As a public opinion interviewer put it,

> We wanted to hold out, to survive, and we feared only that we wouldn't be able to do it and that the Soviets would come. Many people thought anxiously: let's hope the others think the way we do, and that the grumblers won't stab us in the back. But then the elections in December confirmed that nearly all Berliners were of the same opinion.

Another interviewer remarked that people liked to go to political mass meetings partly for the comfort of knowing that their convictions were widely shared. Reading the Berlin press and the minutes of the City Assembly for the blockade period, one gains the definite impression that all signs of solidarity were greeted with relief and enthusiasm. The small number of those who registered for food in the east sector, for example, and the overwhelming acceptance of Allied-sponsored currency were welcome evidence that the city was not being betrayed from within. About thirty of the *Abend* essayists pointed out with satisfaction that only an insignificant number of West Berliners succumbed to the Soviet food offer.

Their growing sense of solidarity helped people to overcome the anxieties that went with the knowledge that communist spies and *agents provocateurs* were constantly around them. A public opinion interviewer wrote:

> From this experience, we became welded together as a community in which each one was dependent on another, and each one had to help the other if he did not want to be condemned by this fighting society. . . . We achieved a sort of indifference to all the Eastern provocations. . . .

Another observer, while agreeing that the feeling of solidarity was an antidote to anxiety, noted no such indifference. Rather, he thought that people attempted to reassure themselves by being ever more outspoken. ("*They* know where I stand; I have nothing to hide; let them do their worst.") This effort also led them to more vigorous participation in anticommunist activities. Under the threat from without, they banded together more tightly than before with those who shared their opinions. And yet, the desire to affirm their position did not lead people to expose themselves unnecessarily. The Social Democratic Party, for instance, which included the largest proportion of the hard-core resisters, did not gain appreciably in membership. There was no rush to jump on the bandwagon, no effort to take the most advanced stand. People merely tried to live up to the norms of the group.[57]

Forces Sustaining Morale Over Time

One of the distinctive features of the Berlin blockade was that it continued for so long. People were forced to endure privations month after month and, during much of the time, with very little hope for a solution. Why, then, was it that discouragement and hopelessness did not affect resistance morale more adversely? While there is no single answer to this question, a number of possibilities suggest themselves.

First of all, people evidently had expected life in a blockaded city to be very difficult indeed, and they therefore tended to be pleasantly surprised when it turned out to be not quite so hard as they had feared. Their initial expectations are shown by a poll taken in October, when the Opinion Surveys Branch asked a cross-section of West Berliners: "Do you think Berliners will merely be kept alive during the winter, or do you think conditions will be slightly better than that?"[58] Thirty per cent of the respondents thought Berliners would merely be kept alive, and 59 per cent expected conditions to be slightly better. In the same survey, people were asked whether they thought that they would get just enough heating material to survive the winter, or whether they expected to be fairly comfortable. Only 12 per cent of the respondents expected to be fairly comfortable; of the rest, 55 per cent expected to have only enough heating materials to survive, and 33 per cent thought they would get none at all. These low expectations at the start of the winter undoubtedly helped to minimize the effect of material deprivations on the citizens' subsequent attitudes.

Another reason morale was sustained over so long a period was that people at first were not aware that they were facing the specter of an eleven-month blockade; they expected it to be a matter of weeks or, at the most, a few months. By the time it became apparent that the blockade would be a long one, Berliners had gained considerable confidence in their own ability to hold out. This is confirmed by the replies to two questions asked by the Opinion Surveys Branch first in July and again in October.[59] The first question in each survey was: "Do you think that the present situation in Berlin will remain unchanged all through the winter, or not?" In July, only 10 per cent of the respondents thought that the situation would remain unchanged (i.e., that the blockade would continue); by October, 71 per cent thought so. Next, the respondents were asked: "How long do you think the Berlin people will be able to bear the restrictions brought about by the blockade?" Responses to this question once again varied widely in the two surveys (see Table 9), indicating that, by October, the majority of West Berliners were expecting a long blockade and were convinced that they could hold out.

TABLE 9

EXPECTATIONS OF WEST BERLINERS ABOUT LENGTH OF TIME THEY COULD HOLD OUT (AS SHOWN BY CROSS-SECTIONS IN JULY AND OCTOBER)[60]

	July		*October*	
No longer	–%	64%	1%	23%
A short time (up to 2 weeks)	21		3	
3–4 weeks	12		–	
1–2 months	6		3	
Until the winter	25		16	
Through the winter (5 or more mo.)	–	25	42	73
A very long time	12		15	
Indefinitely	13		16	
Don't know	11		4	
	100%		100%	

If all the blockade restrictions had been imposed simultaneously, the strain on morale might have been great. But the hardships of the blockade did not come all at once. At first, people were able to supplement their rations by trips to the countryside, and during the summer they did not feel the lack of fuel so keenly. As the blockade was tightened, the capacity of the airlift increased, and it even became possible to fly out some exports from the city.

Two men, one of them a political leader in Berlin and the other a public opinion interviewer, have independently advanced the hypothesis that the morale of the population would have declined seriously during the winter, had it not been sustained by a series of "booster" events. Some of these were actions by Eastern authorities, some were actions by the West. Still others were outside the control of either side. Whenever the morale curve showed a tendency to drop, something would happen to raise it again. This theory is borne out by the following recollection of another public opinion interviewer:

> When, in connection with the great demonstration in September 1948, there were incidents at the Brandenburg Gate, and the people's police shot into the crowd, the hate and revulsion which the Berliners felt against the East was increased. They were not intimidated, but took a firmer position. Also, the verdicts against the young people, who were arrested in the east sector after the demonstration and sentenced to long prison terms, strengthened the West Berliners in their behavior.

A number of the *Abend* essayists also mention specific occurrences as having fortified them, or others, in the resolution to hold out. The mass meeting before the Reichstag in September, the increase in rations in November, the overwhelming victory of democratic forces in the December elections, and the special Christmas rations were among the events cited. The confiscations, kidnapings, and other measures of violence by the Soviet and East German authorities also spurred people to resistance. Over a dozen essayists mentioned their surprise and satisfaction when the Western powers started to fly in heavy machinery with which to build a modern power plant in West Berlin. This gave promise that the electricity shortage might be alleviated even under the blockade. The strongest "booster shots" for morale, however, were the increase in airlift capacity during the fall of 1948, and the coming of spring in March and April of 1949.

Finally, the Berliners' sustained capacity for holding out might be explained, at least in part, by the fact that morale itself became institutionalized. At first, the individual was affected directly by encouraging and discouraging events. But, as time went on, certain modes of behavior and certain attitudes came to be accepted as norms, and whoever deviated from these norms was subjected to pressure from his fellow-citizens. Many people might have been far more discouraged by the rigors of the winter than they actually were, had not their morale been sustained by the collectivity. Society was the stabilizing force that made it difficult for the individual to succumb to demoralizing effects of his personal experience.

The Omnipresence of the Airlift

As has been suggested already, the airlift played a prominent part in the formation and maintenance of resistance morale. It changed people's attitudes toward the Western powers, raised their esteem for Western strength, and reassured those who were anxious. It contributed toward a feeling of partnership, and served to establish a bond between Berlin and the West. It represented a blow struck in the cause of peace, freedom, and democracy. Above all, it made people feel that resistance could succeed.

This extraordinary impact of the airlift may be ascribed chiefly to its physical omnipresence, and to the fact that most Berliners participated in it, either directly or in an emotional sense.

It is interesting to note which aspects of the total operation impressed Berliners the most. The following table lists some of the things about the airlift that were mentioned most frequently by the *Abend* essayists, presumably because they had left the deepest impression.

TABLE 10

ASPECTS OF THE AIRLIFT RECALLED FREQUENTLY BY ESSAY-WRITERS

Aspect	*Number of Persons Mentioning*
Noise of aircraft engines	93
The technical miracle; amazing organization and development	81
Casualties; Air Force personnel and German civilians	66
Achievements and sacrifices of Air Force personnel (other than casualties)	23
Transportation of coal	17
Flying in parts for electric power plant	15
The beauty of the airlift	15
Dropping of candy	7

Many of the available recollections and other comments convey the clear impression that the airlift was not a thing people perceived casually. For many it had an overpowering quality, and aroused emotions of the kind men experience on seeing a great waterfall or a giant mountain. This emotional reaction was reflected by some in the use of superlatives; others showed it in the almost lyrical quality of their descriptions, of which the following passage, from the essay of a 31-year-old clerk, is but one example:

> Every two minutes a plane arrives from West Germany, loaded with food for West Berlin! The sound of engines can be heard constantly in the air, and is the most beautiful music to our ears. One could stand for hours on the Tempelhof elevated station platform and watch the silver birds landing and taking off. And at night the brightly illuminated airfield with its countless little colored lights is like something out of a phantasy. It is a wonderful sight, which I shall never forget!

Being omnipresent and impressive, the airlift assumed, in the eyes of many people, a symbolic significance which far transcended its announced purpose of transporting supplies.

The physical presence of the airlift was such that nobody could ignore it. Day and night, almost without a break, from July 1948 to August 1949, planes circled the city, landed, and took off again at intervals of only a few minutes. The location of the three airfields in widely separated parts of West Berlin meant that landing and takeoff patterns covered nearly the entire city. For most West Berliners the airlift was an ever-present phenomenon.

In recalling blockade days, Berliners frequently said that the airlift became a part of their daily lives, that it was accepted as a normal phenomenon, or that it was regarded as something belonging to the population, rather than as an external event. Indeed, it was often mentioned possessively as "our" airlift. One reason for this identification with the airlift was that Berliners participated in it heavily both in a physical and an emotional sense.

Direct physical participation was limited to those employed at one of the airfields in construction, administration, maintenance, or transportation work. Their number varied greatly at different periods. At the highest point of employment, approximately thirty thousand Berliners worked at the airfields; at the lowest point, the number may have been ten thousand. Several thousand more were engaged by trucking firms to transport supplies from the fields to warehouses.

The men and women who worked at the airfields were, for the most part, people who had come from other professions and trades; only a small core were trained mechanics or regular airfield personnel. Several former airlift workers among the *Abend* essayists mention the strange blend of professional, white-collar, skilled, and unskilled workers of which the total labor force was made up. In spite of these diverse origins, morale among airfield personnel apparently was excellent. Those essayists who discussed the morale of airlift workers agreed that most personnel "preserved their humor" even if they were employed in less skilled labor than that for which they had been trained. Supervisors at Tempelhof reported that many employees voluntarily worked overtime without pay, and that nearly all of them had a sense of the importance of their task. The personnel who unloaded and cleaned the arriving aircraft were particularly anxious to help establish new records. One essayist, who had been so employed, recalled that he and his colleagues were particularly gratified at the recognition they received in the press whenever a record was broken. Competition among various shifts and unloading crews was frequently intense, and from time to time, small prizes were offered to the most efficient crews. A German supervisor at Tempelhof stated:

> We worked in three shifts, but quite often men would not be able to finish their work before the end of the shift and would voluntarily stay on extra time in order to complete a job. Morale was excellent. In spite of the fact that public transportation was operating only very spasmodically, and many of the men had to walk for more than an hour to work, they were seldom late. . . . In general, holidays were simply disregarded. If there was work to do, the men came.

The high morale among airlift workers in Berlin contrasted favorably with that at airfields in West Germany, where, from all accounts, problems of absenteeism and turnover were considerably greater.

To a limited extent, the airlift workers shared their experiences and attitudes with other Berliners, as in the following, typical letter to the *Tagesspiegel*:

> Admiration fills the heart of the Berliner when he sees the way the Allied aircraft zoom above him day after day. For us the pilots are performing a difficult service. An acquaintance who works at Gatow airfield told us that, one night about four o'clock, the crew of a Sunderland flying boat came into the mess hall, freezing and dead-tired. Since too few personnel were there, the fliers cheerfully helped with the serving and washing up. Then they went to sleep in their chairs at the table. The cook, the waitress, and the girl who washes dishes dragged them to armchairs and couches without their waking up. A few hours later, they took off again. . . .[61]

In general, however, one is struck by how rarely these airfield workers are quoted by other Berliners as a source of information about the airlift. One reason for this may have been that they had little opportunity to communicate their knowledge and their attitudes to the rest of the citizens. As a German supervisor at Tempelhof pointed out, contact between airlift workers and other Germans was really quite limited. The men and women employed at the airfields worked at a furious pace, usually to the point of exhaustion, and many of them then faced a long walk home. Consquently, most workers went directly to bed as soon as the working day was over. The supervisor added that he personally had had neither time nor energy for any social life at all.

In addition to those who participated in the airlift, either directly at the airfields or indirectly in connection with transportation and distribution of supplies, there were many who sought employment unsuccessfully, and a smaller but significant number who, although not employed by the airlift, took a serious interest in its technical aspects. Supervisory personnel at Tempelhof said that, throughout the blockade, they were deluged with letters from former Lufthansa and German airforce personnel who offered their services. RIAS received similar letters, including one, in December of 1948, from a former combat flier and flight-leader in a night-pursuit squadron, who said that he would like to work on the airlift even though he had a good job and did not need the employment. No German could become a member of an air crew, but a considerable number of former pilots worked in various capacities on the ground.

Not infrequently, German technicians offered ideas for improving the operation of the airlift. *Task Force Times* reported on March 19, 1949, that a German radio operator had designed an alarm device for use in beacon failure. Another technically-inclined Berliner wrote to RIAS to suggest methods for facilitating landings during fog. A number of technical suggestions were addressed directly to the commanders of the three airfields. Whether or not these suggestions were actually adopted, those who made them clearly showed their sense of participation in the airlift. It was to them a joint venture, rather than the sole responsibility of the Western powers.

Even more far-reaching than this technical interest of a relatively small group was the strong emotional participation of a large segment of the population. It was expressed in a variety of ways. Approximately one-third of the *Abend* essayists indicated sympathy with the fliers, and concern about their safety. Several spoke of waving to the pilots passing overhead; a few thought that pilots had waved to them. Some said that they had to hold out because they "couldn't be untrue to the pilots." Others spoke of their feeling of friendship for the distant airmen. A policeman wrote that he could sympathize with the flying personnel all the more keenly because he, too, had to be out for long periods in all kinds of weather. One lady had included the pilots in her prayers during the airlift. Yet not one of the essayists mentioned ever having met a member of the Allied air forces in person.

People also showed their participation through small gifts to airlift personnel. In the borough of Neukölln, a collection was taken up to buy handmade wood and metal plaques, which were inscribed: "To the U.S. pilots for their tireless efforts, from the grateful citizens of Berlin."[62] Public-information officials at Tempelhof airfield recalled that several hundred cigaret lighters, many of them handmade, had been donated by Berliners as souvenirs for flying personnel. Gifts of dogs finally had to be discouraged because of the difficulty of taking care of them. Books were another favorite gift item. One Berliner wrote to RIAS asking whether some pilot would like a copy of *Kaiser Wilhelm II und die Marine.* The mother of a German pilot who had died in a wartime air accident wrote in her essay that she had wanted to give one of her son's books to an airlift pilot; she had written to Military Government about this, but had received no answer.

The list of gifts and eager givers could be extended almost indefinitely. A U.S. Air Force officer, whose work in Berlin included providing information to German civilians who came to make inquiries at Tempelhof airfield, reported:

> Seems to me I've met every German in Berlin. They come down here, clutching extremely valuable heirlooms against their breasts, and want to make a little ceremony of giving the stuff to the pilots. Or some child will show up with flowers or a valued picture book. It's no act, either. An old man so thin you could see through him showed up a few days ago with a watch that would have fed him for months on the black market. He insisted on giving it to an American. He called it "a little token from an old and grateful heart."[63]

Emotional participation was exhibited also in the prolonged discussion of a memorial for personnel who had lost their lives in the airlift, which culminated in the decision to raise a monument, paid for by popular subscription, in the square outside Tempelhof airport.

In some respects, the airlift took on the characteristics of a competitive sport. Several essayists recalled following the airlift-tonnage figure in the newspapers in great detail. A 17-year-old student wrote that the airlift was always the first subject for discussion and the most important news in the paper. Many people went down to the airfields to watch the airlift in operation much as they would watch a football game. Twenty-five of the essayists mentioned having made such visits, and officials at Tempelhof remembered that the elevated railway station, which commanded a good view of the landing field, was always black with people. Children, and even some adults, made a hobby of collecting aircraft numbers. One public opinion interviewer recalled the more serious aspects of the game:

> Often one could see in the subway or the elevated that people were happy and relieved when the airlift had broken another record. Similarly, they were disappointed and downcast when, because of bad weather or for some other reason, the tonnage figures sank for a few days. I think that was the case not so much out of fear that supplies might not be adequate, but much more because of the feeling that "the others over there," the Russians, would be rubbing their hands and finding support for their eternally repeated theme that the airlift would never be able to bring in enough.

The airlift played a central part in the life of the children. Candy fluttering down out of the sky on midget parachutes delighted the youngest,* and the aircraft themselves became a natural focus for the imagination and the games of the older ones:

> When they travel in the elevated past Tempelhof airfield all Berlin children wish that the train would go slower. They would like to see a little more of the airlift, which for weeks has been the center of their conversations, their games, and perhaps their dreams.[64]

Some of the essayists who mentioned the airlift's impact on the young had themselves been school children at the time; others had been parents of young children. A 16-year-old apprentice wrote:

> In spite of all these vitally important flights, the Americans remembered, as they had many times before, to make the children happy. On a beautiful, clear, sunny weekday, a large crowd of children swarmed around the entrance to the airfield. They had been allowed to leave school earlier than usual because the airfield had been thrown open to visitors. In droves the children threw themselves upon the planes, each according to his own interest, or got friendly "Amis" to explain other things to them. In the afternoon came the surprise. A transport machine landed and a living camel got out. The same machine brought a large quantity of candy, which was thrown to the jubilant bunch of children. Until late in the evening, the small fry, with chocolate smeared over their faces, talked about the wonderful day.
>
> And one day there was another novelty for us children, which all the newspapers featured with pictures and headlines. The British introduced a type of aircraft into the airlift which was entirely new to us. It was the Sunderland "flying boat," which landed in the water by Schwanenwerder. But only a few landed each day. We often begged our parents to arrange our Sunday afternoon walk in such a way that, after going through the woods, we arrived at the water. There it usually was some time before a plane, heralded by the cries and gestures of the children, landed on the water. With interest we followed the unloading and loading. We longed to be allowed to fly in one of these water birds. . . .

* The practice of dropping candy bars on hand-made parachutes was started by U.S. Air Force Lt. Gail S. Halvorsen as a personal project. It later was taken up by other pilots and reached substantial proportions.

Many school children, as part of their class work, were asked to draw pictures of the airlift. Of the nine such drawings reproduced in the Magistrat's pictorial report, *Luftbrücke Berlin,* all but two show Berliners participating in the airlift in some way, as transport workers, joyful observers, or enthusiastic recipients. A 12-year-old drew a family (complete with cat and dog) standing on the roof of their house and looking up at parachutes fluttering down from the sky with appropriate items for each: a bone for the dog, a mouse for the cat, a toy train for the little boy, and what appears to be a food package for the mother. Even one of the two drawings that pictured no direct participation in the airlift nevertheless showed the child's emotional participation. It was captioned: "This is the way the airlift looks to me every day from our balcony." The young artists did not view the airlift as an external phenomenon, but as something directly related to their own lives.

Emotional participation of still another kind was suggested by the public opinion interviewer who described the vicarious satisfaction that derived from the airlift as a means of striking back at the Soviets:

> Except for the few SED adherents, everybody had a "stomach full of anger" . . . everybody developed a desire for revenge, which was then later satisfied in part by the colossal development of the airlift, since every plane which flew in was a sign that the Soviet designs had failed.

One of the essayists alluded to much the same psychological reaction when he said that each oncoming aircraft represented a slap in the face for the Soviets.

The airlift, in the words of one essay-writer, had become *"volkstümlich."* Freely translated, this means that it had become a part of the life of the community. Because it was omnipresent and gave Berliners opportunities for participation, the airlift inevitably reinforced many of the existing trends toward resistance. The planes were a communication device in the sense that they symbolized, or called to mind, other aspects of the blockade situation. Each person could read into them the particular meaning to which he was most receptive. They were like blank posters in the sky, on which each anticommunist West Berliner could write his own slogan for resistance. People who were spurred on by the feeling that the eyes of the world were upon them would construe the sight or sound of the aircraft as proof that they were in the center of attention. Those conscious of being engaged in a partnership with the Western powers were reminded of this partnership by the aerial activity. The planes reinforced even those basic motivations toward resistance—fear and hate of the Soviets—for each aircraft was a reminder that Berlin was being blockaded and threatened with engulfment.

The way in which the meaning of the airlift varied with the individual's attitude toward it is well illustrated by the case of a 61-year-old typist, who recalled that at first the noise of the airlift had been irritating to her, and that one day she said as much to a friend whom she was visiting. The friend was incredulous:

> "But that is *our* airlift! The noise of engines is like music to my ears. Don't forget that the airlift brings us food; it keeps us from perishing."
>
> I was somewhat ashamed, naturally agreed with my hostess, and from that time on I saw and heard the planes of our airlift with different eyes and different ears.

Many of the associations aroused by the planes probably were in the subconscious. A public opinion interviewer thought that the airlift had somehow become symbolic of the social solidarity of the blockade time, to the point where Berliners were almost loathe to see it end:

> As the airlift was gradually brought to an end, people had a rather uncomfortable feeling, but did not quite know why. My interpretation of this is that the noise had somehow become associated with a sense of comradeship among all groups in the population, and that, as the noise became less prominent, people again felt separated from each other.

But most of all, the omnipresence of the airlift provided constant reassurance. At a time when nobody could be entirely sure that Soviet troops would not march into West Berlin at any moment, or that the Western powers would not finally decide that it was inexpedient and too expensive to support Berlin by air, nothing was more reassuring than the actual sight of airlift planes; it meant that West Berlin was still free and that the Western powers were still on the job.

Of the many *Abend* essayists who conveyed this idea, twenty-six stated quite specifically that they felt reassured when they heard or saw aircraft. An elderly lady wrote: "At night we heard the good fliers and we knew that we would not starve." A bank employee recalled:

> For me personally it gradually became a habit before I went to bed, first to look out the window in order to see in the sky the unswerving position lights of the aircraft roaring over us. Then, reassured, I went to bed. . . .

Or, in the words of an unskilled worker,

> Early in the morning, when we woke up, the first thing we did was to listen to see whether the noise of aircraft engines could be heard. That gave us the certainty that we were not alone, that the whole civilized world took part in the fight for Berlin's freedom.

To a women whose job during the blockade had been to clear away rubble, the engines seemed to repeat a line from the song "Watch on the Rhine"—*Lieb Vaterland magst ruhig sein* (Dear Fatherland, you may be calm). A public opinion interviewer reported: "Every morning when we woke up, our first thought was: Are we still free, or have the Russians already occupied West Berlin? The aircraft engines usually answered this question immediately.

Conversely, when the noise of engines could not be heard, doubt began to gnaw at the hearts of thousands of Berliners. An essayist who did not identify his profession, but whose proficiency in graphic description suggests that he may have been a professional writer, told what happened when, at night, the sound of aircraft stopped:

> Suddenly, outside the windows and above the roofs, there is a paralyzing silence. It lurks there like a mysterious black animal, which one can sense but not see. It is uncannily threatening, this silence. It weighs on one like the silence of a corpse. All at once a whole city is listening to this stillness, and in the breasts of hundreds of thousands terrible uncertainty begins to arise. The airlift has stopped. What has happened? Are they going to abandon us? Will we have to submit? It seems as if all life is suspended for several minutes. Then—after an eternity—the roar can be heard again, and there are a hundred thousand sighs of relief.

Berliners who lived near one or another of the airfields recalled that, whenever there was a longer pause than usual at night, they would wake up, uneasily wondering what had happened. General

Clay, whose Berlin residence was directly under the approach to Tempelhof airfield, had the same experience.[65]

It is remarkable how often those who wrote about the blockade referred to the planes as "talking" to people on the ground. Their engines "spoke" to West Berliners with words of reassurance or defiance: to some they promised aid in the present, to others prosperity in the future. The airlift was a most effective means of communication; whatever the planes said was bound to be impressive and relevant, for the message originated in the minds of the audience.

The Favorable Balance: A Summary

"We didn't think of the possibility that our behavior, which we saw simply as a matter of course, would later be interpreted as heroism," wrote a 31-year-old white-collar worker. And a public opinion interviewer observed: "People didn't ask whether they themselves or others had good morale or not; they just went ahead and did what was necessary." Indeed, some Berliners expressed mild irritation when asked about the state of popular morale during the blockade; they argued that it was senseless to ask why people held out when no other course of action was open to them.

What these people seemed to be saying was that the combination and interplay of pressures bearing on Berliners was such that resistance was almost inevitable. When we say that most Berliners had good morale, we are implying that, in the balance of internal and external forces which determined their behavior, the forces predisposing toward resistance were stronger than the forces working in the other direction. Had the two sets of pressures been of approximately equal force, resistance might have been the subject of more conscious deliberation, and more people might have adopted an escapist or neutralist position. But, since the individuals regarded their behavior as natural, or a matter of course, the imbalance between the two opposing forces must have been very great.

In a fair presentation of this balance of forces, however, it is necessary to make two reservations. First, when we say that morale in blockaded Berlin was excellent, we do not mean that all, or even nearly all, individuals were willing to resist at all costs, or that they were completely devoted to the ideals of freedom. Although Berlin was one of the politically most sophisticated cities in the world, there were still many individuals who took an essentially passive attitude, and who accepted the norms of the larger group only under pressure. A large proportion of the population remained more interested in economic security than in political freedom, and at least one-third would have liked to leave Berlin.[66] Any statements about morale, therefore, apply to the group, not necessarily to all individuals in the group.

Second, good morale did not spring forth suddenly; it grew organically. Our discussion of this subject thus far has dealt largely with the pattern of resistance at the height of its development. To give an accurate picture of its gradual growth would be far more difficult. Not only did it vary with the individual, but we are often at a loss for satisfactory milestones by which to gauge the passage of time in social and psychological developments. One can therefore attempt to give no more than a very rough picture of the temporal stages in which resistance tendencies among Berliners emerged and become solidified.

As of the outset of the blockade, the population could be divided into four main groups. The first was the hard core of politically educated resisters, and it included many of the active members of the political parties and free trade unions, and a few intellectuals. For them, the Rubicon had been crossed before the blockade, and they would have held out even if they had seen little chance for success. This group probably did not number more than 5 per cent of the population. A second, far larger group was composed of politically conscious individuals who wanted desperately to avoid Soviet domination, but who could not conceive of this possibility without the active support of the Western powers. They attended mass meetings in the spring of 1948 and were devoted to the democratic leaders, but most of them at that time refrained from taking any steps that would have exposed them to Communist reprisals if the Soviets had succeeded in swallowing the whole city. Only when it became clear that the Western powers would defend their position, and when the airlift began to give promise of success, did this group—possibly one-third of the population—join the first group in active resistance.

A third group was composed of those without strong political convictions, who were willing to accept whatever political regime was imposed upon them. Most of them had political preferences and would rather have lived under a Western, or at least a quadripartite, regime than under Soviet domination. But either they did not see how their own individual actions could affect the political future, or else they allowed the problem of daily living to overshadow their political preferences. This passive group tends to be the largest in almost any society. In Berlin, it probably accounted for more than half the population at the start of the blockade, but became smaller as time went on.

Finally, there were the Communists and their sympathizers. We would probably not be far off in estimating that their number decreased from 10 per cent of the population early in the blockade to barely 5 per cent toward the end.

This, then, was the approximate composition of the society that was exposed to the intense psychological pressure and physical hardship of the blockade. The development of resistance morale was marked by the tendency of the second group to move closer to the hard-core resisters, and by the depletion of the ranks of the uninvolved, many of whom moved up into group two. This process began immediately after the imposition of the blockade, and was almost complete by October. Finally, a substantial number of Communist smypathizers, and possibly even a few actual Communists, appear to have moved into the ranks of the uninvolved, if not into the group of those who made efforts to resist.

More important than the numbers in each group, however, is the fact that those Berliners who were determined to hold out were able to establish the pattern of behavior that was followed by the overwhelming majority of the population. For most people resistance soon ceased to be a subject for conscious deliberation, and became simply a part of their way of life, as forces making them want to hold out more and more outweighed tendencies toward apathy or neutralism. Resistance morale finally became so firmly anchored that far heavier blows would have been required to shake it.

CHAPTER IX

PUBLIC OPINION AND POLITICAL DECISION

FOUR major factors played a role in Berlin's ability to hold out during the blockade. The first and most obvious of these was the decision of the Western powers to defend their position in the city. This decision was given outward expression primarily by the airlift, which supplied material necessities of life to the population and also provided Berliners with constant reassurance.

The second major factor was the corps of strong, democratic leaders in the city. Repeated communist efforts to intimidate the Acting Mayor, the Speaker of the City Assembly, and individual city councilmen and assemblymen failed. They refused to surrender their prerogatives to Soviet puppets and likewise refused to enact legislation that would have given the Soviets sweeping controls over the economy of the city. At the same time, they did their utmost to rally public opinion both in Berlin and throughout the world to oppose Soviet aggression. This corps of tough-minded officials, highly resistant to communist intimidation, had developed during the stormy period of Berlin's history from 1945 to 1948.

A third, and related, factor was that efficient institutions of administration and leadership were at the disposal of the democratic German leaders. The existence of an adequate city bureaucracy, democratic political parties, free labor unions, and noncommunist media of communication helps to explain why Berlin's social and governmental processes never broke down during the blockade, although they were at times badly strained. Without these efficient mechanisms for leadership and administration the influence of Berlin's democratic officials would have been far weaker. In the absence of an efficient rationing system, for example, West Berliners would have been more tempted to register for food in the Soviet sector, while without democratic political party machinery and a free press it would have been far more difficult to overcome the influence of communist agitators.

A final major factor was the resistance morale, which played so large a part in determining the behavior pattern of the city's population at large. As a result of this widespread will to resist, most people spontaneously did everything they could to defeat the blockade, and they tried to keep in check those who for reasons of selfishness, political indifference or pro-communism were inclined to do things that were likely to help the Soviets.

Examination of these four requirements for Berlin's defense strongly suggests that the absence or insufficiency of any one of them would have made it necessary for the Western powers to face the difficult choice the Soviets were trying to force on them: namely, to surrender West Berlin or give up their plans in West Germany. The crucial nature of the first three is immediately apparent. If the airlift had failed, the Berliners would have had to choose between perishing and surrendering to the Soviets. If the Magistrat and Assembly had given in to communist demands, the Western powers would have found themselves almost totally deprived of influence on the city's administration. If the Soviets had controlled the police force and the labor unions in West Berlin it is difficult to see how public order could have been maintained or the airfields operated. The importance of the fourth requirement—good resistance morale—is not so immediately apparent, but good popular morale was no less vital to the defense of Berlin.

The Significance of Popular Resistance

It is fairly certain that the Western powers would not have started the airlift if they had not believed that their policy would receive the wholehearted backing of the Berliners. Administration of the city and the conduct of the airlift in the face of an apathetic or hostile population would have been difficult indeed. Even sporadic labor stoppages could have dislocated the air supply operation. Furthermore, the Western powers were engaged in delicate negotiations regarding the establishment of a West German government. To have attempted an unpopular policy in Berlin at that moment would have had extremely unfavorable repercussions in West Germany. Finally, riots or anti-Western demonstrations in West Berlin would have greatly strengthened the hand of those Western critics who believed that Berlin was a liability to be liquidated at the first opportunity, and might even have led to Soviet intervention.

There is no lack of testimonials by Western leaders to the dependence that they felt on the Berlin population. General Clay, before deciding to launch the airlift, called in Mayor Reuter to ask whether the Western powers could count on the support of the Berliners. Shortly after the start of the blockade, Clay was quoted in the Berlin press as saying that the determination of the Berliners to preserve their freedoms was a necessary condition for the Western powers remaining.[1] On September 22 Ernest Bevin in the House of Commons paid high tribute to the Berliners, saying that their reaction had dismayed and upset the calculations of those who thought the Western powers would be out of Berlin in a few weeks.[2] General Clay later stated that the airlift could not have succeeded had it not been for the people of Berlin under the able leadership of their Magistrat.[3] An official who had occupied a high position in U.S. Military Government went so far as to say, several years after the event, that the behavior of the German population had been one of the main factors in keeping up the determination of the occupation authorities to defend their position. Ambassador Smith noted in his memoirs that during the Moscow negotiations he had been encouraged by the mass meetings and other signs of good resistance morale in West Berlin.[4]

Furthermore, a feeling grew among Allied statesmen, and in the West generally, that it would be unpardonable to betray the courageous Berliners to the Soviets. At the outset of the blockade, General Clay teletyped Washington: "Every German leader, except SED leaders, and thousands of Germans have courageously expressed their opposition to communism. We must not destroy their confidence by any indication of departure from Berlin."[5] As the facts about the Berliners' resistance became known, and their behavior was acclaimed by the free world in more and more lyrical terms, the feeling that it would constitute a serious moral and political liability to abandon the fighting population gained ground in both Washington and London.

Indirectly, the resistance of Berliners contributed to the Allied determination to stay in Berlin in still another and very important way: it created a very strong impression among the politically most influential groups in West Germany, even if a less strong impression among the West German population at large. The repercussions in West Germany of the events in Berlin were such that the Western powers could not have abandoned the city without alienating just those political leaders on whom their plans for a West German government depended.

Good popular morale contributed also to the resolution of Berlin's officials. The overwhelming majority of the people were vocally anticommunist, and expected their leaders in turn to give expression to anticommunist feelings. If, as in the case of Dr. Ostrowski, a leader did not live up to these expectations, he ceased to be a leader. Some years after the blockade, several of the Berlin officials, when asked to explain the source of their courage at the time, denied strenuously that they had shown an unusual degree of courage. "We just did what was expected of us" or "we only did our duty" were stock answers. This modesty should not be allowed to obscure the fact that the path of duty was not easy. But the pressure from below, in the form of popular demands and expectations, made the courageous course appear to be the only one possible. Furthermore, the popular devotion accorded those officials who defied the Communist was a moving reward for a job well done. One has only to think of the encomium paid by the Berliners to Louise Schroeder on several occasions.

Finally, popular resistance made it possible for the city's political machinery to operate effectively. Prior to the blockade, small groups of democratic leaders had slowly and painfully wrested control of Berlin's governmental and trade-union structure from the Communists, and had built up viable political parties. But control of these vital political institutions alone would have counted for little if parallel institutions—neutralist or communist—had been able to command the allegiance of major segments of the population. The ability of West Berlin's police, rationing authorities, labor offices, and other public bodies to function effectively rested not only on support by the occupying powers but on the fact that they were approved by all but a small minority of the population. Much the same was true of the independent labor unions, the democratic parties, and private economic institutions. In short, without mass support from the Berliners, the Western powers probably could not have retained their authority in the city even if they had attempted to do so. Berlin's democratic institutions would have proved inadequate, and the authority and resolution of Berlin's democratic leaders would have been gravely weakened. Under these circumstances, the Soviet strategy might well have succeeded.

The Role of Public Opinion Outside Berlin

Public opinion in West Germany, in East Germany, and in the Western democracies also affected the course of developments during the blockade, although political attitudes in these areas were ordinarily of lower intensity than those in Berlin, and had a more indirect bearing on the outcome of the crisis.

In the three west zones nearly every political leader (except communist leaders) was strongly convinced of the necessity of defeating the Soviet assault on Berlin and was also convinced that st Germany should do everything in its power to assist the Berliners. The West German man in the street, on the other hand, while he showed enthusiasm and support for Berlin when the blockade was first imposed, soon began to resent the demands that were made on him in connection with it. His attention was focussed intensely on his personal economic recovery, and anything that distracted him from this goal was regarded as a nuisance if not a threat. Nevertheless, his feeling of national solidarity with the Berliners and his distrust of communism were sufficient to keep him from making effective protests when his political leaders took action to assist the blockaded capital.

West German leaders and the public in the three west zones interacted in a complex fashion with Berlin's leaders and public. The West German politicians responded to Berlin's appeals for help by extending credit and trying to whip up popular enthusiasm. This greatly encouraged the Berlin population and was an important factor in building resistance morale. Berlin's political leaders, their authority greatly enhanced by the stalwart behavior of their own population, then used this authority to urge the West Germans to hasten with the formation of the Federal Republic. Meanwhile, the West German population, its uncertainty as to whether its economic and political future lay with the East or the West removed in large part by the vigorous defense of Berlin by the Western powers, was bending every effort toward the creation of economic wealth. This rapidly-growing wealth gave promise that the West German state would possess a significant degree of power and also served as another powerful incentive to the Berliners to hold out, since they now hoped to share ultimately in the prosperity of the West.

In East Germany and East Berlin there were few political mechanisms through which public opinion could express itself. Nevertheless, it was not totally without influence. By smuggling small gifts of coal and potatoes to friends in West Berlin, by writing letters to relatives in the West zone, by communicating with West Berlin's newspapers and radio stations, and by other actions of a similar nature, Germans from Soviet controlled territories contributed to West Berlin's resolve to hold out and to West German sentiment favoring aid to Berlin.

In the Western democracies popular opinion about the Berlin crisis seems to have been dominated by three attitudes: admiration for the Berliners, pride and delight in the accomplishments of the airlift, and the desire to have an uncomfortably tense situation resolved. All three attitudes were politically significant. Admiration for the Berliners helped strengthen resistance morale within the blockaded city. Both this admiration and popular pride in the airlift tended to bolster the position of Allied political leaders who were in favor of defending the Western position in Berlin. The widespread desire to escape from the tense political situation led to great pressure on Western politicians to come to some kind of an agreement with the Soviets. This pressure for agreement, even at the cost of Western concessions, was felt by statesmen of all three Western powers, but probably most by the French and least by the Americans, with the British in a middle position.

Domestic opinion made itself felt with particular forcefulness during negotiations. Since Western leaders believed it necessary to reassure their own nationals that all possible peaceful avenues for a solution would be explored, they simultaneously reassured the Soviets that the Allies were not about to respond to communist aggression with military action. Popular pressure for an agreement thus limited the freedom of Western negotiators and made it more difficult for them to defend and advance the interests of their nations.

On the other hand, once informed and aroused, public opinion in the democracies proved a powerful prop to those who insisted on the maintenance of a free Berlin. The degree to which resources of ingenuity and devotion could be tapped by Western leaders depended in part on the commitment which millions of people felt to the cause in question. Furthermore, the pressure of domestic opinion exercised a powerful veto to any tendencies democratic leaders may have had to sacrifice decency for cleverness. Western humanitarianism and decency were guaranteed by the fact that democratic policy makers were answerable for their actions. In the last analysis, this guarantee exercised an important influence in reassuring the Berliners and many West German leaders, and thus protected one of the great strengths in Western policy.

Soviet and Western Efforts to Manipulate Public Opinion

Both sides attempted to manipulate public opinion during the blockade. The Soviets and German communists ordinarily did so in two ways. They appealed to public opinion to justify or to provide an occasion for politically-expedient actions, and they tried to bring popular pressure on German and Allied leaders as one means of influencing their decisions.

Communist use of supposed manifestations of public opinion to legitimize politically expedient actions or policies could be noted at many points during the blockade. Large crowds in East Berlin demonstrated against the Magistrat for several days before the communist authorities, "responding to the popular will," set up a separate east sector government. Certain West Berlin newspapers were excluded from East Berlin because "the workers had objected to them." Factory hands were said to have protested against the decision of the city assembly to hold new municipal elections. The Communists seemed to feel that if they could gain some expression of support for a policy from a few thousand people, even if many of these were children brought willy-nilly to mass demonstrations by the school authorities, this was sufficient to make the policy a legitimate one.

Attempts to use popular pressure to influence democratic leaders were also carried out in a crude manner. The blockade itself was apparently designed as a method of extorting concessions from the Western powers by turning the Berlin population against them. Mob demonstrations at the City Hall were obviously intended as one means of persuading the city government to give in to communist demands. Communist-inspired resolutions opposing the Special Berlin Tax in West Germany were aimed directly at the legislatures that considered this tax. Mass demonstrations in Soviet-controlled areas against Western actions, for instance against establishment of a West German government, appear to have been designed both to bring whatever pressure possible on Western leaders and also to legitimize the Soviet position.

Although the obvious manner in which all these alleged manifestations of public attitudes were engineered detracted from their effectiveness, the Communists did show clearly that they understood the relationship between popular opinion and political decision making. In almost every case the demonstration that was supposed to reveal the people's will could be related to some specific action on which the Soviets themselves had already decided or to some decision that they wished the Western powers to take.

Ernst Reuter and some of the other democratic leaders in Berlin were also conscious of the usefulness of public opinion in bringing strategically-located political figures to make certain decisions. In this case there was no need for forced or engineered demonstrations, but Berlin's leaders did everything they could to promote the formation of resistance morale and then to see that this was given emphatic expression. Also, although Reuter knew what he wanted, his aims were more general. Most of all, he wanted the Western powers to defend their position in Berlin by all means possible. The Herculean work of rousing public opinion both in and outside Berlin that he and his associates performed was primarily aimed at influencing Western leaders in this direction.

References to public opinion before and during the blockade came most frequently from leaders of the Western powers. Shortly before the Soviets finally cut the communications between Berlin and West Germany, several Allied officials expressed the belief that a blockade was unlikely because it would influence public opinion, and especially German public opinion, in a manner unfavorable to Moscow. After the blockade began one could hear statements in Allied quarters to the effect that the Soviets would soon have to back down because they would lose what little good will they still possessed in Germany. The Berlin problem was finally laid before the United Nations by the Western powers not so much in hopes that the world body would be able to find a solution as in order to place it squarely before world opinion.

These appeals to public opinion appear to have been unrealistic, because they left unanswered the question as to just how public opinion was to affect the Soviet leaders. Who was to do what, and through what means? Certainly there were no mechanisms in Germany or the Soviet Union through which public attitudes could be brought to bear on Soviet leaders with sufficient force to make them alter their decisions. The electoral system in European democracies offered a way that Europeans could show their indignation by punishing local Communist Parties at the polls, but it is probable that the Soviets were correct if they calculated that a major defeat for the Western powers in Germany would gain communism far more votes than it lost.

Indeed, the Western leaders themselves were the only ones who were in a position to take action to force the Soviets to alter their policies. There were no other instrumentalities through which public opinion could work. By making decisions to provide planes for the airlift, to institute economic sanctions against East Germany, to strengthen the European defense and economy, and to take other measures that had the effect of altering the world situation to the disadvantage of the Soviets, Western statesmen did in fact finally bring about a change of policy in Moscow. But the only way in which world opinion could help them was to support their policies after these had been enunciated. Appeals to the public were no substitute for working out specific measures. In the end, the Western leaders served as agents of the free world public opinion to which they had at first appealed.

Another aspect of the relationship between leadership and opinion could be observed at the start of the blockade. In spite of preparatory work, public opinion in Berlin and the free world was not yet fully developed when the full force of the crisis struck. Not for at least a week after the full blockade had been imposed were there any widespread expressions of support for Berlin from West Germany and the free world. In Berlin itself there was a period of hesitation, and the city's democratic leaders had to increase the tempo of their resistance appeals to the population. During this incubation period for public sentiment, General Clay, Mayor Reuter, and other German and Allied leaders, had to stand up against the communist onslaught on their own authority. Only later did their actions prove to have been those that would be backed to the full by the popular will.

Political Communications

The mass media played an important part in the development of Berlin's resistance spirit and of world opinion in support of the Berliners. Press and radio provided facilities for communication between leaders and masses, and among groups in different geographical areas. They brought reassurance to the Berliners, and nullified many of the effects of communist agitation.

The role of press and radio as a link between Berlin's leaders and masses was relatively unspectacular but extremely important, for it was the ready availability of these media that enabled the city government and political parties to rally the people in support of their city's freedom. Daily reports about the crisis permitted the citizens to participate emotionally in the struggle. One of the most dramatic instances of this was a "live" RIAS broadcast of a City Assembly meeting that was broken up by communist rowdies. Two radio reporters present were themselves beaten up, but continued broadcasting even as they were being beaten. The newscast made such an impression on the listeners that many of them recalled it vividly several years later.

Communications media played a central part in reinforcing, if not actually creating, the Berliners' sense of being at the center of world attention. Press and radio carried reports of the stalwart behavior of the blockaded citizens to all parts of the free world, and the expressions of admiration that these reports elicited were immediately carried back to Berlin and served to bolster the Berliners' determination to hold out.*

Press and radio also helped to give individual Berliners the reassuring awareness that their opinions were shared by others in the city. Even those who were unable to attend mass meetings could hear or read about these mighty demonstrations and take comfort in the thought that the overwhelming majority of Berliners were united in the struggle. Further reassurance came from the knowledge of foreign support, from printed and broadcast statements of Western leaders, and from reports of the growth of Allied air strength in Europe. Above all, ample news coverage reassured people that nothing terrible had happened, that Soviet troops had not yet marched. Reports from the blockade period mention again and again the "nervous haste" with which the newspaper was read, and the sense of taut anticipation with which people tuned in on the radio newscast. On discovering that no catastrophe had taken place, they would go back to their daily pursuits.

The ready availability of all media of information did much to nullify the effects of communist propaganda and agitation. If the Communists had enjoyed a monopoly, or even a near-monopoly, of the dissemination of information, they would have found it easier to promote panic or defeatism. As it was, people were able to check reports from communist sources against the media they believed to be reliable.

Propaganda—in the sense of a planned effort to influence public opinion through communications—played a small part in the blockade. Except for some minor successes in West Germany, all the vigorous communist propaganda efforts were almost totally ineffectual. Official propaganda from the West also seemed to have few direct effects. An exception to this generalization, in the early days of the blockade, was provided by the Voice of America broadcasts assuring Berliners of American support. They were picked up and widely publicized by the West Berlin press, for they gave the hard-pressed citizens information they needed in order to decide how

* For a fuller description of this reinforcement process, see W. Phillips Davison, "Political Significance of Recognition via Mass Media—An Illustration from the Berlin Blockade," *Public Opinion Quarterly*, Spring, 1956.

to conduct themselves. The Voice of America and the BBC continued to be a supplementary source of reassurance to Berliners, and their listening audiences were substantial. Their chief importance, however, lay in transmitting facts and opinions from the Western world rather than in their ability to influence attitudes or behavior directly.

One reason for the relatively small role played by political propaganda was the fact that most Berliners were able to observe certain important facts directly and at close range. They could see the airlift planes passing overhead, and they could watch them land at the airfields; they could reassure themselves that Berlin was still free, and that the city government was still functioning. Any communication which did not accord with these facts was immediately dismissed.

A second reason, which was cited by many observers of the blockade, was that Berliners had become highly critical of propaganda. They had been exposed to the full violence of Nazi propaganda, and had seen it exploded by defeat. They had then lived through a brief period when the Soviets had a monopoly of the media of information, and this had been followed by the time of Western "re-education" efforts, with their large admixture of propaganda. As a result, Berliners were inclined to question the motives of anyone who sought to influence their opinions, and to reject all judgments that did not accord with the view of the world which they had acquired in the course of their harrowing but enlightening experiences.

The Narrow Margin of Success

Berlin succeeded in holding out by a very narrow margin. There were many times, both before and during the blockade, when the scales could easily have tipped in favor of the Soviets. The Social Democratic Party, which was the principal political focus of resistance in Berlin, came very close to being absorbed by the communist-dominated SED in 1946. Berlin's democratic Magistrat considered abandoning its political leadership as a protest against Allied interference in the following year. Any delay in starting the airlift, or any sign of retreat by the Western powers, might well have produced defeatism among the population when the blockade was first imposed. Allied eagerness to achieve an agreement with the Soviets, combined with a lack of appreciation for the potentialities of the airlift, led to an over-hasty diplomatic compromise which under slightly different circumstances might have assured the Soviets a dominant position in Berlin. Finally, in spite of its magnificent accomplishments, the airlift just barely succeeded in maintaining a minimum standard of living in Berlin throughout the winter. A relatively small decline in the tonnage of coal flown in could have led to the breakdown of essential services.

The narrow margin by which the blockade was defeated underlines the important part played by public opinion in deciding the outcome of the crisis. Deterioration of morale in Berlin, or even strongly negative developments in public opinion in West Germany or among the Allies could have led to a major Western defeat. Public opinion was not necessarily the most single factor on which the outcome of the blockade depended, but it was a vital one.

In the last analysis, the state of public opinion depended principally on a few individuals. For Berlin's resistance, which so roused the admiration of the free world, was forged over a period of time by a handful of rather obscure figures in government, political parties, trade unions, and the press. Without their dedicated work, long before the blockade itself, the resistance spirit would never have grown into the powerful force it became. The Soviet assault on Berlin was defeated by the smooth teamwork of thousands of men operating hundreds of aircraft, and by millions of others who were engaged in reconstructing damaged economies and conducting the daily business of the democracies. But their efforts would have been in vain, if, many months before the crisis, a few men in Berlin had not decided that freedom was worth a fight.

APPENDIX A

Notes on Source Material

Investigation of any historical phenomenon from a social scientific point of view presents the student with a number of characteristic problems. Unless he recognizes in advance the probable future significance of major events, he will have to gather his data after the events are past, and at a time when the human beings in whom he is interested are preoccupied with other matters. As a rule, it is only in situations such as elections, where time, place and nature of events are more or less determined by law or custom, that the social scientist is fortunate enough to be able to make his observations while the event is actually happening. When it comes to gathering information about the attitudes of men and the working of institutions in the past, he is forced to rely on whatever observations journalists, government officials, and others may have recorded at the time, and on the subsequent recollections of people who participated in the event.

This study, having been conceived only after the Berlin blockade, has had to rely on those two kinds of data, neither of which proved completely satisfactory. The first category consisted of information gathered at the time by a variety of persons who had a variety of purposes in mind. Most important in this category were publications that appeared in Berlin during the blockade, letters written to newspapers and radio stations, and a few public-opinion surveys conducted by the Opinion Surveys Branch of U.S. Military Government. The second category was composed of written and oral accounts given several years after the blockade, and hence subject to the biasing effect of the passage of time. It included the memoirs of a number of American and German officials, twenty interviews conducted by the author with leading personalities who were active in Berlin during the blockade period, ten reports written at the author's request by staff members of a public-opinion research organization in Berlin, and more than three hundred essays submitted in connection with a prize contest sponsored by a Berlin newspaper. Since the essays turned out to be the richest source of data on the attitudes and behavior of West Berliners during the blockade, the conditions of the contest and the background of the essayists will be described in some detail.

Der Abend, a Berlin evening newspaper with a circulation of approximately 100,000, has for several years sponsored periodic prize contests in various fields. On January 18, 1952, it announced one of these under the headline: "WHAT DO YOU REMEMBER ABOUT THE AIRLIFT?" A translation of the major portion of this announcement reads as follows:

> Mayor Ernst Reuter recently said in a speech at the radio tower that Berlin's problems are still the same ones which it faced at the time of the blockade. But he also admonished all those who were impatient to look back at the past three years, in which Berlin has accomplished a great deal. This causes the *Abend* to approach its readers with a question:
>
> Do you often think of the blockade times? Of the airlift? Please write and tell us what personal impressions and experiences stick in your memory. *Der Abend* will give the following prizes for the best contributions:
>
> One first prize of 100 marks
> Four second prizes of 50 marks each
> Ten third prizes of 30 marks each
>
> To make it easier for you we will make a few suggestions, for instance:
>
> To what degree did the blockade and airlift affect your life, your work, and your political attitudes?
>
> During the first few days of the blockade, what did you think would happen?
>
> Did you think that the airlift would succeed? Or did you think there was a possibility that war might break out?
>
> What did your neighbors say, and what did you hear from your relatives or acquaintances in East and West Germany?
>
> Remember, these are only suggestions. You are entirely free to write about anything that seems important to you in connection with this subject. There is no limit to the length of the contributions, and the style will not be decisive when the entries are judged. The judges will not decide with reference to stylistic skill, but on the basis of the importance of the content and the amount of detail included. Most important from the point of view of the judges will be the degree to which portrayals describe, in the most true-to-life fashion, the actual

events and their effects on the thinking and feeling of the Berliners.

The announcement specified further that entrants mention their age, occupation, and the section of the city or part of Germany in which they had lived during the blockade. Arrangements were also made whereby persons in East Berlin or East Germany could enter the contest without getting into trouble with the communist authorities.

In the course of the competition, 342 essays were submitted, ranging in length from five to thirty-six hundred words. The median length was about seven hundred words. To judge by what we know of their sex, age, occupation, and area of residence, the writers of the essays represent all major segments of the West Berlin population, although they do not by any means constitute the equivalent of a random sample.

TABLE 1

CHARACTERISTICS OF ESSAY-WRITERS COMPARED WITH THOSE OF A RANDOM SAMPLE OF THE WEST BERLIN ADULT POPULATION[a]

	Essay-Writers	*Random Sample*
A. SEX[b]		
Male	57.5%	43%
Female	42.5	57
	100.0%	100%
B. AGE[c]		
18&19	0.0%	4%
20–29	8.3	14
30–39	12.5	18
40–49	24.8	25
50–59	27.6	21
60–69	18.9	14
Over 69	7.9	4
	100.0%	100%

[a] The writer is indebted to Dr. Leo Crespi, former Chief of the Reactions Analysis Staff of the Office of the U.S. High Commissioner, for the data on the random sample cited here. These figures are based on the analysis of twelve probability samples taken in 1951.

[b] The sex of 12 essay-writers was not given. Therefore, N is 330 for this group.

[c] The age of 77 writers was not given, and 11 were under 18. Therefore, N is 254.

TABLE 1, concluded

	Essay-Writers	*Random Sample*
C. OCCUPATION[d]		
Professional	7.9%	5%
Business	6.1	6
White Collar	16.3	12
Skilled Workers	10.8	10
Semi-skilled and Unskilled Workers	10.1	12
Domestic and Service	2.9	4
Housewives	18.1	21
Pensioners and Students	16.3	16
Unemployed	11.6	14
	100.1%	100%
D. BOROUGH OF RESIDENCE[e]		
Tiergarten	4.4%	5%
Wedding	5.7	11
Kreuzberg	11.3	10
Charlottenburg	9.4	10
Spandau	4.7	8
Wilmersdorf	10.7	7
Zehlendorf	3.8	4
Schöneberg	12.6	9
Steglitz	7.5	7
Tempelhof	11.9	6
Neukölln	13.2	13
Reinickendorf	4.7	10
	99.9%	100%

[d] The occupation of 65 writers either was not given or could not be classified in the given categories. Therefore, N is 277.

[e] Area of residence for essay-writers was classified as of time of writing, rather than as of the blockade period. In 24 cases, residence could not be determined or was outside West Berlin. Therefore, N is 318.

From this table it is clear that, as compared with West Berlin's population as a whole, the essay-writers were over-weighted with males and with older persons. Also, the competition attracted a disproportionately large number of white-collar and professional people. The distribution over districts of residence may reflect geographic characteristics of the circulation of *Der Abend.* Most striking here is the relatively weak representation in the two boroughs of the French sector (Wedding and Reinickendorf) and the heavy representation from the American sector borough of Tempelhof. In spite of these qualifications, the essay-writers can be said to represent a fairly adequate cross-section of the West Berlin population when it comes to age, occupation, and place of residence.

In certain other characteristics, however, the essay-writers can be expected to differ very appreciably from a random sample of the West Berlin population. In particular, we must assume that they are more articulate, that they have time to write, and that they have more than an average interest in prize competitions. For these reasons, and also because the essays each follow their own pattern, their contents cannot be treated statistically in the manner of answers to questions in a public-opinion survey, and analysis must be mainly qualitative. However, a few very rough quantitative judgments are possible. The essays show, for instance, which features of the blockade period were most vividly recalled and commented upon. They also indicate which attitudes were remembered as preponderant and which were believed less common. On the actual historical events the essays proved to be surprisingly accurate.

The various sources of information about the blockade period inevitably left some gaps in the total picture or gave rise to conflicting interpretations. Insofar as possible, the author has tried to deal with these shortcomings by applying standards of internal consistency, and by consulting observers who lived in Berlin at the time or were otherwise concerned with the events of the blockade.

APPENDIX B

Chronology of Events

1948

International	*Germany*
JANUARY 12. Secretary of State Marshall urges Congress to approve European Recovery Program.	
	MARCH 20. Soviets walk out of Allied Control Council.
	APRIL 1. Soviets impose rail and road restrictions on Allied traffic from western zones to Berlin. Allies counter with "little airlift" to supply occupation forces in Berlin.
JUNE 7. London Recommendations announced by U.S., U.K., France, and Benelux nations.	
	JUNE 11. Soviets halt rail traffic between Berlin and West Germany for two days.
	JUNE 12. Highway bridge on road to Berlin closed for "repairs."
JUNE 17. European Recovery Program bill approved by Congress.	JUNE 16. Soviets walk out of Allied Kommandatura.
	JUNE 18. Western powers announce currency reform for West Germany but not Berlin.
JUNE 23. Conference of Soviet Union and satellite foreign ministers meets at Warsaw.	JUNE 23. Soviets order currency reform in East Germany and all Berlin. Western powers order currency reform in West Berlin. City hall riots.
	JUNE 24. Soviets impose full blockade on Berlin.

International	*Germany*
	JUNE 26. Airlift to supply German civilians in Berlin is started.
JULY 16. U.S. dispatches 60 B-29 bombers to British bases.	JULY 19. Soviets offer to supply food to all Berlin.
AUGUST 2. Western representatives meet with Soviets in Moscow. Discussions continue during August.	
AUGUST 30. Moscow Agreement provides for introduction of Soviet-sponsored currency under four-power control in all Berlin.	AUGUST 26–SEPTEMBER 6. Second city hall riots.
	SEPTEMBER 1-7. Four military governors meet in fruitless attempt to implement Moscow Agreement.
	SEPTEMBER 9. Reichstag mass meeting.
SEPTEMBER 29. Western powers refer Berlin dispute to the United Nations.	
OCTOBER 4. U.N. Security Council begins consideration of Berlin dispute at Paris meeting.	OCTOBER 20. USAF and RAF units merged to form Combined Airlift Task Force. West German Parliamentary Council meets at Bonn to start drafting a constitution for West Germany.
OCTOBER 25. Security Council's draft resolution for settling Berlin dispute vetoed by Soviets.	
NOVEMBER 30. Security Council establishes Technical Committee to study Berlin currency problem.	NOVEMBER 30. Berlin Communists split city government by establishing a new government in East Berlin.
	DECEMBER 5. Elections in West Berlin show overwhelming support for democratic parties.

1949

International	*Germany*
JANUARY 3. U.N. Technical Committee submits study of currency problem to the four governments involved.	
JANUARY 31. In press interview Stalin states conditions for ending blockade without reference to currency problem.	
FEBRUARY 4. Western powers report to Technical Committee that its draft proposal not feasible unless Berlin is reunified.	FEBRUARY 4. West tightens counterblockade, stopping all truck traffic between west zones and Soviet zone.
FEBRUARY 15. Start of informal Jessup–Malik talks on Berlin issue.	
	MARCH 19. Communist-dominated People's Council approves constitution for East German government.
	MARCH 20. Western powers announce west mark will be sole legal tender in West Berlin.
APRIL 4. North Atlantic Treaty signed in Washington.	
	APRIL 16. Airlift "Easter Parade" breaks all tonnage records by lifting 12,940 tons of food and coal to Berlin in 24 hours.
APRIL 20. Communist "peace" conference opens in Paris.	
MAY 4. Four powers announce agreement to end blockade.	
	MAY 12. Blockade ends.

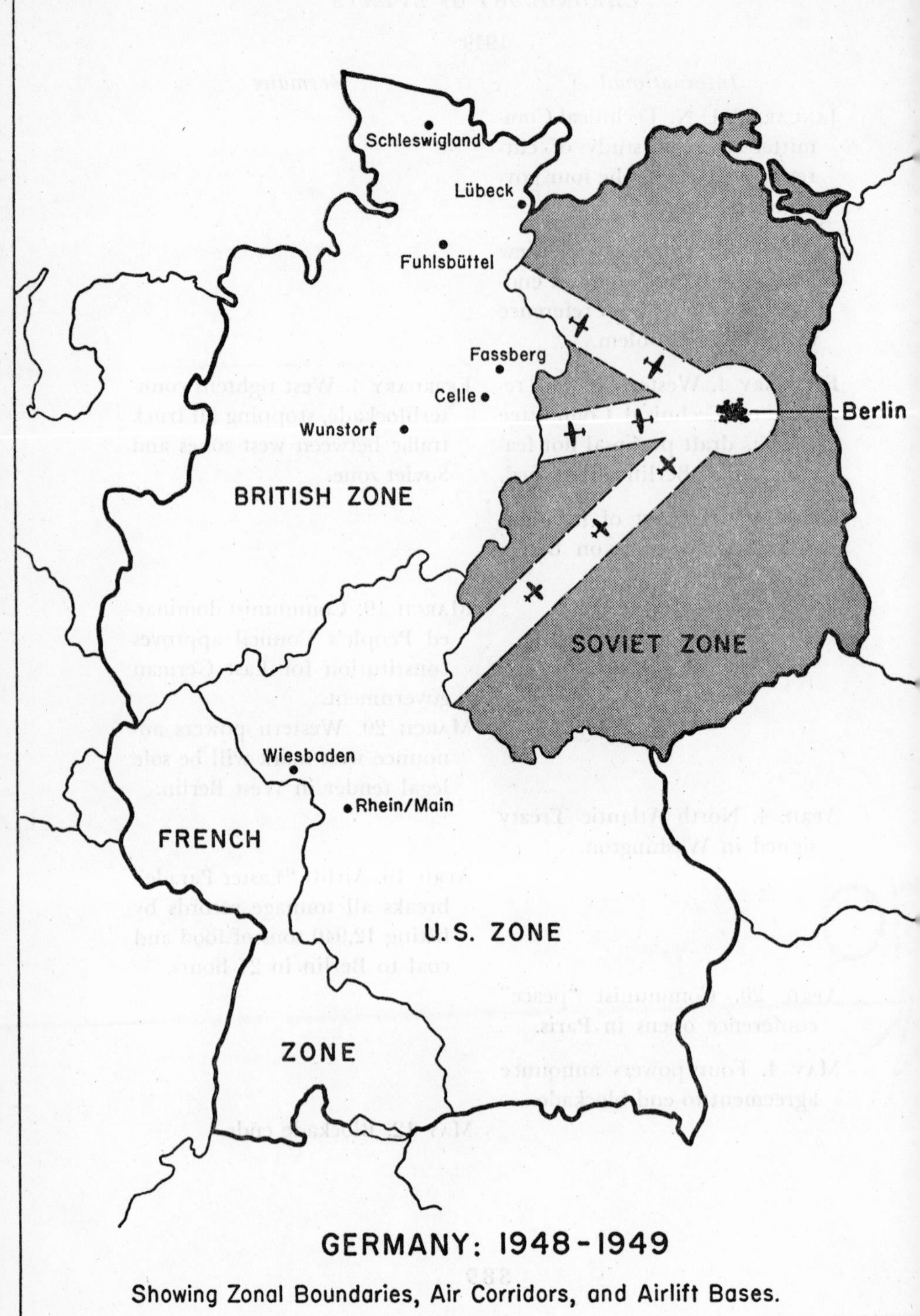

GERMANY: 1948-1949

Showing Zonal Boundaries, Air Corridors, and Airlift Bases.

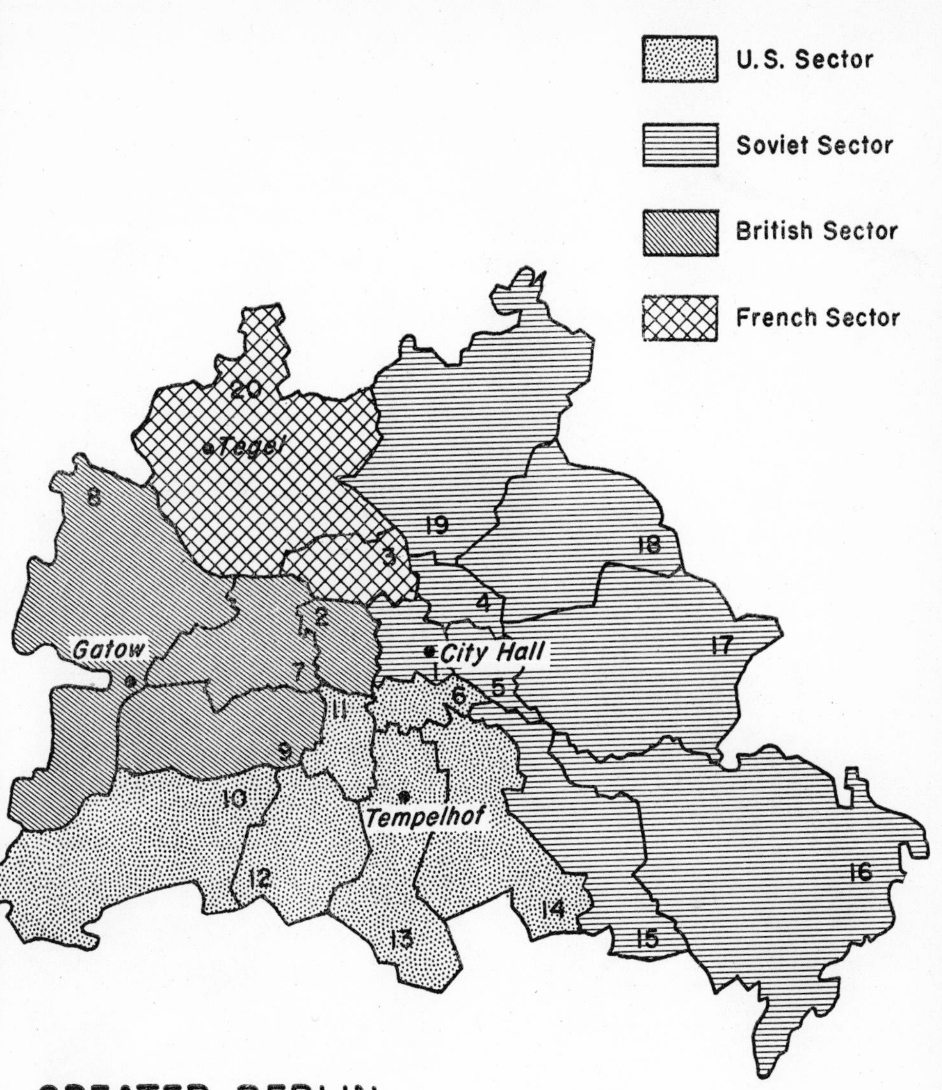

GREATER BERLIN

Showing Sector Boundaries and West Berlin Airfields

The Boroughs of Greater Berlin

1. Mitte
2. Tiergarten
3. Wedding
4. Prenzlauer Berg
5. Friedrichshain
6. Kreuzberg
7. Charlottenburg
8. Spandau
9. Wilmersdorf
10. Zehlendorf
11. Schöneberg
12. Steglitz
13. Tempelhof
14. Neukölln
15. Treptow
16. Köpenick
17. Lichtenberg
18. Weissensee
19. Pankow
20. Reinickendorf

BIBLIOGRAPHICAL NOTES

Chapter I

1. Philip E. Mosely, "The Occupation of Germany," *Foreign Affairs*, July, 1950, p. 593.

2. Boris Meissner, *Russland, die Westmächte und Deutschland*, H. H. Nölke Verlag, Hamburg, 1953, pp. 62-63.

3. *Ibid.*, p. 59.

4. *Ibid.*, pp. 60-76; and General Lucius D. Clay, *Decision in Germany*, Doubleday & Company, New York, 1950, pp. 39-45.

5. Summarized from the *Official Gazette of the Control Council for Germany*, Supplement to Issue No. 1, October 29, 1945, "Documents Relating to the Establishment of the Allied Control Authority," pp. 13-19.

6. Clay, *op. cit.*, pp. 25-26.

7. Frank Howley, *Berlin Command*, Putnam, New York, 1950, pp. 25-32.

8. *Ibid.*, pp. 47-52.

9. Clay, *op. cit.*, pp. 109-110.

10. *Ibid.*, p. 112.

11. *Ibid.*, p. 30.

12. *Ibid.*, pp. 124-125.

13. *Ibid.*, p. 123.

14. *Official Gazette of the Control Council for Germany*, No. 5, March 31, 1946.

15. *Ibid.*, No. 19, August 31, 1948.

16. Howley, *op. cit.*, p. 61. For a description of these training schools in Russia see Graf Heinrich von Einsiedel, *Tagebuch der Versuchung*, Pontes-Verlag, Berlin-Stuttgart, 1950.

17. Cf. *Tagesspiegel*, December 8, 1946; *Neues Deutschland*, January 22, 1947.

18. Cf. Vorwärts, December 31, 1946, January 2 and 14, 1947; *Sozialdemokrat*, January 4, 1947; *Tagesspiegel*, November 2, 1946.

19. J. P. Nettl, *The Eastern Zone and Soviet Policy in Germany, 1945-1950*, Oxford University Press, London, 1951, pp. 88-89. For a more detailed account of the merger see *Military Government Information Bulletin*, U.S. Office of Military Government for Germany, June 1, 1948, pp. 22*ff*.

20. Nettl, *op. cit.*, p. 137.

21. Vladimir Rudolph, "The Agencies of Control: Their Organization and Policies," in Slusser (ed.), *Soviet Economic Policy in Postwar Germany*, Research Program on the U.S.S.R., New York, 1953, p. 57.

22. *Ibid.*, p. 66; and Nettl, *op. cit.*, pp. 132-134.

23. Interview with Major Guy Lloyd, the *London Times*, December 24, 1946.

24. Herbert Hoover, *German Agriculture and Food Requirements*, Report No. 1, The President's Economic Mission to Germany and Austria, February 28, 1947, pp. 3-4 and 7-8.

25. Clay, *op. cit.*, p. 122.

26. *Ibid.*, pp. 165-168; and the *New York Times*, July 30, 1946.

27. *Department of State Bulletin*, September 15, 1946, pp. 496-501.

28. Clay, *op. cit.*, p. 169.

29. *Ibid.*, pp. 174-184; see also *Germany 1947-1949: The Story in Documents*, Department of State Publication 3556, Government Printing Office, Washington, 1950, pp. 450, 466-467.

30. *Chronology of International Events and Documents*, a supplement to *The World Today*, Royal Institute of International Affairs, April 16, 1948, p. 258.

31. Emil Schäfer, *Von Potsdam bis Bonn*, Moritz Schauenburg Verlag, Lahr, 1950, pp. 37-38.
32. *Chronology of International Events and Documents*, January 12, 1948, p. 35.
33. Schäfer, *op. cit.*, pp. 48-49.
34. The *New York Times*, February 3, 1948.
35. Heinz Sauermann, "Der amerikanische Plan für die deutsche Währungsreform," *Zeitschrift für die gesamte Staatswissenschaft*, No. 2, 1955, p. 196. See also Jack Bennett, "The German Currency Reform," *Annals of the American Academy of Political and Social Science*, January, 1950, pp. 43-45.
36. The *New York Times*, August 10, 1947.
37. The *London Times*, February 5, 1948.
38. *Ibid.*
39. Clay, *op. cit.*, pp. 208-211.
40. *Ibid.*, p. 157.
41. *Ibid.*, p. 161. See also the *New York Times*, January 21, 1948; February 20, 1948; and March 11, 1948.
42. Meissner, *op. cit.*, p. 83.
43. James F. Byrnes, *Speaking Frankly*, Harper & Brothers, New York, 1947, pp. 171-178.
44. *Ibid.*, p. 159.
45. *Ibid.*, p. 180.
46. Meissner, *op. cit.*. p. 126.
47. *Ibid.*, p. 150.
48. *Ibid.*, pp. 146-147.
49. Clay, *op. cit.*, p. 348.
50. Royal Institute of International Affairs, *Survey of International Affairs, 1947-1948*, Oxford University Press, London, 1952, p. 240.
51. *Neues Deutschland*, January 16, 1948.
52. *Military Government Information Bulletin*, U.S. Office of Military Government for Germany, May 4, 1948, p. 23.
53. *Neues Deutschland*, March 18, 1948.
54. *British Zone Review*, published for British occupation personnel by the Control Commission for Germany (British Element), May 29, 1948, p. 2.
55. *Neues Deutschland*, June 15, 1948.
56. The *New York Times*, February 17, 1948.
57. Clay, *op. cit.*, p. 355.
58. Clay, *op. cit.*, p. 349.
59. The Council on Foreign Relations, Inc., *The United States in World Affairs, 1948-1949*, Harper & Brothers, New York, 1950, pp. 71-76.
60. *Germany 1947-1949: The Story in Documents*, p. 75.
61. Clay, *op. cit.*, p. 356.
62. The *New York Times*, March 23, 1948.
63. Clay, *op. cit.*, p. 357.
64. *Ibid.*, pp. 212-214.
65. Quoted in Edward Hallett Carr, *German-Soviet Relations between the Two World Wars, 1919-1939*, The Johns Hopkins Press, Baltimore, 1951, p. 65.
66. Quoted in Lionel Kochan, *Russia and the Weimar Republic*, Bowes and Bowes, London, 1954, p. 83.
67. *USSR Information Bulletin*, the Soviet Embassy, Washington, D.C., July 14, 1948, p. 398.
68. Meissner, *op. cit.*, p. 147.
69. *Ibid.*, p. 92.
70. Franz Neumann, "Soviet Policy in Germany," *Annals of the American Academy of Political and Social Science*, May, 1949, p. 175.

NOTES

Chapter II

1. Frank Howley, *Berlin Command*, Putnam, New York, 1950, pp. 44-45.

2. *Ibid.*, p. 97. See also *Berliner Schicksal, 1945-1952*, a collection of official documents published by the government of Berlin, 1952, pp. 37-38.

3. *Berlin Sector: A Four Year Report, July 1, 1945-September 1, 1949*, Office of Military Government, U.S. Sector, Berlin, pp. 81-82.

4. Howley, *op. cit.*, p. 98; and Berliner Schicksal, p. 38.

5. *Berliner Schicksal*, pp. 38-39.

6. *Der Abend*, January 18, 1947.

7. Boris Meissner, *Russland, die Westmächte und Deutschland*, H. H. Nölke Verlag, Hamburg, 1953, p. 59, and *Berliner Schicksal*, p. 10. See also Gustav Klingelhöfer, "The Political Awakening," *Berliner Stimme*, June 18, 1955, for a detailed account of the postwar revival of the Social Democratic Party.

8. Harold Hurwitz, "Military Government and The German Press: An Experiment in Cross-Cultural Institutional Change," unpublished Master's Thesis, Department of Sociology, Columbia University, 1953, pp. 188-191.

9. Howley, *op. cit.*, p. 79.

10. *Official Gazette of the Control Council for Germany*, Supplement to Issue No. 1, October 29, 1945, "Documents Relating to the Establishment of the Allied Control Authority," p. 11.

11. Howley, *op. cit.*, pp. 52-62. See also *Berlin Sector*, p. 25.

12. Howley, *op. cit.*, p. 56.

13. Lucius D. Clay, *Decision in Germany*, Doubleday & Company, New York, 1950, p. 26; and Philip E. Mosely, "The Occupation of Germany," *Foreign Affairs*, July, 1950, p. 587.

14. Article 2, No. 41.

15. Title 21, paragraph 157.

16. Howley, *op. cit.*, pp. 93 and 114.

17. *Ibid.*, pp. 110-112.

18. Hurwitz, *op. cit.*, p. 190.

19. Howley, *op. cit.*, p. 72.

20. *Ibid.*, p. 93.

21. *Berlin Sector*, p. 63.

22. Clay, *op. cit.*, p. 115.

23. *The Berlin Crisis: A Report on the Moscow Discussions, 1948*, Department of State Publication 3298, U.S. Government Printing Office, Washington, September, 1948, p. 48.

24. *British Zone Review*, published for British occupation personnel by the Control Commission for Germany (British Element), March 19, 1949, pp. 19 and 21.

25. *Berlin in Zahlen, 1947*, Hauptamt für Statistik von Gross-Berlin, Kulturbuch-Verlag, 1949, p. 186.

26. Klingelhöfer, *op. cit.*

27. *Ibid.*

28. *Manchester Guardian Weekly*, April 12, 1946.

29. Howley, *op. cit.*, p. 106.

30. *Ibid.*

31. *Ibid.*, pp. 104-106.

32. *Ibid.*, pp. 107-110.

33. *Ibid.*, pp. 120-121; see also Clay, *op. cit.*, p. 132.

34. Howley, *op. cit.*, p. 121.

35. *Ibid.*, pp. 121-129.

36. *Ibid.*, pp. 131-132.
37. *Berlin in Zahlen, 1947*, p. 424.
38. Quoted in *Die städtischen Körperschaften in der Berliner Krise, Tatsachen und Dokumente*, published by the city government, Berlin, 1949, pp. 4-5.
39. Howley, *op. cit.*, pp. 139-140. See also Stenographic Minutes of the Berlin City Assembly, I, 5th Session, December 12, 1946.
40. Cf. Stenographic Minutes of the Berlin City Assembly, I, 25th Session, April 11, 1947, especially the remarks of Karl Litke (SED).
41. *Ibid.*
42. Howley, *op. cit.*, pp. 145-146.
43. *Ibid.*, p. 147.
44. The *New York Times*, September 10, 1947.
45. Stenographic Minutes of the City Assembly, I, 36th Session, June 24, 1947.
46. *Berliner Schicksal*, p. 44.
47. Cf. the remarks of Deputy Landsberg (CDU), Stenographic Minutes of the City Assembly, I, 37th Session, July 11, 1947.
48. *Berliner Schicksal*, p. 43.
49. The *New York Times*, January 25, 1947.
50. *Ibid.*
51. *Berliner Schicksal*, p. 50.
52. Howley, *op. cit.*, p. 165.
53. *Berliner Schicksal*, pp. 44-45.
54. *Ibid.*, p. 49.
55. *Ibid.*, pp. 49-50.
56. *Soviet News*, Press Department of the Soviet Embassy, London, April 28, 1948, p. 3.
57. The *New York Times*, May 14, 1948.
58. *Berliner Schicksal*, p. 292.
59. *Ibid.*, pp. 299-301.
60. *Ibid.*, p. 298.
61. For a detailed account of the communist attempt to gain control of the Berlin LDP, see *Für Recht und Freiheit*, printed speech delivered on January 25, 1948, by Karl Hubert Schwennicke, chairman of the Berlin LDP.
62. *Tagesspiegel*, January 21, 1947.
63. *Unser Wirken 1948-50*, Gesamtverband der öffentlichen Betriebe und Verwaltungen, p. 15.
64. Cf. editorial in *Tagesspiegel*, December 8, 1946.
65. *Ibid.*
66. The *New York Times*, March 31, 1947.
67. Cf. *Sozialdemokrat*, January 4, 1947; and *Abend*, January 11, 1947.
68. The *New York Times*, February 4, 1947; the *New York Herald Tribune*, February 2, 1947; Howley, *op. cit.*, pp. 151-153.
69. The *New York Times*, February 12, 1947.
70. Howley, *op. cit.*, p. 152.
71. *Sozialdemokrat*, January 18, 1947.
72. *SPD Gross-Berlin 1947-48*, Annual Report of the Executive Committee, printed for the use of delegates to the Landesparteitag on May 8-9, 1948.
73. Cf. *Wir klagen an!*, a pamphlet published by the Unabhängige Gewerkschafts-Organisation (Independent Union Organization) of Greater Berlin, 1948.
74. The *New York Times*, August 6, 1947.
75. Clay, *op. cit.*, p. 351.
76. The *New York Times*, May 29, 1948.
77. Cf. the *New York Times*, April 22, 1947, and August 6, 1947.
78. *Ibid.*, October 12, 1947.

79. *Ibid.*, January 12, 1948.
80. *Neues Deutschland*, April 15, 1948.
81. *Notes on the Blockade of Berlin*, issued by the Control Commission for Germany (British Element), February, 1949, pp. 8-9.
82. The *London Times*, March 31, 1948.
83. The *New York Times*, April 2, 1948.
84. Howley, *op. cit.*, p. 193.
85. Clay, *op. cit.*, pp. 358-359.
86. Lowell Bennett, *Bastion Berlin*, Friedrich Rudl, Frankfurt, 1951, pp. 35-39.
87. The *London Times*, April 13, 1948; also Clay, *op. cit.*, p. 361.
88. Stenographic Minutes of the Berlin City Assembly, I, 64th Session, April 15, 1948.
89. Cf. the *London Times*, June 11 and 14, 1948; *Tagesspiegel*, June 11, 16, and 18, 1948. For a general treatment of Soviet restrictions on traffic between West Germany and Berlin, see also *The Berlin Crisis: A Report on the Moscow Discussions, 1948*, pp. 1-6.
90. The *New York Times*, March 25, 1948.
91. *Ibid.*, April 6, 1948.
92. *Ibid.*
93. *Ibid.*, April 8, 1948.
94. *Ibid.*, April 10, 1948.
95. *Ibid.*, April 14, 17, 18, 20, 23; May 2, 21, 1948.
96. *Ibid.*, April 11, 1948.
97. *Soviet News*, London, April 26, 1948, p. 3.
98. The *New York Times*, April 15, 1948.
99. *Ibid.*, May 9, 1948.
100. *Ibid.*, April 25, 1948.
101. *Tagesspiegel*, June 18, 1948.
102. *Ibid.*, June 5, 1948.
103. *Neues Deutschland*, June 13, 1948.
104. The *London Times*, November 11, 1947.
105. *Ibid.*, May 29, 1948.
106. *Die städtischen Körperschaften in der Berliner Krise*, p. 11.
107. Stenographic Minutes of the Berlin City Assembly, I, 49th Session, December 4, 1947; also personal interviews.
108. *Berliner Schicksal*, p. 46.
109. *Ibid.*, pp. 268-269.
110. *Notes on the Blockade of Berlin*, pp. 61-62.
111. *Die städtischen Körperschaften in der Berliner Krise*, pp. 11-12.
112. Howley, *op. cit.*, p. 174.
113. The *London Times*, June 14, 1948.
114. Howley, *op. cit.*, pp. 179-182; see also *Military Government Information Bulletin*, August 24, 1948, p. 19, and the monthly *Report of the U.S. Military Governor* for June, 1948, pp. 1-2.
115. The *New York Times*, June 17, 1948.
116. Clay, *op. cit.*, p. 159.
117. Frank L. Howley (as told to J. P. McEvoy), "I've Talked 1600 Hours with the Russians," *Reader's Digest*, May, 1949, pp. 75-76.
118. The *New York Times*, January 12, 1948.
119. *Ibid.*, January 13, 1948.
120. *Ibid.*
121. *Department of State Wireless Bulletin*, January 14, 1948.
122. Walter Millis (ed.), *The Forrestal Diaries*, The Viking Press, New York, 1951, p. 387.

123. *Ibid.*, p. 395.
124. *Ibid.*, p. 408.
125. *Ibid.*, p. 411.
126. The *New York Times*, April 2, 1948.
127. Clay, *op. cit.*, p. 358.
128. *Ibid.*, p. 360.
129. *Ibid.*, p. 361. (Copyright 1950 by Lucius D. Clay. Reprinted by permission of Doubleday & Co., Inc.)
130. Howley, *Berlin Command*, pp. 174-175 and 200-202.
131. Cf. Dwight Boyd Mitchell, "The Berlin Problem 1943-49" (unpublished Master's thesis, Department of Political Science, University of Illinois, 1949).
132. *The Forrestal Diaries*, p. 444.
133. Howley, *Berlin Command*, pp. 186-187; see also Jack Bennett, "The German Currency Reform," *Annals of the American Academy of Political and Social Science*, January, 1950, p. 46.
134. The *New York Times*, June 20, 1948.
135. *Ibid.*, June 21, 1948.
136. Ferdinand Friedensburg, *Berlin—Schicksal und Aufgabe*, Pädagogischer Verlag Berthold Schulz, Berlin, 1953. p. 25.
137. *Ibid.*
138. Cf. *Der Sozialdemokrat*, October 20, 1947.
139. *Berliner Schicksal*, pp. 47-48.
140. *Ibid.*, pp. 51-52.
141. Cf. Howley, *Berlin Command*, pp. 122-123.
142. *Ibid.*, pp. 141-143.
143. Speech at the SPD Party Day in Nürnberg, June 30, 1947.
144. *Neue Zeitung* (Berlin edition), April 30, 1948.
145. Ernst Reuter, "Ein Jahr in Berlin," in *Sozialdemokrat*, December 16, 1947.
146. *Tagesspiegel*, March 20, 1948.
147. *Ibid.*
148. *Ibid.*, May 4, 1948.

Chapter III

1. *Tagesspiegel*, June 19, 1948.
2. Jack Bennett, "The German Currency Reform," *Annals of the American Academy of Political and Social Science*, 1950, p. 51.
3. *Neues Deutschland*, June 19, 1948.
4. *Ibid.*
5. *Tagesspiegel*, June 20, 1948.
6. The *New York Times*, June 20, 1948.
7. *Berliner Schicksal 1945-1952*, a collection of official documents published by the government of Berlin, 1952, pp. 52-53.
8. *Tagesspiegel*, June 20, 1948.
9. *Report of the U.S. Military Governor* for June, 1948, p. 7.
10. *Ibid.*
11. *Tagesspiegel*, June 22, 1948.
12. The *New York Times*, June 22, 1948. See also Jack Bennett, *op. cit.*, pp. 53-54.
13. The *New York Times*, June 25, 1948.
14. The *London Times*, June 24, 1948, and *Report of the U.S. Military Governor* for June, 1948, p. 7; see also Jack Bennett, *op. cit.*, pp. 51-52.
15. Jack Bennett, *op. cit.*, p. 52.

16. *Die städtischen Körperschaften in der Berliner Krise, Tatsachen und Dokumente,* published by the city government, Berlin. 1949, p. 19.
17. *Soviet News,* Soviet Embassy, London, June 24, 1948.
18. *Die städtischen Körperschaften in der Berliner Krise,* p. 19.
19. Lucius D. Clay, *Decision in Germany,* Doubleday & Company, New York, 1950, p. 364.
20. Frank Howley, *Berlin Command,* Putnam, New York, 1950, pp. 186-188.
21. *Tagesspiegel,* June 24, 1948.
22. *Die städtischen Körperschaften in der Berliner Krise,* pp. 19-23.
23. *Ibid.,* p. 22.
24. *Tagesspiegel,* June 26, 1948.
25. Howley, *op. cit.,* pp. 196-197.
26. *Ibid.,* p. 203; also *Tagesspiegel,* June 25, 1948.
27. *Notes on the Blockade of Berlin,* issued by the Control Commission for Germany (British Element), February, 1949, p. 12.
28. The *New York Times,* June 25, 1948.
29. *Ibid.,* June 26, 1948.
30. *Ibid.,* June 25, 1948.
31. Cf. *Tagesspiegel* and *Telegraf,* June 25, 1948.
32. *Report of the U.S. Military Governor* for June, 1948, pp. 22-23.
33. The *New York Times,* June 25, 1948.
34. "A Special Study of Operation 'Vittles'," *Aviation Operations Magazine,* April, 1949, p. 8.
35. *Berlin Airlift—A* USAFE *Summary,* Hq. U.S. Air Force, Europe, 1949, p. 3.
36. C. J. V. Murphy, "The Berlin Airlift," *Fortune,* November, 1948, p. 90.
37. Clay, *op. cit.,* p. 366. (Copyright 1950 by Lucius D. Clay. Reprinted by permission of Doubleday & Co., Inc.)
38. Walter Millis (ed.), *The Forrestal Diaries,* The Viking Press, New York, 1951, pp. 451-452.
39. The *New York Times,* June 27, 1948.
40. The *London Observer,* June 27, 1948.
41. The *New York Times,* June 27, 1948.
42. "A Special Study of Operation 'Vittles'," *op. cit.,* p. 8.
43. Harry S Truman, *Years of Trial and Hope,* Doubleday & Company, New York, 1946, p. 123.
44. *Ibid.*
45. Howley, *op. cit.,* p. 204.
46. *The Forrestal Diaries,* pp. 452-453.
47. *Ibid.,* pp. 453-454.
48. *Ibid.,* pp. 454-455.
49. *Ibid.*
50. *Tagesspiegel,* June 29, 1948.
51. *Ibid.*
52. "One Year of the Berlin Airlift," *Fighting Forces,* August, 1949, p. 145.
53. *Telegraf,* June 29, 1948.
54. *Tagesspiegel,* June 30, 1948.
55. *Berlin Airlift—A* USAFE *Summary, op. cit.,* pp. 4-5; and personal interviews.
56. Paul W. Fisher, "Berlin Airlift," special issue of *The Bee Hive* (quarterly), United Aircraft Corporation, East Hartford, Conn., Fall, 1948, p. 9.
57. Stenographic Minutes of the Berlin City Assembly, I, 75th Session, June 29, 1948.
58. *Ibid.*
59. *Luftbrücke Berlin,* a pictorial report published by the Magistrat of Greater Berlin, Arani Verlag, 1949, p. 15.

60. Stenographic Minutes of the Berlin City Assembly, I, 75th Session, June 29, 1948.

61. UGO—*Erster Geschäftsbericht*, Unabhängige Gewerkschafts-Organisation (Independent Union Organization) of Greater Berlin, 1949, pp. 140-141.

62. *Ibid.*, p. 139.

63. *Tagesspiegel*, June 30, 1948.

64. *Ibid.*

65. *Ibid.*, and the *New York Times*, June 30, 1948.

66. The *New York Times*, June 29, 1948.

67. *Ibid.*, July 1, 1948. For the full text of Bevin's remarks, see Beate Ruhm von Oppen (ed.), *Documents on Germany Under Occupation*, Royal Institute of International Affairs, Oxford University Press, London, 1955, pp. 308-314.

68. *Documents on Germany Under Occupation*, p. 313.

69. The *New York Times*, July 1, 1948.

70. *Tagesspiegel*, July 2, 1948; and *Die Welt*, July 1, 1948.

71. *Neues Deutschland*, June 30, 1948.

72. *Telegraf*, July 2, 1948. For the full text of the Soviet pronouncement, see *Documents on Germany Under Occupation*, pp. 314-315.

73. *Berlin Sector*, p. 26.

74. *Report of the U.S. Military Governor* for July, 1948, p. 1.

75. The *New York Herald Tribune*, July 2, 1948.

76. *Telegraf*, July 2, 1948.

77. *Tagesspiegel*, July 1, 1948.

78. *Die Welt*, July 1, 1948.

79. *Telegraf*, July 2, 1948.

80. *Ibid.*, and *Tagesspiegel*, July 2, 1948.

81. *Telegraf* and *Tagesspiegel*, July 2 and 3, 1948.

82. *Tagesspiegel*, July 2, 1948.

83. The *New York Herald Tribune*, June 3, 1948.

84. *Telegraf*, July 3, 1948.

85. *The Forrestal Diaries*, pp. 455-456.

86. *Telegraf*, July 3, 1948.

87. The *New York Times*, July 3, 1948.

88. *Telegraf*, July 3, 1948.

89. *Ibid.*

90. *Ibid.*

91. *Tagesspiegel*, July 3, 1948.

92. Clay, *op. cit.*, p. 367.

93. *The Berlin Crisis: A Report on the Moscow Discussions, 1948*, Department of State Publication 3298, U.S. Government Printing Office, Washington, September, 1948, pp. 7-8.

94. The *New York Times*, July 7 and 8, 1948.

95. *Telegraf* and *Tagesspiegel*, July 6, 1948.

96. *Tagesspiegel*, July 6 and 7, 1948.

97. *Ibid.*, July 8, 1948.

98. "A Special Study of Operation 'Vittles'," *op. cit.*, p. 8.

99. *U.S. News and World Report*, July 9, 1948, pp. 11 and 13.

100. The *New Statesman and Nation*, July 10, 1948, p. 21.

101. *Ibid.*

102. Howley, *op. cit.*, p. 212.

103. Clay, *op. cit.*, p. 374.

104. *Ibid.*

105. The *New York Times*, July 11, 1948.

106. *Ibid.*

107. *Tagesspiegel*, July 13, 1948.
108. *Telegraf*, July 12, 1948.
109. *Tagesspiegel*, July 13, 1948.
110. *Ibid.*, July 14, 1948.
111. *The Berlin Crisis*, pp. 10-15.
112. The *London Times*, July 16, 1948.
113. The *New York Times*, July 16, 1948.
114. *Ibid.*
115. *The Bee Hive, op. cit.*, p. 7.
116. *The Forrestal Diaries*, p. 457.
117. The *New York Times*, July 16, 1948.
118. "The Radio Audience in Amzone, Berlin and Bremen," Report No. 106, March 27, 1948, Opinion Surveys Branch. Office of Military Government (U.S.).
119. "Berliners View the Czechoslovak Situation," Report No. 117, April 27, 1948.
120. Stenographic Minutes of the Berlin City Assembly, I, 75th Session, June 29, 1948.
121. UGO—*Erster Geschäftsbericht*, pp. 83-84.
122. *Ibid.*, p. 112.
123. *Telegraf*, July 11, 1948.
124. "Berlin Reactions to the Airlift and the Western Powers," Report No. 130, July 23, 1948.
125. Louis Glaser, "Berlin Divided," *Military Government Information Bulletin*, October 19, 1948, p. 3.
126. Curt Reiss, *The Berlin Story*, Dial Press, New York, 1952, pp. 197-198.
127. *The Forrestal Diaries*, pp. 481-483.
128. W. Bedell Smith, *My Three Years in Moscow*, J. B. Lippincott Company, Philadelphia and New York, 1950, p. 253; and Howley, *op. cit.*, pp. 194-195.
129. Reiss, *op. cit.*, p. 177.
130. Clay, *op. cit.*, p. 361.
131. Joseph and Stewart Alsop, "How Our Foreign Policy Is Made," the *Saturday Evening Post*, April 30, 1949.
132. *U.S. News and World Report*, July 9, 1948, p. 11.
133. Alsop, *op. cit.*

Chapter IV

1. The *New York Times*, July 17, 1948.
2. Drew Middleton, *The Struggle for Germany*, Allan Wingate, London and New York, 1950, p. 158.
3. Lucius D. Clay, *Decision in Germany*, Doubleday & Company, Inc., New York, 1950, p. 368.
4. The *New York Times*, July 21, 1948.
5. *Ibid.*, July 19 and 21, 1948.
6. Walter Millis (ed.), *The Forrestal Diaries*, The Viking Press, New York, 1951, pp. 459-460 (entry for July 21, 1948). See also Harry S Truman, *Years of Trial and Hope*, Doubleday & Company, Inc., New York, 1956, p. 124.
7. The *New York Times*, July 19, 1948.
8. *The Forrestal Diaries*, p. 459.
9. Clay, *op. cit.*, p. 368. See also Truman, *op. cit.*, p. 124.
10. Truman, *op. cit.*, p. 125.
11. *The Forrestal Diaries*, p. 459.
12. Truman, *op. cit.*, p. 125.

13. The *New York Times,* July 26, 1948. See also *Chronology of International Events and Documents,* a supplement to *The World Today,* Royal Institute of International Affairs, July 25, 1948, p. 519.
14. *Die Welt,* July 17, 1948.
15. The *New York Times,* July 31, 1948.
16. *Ibid.,* July 17, 1948.
17. *Ibid.,* July 28 and 31, 1948.
18. *Tagesspiegel,* August 10, 1948.
19. The *New York Times,* July 27, 1948.
20. *The Forrestal Diaries,* p. 459.
21. *Ibid.,* pp. 461-462.
22. *Ibid.,* p. 460.
23. The *New York Times,* April 8, 1947.
24. *The Forrestal Diaries,* p. 457.
25. *Ibid.*
26. *The Berlin Crisis: A Report on the Moscow Discussions, 1948,* Department of State Publication 3298, U.S. Government Printing Office, Washington, September, 1948, pp. 15-17.
27. W. Bedell Smith, *My Three Years in Moscow,* J. B. Lippincott Company, Philadelphia and New York, 1950, p. 242.
28. *Ibid.*
29. *The Berlin Crisis,* pp. 17-20. See also *The Forrestal Diaries,* p. 469.
30. Smith, *op. cit.,* p. 247; and *The Berlin Crisis,* pp. 22-35.
31. *The Berlin Crisis,* p. 36.
32. Smith, *op. cit.,* pp. 249-250.
33. *Ibid.,* p. 252.
34. *The Berlin Crisis,* pp. 40-41. See also *The Soviet Union and the Berlin Question,* Vol. 1, a collection of documents published by the Ministry of Foreign Affairs of the U.S.S.R., Moscow, 1948, pp. 47-48.
35. Smith, *op. cit.,* p. 251.
36. *The Forrestal Diaries,* pp. 479-480.
37. Clay, *op. cit.,* pp. 369-370.
38. *The Observer,* August 29, 1948.
39. The *London Times,* August 2, 1948.
40. *Tagesspiegel,* August 21, 1948.
41. *Ibid.,* August 22, 1948.
42. *Neues Deutschland,* August 18, 1948.
43. *Ibid.,* August 29, 1948.
44. *Ibid.,* July 17, 1948.
45. *Ibid.,* August 7 and 13, 1948.
46. *USSR Information Bulletin,* Soviet Embassy, Washington, D.C., August 11, 1948, p. 459.
47. *Tagesspiegel,* July 24 and September 16, 1948. See also Frank Howley, *Berlin Command,* Putnam, New York, 1950, p. 245.
48. *Berlin in Zahlen 1950,* Hauptamt für Statistik von Gross-Berlin, Kulturbuch-Verlag, 1950, p. 180.
49. *Tagesspiegel,* July 25, 1948.
50. *Ibid.,* July 22 and 25, 1948.
51. Bezirksbürgermeister Ryneck at the SPD Party Congress, as quoted in *Tagesspiegel,* August 1, 1948.
52. City Councilman Füllsack, as quoted in *Tagesspiegel,* August 4, 1949.
53. *Report of the U.S. Military Governor* for September, 1948, p. 2.
54. *Berlin 1948,* an annual report published by the Magistrat of Greater Berlin, Kulturbuch-Verlag, Berlin, 1950, p. 87.

55. *Notes on the Blockade of Berlin,* issued by the Control Commission for Germany (British Element), February, 1949, pp. 16-17.
56. *Tagesspiegel,* July 20, 1948.
57. *Ibid.,* July 27, 1948.
58. *Ibid.,* July 29, 1948.
59. Howley, *op. cit.,* pp. 220-221.
60. *Tagesspiegel,* July 6, 1948.
61. Cf. the remarks of Dr. Friedensburg, Stenographic Minutes of the City Assembly, I, 79th Session, July 29, 1948.
62. *Neues Deutschland* and *Tagesspiegel,* July 27, 1948.
63. *Tagesspiegel,* July 29, 30 and 31, 1948.
64. *Ibid.,* August 3, 1948.
65. *Ibid.,* August 18, 1948.
66. *Ibid.,* November 23, 1948.
67. *Ibid.,* July 27 and 29, 1948.
68. *Ibid.,* August 4, 1948.
69. *Ibid.,* August 13, 1948.
70. *Die städtischen Körperschaften in der Berliner Krise, Tatsachen und Dokumente,* published by the city government, Berlin, 1949, pp. 43-47.
71. For a detailed account of these events, see *Berlin 1948, op. cit.,* pp. 83-84.
72. *Report of the U.S. Military Governor* for July, 1948, p. 6.
73. *Ibid.,* August, 1948, p. 3.
74. The *New York Herald Tribune,* August 2, 1948.
75. The *London Times,* August 2, 1948.
76. The *New York Times,* August 7, 1948.
77. *Ibid.*
78. *Ibid.,* August 12, 1948.
79. *Tagesspiegel,* August 25, 1948.
80. *Report of the U.S. Military Governor* for August, 1948, p. 4.
81. Howley, *op. cit.,* p. 212.
82. The *London Times,* August 26, 1948.
83. *Berliner Schicksal, 1945-1952,* a collection of official documents published by the government of Berlin, 1952, pp. 65-67.
84. *Ibid.* See also *Tagesspiegel,* August 25 and September 2, 1948.
85. *Tagesspiegel,* August 26, 1948.
86. *Ibid.,* August 27, 1948.
87. *Neues Deutschland,* August 26 and 27, 1948.
88. *Tagesspiegel,* August 27, 1948.
89. *Berliner Schicksal,* p. 69.
90. *Ibid.,* pp. 71-72.
91. *Tagesspiegel,* September 1, 1948.
92. Smith, *op. cit.,* p. 252; and *The Berlin Crisis,* pp. 41-42.
93. *Tagesspiegel,* July 27, 1948.
94. *Ibid.,* August 1, 1948.
95. *Ibid.,* August 3, 1948.
96. Howley, *op. cit.,* p. 212.
97. *The Forrestal Diaries,* p. 484.
98. *Tagesspiegel,* September 2, 1948.
99. *The Berlin Crisis,* pp. 42-44; Clay, *op. cit.,* p. 371.
100. The *New York Herald Tribune,* September 9, 1948.
101. *The Forrestal Diaries,* pp. 481-484.
102. The *New York Times,* September 8, 1948.
103. *Tagesspiegel,* September 4, 1948.
104. *Ibid.,* September 7 and 8, 1948. See also Howley, *op. cit.,* pp. 215-217.

105. The *London Times,* September 10, 1948.

106. *Neues Deutschland,* September 8 and 9, 1948.

107. *The Soviet Union and the Berlin Question,* Vol. 1, a collection of documents published by the Ministry of Foreign Affairs of the U.S.S.R., 1948, p. 83.

108. Cf. Boris Shub, *The Choice,* Duell, Sloan and Pearce, New York, 1950, pp. 142-158. See also *Tagesspiegel,* September 9 and 10, 1948; and Howley, *op. cit.*, pp. 217-218.

109. *Neues Deutschland,* September 10, 1948.

110. *The Forrestal Diaries,* p. 483.

111. Clay, *op. cit.*, pp. 370-371.

112. Truman, *op. cit.*, p. 128.

113. Smith, *op. cit.*, p. 247; The *New York Times,* August 25, 1948.

114. Smith, *op. cit.*, p. 251.

Chapter V

1. *Berlin 1948,* an annual report published by the Magistrat of Greater Berlin, Kulturbuch-Verlag, Berlin, 1950, p. 90.

2. *Notes on the Blockade of Berlin,* issued by the Control Commission for Germany (British Element), February, 1949, p. 14.

3. The *New York Herald Tribune,* October 17, 1948.

4. The *London Times,* October 20, 1948.

5. *Tagesspiegel,* October 29, 31, and November 10, 1948.

6. German Press Service (DPD) dispatch, November 2, 1948.

7. *Report of the U.S. Military Governor* for December, 1948, p. 6.

8. *Tagesspiegel,* October 29, 1948.

9. *Berlin Sector: A Four Year Report, July 1, 1945-September 1, 1949,* Office of Military Government, U.S. Sector, Berlin, p. 93.

10. The *New York Times,* September 25, 30; October 3, 6, 7, 8; November 11, 1948.

11. *Ibid.*, October 4, 1948.

12. *Ibid.*, November 11 and 13, 1948.

13. *Ibid.*, September 11, 1948.

14. *The Berlin Crisis: A Report on the Moscow Discussions, 1948,* Department of State Publication 3298, U.S. Government Printing Office, Washington, September, 1948, p. 48. For the text of this and the following communication, see also *The Soviet Union and the Berlin Question,* Vol. 1, a collection of documents published by the Ministry of Foreign Affairs of the U.S.S.R., 1948, pp. 49-57.

15. *The Berlin Crisis,* p. 48.

16. *The Soviet Union and the Berlin Question,* Vol. I, p. 56.

17. The *New York Times,* October 27 and 28, 1948.

18. J. P. Nettl, *The Eastern Zone and Soviet Policy in Germany, 1945-1950,* Oxford University Press, London, 1951, p. 109.

19. *Neues Deutschland,* July 22, 1948.

20. Nettl, *op. cit.*, pp. 247*ff*. and *passim.*

21. The *New York Herald Tribune,* August 4, 1948.

22. The *New York Times,* September 21, 1948.

23. *Ibid.*, October 7, 1948.

24. *Ibid.*, October 20, 1948.

25. Stenographic Minutes of the Berlin City Assembly, I, 87th Session, October 25, 1948.

26. The *New York Times,* September 19 and October 20, 1948.

27. The *New York Herald Tribune,* October 17, 1948.

28. *Tagesspiegel,* September 23 and 30, 1948.

29. The *London Times*, November 30, 1948.
30. Stenographic Minutes of the Berlin City Assembly, I, 83rd Session, September 20, 1948.
31. *Zwei Jahre Kommunalarbeit in Gross-Berlin*, published by the Berlin SPD for use of party workers in the 1948 election, p. 95.
32. *Tagesspiegel*, October 10, 1948.
33. *Ibid.*, March 5, 1949.
34. *Ibid.*, November 25, 1948.
35. *Zwei Jahre Kommunalarbeit in Gross-Berlin*, pp. 94 and 95.
36. *Tagesspiegel*, October 8, 1948.
37. *Ibid.*, October 10, 1948.
38. *Zwei Jahre Kommunalarbeit in Gross-Berlin*, p. 96.
39. *Tagesspiegel*, December 9, 1948.
40. *Ibid.*, March 5, 1949.
41. *Zwei Jahre Kommunalarbeit in Gross-Berlin*, p. 96.
42. *Tagesspiegel*, October 10, 1948.
43. *Report of the U.S. Military Governor* for November, 1948, pp. 35-36.
44. Cf. UGO—*Erster Geschäftsbericht*, Unabhängige Gewerkschafts-Organisation (Independent Union Organization) of Greater Berlin, 1949, p. 136.
45. *Ibid.*, p. 101.
46. *Report of the U.S. Military Governor* for August, 1948, p. 22.
47. UGO—*Erster Geschäftsbericht*, p. 79. (Figures have been rounded to the nearest thousand.)
48. *Tagesspiegel*, September 24, 1948.
49. *Ibid.*, September 25, 1948.
50. *Ibid.*, September 26 and 28, 1948.
51. *Ibid.*, October 3, 1948.
52. *Ibid.*, October 6, 1948.
53. *Ibid.*, January 21, 1949.
54. *Ibid.*, November 16, 1948.
55. Lowell Bennett, *Bastion Berlin*, Friedrich Rudl, Frankfurt a/M, 1951, p. 176.
56. *Tagesspiegel*, October 9, 1948.
57. Cf. Frank Howley, *Berlin Command*, Putnam, New York, 1950, p. 215.
58. *Tagesspiegel*, September 30, 1948.
59. *Ibid.*, October 2, 1948.
60. The *New York Times*, October 2, 1948.
61. *Ibid.*, October 1, 1948.
62. "Statement of the Information Bureau of the Soviet Military Administration in Germany," released December 21, 1948, as quoted in *The Soviet Union and the Berlin Question*, Vol. 2, a collection of documents published by the Ministry of Foreign Affairs of the U.S.S.R., 1949, p. 28.
63. *Berliner Schicksal, 1945-1952*, a collection of official documents published by the government of Berlin, 1952, p. 63.
64. *Tagesspiegel*, August 20, 1948.
65. *Berliner Schicksal, 1945-1952*, p. 63.
66. *Tagesspiegel*, October 9, 14 and 17, 1948.
67. *Neues Deutschland*, October 16, 1948.
68. *Tagesspiegel*, October 30, 1948.
69. *Ibid.*, October 21, 1948.
70. *Ibid.*, October 31, 1948.
71. *Ibid.*, October 24, 1948.
72. *Ibid.*, November 9, 1948.
73. *Berliner Schicksal, 1945-1952*, p. 83.

74. *Tagesspiegel,* November 21, 1948.
75. *Berliner Schicksal, 1945-1952,* p. 73.
76. *Tagesspiegel,* November 16, 1948.
77. *Ibid.,* November 17, 1948.
78. The *London Times,* November 22, 1948.
79. *Berliner Schicksal, 1945-1952,* p. 83.
80. *Ibid.,* p. 82.
81. *Neues Deutschland,* November 21, 1948; and the *London Times,* November 22, 1948.
82. *Neues Deutschland,* November 27 and 28, 1948.
83. *Ibid.,* November 30, 1948.
84. *Berliner Schicksal, 1945-1952,* p. 84.
85. *Tagesspiegel,* November 30, 1948.
86. *Berliner Schicksal, 1945-1952,* pp. 84-85.
87. *Neues Deutschland,* December 1, 1948.
88. *Chronology of International Events and Documents,* a supplement to *The World Today,* Royal Institute of International Affairs, December 21, 1948, p. 838.
89. *Berliner Schicksal, 1945-1952,* pp. 85-87.
90. *Tagesspiegel,* December 3, 1948.
91. *Ibid.*
92. *Berliner Schicksal, 1945-1952,* p. 87.
93. *The Soviet Union and the Berlin Question,* II, *op. cit.,* p. 28.
94. Ferdinand Friedensburg, *Berlin—Schicksal und Aufgabe,* Pädagogischer Verlag Berthold Schulz, Berlin, 1953, p. 40.
95. The *London Times,* December 2, 1948.
96. *Berliner Schicksal, 1945-1952,* p. 78.
97. The *New York Herald Tribune,* September 15, 1948.
98. *Tagesspiegel,* September 24, 1948.
99. *Berliner Schicksal, 1945-1952,* pp. 78-79.
100. Stenographic Minutes of the Berlin City Assembly, I, 86th Session, October 21, 1948.
101. *Tagesspiegel,* October 22, 1948.
102. Stenographic Minutes of the Berlin City Assembly, I, 87th Session, October 25, 1948.
103. *Berliner Schicksal, 1945-1952,* p. 81.
104. *Ibid.,* p. 84.
105. *Ibid.*
106. *Tagesspiegel,* November 16, 19 and 23, 1948.
107. *Ibid.,* December 5, 1948.
108. *Neues Deutschland,* November 12, 27, 28 and December 3, 1948.
109. The *New York Times,* November 13, 1948.
110. *Berlin Sector,* p. 20.
111. *Tagesspiegel,* October 27, 1948.
112. *Ibid.,* November 6, 1948.
113. *Ibid.,* November 9, 1948.
114. *Neues Deutschland,* November 10, 1948.
115. *Tagesspiegel,* November 11, 1948.
116. *Ibid.,* November 13, 17, 21, 23, and 24, 1948.
117. *Neues Deutschland,* October 3, 1948.
118. *Ibid.,* October 14, 1948.
119. *Ibid.,* October 9, 1948.
120. *Tagesspiegel,* November 3, 1948.
121. *Ibid.,* September 16, 1948.
122. *Ibid.,* September 19 and 22, 1948.

123. The *New York Times*, October 24, 1948.

124. *Tagesspiegel*, October 26, 1948.

125. E.g., *Neues Deutschland*, November 17, 1948.

126. *Ibid.*, October 21, 1948.

127. *Ibid.*, October 22 and 28, 1948.

128. *Tagesspiegel*, November 26 and 30; December 3 and 4, 1948.

129. The *New York Times*, December 4, 1948.

130. *Neues Deutschland*, November 13, 1948.

131. *Tagesspiegel*, November 25, 1948.

132. *Ibid.*, December 2, 1948.

133. *Ibid.*, December 5, 1948.

134. *Ibid.*, December 6, 1948.

135. The *London Times*, December 6, 1948.

136. *Berlin in Zahlen 1950*, Hauptamt für Statistik von Gross-Berlin, Kulturbuch-Verlag, 1950, p. 265.

137. *Report of the U.S. Military Governor* for November, 1948, p. 13.

138. *Berlin 1948*, p. 130.

139. *British Zone Review*, published for British occupation personnel by the Control Commission for Germany (British Element), October 15, 1948, p. 2.

140. The *New York Times*, October 7 and 8, 1948.

141. *Tagesspiegel*, October 9, 1948.

142. The *New York Times*, November 21, 1948.

143. From materials collected and made available in memorandum form by Harold Hurwitz.

144. UGO—*Erster Geschäftsbericht*, p. 141.

145. The *New York Times*, December 8 and 22, 1948; *Tagesspiegel*, January 5, 1949.

146. Stenographic Minutes of the Berlin City Assembly, I, 94th Session, December 7, 1948.

147. *Tagesspiegel*, December 8, 1948.

148. *Neues Deutschland*, December 17, 1948.

149. *Ibid.*

150. *Chronology of International Events and Documents*, December 19 and 21, 1948, pp. 837-838.

151. *Tagesspiegel*, December 21, 1948.

152. *Ibid.*, March 4 and April 5, 1949.

153. Walter Millis (ed.), *The Forrestal Diaries*, The Viking Press, New York, 1951, p. 485.

154. *The Berlin Crisis*, pp. 44-46.

155. *Ibid.*

156. The *New York Times*, September 17, 1948.

157. *Chronology of International Events and Documents*, October 19, 1948, p. 717.

158. *The Soviet Union and the Berlin Question*, Vol. I, pp. 50-51.

159. *The Berlin Crisis*, pp. 46-50.

160. *Ibid.*, pp. 50-51.

161. The *New York Times* and the *London Times*, September 24, and 25, 1948.

162. *The Soviet Union and the Berlin Question*, Vol. 1, pp. 54-57; see also *The Berlin Crisis*, pp. 51-54.

163. Reprinted in the *USSR Information Bulletin*, Soviet Embassy, Washington, D.C., October 6, 1948.

164. *The Berlin Crisis*, pp. 56-61; and the *New York Times*, September 27, 1948.

165. *Chronology of International Events and Documents*, September 29, 1948, pp. 674-675.

166. *The Forrestal Diaries*, p. 486.

167. *Ibid.*, pp. 489-490.

168. The *London Times*, September 23, 1948.

169. The *New York Times*, September 24, 1948.

170. *Ibid.*, September 25, 1948.

171. *The Berlin Crisis*, pp. 55*ff*.

172. *An Account of Events Leading up to a Reference of the Berlin Question to the United Nations*, H.M. Stationery Office, London, October 11, 1948.

173. The *New York Times*, September 27, 1948.

174. For the full statement see *The Soviet Union and the Berlin Question*, Vol. 1, pp. 58-72.

175. The *London Times*, October 5, 1948.

176. *Chronology of International Events and Documents*, October 4 and 5, 1948, pp. 675-677. The full text of the debates is contained in the *Official Records* of the Security Council, third year. See especially No. 113 (361st meeting: 4 October 1948)—No. 120 (372nd meeting: 25 October 1948).

177. *Chronology of International Events and Documents*, October 6, 1948, pp. 677-680.

178. The *New York Times*, October 11, 1948.

179. *Chronology of International Events and Documents*, October 15, 1948, p. 715.

180. *Ibid.*, October 22 and 25, 1948, pp. 742-744.

181. *The Soviet Union and the Berlin Question*, Vol. 2, p. 6.

182. *Ibid.*

183. *Chronology of International Events and Documents*, October 28, 1948, p. 745.

184. *The Soviet Union and the Berlin Question*, Vol. 2, pp. 10-11.

185. Trygve Lie, *In the Cause of Peace*, Macmillan, New York, 1954, pp. 203-209.

186. *Ibid.*, pp. 209-210.

187. *Ibid.*, pp. 211-215.

188. *Ibid.*, p. 216.

189. The *New York Times*, November 21, 1948; and *The Soviet Union and the Berlin Question*, Vol. 2, pp. 17-18.

190. *Chronology of International Events and Documents*, November 26, 1948, pp. 817-818.

191. The *New York Times*, December 2, 1948.

192. *Chronology of International Events and Documents*, December 1, 1948, p. 818.

193. The *New York Times*, December 2 and 10, 1948.

194. The *London Times*, December 6 and 10, 1948.

195. Clay, *op. cit.*, p. 379.

196. *The Soviet Union and the Berlin Question*, Vol. 2, pp. 19-23.

197. Report of the chairman of the committee of neutrals, as summarized in *Chronology of International Events and Documents*, March 16, 1949, pp. 186-187. See also *The Soviet Union and the Berlin Question*, Vol. 2, pp. 31-84.

198. *Chronology of International Events and Documents*, March 16, 1949, p. 173.

199. For the full report see *The Soviet Union and the Berlin Question*, Vol. 2, pp. 73-84.

200. Clay, *op. cit.*, pp. 375-377.

201. *Ibid.*, p. 376.

202. *The Forrestal Diaries*, p. 486.

203. Lie, *op. cit.*, p. 210.

204. *Ibid.*, pp. 203 and 210.

205. Harry S Truman, *Years of Trial and Hope*, Doubleday & Company, New York, 1956, p. 129.

206. Howley, *op. cit.*, pp. 228-229.

207. E.g., the *New York Times*, December 4, 1948.

208. The *New York Times*, October 22, 1948.

209. *Ibid.*, September 29, 1948.

210. Cf. The Council on Foreign Relations, Inc., *The United States in World Affairs, 1948-49*, Harper & Brothers, New York, 1950, *passim*.

211. *Report of the U.S. Military Governor* for October, 1948, p. 44.

212. *The United States in World Affairs, 1948-49*, pp. 157-158.

Chapter VI

1. *The Soviet Union and the Berlin Question*, Vol. 2, a collection of documents published by the Ministry of Foreign Affairs of the U.S.S.R., 1949, p. 8.

2. The *New York Times*, January 9 and 13, 1949.

3. *Ibid.*, February 3 and 4, 1949.

4. *Department of State Bulletin*, May 8, 1949, p. 591.

5. The *London Times*, January 28, 1949.

6. *Tagesspiegel*, January 28, 1949.

7. The *New York Times*, January 28, 1949.

8. *Tagesspiegel*, January 30, 1949.

9. *Ibid.*, January 21, 1949.

10. *Ibid.*, March 12, 1949; the *New York Times*, March 13, 1949.

11. *Tagesspiegel*, March 12, 1949.

12. *Ibid.*, February 5, 1949.

13. *Ibid.*, February 15, 1949.

14. *Ibid.*, January 7, 1949.

15. *Ibid.*

16. The *New York Times*, February 18, 1949.

17. *Berlin Sector: A Four Year Report, July 1, 1945-September 1, 1949*, published by the Office of Military Government, U.S. Sector, Berlin, p. 38.

18. *Tagesspiegel*, April 29, 1949.

19. *Ibid.*, April 30, 1949.

20. *Ibid.*, February 9, March 2 and 3, 1949.

21. *Ibid.*, January 7 and 8 and March 2, 1949.

22. *Report of the U.S. Military Governor* for January, 1949, pp. 2-3; see also the *New York Times*, January 8, 1949.

23. *Neues Deutschland*, March 1 and 2, 1949.

24. E.g., *ibid.*, March 25, 1949.

25. *Berlin Sector*, p. 41; see also *Tagesspiegel*, January 5, 1949.

26. *Berlin Sector*, pp. 31-32; see also Frank Howley, *Berlin Command*, Putnam, New York, 1950, p. 231.

27. *Berlin Airlift—A* USAFE *Summary*, Hq. U.S. Air Force, Europe, 1949, p. 12.

28. The *London Observer*, April 17, 1949.

29. The *New York Times*, April 17, 1949.

30. *Berlin in Zahlen, 1950*, Hauptamt für Statistik von Gross-Berlin, Kulturbuch-Verlag, 1950, p. 140.

31. German Press Service (DPD) dispatch, Hamburg, March 25, 1949.

32. *Tagesspiegel*, January 26 and April 30, 1949.

33. *Ibid.*, February 2, 1949.

34. *Berlin 1948*, an annual report published by the Magistrat of Greater Berlin, Kulturbuch-Verlag, Berlin, 1950, p. 97.

35. *Berliner Schicksal, 1945-1952*, a collection of official documents published by the government of Berlin, 1952, p. 81.

36. *Chronology of International Events and Documents*, a supplement to *The World Today*, Royal Institute of International Affairs, March 16, 1949, pp. 186-187.

37. Howley, *op. cit.*, pp. 254-255.

38. Stenographic Minutes of the Berlin City Assembly, II, 8th Session, March 21, 1949.

39. "West Berlin's Reaction to a Single Currency," Report No. 186, April 27, 1949.

40. *Neues Deutschland*, March 22, 1949.

41. *Ibid.*, March 26 and 27, 1949.

42. *Tagesspiegel*, March 22, 1949.

43. *Berlin 1948*, p. 96.

44. The *London Times*, February 5, 1949.

45. *Telegraf*, February 27, 1949.

46. *Tagesspiegel*, January 19 and 27, 1949; see also Howley, *op. cit.*, p. 254.

47. *Tagesspiegel*, February 3 and 5, 1949.

48. Cf. *Telegraf*, February 25, 1949.

49. *Tagesspiegel*, January 1, 1949.

50. *Ibid.*, January 7, 1949.

51. *Ibid.*, January 5, 1949.

52. *Ibid.*, February 3, 1949.

53. *Ibid.*, February 17, 1949.

54. *Ibid.*, February 12, 1949.

55. *Ibid.*, February 19, 1949.

56. *Ibid.*, January 6, 1949.

57. *Ibid.*, February 19, 1949.

58. *Ibid.*, March 5 and 22, 1949.

59. Stenographic Minutes of the Berlin City Assembly, II, 10th Session, April 7, 1949.

60. *Berlin 1949*, an annual report published by the Magistrat of Greater Berlin, Kulturbuch-Verlag, Berlin, September 1, 1950, p. 7.

61. Harry S Truman, *Years of Trial and Hope*, Doubleday & Company, New York, 1956, p. 130.

62. The Council on Foreign Relations, Inc., *The United States in World Affairs, 1949*, Harper & Brothers, 1950, pp. 534 and 537.

63. The *New York Times*, January 29, 1949.

64. *Ibid.*, March 24, 1949.

65. *Ibid.*, April 15 and 18, 1949.

66. *Ibid.*, April 20, 1949.

67. *Ibid.*, February 23 and 24, 1949.

68. The *New York Herald Tribune*, March 19, 1949.

69. The *New York Times*, March 20, 1949.

70. The *New York Herald Tribune*, March 31, 1949.

71. The *New York Times*, April 23 and 29, May 12, 1949.

72. *Ibid.*, March 8, 1949.

73. The *London Times*, April 20, 1949.

74. The *New York Times*, March 17-31, 1949. For a detailed Soviet account, see *USSR Information Bulletin*, Soviet Embassy, Washington, D.C., April 8, 1949.

75. The *New York Times*, April 20-26, 1949.

76. *Ibid.*, April 3, 1949.

77. *Department of State Bulletin*, May 8, 1949, p. 591.
78. *Ibid.*, May 15, 1949, p. 631.
79. The *New York Times*, May 10 and 11, 1949.
80. The *Christian Science Monitor*, April 16, 1949; and the *New York Times*, April 20, 1949.
81. General Lucius D. Clay, *Decision in Germany*, Doubleday & Company, New York, 1950, p. 390.
82. The *New York Times*, March 30, 1949.
83. Stenographic Minutes of the Berlin City Assembly, II, 12th Session, May 12, 1949.
84. *Tagesspiegel*, May 13, 1949.
85. W. Bedell Smith, *My Three Years in Moscow*, J. B. Lippincott Company, Philadelphia and New York, 1950, p. 257.
86. J. P. Nettl, *The Eastern Zone and Soviet Policy in Germany, 1945-1950*, Oxford University Press, London, 1951, pp. 276-277.
87. Clay, *op. cit.*, p. 389.
88. Trygve Lie, *In the Cause of Peace*, Macmillan, New York, 1954, pp. 217-218.
89. F. Federau, "Der Interzonenhandel Deutschlands von 1946 bis Mitte 1953," *Vierteljahreshefte zur Wirtschaftsforschung*, 1953, No. 4.
90. Klaus Mehnert and Heinrich Schulte (eds.), *Deutschland-Jahrbuch 1949*, West-Verlag, Essen, 1949, p. 221.
91. *The United States in World Affairs*, 1949, p. 39.
92. The *New York Times*, April 17, 1949.
93. The *New York Herald Tribune*, April 19, 1949.

Chapter VII

1. Lucius D. Clay, *Decision in Germany*, Doubleday & Company, New York, 1950, p. 361.
2. The *New York Times*, June 28, 1948.
3. *Ibid.*, July 4, 1948.
4. "Breakdown of Four-Power Rule in Berlin," *The World Today*, August, 1948, p. 331.
5. E.g., *Report of the U.S. Military Governor* for February, 1949, p. 3.
6. *Germany 1947-1949: The Story in Documents*, Dept. of State Pub. 3556, Government Printing Office, Washington, 1950, pp. 275-277.
7. *Süddeutsche Zeitung*, July 3, 1948.
8. Article by Adenauer in *Die Welt*, June 10, 1948.
9. *Schleswig-Holstein, 13. Tagung*, July 6, 1948, pp. 9-10.
10. *U.S. Military Government Information Bulletin*, August 10, 1948, p. 9.
11. *Nordrhein-Westfalen, 50. Sitzung*, July 15, 1948, p. 690.
12. *Württemberg-Hohenzollern, 57. Sitzung*, March 24, 1949, p. 1023.
13. *Süddeutsche Zeitung*, July 3, 1948.
14. *Rheinische Zeitung*, as quoted in the *British Zone Review*, October 15, 1948, p. 14.
15. *Süddeutsche Zeitung*, July 10, 1948.
16. *Nordrhein-Westfalen, 50. Sitzung*, July 13, 1948, pp. 689-690.
17. *Tagesspiegel*, June 29, 1948.
18. Harry S Truman, *Years of Trial and Hope*, Doubleday & Company, New York, 1956, p. 127.
19. *Tagesspiegel*, July 3, 1948.
20. *Niedersachsen*, 39. Sitzung, July 13, 1948, p. 1978.
21. *Schleswig-Holstein, 13. Tagung*, July 6, 1948, p. 13.

22. *Tagesspiegel,* July 3, 1948.
23. *Nordrhein-Westfalen, 50. Sitzung,* July 15, 1947, pp. 689-690.
24. *Württemberg-Hohenzollern. 48. Sitzung,* December 16, 1948, pp. 825-826.
25. Drew Middleton, *The Struggle for Germany,* Allan Wingate, London and New York, 1950, pp. 151-152.
26. *Württemberg-Hohenzollern, 57. Sitzung,* March 24, 1949, p. 1024.
27. *Tagesspiegel,* September 1, 1948.
28. "Hessians Consider the Effect of Lifting the Blockade on West German Government," Report No. 174, May 27, 1949.
29. *Tagesspiegel,* July 11 and 17, 1948, citing the German News Agency (DENA) and the German Press Service (DPD).
30. This and much of the information following came from a file of memoranda originally maintained at the bizonal Länderrat, and made available to the author through the courtesy of officials of the German Bundesrat in Bonn. It will be referred to as "Bundesrat Berlin File."
31. *Wiesbadener Kurier,* July 2, 1948.
32. *Tagesspiegel,* July 11, 1948.
33. *Hessen, 59. Sitzung,* May 20, 1949, p. 2117.
34. This summary of the communist argument is based on minutes of the following: Economic Council, *23. Vollversammlung,* October 19, 1948, pp. 1051-1052 and 1054-1056; *Nordrhein-Westfalen, 50. Sitzung,* July 15, 1948, pp. 694-702; *Württemberg-Hohenzollern, 31. Sitzung,* July 13, 1948, pp. 426-427, and *48. Sitzung,* December 16, 1948, p. 824; and *Hessen, 48. Sitzung,* October 20, 1948, pp. 1723-1724, and *59. Sitzung,* May 20, 1949, p. 2122.
35. *Hessen, 48. Sitzung,* October 20, 1948, pp. 1723-1724.
36. *Hessen, 43. Sitzung,* July 13, 1948, p. 1523, and Hessischer Landtag, *Drucksache,* Abteilung I, No. 851.
37. Economic Council, *23. Vollversammlung,* October 19, 1948, p. 1055.
38. *Ibid.,* p. 1051.
39. *Hessen, 46. Sitzung,* September 22, 1948, p. 1646.
40. *Württemberg-Hohenzollern, 48. Sitzung,* December 16, 1948, p. 826.
41. *Nordrhein-Westfalen, 49. Sitzung,* July 14, 1948, p. 655.
42. Economic Council, *23. Vollversammlung,* October 19, 1948, p. 1054.
43. *Württemberg-Hohenzollern, 31. Sitzung,* July 13, 1948, p. 427.
44. *Tagesspiegel,* July 1, 1948.
45. *Nordrhein-Westfalen, 50. Sitzung,* July 15, 1948, p. 707.
46. *Tagesspiegel,* July 22, 1948.
47. E.g., Economic Council, *35. Vollversammlung,* March 24-25, 1949, p. 1555.
48. Office of the U.S. High Commissioner for Germany, *Elections and Political Parties in Germany 1945-1952,* June 1, 1952, *passim.* (Prepared by Policy Reports Secretary, Office of Executive Secretary.)
49. *Württemberg-Hohenzollern, 48. Sitzung,* December 16, 1948, p. 825.
50. Economic Council, *23. Vollversammlung,* October 19, 1948, p. 1052.
51. Economic Council Document, No. 238, 1948.
52. Bundesrat Berlin File.
53. *Ibid.*
54. *Ibid.*
55. *Ibid.*
56. *Ibid.*
57. *Ibid.*
58. *Ibid.*
59. Economic Council, *23. Vollversammlung,* October 19, 1948, p. 1049.
60. *Ibid.,* pp. 1049-1056 and 1064-1067.
61. *Ibid.*

62. Stenographic Minutes of the Berlin City Assembly, I, 81st Session, September 6, 1948, pp. 56-57.

63. *Tagesspiegel*, July 2, 1948.

64. Opinion Surveys Branch, Office of Military Government (U.S.), Report No. 144, October 26, 1948, p. 2.

65. *Württemberg-Hohenzollern, 57. Sitzung*, March 24, 1949, pp. 1020-1021.

66. *Ibid.*, p. 1021.

67. *Ibid.*, p. 1024.

68. *Ibid., 48. Sitzung*, December 16, 1948, p. 824.

69. Drew Middleton, *op. cit.*, p. 152.

70. Paul F. Myers and W. Parker Mauldin, *Population of the Federal Republic of Germany and West Berlin*, U.S. Bureau of the Census, Washington, 1953, p. 7.

71. *Ibid.*, p. 7.

72. Opinion Surveys Branch, Report No. 144, October 26, 1948.

Chapter VIII

1. Opinion Surveys Branch, "How Berliners Expect and Want the Crisis Settled—With Their Recommendations," Report No. 147, November 17, 1948.

2. William Buchanan and Hadley Cantril, *How Nations See Each Other*, University of Illinois Press, Urbana, Ill., 1953, pp. 162-163.

3. "Attitudes and Resources of Berliners as They Look Forward to a Blockaded Winter," Report No. 150, December 15, 1948, p. 2.

4. From materials collected and made available in memorandum form by Harold Hurwitz. (This source will be referred to hereafter as "Blockade Memorandum.")

5. Office of Military Government, Opinion Surveys Branch, "West Berlin's Reactions to a Single Currency," Report No. 168, April 27, 1949.

6. Opinion Surveys Branch, Report No. 150, *op. cit.*, p. 9.

7. *Berlin Sector: A Four Year Report, July 1, 1945-September 1, 1949*, published by the Office of Military Government, U.S. Sector, Berlin, p. 47.

8. *Report of the U.S. Military Governor* for May, 1948, Statistical Annex, p. 18.

9. *Berlin 1948*, an annual report published by the Magistrat of Greater Berlin, Kulturbuch-Verlag, Berlin, 1950, p. 91.

10. *Ibid.*

11. Frank Howley, *Berlin Command*, Putnam, New York, 1950, p. 201.

12. *Notes on the Blockade of Berlin*, issued by the Control Commission for Germany (British Element), February, 1949, p. 35.

13. *Ibid.*, pp. 32-34.

14. Report No. 150, *op. cit.*, p. 4.

15. *Notes on the Blockade of Berlin*, p. 47.

16. *Berlin in Zahlen 1950*, Hauptamt für Statistik von Gross-Berlin, Kulturbuch-Verlag, 1950, pp. 114 and 116.

17. *Ibid.*, p. 56.

18. *Notes on the Blockade of Berlin*, p. 55.

19. Howley, *op. cit.*, p. 202.

20. Report No. 150, *op. cit.*, p. 8.

21. *Tagesspiegel*, August 29, 1948.

22. *Ibid.*, July 15, 1948.

23. *Ibid.*, August 13, 1948.

24. *Berlin 1948*, p. 97.

25. All figures are from *Berlin in Zahlen* (*1947, 1950*, and *1951*) unless otherwise identified.

26. *Notes on the Blockade of Berlin*, p. 63.

27. Lowell Bennett, *Bastion Berlin*, Friedrich Rudl, Frankfurt, 1951, pp. 157-158.

28. *Württemberg-Hohenzollern, 48. Sitzung*, December 16, 1948, p. 826.

29. Howley, *op. cit.*, pp. 231-232.

30. *British Zone Review*, published by the Control Commission for Germany (British Element), November 20, 1948, pp. 1-2.

31. *Ibid.*, p. 2.

32. Lowell Bennett, *Bastion Berlin*, Friedrich Rudl, Frankfurt, 1951, p. 83.

33. *Tagesspiegel*, July 10, 1948.

34. "Berlin Reactions to the Airlift and the Western Powers," Report No. 130, July 23, 1948, p. 6.

35. Buchanan and Cantril, *op. cit.*, p. 168.

36. "Summary of Reactions to the End of the London Conference," Report No. 86, December 17, 1947.

37. Opinion Surveys Branch, "Bremen Attitudes Compared with Berlin and Amzone," Report No. 110, April 15, 1948.

38. Report No. 147, *op. cit.*

39. *Tagesspiegel*, January 9, 1949.

40. "Berlin Attitudes on the Airlift—Further Trends," Report No. 141, October 4, 1948, p. 1.

41. Report No. 147, *op. cit.*

42. Opinion Surveys Branch, Report No. 130, *op. cit.*, p. 2.

43. *Ibid.*

44. *Ibid.*, p. 6.

45. *Tagesspiegel*, July 11, 1948.

46. Ferdinand Friedensburg, *Berlin—Schicksal und Aufgabe*, Pädagogischer Verlag Berthold Schulz, Berlin, 1953, p. 48.

47. *Berlin 1949*, Kulturbuch-Verlag, September 1, 1950, p. 13.

48. Friedensburg, *op. cit.*, p. 48.

49. Bennett, *op. cit.*, p. 82.

50. UGO—*Erster Geschäftsbericht*, published by the Unabhängige Gewerkschafts-Organization (Independent Union Organization) of Greater Berlin, 1949, p. 129.

51. *Telegraf*, July 9, 1948.

52. "Security *versus* Freedom in Blockaded Berlin," (Report No. 151, December 18, 1948).

53. *Cf.* Theunissen, "Berlin als Politische Aufgabe," *Berliner Almanach 1948*, Berlin, 1948; also "Life in Berlin Today," *The World Today*, December, 1948, p. 503.

54. Stenographic Minutes of the Berlin City Assembly, I, 75th Session, June 29, 1948.

55. *Tagesspiegel*, July 4, 1948.

56. "Some Trends in Berlin Morale with Sidelights on Recreation," Report No. 134, September 2, 1948, p. 3.

57. Hurwitz, "Blockade Memorandum."

58. Report No. 150, *op. cit.*, p. 2.

59. *Ibid.*

60. *Ibid.*, p. 3.

61. *Tagesspiegel*, July 24, 1948.

62. *Task Force Times*, Bulletin of the Combined Airlift Task Force, August 28, 1948.

63. "Berlin Airlift," special issue of *The Bee Hive*, United Aircraft Corporation, East Hartford, Conn., Fall, 1948, p. 21.

64. *Tagesspiegel*, September 19, 1948.
65. Clay, *op. cit.*, p. 391.
66. Opinion Surveys Branch, Report No. 150, *op. cit.*, *passim.*

Chapter IX

1. *Cf.* "Will to Freedom Decisive," *Tagesspiegel*, July 16, 1948.
2. The *London Times*, September 23, 1948.
3. *Luftbrücke Berlin*, a pictorial report published by the Magistrat of Greater Berlin, Arani Verlag, 1949, p. 2.
4. W. Bedell Smith, *My Three Years in Moscow*, J. B. Lippincott Company, Philadelphia and New York, 1950, p. 242.
5. Lucius D. Clay, *Decision in Germany*, Doubleday & Company, New York, 1950, p. 366.

INDEX

PUBLISHED RAND RESEARCH

PRINCETON UNIVERSITY PRESS, PRINCETON, NEW JERSEY

Approximations for Digital Computers, by Cecil Hastings, Jr., 1955
International Communication and Political Opinion: A Guide to the Literature, by Bruce Lannes Smith and Chitra M. Smith, 1956
Dynamic Programming, by Richard Bellman, 1957

COLUMBIA UNIVERSITY PRESS, NEW YORK

Soviet National Income and Product, 1940-48, by Abram Bergson and Hans Heymann, Jr., 1954
Soviet National Income and Product in 1928, by Oleg Hoeffding, 1954
Labor Productivity in Soviet and American Industry, by Walter Galenson, 1955

THE FREE PRESS, GLENCOE, ILLINOIS

Psychosis and Civilization, by Herbert Goldhamer and Andrew W. Marshall, 1949
Soviet Military Doctrine, by Raymond L. Garthoff, 1953
A Study of Bolshevism, by Nathan Leites, 1953
Ritual of Liquidation: The Case of the Moscow Trials, by Nathan Leites and Elsa Bernaut, 1954
Two Studies in Soviet Controls: Communism and the Russian Peasant, and Moscow in Crisis, by Herbert S. Dinerstein and Leon Gouré, 1955
A Million Random Digits with 100,000 Normal Deviates, by The RAND Corporation, 1955

MCGRAW-HILL BOOK COMPANY, INC., NEW YORK

The Operational Code of the Politburo, by Nathan Leites, 1951
Air War and Emotional Stress: Psychological Studies of Bombing and Civilian Defense, by Irving L. Janis, 1951
Soviet Attitudes Toward Authority: An Interdisciplinary Approach to Problems of Soviet Character, by Margaret Mead, 1951
Mobilizing Resources for War: The Economic Alternatives, by Tibor Scitovsky, Edward Shaw, Lorie Tarshis, 1951
The Organizational Weapon: A Study of Bolshevik Strategy and Tactics, by Philip Selznick, 1952
Introduction to the Theory of Games, by J. C. C. McKinsey, 1952
Weight-Strength Analysis of Aircraft Structures, by F. R. Shanley, 1952
The Compleat Strategyst: Being a Primer on the Theory of Games of Strategy, by J. D. Williams, 1954
Linear Programming and Economic Analysis, by Robert Dorfman, Paul A. Samuelson and Robert M. Solow, 1958

PUBLIC AFFAIRS PRESS, WASHINGTON, D.C.

The Rise of Krushchev, by Myron Rush, 1958
Behind the Sputniks: A Survey of Soviet Space Science, by F. J. Krieger, 1958

ROW, PETERSON & COMPANY, EVANSTON, ILLINOIS

German Rearmament and Atomic War: The Views of German Military and Political Leaders, by Hans Speier, 1957
West German Leadership and Foreign Policy, edited by Hans Speier and W. Phillips Davison, 1957

PUBLISHED RAND RESEARCH

PRINCETON UNIVERSITY PRESS, PRINCETON, NEW JERSEY

Approximations for Digital Computers, by Cecil Hastings, Jr., 1955
International Communication and Political Opinion: A Guide to the Literature, by Bruce Lannes Smith and Chitra M. Smith, 1956
Dynamic Programming, by Richard Bellman, 1957

COLUMBIA UNIVERSITY PRESS, NEW YORK

Soviet National Income and Product, 1940–48, by Abram Bergson and Hans Heymann, Jr., 1954
Soviet National Income and Product in 1928, by Oleg Hoeffding, 1954
Labor Productivity in Soviet and American Industry, by Walter Galenson, 1955

THE FREE PRESS, GLENCOE, ILLINOIS

Psychosis and Civilization, by Herbert Goldhamer and Andrew W. Marshall, 1953
Soviet Military Doctrine, by Raymond L. Garthoff, 1953
A Study of Bolshevism, by Nathan Leites, 1953
Ritual of Liquidation: The Case of the Moscow Trials, by Nathan Leites and Elsa Bernaut, 1954
Two Studies in Soviet Controls: Communism and the Russian Peasant, and Moscow in Crisis, by Herbert S. Dinerstein and Leon Gouré, 1955
A Million Random Digits with 100,000 Normal Deviates, by The RAND Corporation, 1955

McGRAW-HILL BOOK COMPANY, INC., NEW YORK

The Operational Code of the Politburo, by Nathan Leites, 1951
Air War and Emotional Stress: Psychological Studies of Bombing and Civilian Defense, by Irving L. Janis, 1951
Soviet Attitudes Toward Authority: An Interdisciplinary Approach to Problems of Soviet Character, by Margaret Mead, 1951
Mobilizing Resources for War: The Economic Alternatives, by Tibor Scitovsky, Edward Shaw, Lorie Tarshis, 1951
The Organizational Weapon: A Study of Bolshevik Strategy and Tactics, by Philip Selznick, 1952
Introduction to the Theory of Games, by J. C. C. McKinsey, 1952
Weight-Strength Analysis of Aircraft Structures, by F. R. Shanley, 1952
The Compleat Strategyst: Being a Primer on the Theory of Games of Strategy, by J. D. Williams, 1954
Linear Programming and Economic Analysis, by Robert Dorfman, Paul A. Samuelson, and Robert M. Solow, 1958

PUBLIC AFFAIRS PRESS, WASHINGTON, D.C.

The Rise of Khrushchev, by Myron Rush, 1958
Behind the Sputniks: A Survey of Soviet Space Science, by F. J. Krieger, 1958

ROW, PETERSON & COMPANY, EVANSTON, ILLINOIS

German Rearmament and Atomic War: The Views of German Military and Political Leaders, by Hans Speier, 1957
West German Leadership and Foreign Policy, edited by Hans Speier and W. Phillips Davison, 1957